RESISTANCE MONEY

Bitcoin isn't just for criminals, speculators, or wealthy Silicon Valley entrepreneurs – despite what the headlines say. In an imperfect world of rampant inflation, creeping authoritarianism, surveillance, censorship, and financial exclusion, bitcoin empowers individuals to elude the expanding reach and tightening grip of institutions both public and private. So although bitcoin is money, it isn't just money. Bitcoin is *resistance* money.

Resistance Money: A Philosophical Case for Bitcoin begins by explaining why bitcoin was invented, how it works, and where it fits among other kinds of money. The authors then offer a framework for evaluating bitcoin from a global perspective and use it to examine bitcoin's monetary policy, censorship-resistance, privacy, inclusion, and energy use. The book develops a comprehensive and measured case that bitcoin is a net benefit to the world, despite its imperfections. *Resistance Money* is intended for all, from the clueless to the specialist, from the proponent to the die-hard skeptic, and everyone in between.

Key Features:

- Provides a philosophical approach that makes use of multiple disciplines in its analysis
- Offers a clearly written, measured academic treatment of bitcoin, comprehensive in scope and free of ideological baggage
- Includes information on the financial, social, and environmental costs of bitcoin, how these costs are sometimes exaggerated, and how they might be mitigated
- Addresses the strongest arguments against bitcoin and shows how some succeed and most come up short.

Andrew M. Bailey is Associate Professor of Humanities at Yale-NUS College, Singapore.

Bradley Rettler is Associate Professor of Philosophy at the University of Wyoming in Laramie, Wyoming, USA.

Craig Warmke is Associate Professor of Philosophy at Northern Illinois University in DeKalb, Illinois, USA.

RESISTANCE MONEY

A Philosophical Case for Bitcoin

Andrew M. Bailey, Bradley Rettler, and Craig Warmke

Routledge
Taylor & Francis Group

NEW YORK AND LONDON

Designed cover image: by @bitcoinfool

First published 2024
by Routledge
605 Third Avenue, New York, NY 10158

and by Routledge
4 Park Square, Milton Park, Abingdon, Oxon OX14 4RN

Routledge is an imprint of the Taylor & Francis Group, an informa business

ISBN: 978-1-032-77778-8 (hbk)
ISBN: 978-1-032-77780-1 (pbk)
ISBN: 978-1-003-48472-1 (ebk)

DOI: 10.4324/9781003484721

Typeset in Sabon LT Pro
by Apex CoVantage, LLC

To Satoshi

CONTENTS

ACKNOWLEDGMENTS

For comments, critique, conversation, or camaraderie, we thank the following: Adrian Yee, Adriel Yong, Akın Heper, Alaukik Pant, Alex Gladstein, Allen Farrington, Andrew Perkins, Bas Wisselink, Ben Schupmann, Benjamin Peck, Bennett Tomlin, Bradley Monton, Brady Dale, Brandon Warmke, Brett Scott, Bryon Bothun, Burak Tamaç, Calle, Carl Steib, Cas Piancey, Chan Shawn Kit, Chris Berg, Chris Blec, Dan Clarke, Daniel Kuhn, Danny Knowles, David Waugh, David Zell, Dea Rezkitha, Dennis Porter, Dennis Porto, Eric Schliesser, Eugene Gant, Franz-Peter Griesmaier, Gerald Glickman, Grant McCarty, Gwart, Gytis Greicius, Hass McCook, Henry Magram, Hunter Trujillo, James Pierog, Jan May, Jason Maier, Jeremy Poley, Jerry Brito, Jim Gibson, Joe Kelly, Johann Wah, John Light, Josh Hendrickson, Joshua Rasmussen, Justin Foo, Kale Hyder, Kaushik Swaminathan, Keith Buhler, Keith Hankins, Kevin Vallier, Khizer Khan, Kyle Saunders, Laura Warmke, Leonidas Zelmanovitz, Level39, Lindsay Rettler, Lloyd Koh, Lyn Alden, Lydia Mashburn, Manka Bajaj, Margot Paez, Mark Casey, Mark Stephany, Martin Lipman, Matthew McKeever, Matthew Pines, Matt Rotando, Micah Warren, Michael Casey, Michael Rea, Mike Brock, Murch, Natalie Smolenski, Nate Harmon, Nathan Ballantyne, Niaz Chowdhury, Nic Carter, Nick Almond, Nick Anthony, Noelle Acheson, Paul Dylan-Ennis, Paola A. Suarez, Pete Rizzo, Peter McCormack, Peter Ryan, Peter St Onge, Raphael Schön, Rene Pickhardt, Richard Kim, Rob Colter, Rocket, Roger Ver, Rohan Mukherjee, Rohan Naidu, Ryan Foo, Scott Hagaman, Shane M. Wilkins, Spandana Bhattacharya, Steven Lubka, Thomas Hogan, Tim Bouma, Timothy Heggem, Tony Cai, Troy Cross, Tuur Demeester, Waihuini Njoroge, William

Luther, Yves Bennaïm, and Zach Mahon. And a mighty host of anonymous plebs – you know who you are. We extend special thanks to our editor at Routledge, Andrew Beck, for believing in our project.

For research support, we thank Yale-NUS College, the National University of Singapore, the Singapore Ministry of Education, the University of Notre Dame, Northern Illinois University, the Wyoming Institute for Humanities Research, and the University of Wyoming for a College of Arts and Sciences Research Activity Grant that brought the authors together for two weeks in Summer 2022. We also thank the Bitcoin Policy Institute and the American Institute for Economic Research for supporting a manuscript workshop.

1

BITCOIN'S GENESIS

1.1 Welcome to bitcoin

Bitcoin is for criminals. It's a tool for terrorists, drug dealers, and hackers, and a plaything for degenerate speculators.

Bitcoin is for protestors. It's a tool for Alexei Navalny and other Russian dissidents. It's for Roya Mahboob and women under patriarchal rule. It's for underbanked Black Americans, North Korean and Ukrainian refugees, Venezuelan farmers suffering under hyperinflation, and whistleblowers like Julian Assange and Edward Snowden.

Bitcoin is resistance money.

Bitcoin is money. Though not created or maintained by any nation state, it has higher volume and more users than many national currencies.[1] But it's not just money. It's money for resistance. It's money for people on the margins. This doesn't necessarily make bitcoin good or bad. Resistance is itself neither good nor bad; it matters what's being resisted. We can resist bad things – that's good. But we can also resist good things – that's bad.

No doubt, bitcoin has empowered wrongdoers. That's why they've used it. But bitcoin also empowers those on the margins. In so doing, it serves as a check against the authority and overreach of corporations, states, and anyone else who would stand between people and their money.

Headlines about bitcoin fixate on price, often to the exclusion of all else. This book, by contrast, concerns the nature of bitcoin and its global consequences. We grant that bitcoin has some bad consequences. Even so, we suspect that after you finish this book, you'll prefer to live in a world with bitcoin – a world with resistance money – rather than without.

DOI: 10.4324/9781003484721-1

We begin with the basics – bitcoin's origin and purpose.
It starts with the cypherpunks.

1.2 The cypherpunk dream

Judith Milhon was a force of nature. She had issues with authority. Indeed, she was a criminal, arrested several times for organizing and participating in the 1960s civil rights protests. When St. Jude (as she was known) set her mind to a task, few could dissuade her. And if there wasn't a way, she made one.[2]

As a self-taught programmer, St. Jude became an early and powerful advocate for women in computing and hacking. "Girls need modems," she often said. In the emerging digital world, St. Jude's rebellious spirit found fresh expression. Like the do-it-yourself hippies of the 1970s, hackers in St. Jude's mold wouldn't rely on legacy institutions to accomplish their goals.[3] They would do it themselves – and pay little heed to any rules and rulers in the way.

St. Jude's advocacy and attitude were prescient.

In the 1980s and 90s, cyberpunk stories like *Neuromancer, Blade Runner*, and *Snowcrash* depicted a grim future where society has cut an unholy deal with digital autocrats. The autocrats supply channels for communication and commerce, ways to send and receive messages and money. Then, as we use their channels, the autocrats collect our personal information for power and profit. They can also kick us to the curb – at any time and for any reason. Many self-censor in both talk and trade to prevent the digital autocrats from censoring them first. Sound familiar? It's reality for many worldwide.

To counter these forces, some turn to politicians. They hope for regulatory solutions. They vote for a better world. They might even run for office. Others – the Unabomber types – resort to violence. And some retreat, hoping to find peace elsewhere. Senator, menace, or monk. Until recently, such were the posts in the nascent war against digital authoritarianism.

Those in St. Jude's mold forged another path. Decades before the iPhone, they began to meet regularly in the California Bay Area to discuss how they could avoid a world of digital autocrats with terrifying new powers. They thought cryptography could turn computers into engines of freedom rather than oppression. They didn't primarily rely on politicians, projectiles, or prayer.

Instead, they wrote code.[4] St. Jude dubbed them *cypherpunks*.[5]

The cypherpunks didn't just write code; they wrote *a lot* of code. You may have heard about some of it. The cypherpunks were responsible for Pretty Good Privacy, aka "PGP" (Philip Zimmermann and Hal Finney),

BitTorrent (Bram Cohen), and Wikileaks (Julian Assange), to start. Their work made possible the end-to-end encrypted messaging you might use in Signal or WhatsApp and anonymous internet browsing through Tor. The cypherpunks created pathways for private and secure communication, tore down the walls of intellectual property, fought for civil liberties, and revealed surveillance programs and war crimes to the world. But in our view, perhaps the most important cypherpunk creation is bitcoin.

We use money to express our values and preferences. Our transactions encode our dreams and desires. Money shapes the world. And as the world digitizes, so, too, does the money that makes it go 'round. Since digital money flows through financial institutions, they see every transaction and can stop any one of them. The digital money of banks and payment processors enables the dystopian future the cypherpunks feared.

To protect our privacy and autonomy, we need digital cash – money in the digital world that works like cash in the physical world. Physical cash resists surveillance and control. Unlike the digital money we more often use, physical cash requires no trusted intermediaries to hold and transfer funds. With cash, one party simply hands some bills over to the other. In software speak, cash is "peer-to-peer." So if you'd like to spy on a cash transaction in Chicago, you need eyes in Chicago. Or if you'd like to block one in Singapore, you must prevent the exchange in Singapore. The cypherpunks dreamed of a digital instrument with similar features – digital cash. Digital cash would preserve our privacy and autonomy even as we transact over the internet.

Serious obstacles stood in the way. The big one was the *double-spending problem*. Anyone would love to spend one and the same dollar bill twice – much like we'd love to have our cake and eat it too. But we can't for a couple reasons. First, we don't have a cheap and effective replicator. At least for now, we can't shove a dollar bill in a black box and then, for pennies, withdraw several perfect copies. Second, the Treasury's rules state that more than 50% of a bill must remain in exchange for new currency.[6] So thanks to the laws of physics and the power of a central authority, we can't expand the money supply with the cunning use of scissors.

Digital US dollars work differently, of course. We can't double-spend them because banks and other holders of digital money keep detailed financial records of who has which amounts. And like anyone who counterfeits physical dollars, anyone who cooks the digital books would face severe consequences. So we avoid dollar double-spends, whether physical or digital, with the help of central authorities.

The digital dollars in our bank accounts aren't digital cash because digital dollars aren't peer-to-peer. Truly digital cash, without central authorities, poses a major challenge. Digital cash would be, of course, digital – the sort of thing that inhabits computers. But digital things are easy to copy and paste – just press CTRL+C/CTRL+V. That's a cheap and effective replicator in the digital realm. Few would use your digital trinkets as money if any 10-year-old could increase the supply with a few keystrokes. The marginal price of such a trinket would rapidly drop to zero.

To protect against digital counterfeiting, we might introduce a central authority to keep a ledger that tracks the ownership of each digital coin. Such an authority could block any attempt to spend one and the same coin twice. The authority could even provide significant privacy assurances. Thanks to advances in cryptography, the authority could block attempted double-spends without knowing the amounts or the parties involved.[7] But such designs reintroduce a trusted party, making the money much less cash-like and easier to block. Indeed, the system as a whole would have a single point of failure, the central ledger tracking all transactions. It would resemble traditional digital money more than digital cash.

Prior to bitcoin, *digital* seemed incompatible with *cash*. In *Digital Cash*, Finn Brunton captures the apparent paradox:

> The work of making cash digital means creating an object that is trivial to transact over networked computers and easy to verify – to prove that it is what it appears to be – but impossible to forge or duplicate, and that can carry the information about what it is and what it is worth, without generating any information about how it is used or by whom.
>
> This is a set of seemingly paradoxical and impossible demands: it must be available but scarce, unique and anonymous but identifiable and reliable, and easy to transmit but impossible to copy. It must have all these attributes in the context of technologies that were designed and built to make copies in their very functioning – costlessly, immediately, and perfectly.[8]

For several years and across various meetups and mailing lists, cypherpunks and their allies plugged away. Perry Metzger, one of the most prolific writers on the cypherpunk mailing list and a moderator of its successor, the cryptography mailing list, says that discussions about digital cash "percolated in the mailing lists more or less constantly for over 15 years."[9] Most attempts to make digital cash never launched. The ones that did, failed.[10]

And then there was bitcoin.

1.3 How bitcoin fulfills the cypherpunk dream

Cash is peer-to-peer. We can save it and spend it without depending on others. When it comes to money that isn't cash, we trust individuals and institutions to provide financial services for us. When things go well, these providers take on certain roles and thus make our lives much easier. But they also bring risk. When these risks materialize, these providers make our lives much harder. To gain a better appreciation for digital cash, we'll focus on three functions or roles within the monetary domain and the risks associated with each: managing, mediating, and making money.[11]

1.3.1 Managers

Few store their life savings in cash under a pillow. Instead, we have others store our savings for us – managers. They usually have expertise, resources, and staff to provide security. Banks serve as managers most often. We entrust them with our funds because we think it's riskier to hold the funds ourselves.

Yet managers could lose our funds too. When banks hold funds, we trust them to keep funds safe from loss or theft. But banks usually don't store funds in vaults, physical or otherwise. They lend our money to others for profit. So by enlisting a bank to store our funds, we must also trust them to do so responsibly. If they do it irresponsibly, we might lose some or all of our funds.

1.3.2 Mediators

When using cash, you hand over some dollar bills, and the transaction is complete. No one else needs to know what happened, and no one else needs to cooperate for full settlement to occur. The handover is the settlement. In modern electronic payment systems, the "handover" often involves a complex web of trusted parties. These are the mediators.

With a tap of your Visa card, you can leave the store with Flintstone vitamins in hand. But the transaction isn't actually complete. *Provisional* settlement – a conditional and easily revocable state – occurs when Visa initially approves the transaction. But *final* settlement – unconditional and not easily revocable – typically takes days or weeks. In that time, money will travel through Visa, your bank, and the merchant's bank. It ultimately settles through master central bank accounts but might first wind through corresponding banks that facilitate inter-bank transfers.

Thanks to mediators, merchants themselves don't need to extend you credit or know who you are or where you live. But under the hood, mediators involve significant complexity. Your card has the Visa logo. The merchant trusts Visa. Visa trusts your bank. Your bank trusts you. Trust expands our financial powers and provides convenience. Thanks to mediators, we can also transact over great physical distances – good luck doing that with physical cash.

The system works only if mediators deal quickly, honestly, and with few mistakes. But each mediator is a potential point of failure. If they fail, convenience vanishes. You might get stuck in an infinite loop of Muzak and customer service representatives, hoping for someone to put Humpty back together again before dinnertime.

In the web of managers and mediators, some entities play both roles. Banks play both, for example. But whether service providers manage funds, facilitate transactions, or both, they know quite a bit about us. We provide personal information when we sign up for their services. And as we use those services, they collect even more personal information. So we have to trust that they'll steward this information responsibly – to protect it from prying eyes and to surrender it to authorities only with due cause.

Despite the overlap between mediators and managers, only when a provider serves as a mediator does it also serve as an *intermediary* between you and your counterparty in a financial transaction. That is, while both managers and mediators are *trusted parties* in the sense given earlier, mediators are also trusted *third* parties. To make this more vivid, imagine a cash transaction where you hand a dollar bill to a middleman, who then hands it to the merchant. Middlemen are often unnecessary for cash transactions. They are also risky: middlemen might delay or block the transaction or even take a cut for themselves. But modern electronic transactions require middlemen. When things operate smoothly, our trust and their trustworthiness together yield all manner of convenience.

1.3.3 Makers

Under the watchful eye of the Securities and Exchange Commission, American corporations create shares and sell them on the stock market. Corporations that issue stock are *makers*. And holding stock requires trust in its maker. A company that issues more units of stock may dilute the share of the company owned by shareholders, even if those shareholders continue to hold the same number of units. So issuing more stock also makes each unit less valuable.

Money has makers too. Even if you're unfamiliar with corporate finance, you've likely used the dollar, euro, or yen. Their makers are banks. How this happens varies across national boundaries and within them. Typically, *inside money* comes from commercial banks. Your bank account – which is *inside* the private sector – holds inside money. Your bank, in turn, ultimately has a balance at a bank for banks – the central bank, which is *outside* the private sector. Thus, this balance concerns *outside money*.

Inside money is an IOU for outside money.[12] For example, your personal bank account might show a dollar amount. But those aren't real dollars. They are IOUs or claims on real dollars, the things represented by physical dollar bills or in balances that commercial banks hold at the central bank. Whereas commercial banks issue inside money through debt, central banks issue outside money through, well, decree. And either way, we trust banks to create money responsibly.

The most influential central bank in the world is the US Federal Reserve. It provides a monetary asset, the US dollar, around which billions of people coordinate their economic behavior. They carry out their mission by pushing and pulling various levers to help ensure that the US dollar maintains a stable price – or, what's the same, that goods and services enjoy a stable price in dollars.

The Federal Reserve is a trusted party in all three senses of maker, manager, and mediator – it is the monetary trinity. The Fed makes the dollar. The Fed manages the funds of other banks. And the Fed ultimately serves as the central mediator for digital dollar transactions through services like FedWire.

In sum, managers offer convenience and peace of mind. Mediators maintain financial plumbing. And makers enable economic stability and exchange through a common medium. Users of modern money trust these parties to do their jobs well. This is a tradeoff and involves risk. As cypherpunk Nick Szabo says, trusted parties are "security holes."[13] Managers sometimes fail, leaving their customers with pennies on the dollar. Mediators sometimes block lawful commerce. Makers also make mistakes. They might print too much money and, as inflation soars, put on the brakes too late. Then they might slam the brakes too hard and, as a recession looms, keep the brakes on for too long. Sometimes makers know which levels they'll pull and, as private citizens, execute a series of, let's say, well-timed trades in the stock market. This is insider trading, not with company stock, but with what company stocks trade against – a national currency.

As a group, these trusted parties can and sometimes do imperil our financial privacy, our funds, our freedom to use them as we'd like, and their value. Some will judge that the benefits of trusted parties outweigh the risk. They might be right. It might also be true that we would benefit from having options without one or more of these trusted parties so that participating in the economy doesn't force us into a single set of tradeoffs.

1.3.4 Minimizing trust: Cash and bitcoin

Traditional cash doesn't require users to trust managers and mediators. You can custody your own cash and transact without intermediaries. By being your own manager and mediator, you can enhance your financial privacy and freedom. But cash is subject to maker trust. Someone has to print those bills. We trust them to print enough – but not too much – and with effective anti-counterfeiting measures.

Whereas traditional digital money requires trust in managers, mediators, and makers, and physical cash requires trust in makers alone, bitcoin requires trust in none. Or more cautiously, it was created to require trust in none. Here's how Satoshi Nakamoto, the pseudonymous creator of bitcoin, puts it:[14]

> I've developed a new open source P2P [peer-to-peer] e-cash system called Bitcoin. It's completely decentralized, with no central server or trusted parties, because everything is based on crypto proof instead of trust . . .
>
> The root problem with conventional currency is all the trust that's required to make it work. The central bank must be trusted not to debase the currency, but the history of fiat currencies is full of breaches of that trust. Banks must be trusted to hold our money and transfer it electronically, but they lend it out in waves of credit bubbles with barely a fraction in reserve. We have to trust them with our privacy, trust them not to let identity thieves drain our accounts. Their massive overhead costs make micropayments impossible.
>
> A generation ago, multi-user time-sharing computer systems had a similar problem. Before strong encryption, users had to rely on password protection to secure their files, placing trust in the system administrator to keep their information private. Privacy could always be overridden by the admin based on his judgment call weighing the principle of privacy against other concerns, or at the behest of his superiors. Then strong encryption became available to the masses, and trust was no longer required. Data could be secured in a way that was physically impossible for others to access, no matter for what reason, no matter how good the excuse, no matter what.
>
> It's time we had the same thing for money. With e-currency based on cryptographic proof, without the need to trust a third party middleman, money can be secure and transactions effortless.
>
> One of the fundamental building blocks for such a system is digital signatures. A digital coin contains the public key of its owner. To transfer it, the owner signs the coin together with the public key of the next owner. Anyone can check the signatures to verify the chain of ownership. It works well to secure ownership, but leaves one big problem unsolved: double-spending. Any owner could try to re-spend an already spent coin by signing it again to another owner. The usual solution is for a trusted company with a central database to check for double-spending, but that just gets back to the trust model. In its central

position, the company can override the users, and the fees needed to support the company make micropayments impractical.

Bitcoin's solution is to use a peer-to-peer network to check for double-spending. In a nutshell, the network works like a distributed timestamp server, stamping the first transaction to spend a coin. It takes advantage of the nature of information being easy to spread but hard to stifle . . .

The result is a distributed system with no single point of failure. Users hold the crypto keys to their own money and transact directly with each other, with the help of the P2P network to check for double-spending.[15]

There's a lot going on here, including some technical vocabulary that we'll explain in Chapter 2. But even a cursory read will give you a sense of what bitcoin aspires to be: an electronic monetary system, with all the conveniences of modern money and without trusted parties – a system that enables peer-to-peer transfer, in other words. Or in two words: *digital cash*. The cypherpunk dream.

Does bitcoin make good on that promise? Did the dream come true? These are questions we'll take up in more detail in subsequent chapters. But for now, we'll make a few observations about how bitcoin's design matches the digital cash ideal.

Recall the risks associated with trusted parties: privacy leaks, blocked transactions, leakage (high fees extracted by intermediating parties), and irresponsible creation or management of monetary assets.

The cypherpunks feared a dossier society, a future where corporations and governments have the proverbial manila folder on each of us. Each of our digital dossiers would include the details of everything we've ever bought – when, where, and for how much. Despite the cypherpunks' warnings, we now live in a dossier society. When we sign up for credit cards or services like PayPal, we cough up our names and all sorts of personal information. Then everything we ever buy sticks to our real-life identities.

Trust – enabled by knowledge – is what makes the system work, and it goes both ways. To store your funds with a manager or transact using one or more mediators, you must register for an account and pass all manner of security or credit checks, visible and hidden. Your transactions are monitored and recorded, and each is attached to your name, your identity, and all the other information about you on file. Your passwords are on file, too, and these sometimes leak in unfortunate or even life-shattering ways.

Bitcoin, by contrast, requires no registration and collects no personal information. With little more than an internet-connected device, anyone can send or receive bitcoin to anyone else in the world. As with email, sending and receiving bitcoin requires both an address and a password. But unlike email, your bitcoin address and its password are meaningless strings of symbols that bear no tell-tale connection to your real-life identity. Each serves as a pseudonym. You can use as many addresses as you like for as long as you like. Anyone who'd like to build your dossier from your bitcoin behavior has to work much harder to do so.

The previous paragraph is in need of qualification. Unlike the ledgers of typical commercial banks, the bitcoin ledger is open for anyone to read. Even so, bitcoin users can achieve significant levels of financial privacy. We'll explore this subject at much greater length in Chapter 6.

Bitcoin also provides enhanced monetary security. Credit card companies, banks, and payment processors often block transactions and close accounts. Governments sometimes seize money from the accounts of citizens. Although you own the funds in these accounts, you don't possess them. Trusted parties do. And trusted parties work for their own best interests, not ours. So although trusted parties provide valuable services like fraud prevention, they're also security holes. You have to trust them to behave well.

Bitcoin does away with mandatory managers and mediators. You can take custody of your own bitcoin, just as you do with cash. Doing so only requires that you store the relevant password. And since you can send bitcoin to anyone without funneling it through trusted intermediaries, you needn't pass security or credit checks.

Bitcoin also does away with makers in an important sense. The Federal Reserve updates its projections and policies frequently. On a near-monthly basis, millions tune in for the pronouncements from a single man at a podium to guide spending and investment – monetary groundhog day. Bitcoin has no CEO, no central bank, and therefore, no groundhog days. Its monetary policy is non-discretionary. It's also fixed and in two senses. In the first sense, the issuance schedule of bitcoin is planned forever. This is where the supply cap of 21 million bitcoin appears.[16] But some schedules are easier to change than others. And bitcoin's schedule is exceedingly difficult to change; this is how bitcoin's monetary policy is fixed in the second sense. A change in monetary policy would require near unanimity among network participants, an extraordinarily unlikely situation.

Bitcoin promises to combine the conveniences of modern money with the privacy and security assurances of cash but without the risk of makers. It's an enticing promise. So enticing, in fact, that it should also make you very skeptical.

We're skeptical too. Yet we will argue that bitcoin makes good on many of its promises. There are momentous tradeoffs along the way and qualifications aplenty. But fundamentally, bitcoin is what it says on the box: digital cash. And therein lies its power as a tool of liberation and resistance.

We'll say much more about how bitcoin works, its connection to the digital cash idea, and its costs and benefits in the chapters to come. But in what remains of this chapter, we'll describe our method and approach and then briefly preview the rest of the book.

1.4   How we'll proceed

In this book, we explain what bitcoin is and why we think you'd rather live in a world with it rather than without. We consider evidence, data, and arguments from a broad range of disciplines – computer science, law, ethics, finance, economics, climate science, history, international politics, and more. No one, so far as we know, has PhDs in all these areas. And most of these fall far outside our own core expertise in philosophy.

We'd forgive you for thinking that three philosophers aren't up to the task. Wouldn't a book on digital money better suit a computer scientist or economist? Or perhaps better yet, a computer scientist/economist? Maybe so. But not *this* book. Our big question is whether we would rather live in a world with or without bitcoin. To frame this question well, we must consider philosophical issues about bitcoin's nature, the nature of the worlds we're considering, the method for deciding, and the relevant values and moral principles in play.

We need philosophical tools not only to frame the question but to answer it. Now you might propose to answer the question by determining whether bitcoin helps or hurts more people overall. But this strategy treats everyone equally. Perhaps a welfare bump for the poor should trump the costs to the rich. The strategy also neglects the varying degrees to which Bitcoin helps or hurts different people. A person who saves Bitcoin privately to leave an abusive spouse outweighs a person who loses $1,000 in a bitcoin gamble. A full evaluation should also incorporate the degree to which bitcoin benefits and harms each person.

But that alone doesn't suffice either. Both present people and future people matter, not present people alone. Given the world's current state and trajectory, is it *better* that we continue with bitcoin or without? To answer this question, we'll reason from first principles about right and wrong, what money is and could be, which features of money are good features for a money to have, how to balance harm and happiness, and so on. Overall, we use the tool of philosophical argument. And the book revolves around a philosophically-motivated thought experiment to derive our conclusion: that very likely, you would prefer to live in a bitcoin world. So this particular bitcoin book needs philosophy.

We also need more than philosophy. We need the tools of computer science and cryptography to understand bitcoin's technical machinery. We need tools from economics to understand bitcoin's incentives and the possible effects of its monetary policy. We need tools from physics and climate science to understand bitcoin's energy consumption. We also need to observe the world to see how bitcoin currently affects it and speculate reasonably about its future effects, given our current trajectory. We'll use data in the aggregate, as well as particular events. We'll use statistics about banking and finance, for instance, and examine real-world uses of bitcoin. Thus, unlike purely theoretical philosophy books, this one has two feet firmly planted in the concrete world. The task is enormous precisely because so many disciplines bear on it.

Herein lies the danger. Foreigners often get lost. And we are, in all fields except philosophy, foreigners. We are what Nathan Ballantyne calls *epistemic trespassers*, people who pass judgments in an area without having that area's evidence or skills.[17] No one can avoid this while working on the big questions about bitcoin. The questions are too expansive and multidisciplinary. To trespass responsibly, we've shored up our knowledge in other domains and consulted with a range of experts from other disciplines. Although the main argument channels evidence from other disciplines, it nonetheless remains philosophical overall.

This book focuses on the current state of the world, bitcoin's place in it, and the world's potential trajectories. We consider the people bitcoin helps, as well as those it harms. And besides individuals, we consider past, present, and future structural factors in the distribution of goods and power. We firmly believe that anyone who attends solely to bitcoin's benefits misses something, as does anyone who attends solely to its harms. A reasonable view about bitcoin requires considering both. In what follows, you'll find a framework for doing exactly that. And if you use it, you'll likely judge that bitcoin's benefits outweigh its costs.

1.5 Disclosures and denials

Let's clarify what the book doesn't do.

We don't prophesy. Though we'll argue in Chapter 5 that volatility is baked into bitcoin's design, the book makes no systematic bitcoin price predictions. The price of bitcoin will go up. But it will also go down. Up, down, all around. It might even drop to zero. But we care far more about bitcoin's use as resistance money than we do about bitcoin's price. So that's what this book is about.

We don't market. The book doesn't promote or encourage investment in bitcoin.[18] Imagine an overall positive philosophical assessment of the internet from the 1990s. At the time, detractors wouldn't have automatically accused the authors of goading others to "buy the internet." This sounds silly because the main internet protocols were never monetized. But we often meet this sort of response to our work on bitcoin, and it's no wonder why. Bitcoin isn't just monetizable – it's money. And if you squint hard enough, defending anything that has a price resembles marketing. But this book isn't a pamphlet. We don't care whether you buy bitcoin. So we won't explain how to buy, hold, or spend it. We're philosophers. We care more about the truth than about bitcoin. We offer arguments about bitcoin but not arguments to buy bitcoin.

We don't preach – not to the choir, at least. Substantial portions of the book won't please many die-hard bitcoin enthusiasts. We argue for claims that many bitcoin enthusiasts reject or wouldn't say aloud in polite company – that bitcoin and the US dollar are symbiotic, that the world likely won't undergo "hyperbitcoinization" in our lifetimes (where bitcoin becomes the only money), that bitcoin can help ameliorate very real and human-caused climate issues, and so on. Although bitcoin enthusiasts have a diverse set of beliefs, as we discussed earlier, many influential bitcoin enthusiasts do endorse Austrian economics and some form of radical libertarianism or even anarcho-capitalism. We don't, however. And the book doesn't. We have few, if any, ideological arrows in our quiver. We argue from widely held beliefs.

We also acknowledge potential sources of bias. All three of us use bitcoin as money and hold modest amounts of it.[19] This could skew our judgment. We're human. We've all been fellows with the Bitcoin Policy Institute. One of us has also written for a bitcoin company. We appear on bitcoin podcasts, publish in bitcoin venues, and speak at bitcoin conferences. We have social ties across the bitcoin world. These all provide insight. But they also likely skew our judgment.

Some will call us grifters. Suppose we are. Still, our arguments stand or fall on their merits. We submit them for serious consideration. But really, we humbly submit that the grift critique gets things backwards. We advocate for bitcoin because we believe in it after years of study; we didn't study bitcoin for years because we own bitcoin. We've also taken on reputational risk. Academics, for the most part, still associate bitcoin with alt-right political views, gambling, and crime. Any academic who writes positively about bitcoin risks being labeled as a political radical or, yes, a grifter. Indeed, we know many academics who agree with us about bitcoin but who don't say so publicly for fear of reprisal. We've risked our reputations to say publicly what we've discovered privately – that bitcoin is likely overall good. This book is evidence of our skin in the game. We invite you to play, by considering the arguments themselves.

1.6 Audience

If you've made it this far and are curious about what comes next, this book is for you. Bitcoin is complex. But we'll equip you in the pages to come with just about everything you'll need to know to understand it, without fixation on unnecessary technical details.

The book is also for bitcoin skeptics. Skeptics keep us honest. They probe and poke and question. We're here for it. Although we view bitcoin positively, we'll draw throughout on premises that anyone can accept, not just die-hard friends of bitcoin. We'll also present and evaluate several dozen challenges to bitcoin along the way.

Few outsiders realize that crypto enthusiasts number among bitcoin's most ardent skeptics. We've also seen outsiders express surprise at the contempt bitcoin enthusiasts often have for the rest of the cryptocurrency space. Although we think bitcoin is special,[20] we wage no battles on this front. This is a bitcoin book, not an anti-crypto book. In our experience, crypto folk usually respect bitcoin. Some love it. But many such people hide their feelings to avoid bitcoin tribalists. If this is you, think of our book as a bridge back to bitcoin. Come on over for a bit; it's safe.

This olive branch might frustrate some bitcoin enthusiasts. And if they keep reading, we might frustrate them a bit more. As umpires of ideas, we call balls and strikes as we see them, even if we upset the home crowd. Standard pro-bitcoin arguments require significant qualification, and some should be rejected altogether. Tribalism, here as elsewhere, provides an unreliable outlook on the world. Tribes narrow and blur our vision.[21] Despite the hopes of many bitcoin diehards, it won't end war, restore the traditional family, or fix the real estate market. It won't improve nutrition, inspire a return to Renaissance-style art, or revive nineteenth-century architecture. Bitcoin does not fix everything. It fixes a few things – and even breaks some others. But what it does fix is of great consequence.

Many policymakers agree that bitcoin is consequential. Rarely do they treat bitcoin as they once did – as digital pogs or Dutch tulips, a passing fad among the young or degenerate. Even so, policy discussions often miss the mark. Many bitcoin-related policy recommendations would hurt more than they help. We think the main culprit here is ignorance. So policymakers would benefit from a deeper understanding of bitcoin and its global consequences. This book offers exactly that.

On the flip side, concerned voters hear that Governor so-and-so is pro-bitcoin or that Senator such-and-such is anti-bitcoin. We offer no advice about how to weigh political candidates on the basis of their bitcoin stances. But the book will help readers understand bitcoin well enough to evaluate many policy proposals that touch on bitcoin.

Some crystal-ball readers suspect bitcoin is the future of money. And they wonder what the future holds as a result. They'll find valuable ingredients for their mental models in what follows.

Potential investors scrutinize bitcoin's value proposition. Although we would make crummy financial advisors, anyone who hopes to bet on bitcoin's success (or failure) would benefit from a deeper understanding of what bitcoin is and how it fits into the world.

Finally, we come to the philosophers. Our people. Understanding bitcoin requires some familiarity with several disciplines. But the big questions – the most controversial and interesting ones – are essentially philosophical. And this book is packed with controversy. There's some heterodox metaphysics in Chapter 2, unusually non-ideal political philosophy in Chapter 4, strident and liberal anti-censorship and pro-privacy arguments in Chapters 6 and 7, and a pro-bitcoin conclusion in Chapter 12. And then there's Chapter 11 – a compendium of anti-bitcoin arguments and responses to them. Food for thought: enjoy the meal.

1.7 Preview

The central question of the book is whether we ought to prefer a world with bitcoin to a world without bitcoin. So after explaining what bitcoin is and situating it among other cryptocurrencies, we introduce our preferred method of evaluation: the veil of ignorance. We ask the reader to forget who they are in the world and evaluate bitcoin from the supposition that they could turn out to be any actual person. We break the central question into five dimensions: monetary policies and institutions, privacy, censorship-resistance, financial inclusion, and security and energy use. Along each of these dimensions, we argue that bitcoin offers something valuable. With respect to monetary institutions, bitcoin brings the rule of law to the world of money and is an attractive alternative and opt-in money, especially for the billions who suffer under bad monetary rulers. With respect to financial privacy, we show how bitcoin's open architecture enables swapping, joining, and routing techniques that in turn enable privacy by obscurity – just like ordinary physical cash. With respect to censorship, we show that uncensorable money is a powerful tool in the fight against the authoritarian regimes under which half the world's population suffers. When it comes to financial inclusion, we discuss the reasons people are excluded from traditional monetary networks and show that bitcoin does not allow for systemic exclusion. We then turn our attention to bitcoin's security and discuss bitcoin's energy use and the positive and negative externalities that energy use leads to. Having made a case for bitcoin due to the aforementioned features, we then offer and discuss all the best objections to bitcoin.

Where does this all leave us? We conclude with a cumulative evaluation of bitcoin that integrates the results of the previous chapters. If you didn't know who you'd be and were moderately risk averse, we think the balance of the evidence supports a net positive assessment of bitcoin behind the veil. There is room here, though, for reasonable disagreement, and our framework highlights the dimensions that matter, clarifies the fault lines that remain, and helps identify empirical, technical, and normative theses that deserve further attention. We conclude with a meditation on what bitcoin may yet do.

But before all that, you might want to know what bitcoin really is. That's where we turn next. But be warned that the next chapter is technical, especially Section 2.3 and following. Those who aren't interested in those technical details can skip ahead to Chapter 3.

Notes

1. Hazlett and Luther (2020).
2. Halvorson (2021).
3. Schrepel (2021).
4. Hughes (1993).
5. Bartlett (2016) and Levy (2001): Chapter 7.
6. We'll often speak of dollars, or US dollars, because that's a currency with which we and many others are familiar. In most cases, readers can substitute their own state-issued currency.
7. Chaum (1982).
8. Brunton (2020, p. 1).
9. Metzger (2022).
10. The preface to Narayanan et al. (2016) – "The Long Road to Bitcoin" – documents about a hundred cryptographic electronic payment systems, nearly all of which failed.
11. Each kind of trusted party can be found in an early post announcing the creation of bitcoin and explaining its contrast with conventional systems, quoted nearly in full later.
12. Lagos (2008).
13. Szabo (2001).
14. We'll drop the "Nakamoto" from here on out, refer to Satoshi as an individual (although the moniker may well have been operated instead by a collective), and use the pronouns that Satoshi apparently preferred. As for Satoshi's true identity, we'll not speculate on the matter here but refer interested readers to Frisby (2014): Chapter 6 and Appendix II.
15. Nakamoto (2009a). Notably, the post quoted here appeared on the website for the P2P foundation, "The Foundation for Peer to Peer Alternatives," further cementing disintermediated commerce as a central goal in bitcoin's design.

16. In fact, there will eventually be exactly 20,999,999.9769 bitcoin, 20,999,949. 9769 of which will ever be spendable.
17. See Ballantyne (2019a, 2019b, p. 207).
18. For a book that takes up that task, see Edstrom (2019).
19. We have dollars too – American and Singaporean – and use them as money.
20. Bailey and Warmke (2023).
21. Kahan (2016).

2

WHAT BITCOIN REALLY IS

2.1 The book of bitcoin

From March 1836 to October 1837, Boz faithfully published a new installment of his story every month – except for May 1837, when he was mourn-
ing his sister-in-law's passing. We can imagine the process. Every month,
Boz would produce some text. Referees or editors would ensure that it met
various standards. And finally, the publisher, Chapman & Hall, would
disseminate each installment to shops and readers. We now recognize Boz
under his legal name, 'Charles Dickens', and this story as *The Pickwick
Papers*.

Bitcoin works much the same way except that the bitcoin "book" is
digital, lengthy, and boring. There is not one pseudonymous writer but
many. No single grumpy referee or editor has veto power. And a revolving
group of publishers compete to publish an installment every ten minutes.
The bitcoin book has more coauthors than any other work in history. And
it is likely the most secure publicly available document the world has ever
known.

In our view, this ongoing digital book describes the movements of an
abstract substance – bitcoin. Due to the book's content and production,
we can treat the book of bitcoin as a giant ledger where each described
movement of bitcoin serves as a ledger entry. As we'll see, Satoshi created
digital money without trusted parties by inventing a decentralized publication system for a massively coauthored story.

Though it attempts to replicate some key features of both physical cash
and centralized databases typical of other forms of digital money, Satoshi's

DOI: 10.4324/9781003484721-2

system bears little resemblance to either. Why did digital cash take this weird form? Satoshi designed bitcoin to avoid trusted parties: makers, mediators, and managers. In doing so, he also resolved a dilemma. We'll understand bitcoin – and money – better once we see what this dilemma is and how Satoshi resolved it.

2.2   Fail or jail

Satoshi once implied that he began working on bitcoin in mid-2007.[1] By then, he had seen several digital money projects go down in flames. Collectively, these failures provided evidence of a dilemma. On the one hand, you could build a project without trusted parties. But no one knew how to prevent digital counterfeiting, and hyperinflation, without trusted parties. On the other hand, your digital money project could have a trusted party – you, perhaps. Then you could protect the supply's overall integrity and prevent hyperinflation. The downside? If you didn't have the resources to hire the right lawyers, federal agents might shut down your project, seize assets, and even prosecute you as a felon. Hence, you could either create worthless digital tokens or risk a one-way ticket to the slammer. Fail or jail.

Let's review a few examples that Satoshi himself likely witnessed.

You've probably never heard of Mojo Nation. It was a niche network with a short lifespan, from 2000 to 2002. It never had a successful product or a wide user base. But unlike most failed internet companies from the dot-com era, it achieved lasting significance. In fact, Mojo Nation is likely the era's most influential failure.[2]

Cypherpunk Jim McCoy founded Mojo Nation in 2000 to create a peer-to-peer file-sharing application. But it had another main component to incentivize users – digital money, in the form of Mojo tokens. In essence, Mojo Nation tried to create both BitTorrent and bitcoin in a single project. It's no surprise that Mojo Nation buckled under excessive ambition. Mojo Nation's token supply soon went haywire, leading to hyperinflation.

In the wake of Mojo Nation's failure, a former employee discarded the failed digital money component and then simplified and released the file-sharing component as free and open-source software. The result – BitTorrent – has at times purportedly accounted for up to half of all internet traffic, with hundreds of millions of users worldwide. That former employee, cypherpunk Bram Cohen, has called Mojo Nation a "glorious failure." And on the failed experiment in digital cash, he quipped: "Inflation control is easy. Decentralized inflation control is hard."[3]

This point follows from a more general principle. Without trusted parties, it's hard to protect the integrity of a digital monetary asset, whether from people who seek to game issuance or from those who seek to double-spend.

Projects with trusted parties could protect an asset's integrity – but not if federal prosecutors came knocking. Let's review some noteworthy cases where this happened.

E-gold, founded by oncologist Douglas Jackson in 1996, settled transactions in digital grams of gold backed by physical gold held in reserve. Users could also transact nominally in dollars, keep their private information private, and send micropayments over the internet or wirelessly over mobile. Transactions settled quickly with low fees. E-gold processed up to $2 billion per year in 2006 and boasted several million active accounts. But in 2005, the FBI and Secret Service raided e-gold's parent company and seized its financial records.[4] Then in April 2007, just before Satoshi began work on bitcoin, Jackson and his colleagues were indicted for conspiracy to commit money laundering and for operating an unlicensed money-transmitting business. At the same time, the government seized a ton of the company's gold – literally.[5]

In interviews, Jackson has denied that e-gold's centralization led to its downfall. Instead, he has bizarrely blamed both a "very high profile cypherpunk" who sought to kill his business and a corrupt law enforcement agency.[6] But e-gold had custodians, central offices, intermediaries, and a CEO. Without these, would-be attackers would have had little to attack. A knight may fall by the sword, but parading shieldless doesn't help.

Or consider the electronic Liberty Dollar. Its creator, Bernard Nothaus, had a "spiritual epiphany" in 1974 about the importance of gold and, soon after, co-founded the Royal Hawaiian Mint – a decidedly nonroyal mint in Hawaii. Nothaus realizes how whacky his quasi-religious conviction might sound. His defense:

> You can make fun of it if you like. But there are religions where God comes to you on a little wafer. They had some good people selling that one. Imagine marketing a crucifixion as a beautiful experience. Give me a naked woman and a joint.[7]

In 1998, Nothaus created Liberty Dollar to issue a private currency with precious metals. And in 2003, he issued the electronic Liberty Dollar – backed by precious metals. Liberty Dollar had a quarter million users, with $55 million in circulation across 80 cities.

Then in 2006, the US Mint and prosecutors from the Department of Justice announced that using the physical Liberty Dollar was a federal crime. A defiant Nothaus continued to run Liberty Dollar, and in March 2007, he boldly filed suit against Henry Paulson, the Secretary of the Treasury, and

Alberto Gonzales, the US Attorney General. He lost. And on a November 2007 morning, the FBI and Secret Service raided the Liberty Dollar headquarters in an Evansville, Indiana, strip mall. They seized over $8 million in precious metals, including nearly two tons of Ron Paul coins. Although Nothaus seemed to have run the digital Liberty Dollar above board,[8] it died as collateral damage.

Several other projects busied the FBI around the same time. For instance, in 2002, Vladimir Kats and Arthur Budovsky launched Gold Age. By July 2006, they'd been indicted for running a related illegal money-transmitter business. The case "sent shockwaves through the digital currency industry."[9] They pled guilty in 2007 and received five years probation. Soon after, Budovsky fled to Costa Rica and, with Kats and a few others, started Liberty Reserve, a highly popular digital currency business. It was shut down by the US government in 2013. Kats received a ten-year prison sentence in return for pleading guilty and cooperating in the case against Budovsky, who then pled guilty and received a 20-year sentence.

The husband-and-wife team of James and Pamela Fayed founded E-bullion in 2001. Like e-gold, all transactions were instant and final with low fees. The currency was backed by gold bullion, and users could open an account without providing personal information. Among these digital currency projects, E-bullion is special. In 2015, James Fayed explained why:

> All in all, to date no charge against me or my companies regarding illegal or criminal conduct has been proven or survived legal challenges, and this is simply because no criminal activity existed, period.[10]

This is a half-truth, however. The Fayeds avoided prosecution because on July 28, 2008, days before the government unsealed an indictment against E-bullion, Pamela died. James killed her. So technically, Pamela couldn't go to prison because she was dead, and James couldn't go to prison because he was already there. A pyrrhic victory.

You get the picture. The Feds pursued digital cash projects with extreme diligence. But why? Nothaus, the founder of Liberty Dollar, found the situation absurd:

> This is the United States government. It's got all the guns, all the surveillance, all the tanks, it has nuclear weapons, and it's worried about some ex-surfer guy making his own money? Give me a break!

This must have been particularly frustrating for Nothaus, who seems to have run his digital currency business above board. But in the wake of 9/11, the US Patriot Act sought to curb the flow of dark money around the world. And in the eyes of law agencies, digital cash projects outside traditional rails looked like sewers full of dark money. Often, they were. Liberty Reserve, for instance, allegedly handled $6 billion in criminal proceeds.[11]

Now some failed digital cash projects had the corporate structure to run legal money-transmitting businesses. Mondex (1993), acquired by Mastercard in 1997, oddly achieved a circular economy at the University of Exeter. But it was doomed by requiring costly and inconvenient infrastructure. Visacash launched in 1997. They not only mimicked Mondex's failures but also inexplicably marketed their product as an "electronic purse." Neither were native to the internet, and of course, they were centralized. If governments had pressured either to spy on users or shut down accounts, they would have had to comply or suffer the consequences.

Meanwhile, several cypherpunk proposals either never launched or never gained much adoption – DigiCash (1990, David Chaum), hashcash (1997, Adam Back), b-money (1998, Wei Dai), bitgold (1998, Nick Szabo), RPOW (2004, an implementation of bitgold with a trusted server, along with a patched version of BitTorrent to incentivize users, Hal Finney), and Nym (2005, an implementation of Chaum's ecash, Jason Holt). Most lacked ways to protect the integrity of the asset supply or operate without trusted parties. But they made incremental progress. DigiCash, for example, used cryptography to ensure that no one could spend tokens that weren't theirs and implemented cash-like privacy guarantees. In b-money, copies of the entire ledger would be maintained by all network participants.[12] And hashcash – conceived first as an anti-spam measure – deployed expensive computations to ensure that no one could print new tokens at zero cost (b-money did this as well).[13] Each of these innovations would eventually find a home in bitcoin's design.[14]

By mid-2007, when Satoshi began work on bitcoin, he had strong evidence for a dilemma. As a lone individual without a legal team, a new digital cash project had a good chance of failing for one of two reasons:

- corrupted use or supply, without trusted parties, or
- censorship and federal persecution, with trusted parties

Pick your poison – oversupply or FBI. And even if you could avoid these fates, you would need to bootstrap a monetary network from scratch. Both big-time projects (like Mondex) and small-time ones (like DigiCash) would fail at this later step. None of bitcoin's spiritual ancestors would ever achieve a significant level of adoption.

Satoshi deftly steered his project through these obstacles. Above all, he discovered how to protect the integrity of digital money without trusted parties – no makers, mediators, or managers needed. In the failed projects with trusted parties, federal authorities seized the assets of managers, pursued makers for counterfeiting, and charged mediators with money laundering and running unlicensed money-transmitting businesses. Often, a single person served all three roles, making them a lightning rod for government attention. Bitcoin, by design, lacks all three. So bitcoin solved three related challenges.

2.2.1   Issuance without makers

Reflecting in 2007 on the legal troubles of projects like e-gold, Mojo Nation founder Jim McCoy said that you "never want to open this Pandora's box of tying units to any real currency like the dollar."[15] At that time, this was a recipe for being charged for counterfeiting. But if you tied the units of digital cash to something else held in reserve, like precious metals, the FBI could (and did) seize them and make your project worthless anyway. So it was clear that Mojo Nation had the right idea to issue its own native unit without tying it to anything.

However, if you issued a new unit unbacked by anything, then the project must bootstrap itself and somehow scale to wider adoption. Also, without a maker to issue these units, the system must automate issuance. The system must then thwart potential cheaters who seek to exploit the conditions for automated issuance. Otherwise, users will reward themselves too much and too quickly, leading to hyperinflation – like Mojo Nation.

2.2.2   Custody without managers

With few possible exceptions, all the earlier failures in digital cash ultimately required someone else to hold your funds. Users simply held a claim on them. This is even true of David Chaum's privacy project, Digicash, and Hal Finney's implementation of bitgold. As a result, user funds pooled into large honeypots, vulnerable to loss, seizure, and irresponsible investment. A digital cash project that doesn't require managers must allow users to hold money directly. But how can we hold digital money directly? Managers with online financial services have a registry of usernames and passwords to give each user exclusive access to an account. Without a central registry of usernames and passwords, how can users "store" digital cash anywhere?

2.2.3   Payments without mediators

We can copy and paste digital objects like photos and music files. If a piece of cash is also digital, why couldn't we copy and paste it too? Then we could both spend and save the very same stash of money simultaneously. Without a trusted party to track digital cash on a central ledger, the digital cash system must have some other way to prevent double-spending. As we explained in Chapter 1, a digital cash system is worthless without double-spending prevention.

To create digital cash for the masses, Satoshi had to discover how to automate issuance, enable direct custody, and prevent double-spending. It's a tall order. He filled it by creating a decentralized publication system.

Bitcoin is a hodgepodge of techniques and tools glued together to resolve the earlier challenges. Here's a primer, in case you've never quite understood how the main pieces fit together.[16] If you already have a firm grasp of how bitcoin works or are uninterested in the technical details, you can skip to Chapter 3 now without too much loss. When evaluating our later arguments, though, you may want to keep an open mind about revisiting Chapter 2. The issues we explore in the rest of the book will occasionally rest on the details here.

2.3 Bitcoin's ledger

Participants in the Bitcoin network play three different, though sometimes overlapping, roles:

(1) *Users* compose and submit transactions for the ledger.
(2) *Nodes* referee submitted transactions and maintain the ledger.
(3) *Miners* compete with one another to publish updates to the ledger.[17]

In other words, the bitcoin network has writers, referees, and publishers. We'll spiral around these roles to explain how bitcoin secures its ledger without trusted third parties. But we begin with the ledger itself.

Ledgers record transactions. Checkbook ledgers record checks. Bank ledgers record loans given and deposits taken. Likewise, the bitcoin ledger records all bitcoin transactions. From bitcoin's genesis in January 2009 until today, the ledger has recorded every single movement of bitcoin. When a quantity of bitcoin moves from one spot to another – we call these spots *addresses* – the ledger records it.[18]

In fact, the ledger's saying that an address has bitcoin *makes it so*. This contrasts sharply with more familiar ledgers. Mildred might forget to record the check for her babysitter. A bank might record a deposit in the wrong amount. These ledgers can misrepresent. They represent events outside the ledger and may therefore record an event with false details or fail to record an event at all. This was a problem for e-gold, the electronic Liberty Dollar, and other such projects; no matter what these ledgers said you had, the Feds could raid a strip mall and seize the underlying asset. But the bitcoin ledger can't misrepresent bitcoin transactions. It records the truth about all bitcoin transactions and nothing but the truth. This is because the fact that the ledger says it *makes* it true; the truth depends on what the ledger itself records because bitcoin doesn't exist outside of the ledger. So the bitcoin ledger not only records but also *determines* who has which amounts of bitcoin.[19]

Some ledgers are like mirrors. They reflect, perhaps imperfectly, some *other* reality. These are accurate to the extent that they reflect that reality well. Bitcoin's ledger is not like this, for it records no reality beyond the ledger itself.

To be sure, people may send bitcoin to the wrong address or in the wrong amount. But these user errors involve a mismatch between what we intend and what we do. The bitcoin network can't read our minds. In such cases, it doesn't do what we intend. It simply updates the ledger based on what we do. So even though the bitcoin ledger doesn't make mistakes, it can and does embed our own. Imperfect humans. Perfect ledger.

In this way, bitcoin resembles cash. If you drop a $10 bill in the park, neither the Federal Reserve nor the Treasury have erred. If you complain to them and ask for it back, they'd rightly show you the door. When you misplace physical cash, the laws of nature haven't malfunctioned. The physical world hasn't glitched. It simply embeds your mistake.

At this point, you might protest: Doesn't comparing bitcoin to cash undermine the claim that bitcoin is digital cash? After all, real cash needs no ledger. So why does bitcoin have one? But in fact, physical cash has a ledger not unlike bitcoin's own. Each piece of cash – bill or coin – has a path through physical space and time. And at each moment, a bill or coin occupies a location in the form of spatiotemporal coordinates. We possess a bill or coin when those coordinates have some close relation to our own, as when we control access to a purse or vault or back pocket. Changes of possession, then, are written in the dance through these coordinates over time. So in that sense, physical cash has a ledger all right – the physical world itself.[20]

The bitcoin ledger works similarly but uses *mathematical* rather than *physical* space. Bitcoin addresses – i.e., the "places" where we hold bitcoin in the ledger – actually correspond to locations on a geometric curve.[21] And just as the physical laws ensure that chunks of cash don't sit at two or more places at once, the laws of bitcoin ensure that no single chunk of bitcoin sits at two or more addresses at once. In part, Satoshi overcame the double-spending problem by situating digital cash inside mathematical space, much like physical cash sits in physical space. For, as we'll soon explain, the rules in bitcoin's software prohibit quantities of bitcoin from sitting at two mathematical "places" at once.

Thus far, for simplicity, we've spoken of *the* bitcoin ledger. But bitcoin has no central ledger. Instead, Satoshi created a *distributed* system of ledgers with strict rules for how to update them. Anyone who runs the bitcoin software maintains their own copy; there are 47,000 such copies at the time of writing.[22] So no particular person or institution maintains *the* ledger; individuals maintain *a* ledger that, in time, duplicates of everyone else's ledger. All such copies agree, or at least converge towards agreement. They rarely disagree about which transactions have occurred or about how much bitcoin is at which address. But when they do, the network eventually reaches consensus. This is where the nodes and miners come in.

2.4   Nodes and miners

The bitcoin software encodes rules to preserve and update the ledger. Computers that run this software are *nodes*. Nodes check every transaction twice: once before miners see it and once after.[23]

On the first check, nodes serve as referees. After users submit transactions to appear in the ledger, nodes sift out the bad ones. The bad ones lack proper formatting or attempt to spend bitcoin that doesn't exist or has already been spent. Nodes forward the remaining transactions to miners. Miners then compete to publish a bundle of these transactions. Don't worry about mining yet; we'll explain it shortly. But about every ten minutes, a winning miner sends its bundle – called a *block* – back to all the nodes for another check.

At this point, nodes perform the second check, as curators of the ledger. After a miner successfully produces a block of transactions for the ledger, all the nodes verify whether it did indeed win the competition, whether it has the proper format, and whether it includes only good transactions.[24] If so, they add it to their ledger. Nodes continuously update their copies of the ledger, forward their updates to other connected nodes, and so on. In this way, updates to the ledger quickly propagate across the bitcoin network. So nodes both referee and curate the ledger. They don't themselves publish blocks for the ledger. That's what miners do.[25]

That's right: miners aim primarily to publish blocks to bitcoin's ledger. Fundamentally, they are competitive publishers. But they don't compete for nothing. The winning miner receives a reward in bitcoin. They're called *miners*, though, due to how they compete. Each block presents a mathematical challenge, and miners "dig" through mathematical space, rifling through numbers for a potential solution – much like gold miners dig in the ground for precious metal.

Mining solves two challenges at once: first, how to prevent double-spending without mediators and, second, how to issue an asset without makers. We'll briefly explain how mining works, first, and then show how it solves the double-spending and issuance problems.

2.5 How mining works

Miners compete to find a number by trial-and-error. They take node-approved transactions and "scrunch" them.[26] Then – simplifying a bit – they feed the scrunched transactions, data from the prior winning block, and a random number (we call this a *nonce*) into a mathematical function that spews out an unpredictable result. The result is unpredictable in this sense: you can't tell what the output will be from a given input until you actually compute the thing. The slightest change to an input will result in a wildly different output. This aptly named *hash function* spits out a number, and if it's "low enough," the miner wins. Miners feed the hash function repeatedly, cycling through nonces, until the function spews out a low-enough number. A miner wins about every ten minutes.

Let's consider a few basic examples. Suppose our target level for being "low enough" is 00001000. A winning miner must find a nonce that, combined with the prior block data and scrunched transactions, spews out a number at least as low as 00001000 from the hash function. Miners cycle through random nonces until someone hits the jackpot.

Trial 1

Inputs: [prior block data], [scrunched transactions], random nonce: 234609823

Output: 00322934. Too high; try again.

. . .

Trial 289

Inputs: [prior block data], [scrunched transactions], random nonce: 349457532

Output: 00813493. Too high; try again.

. . .

Trial 3,281

Inputs: [prior block data], [scrunched transactions], random nonce: 740761041

Output: 00000231. Low enough; victory!

Miners cycle through random nonces because the function is one-way: although a given input always returns the same output, each output is unpredictable from its input. Computers have no way to work backwards from a desired output to a particular random nonce and no way of ruling out nonces in batches or with useful heuristics. Trial-and-error, then, is the best way to find a lucky nonce. Anyone who's found such a nonce had to do some computational work: 3,281 guesses in this case.[27] Were the target lower – 00000100 instead of 00001000, say – we'd likely need many more guesses.

Of course, a miner could get super lucky. A miner might find a lucky nonce within the first few computations. But on average and over time, the lower the target threshold, the more computational grunt work required. So a miner who presents a winning nonce thereby offers evidence of completed work. For this reason, bitcoin's mining procedure is called "proof of work" – miners submit cryptographic proofs that they have done computational work.

The winning miner combines the prior block data, scrunched transactions, and the nonce into a block and passes it on to the network of nodes for verification. The nodes can quickly verify the block to ensure that its output falls below the threshold. Although finding a lucky nonce is computationally expensive, verification is computationally cheap – and fast. As evidence of bitcoin's elegant engineering, the "prior block data" in each block includes the output of the lucky trial from the *previous* block. This chains the blocks together into a block*chain*.

That's mining in a nutshell. The name of the game is to produce a block of transactions that the nodes will append to their ledgers. Collectively, the nodes are quite powerful then. If they reject a block, the miner receives no reward. Miners have good reason, then, to compile and submit for publication only transactions that nodes would endorse.

Now some have argued that miners serve as the very sort of mediators that bitcoin was designed to avoid, the kinds of mediators that we encounter in more traditional financial services – trusted payment processors, clearinghouses, and so on. The argument goes like this: to send bitcoin, users need miners to cooperate. Therefore, some miners stand between senders and recipients. As a result, miners mediate transactions in precisely the way that Satoshi hoped to avoid.[28]

True, a transaction can't settle without *some* miner publishing it within a block. But it doesn't follow that the cooperation of *any miner in particular* is required to settle a transaction.[29] No particular miner "stands in the middle" with the power to tamper with or block your transaction. Instead, an army of miners are constantly competing for the honor of publishing transactions. Publishing a transaction also nets the miner a transaction fee, which incentivizes each miner not to censor particular transactions.[30] So you don't need to trust all miners to cooperate. As with kidneys and some other bodily organs, you only need one, and it doesn't matter which.

What's more, neither miners nor nodes behave like trusted parties. First, they don't, and can't, custody the funds in the transactions they publish or referee. So users needn't trust them not to seize their funds. Second, entry and exit are permissionless. Miners and nodes enter and exit freely; no one can stop them from doing so. Third, anyone can independently verify all of the relevant activities. All participants run open-source software, and anyone can examine it for security holes. Miners do not merely claim to have done the relevant work. They *prove* it. And a node does not merely announce that a transaction is valid and then forward it on to peers for their immediate acceptance. Other nodes, instead, verify the transaction themselves. They don't trust, they verify.

Nodes also have specific rules about which kinds of blocks they'll accept. And these rules help solve the problems with double-spending and automated issuance. We consider these solutions one at a time.

2.6   Double-spending prevention without mediators

To prevent double-spends from appearing in the ledger, nodes follow two rules.

The first rule is obvious: reject blocks with an attempted double-spend. Under the hood, each transaction cites one or more past transactions as the source of the bitcoin that it spends. In this way, we can tell whether a transaction attempts to spend bitcoin previously spent in a past block. Nodes reject any such simple attempts.

So nodes must know all past transactions. And this requires that they agree on the state of the ledger through the most recent block. Here, the second rule comes in – nodes automatically endorse the *heaviest* version of the ledger. The heaviest version is the one that likely took the most work to produce by cycling through the most nonces. This rule protects against more complex double-spends.

Computing the heaviest version of the ledger requires that blocks have both an order and marker for the work likely required to produce each one. In bitcoin, each block has a piece of data that serves both purposes. It's the output of the hash function that secured the block's victory – the output that must fall below the threshold to win the competition.

To order blocks, each block's winning hash output appears in the next block. Each new block, then, includes a digital fingerprint of its predecessor. But this very fingerprint reveals how much work was likely required to produce it! The lower the output, the more computation cycles its miner likely expended. The hash output, then, serves as both a sequencer and a measurement. Hence, the mining hash function does more than provide the decentralized competition to publish blocks of transactions. Its output also orders blocks and allows nodes to calculate the heaviest chain of blocks.

By the nature of this dual-use fingerprint, nodes can compute the likely amount of work it took to produce a sequence of blocks. Since nodes are programmed to endorse the heaviest chain of blocks, the dual-use fingerprint enables the network to reach consensus about the state of the ledger

Imagine a field strewn with rocks, some stacked into mighty towers. Your job is to find the most massive tower. So you select the tower that took the most physical work to create. Luckily, each rock has its mass etched on the side – 1 kg here, 2.4 kgs there, and so on. With this information in hand, you can calculate which tower is the most massive. Sum up the numbers on the side of every tower's constituent rocks, and you'll know which tower likely required the most work to build. That's your winning tower. Nodes do this with candidate chains of blocks. They survey candidates and endorse the one that likely required the most work.

Here's how the heaviest chain rule helps maintain global agreement about the state of the ledger. Suppose two or more miners produce legitimate blocks at approximately the same time, each with a different attempt to spend the same bitcoin. Some nodes may choose one block while others choose the other. Miners then have a choice: which leading edge of the chain will they use to build the next block?

In the field of rocks, the miners' choice is like choosing between multiple towers with the same aggregate mass. But miners don't suffer like Buridan's ass, caught between competing options forever. They simply pick a chain to build on. Towers continue to receive new rocks, as it were. Soon enough, then, one chain outweighs the others.[31] As a result, the nodes automatically endorse it. This incentivizes miners to follow suit. For if you mine on top of a block that nodes no longer endorse, you lose the bitcoin reward. These miner incentives drive network consensus.

The heaviest chain rule shines brightest while protecting against complex double-spends. Suppose Jim uses bitcoin to buy a chair, and he's soon at home sitting in it. Then he wants his bitcoin back and decides he'd like to "undo" his transaction. Undoing the spend would require Jim to create an alternative series of blocks that diverges just prior to his transaction and that eventually outweighs the original chain. The nodes would then endorse his chain due to the heaviest chain rule.[32]

To succeed, Jim must marshal enough computing power to add enough blocks, one by one, until the nodes recognize his chain as the heaviest. This is called a *51% attack* because an attacker with a majority of the network's total computing power will likely succeed in building the heaviest chain.

51% attacks require expensive hardware and vast amounts of energy to outcompete the original chain as it continues to grow, block by block.

While Jim would likely succeed if he held 51% of the network's computing power, there's no guarantee. Miners on the original chain may devote more resources to defeating the attack. Or Jim might just get unlucky and fall further behind, requiring him to keep his electricity consumption high for far longer than he'd planned. There's another wrinkle too. The higher a bitcoin payment, the longer the seller should wait to hand over the goods. The longer the seller waits, the more blocks the attacker would need to redo, making the attack not just financially unwise but infeasible.

Suppose you wished to construct the most massive rock tower. You'd have to work a lot – more so than any other single individual would while working on the biggest tower. Double-spending is similar. To undo a past transaction, you must outwork the rest of the network in creating an alternative chain. Otherwise, your work counts for nothing. This is how bitcoin prevents double-spending without mediators. Whereas copying-pasting digitized information is extremely cheap and easy, rewriting bitcoin blocks is hugely expensive and comes with a decent chance of failure. So if someone has enough resources, she might as well mine blocks on the original chain and reap the rewards.

Any digital cash system will fail without double-spending prevention. Prior to bitcoin, projects like e-gold and Liberty Reserve used mediators. This made them less cash-like. Bitcoin gave us something new: double-spending prevention without mediators in the digital world. Instead of mediators, bitcoin nodes incentivize miners to secure the network against double-spends.

2.7 Issuance without makers

Satoshi also solved the problem of automated issuance: he figured out how to issue new units of money without centralized makers. To do so, he needed rules for issuance that were extremely hard to game. He needed rules for creating new tokens that would assign them to system participants but without enabling a free-for-all where anyone could mint new tokens and drive the supply to infinity and the value to zero (as with Mojo Nation).

Here's how he did it.

First, Satoshi encoded a long-range schedule for bitcoin's issuance. For now, each block issues new bitcoin. But this won't last forever. The last quantity of bitcoin will be issued in the year 2140, with the maximum supply falling under 21 million total bitcoin. On this schedule, early blocks issued up to 50 freshly minted bitcoin. Then every 210,000 blocks (approximately every four years), each block issues half as much: 50 bitcoin for the first four years, then 25 bitcoin, then 12.5, and so on. At the time of writing, each block issues 6.25 new bitcoin.

Second, bitcoin's issuance goes to the very participants who secure the network – the miners. Thus, bitcoin miners serve a dual purpose as both publishers and conduits of bitcoin issuance. This is crucial for a very simple reason: miners make the issuance schedule hard to game. You might think that bitcoin miners could pull the issuance schedule forward by devoting more computer power to produce blocks more quickly. But in practice, they can't.

Nodes compute the average time to publish a block over two-week periods. If blocks arrive, on average, more quickly than every ten minutes, nodes increase the mining difficulty for the following two weeks by lowering the threshold; lowering the threshold is like shrinking the bullseye. But if blocks come in more slowly than every ten minutes, the difficulty decreases, like enlarging the bullseye. As a result, miners cannot simply devote more computing power and compress the issuance schedule. After two weeks of faster blocks, the network makes mining that much more difficult for the subsequent two-week period. The network self-adjusts like a living organism to ensure that it remains on schedule forever.

Miners work for new coins. But they can't game the total supply or issuance schedule by working harder. Working harder does, however, increase their likely share of fixed rewards and thereby decrease the likely share of others, assuming others don't also work harder. Miners are incentivized to work harder to increase their likelihood of reward, and working harder increases bitcoin's security against double-spending. When miners pursue their own self-interest, they make bitcoin a more viable digital cash – more resistant to double-spending. Pretty clever.

On top of all this, bitcoin's issuance isn't just automated but also publicly auditable. Thanks to bitcoin's public ledger, anyone can audit the entire supply with nothing but a node. By comparing bitcoin's scheduled issuance against its actual issuance, anyone can audit the global supply of a monetary asset in under a second from their basement.

To review: Satoshi designed a technical tango to automate issuance and prevent double-spending without trusted parties. Nodes serve as the lead: miners must satisfy their rules to reap the desired reward. In rewarding bitcoin to dutiful miners, nodes incentivize them to protect their reward's own integrity. So anyone who wants digital cash without trusted parties also has incentive to join this virtuous feedback loop and run a node.

We've covered how bitcoin has issuance without makers and payments without mediators. But we've not yet covered how bitcoin permits custody without managers. For this, we must first explain how users construct transactions.

2.8   Users

The bitcoin ledger looks like a ginormous web of bucket brigades. Each transaction "pours" – and locks – bitcoin into one or more addresses. Once locked, it's ready for pouring again. Pouring also requires unlocking that bitcoin to pour. So every transaction has two halves – unlockings to pour and pourings to lock. The unlockings occur in *transaction inputs,* and the pourings occur in *transaction outputs*. Since inputs depend on previous outputs, we'll cover outputs first.

Warning: this section is fairly technical. Most bitcoin users have little idea about what follows because wallet applications handle this under the hood. But payoffs await those who persevere.

Each output in a transaction pours bitcoin into a new address. So each output has two bits of information:

- An amount of bitcoin to send (e.g., 0.25 bitcoin)
- A recipient address (e.g., bc1qvmvqqr9r0z86kpjzakyew48rsnqejqf56f-zl4u)

A transaction has one or more outputs, and each output has a unique tag in the blockchain. When a transaction appears in the ledger, outputs effectively lock the bitcoin to the recipient addresses.

Each input in a transaction unlocks bitcoin from a past transaction output. Inputs have two main parts too. The first cites the source of bitcoin to unlock:

- A pointer to a previous transaction output

The input also unlocks the bitcoin in that past output. For this, you need a *private key* – a number that works like a fancy password. The private key has two crucial features. First, it generates an address through a one-way function.[33] Because the function is one-way, no one can use the address to compute its private key. As with the hashing function miners use, you can't work backwards from its output to its input.

Second, the private key helps generate verifiable digital signatures. These signatures show that you have the private key for the generated address, without ever revealing the private key itself. A private key is like a digital signet ring. You can use it to prove that you have it. You can stamp messages of varying kinds to show that someone with the ring has endorsed them. Bitcoin transactions are messages, signed by private keys, that say where some bitcoin goes.

So a transaction input not only tags a past output as its source of bitcoin but it also includes a digital signature to prove the spender has the bona fides to spend that bitcoin. To provide these bona fides, you (privately) feed your address's private key along with the rest of the candidate transaction into a special cryptographic algorithm. Your transaction input then includes the result:

- A digital signature from the appropriate private key over the rest of the transaction

No one else sees the private key, but anyone can verify whether the digital signature came from it just by having the rest of the bitcoin transaction. And nodes do exactly that when they serve as referees.

Let's put the pieces together. Suppose you want to send some bitcoin to Liz. You specify an amount to send, an address Liz controls, and an unspent transaction output in which your address received some bitcoin. Your application composes this transaction and sends it along with the appropriate digital signature to the nodes.[34] Nodes verify the signature and check the ledger to make sure that you're not trying to double-spend. They forward it to miners, who race to publish it in the next block.[35] The winning miner sends a block for nodes to verify. Once verified, nodes add the block to their ledgers. Miners then compete to publish the next block. The ledger contains 801,238 blocks at the time of writing. Kerchunk! Make that 801,239.[36]

2.9 Custody without managers

Unlike digital cash, digital money is nothing new. You might own some digital money, for example, in the form of a balance with a commercial bank. By *owning* digital money, you might have moral and legal claims over it.[37] But in the world of traditional finance, digital money requires managers. You don't – and can't – *possess* your own digital money.

Physical cash is different. You can own it, obviously. But you can also hold it yourself. You may own cash *and* possess it. And you can possess it in a way that excludes others from possessing it – in *your* wallet, in *your* piggy bank, underneath *your* mattress. You possess a ten-dollar bill insofar as you control its location. And you control its location when you have the power to move it – from your hand, piggy bank, or whatever. To spend it, you exercise this control to move it from one physical locale to another, like when you hand over a banknote to a merchant.

With bitcoin, Satoshi brought this sort of excludable possession into the digital world. With physical cash, you alone may enjoy exclusive control because, say, you alone have the physical key to a physical vault. With bitcoin, a user enjoys exclusive control when she alone has the private key to unlock bitcoin from a past transaction. To spend bitcoin, users exercise that control to move it from one *mathematical* locale to another.

Let's tease this apart some more. Bob hasn't really sent bitcoin to Alice's address until the transaction appears in the ledger. Once it does, the transaction output locks bitcoin to Alice's address. The output remains an *unspent transaction output* – a UTXO – until Alice unlocks it with a digital signature in a transaction of her own.

UTXOs are like little digital checks; they are digital financial instruments that need an authorized digital signature to spend the quantities of bitcoin they specify. Alice's UTXO specifies a quantity of bitcoin under her control. And it's under her control because she has the private key for the recipient address in the UTXO. With that private key, Alice can produce a verifiable digital signature. As long as Alice retains exclusive access to this private key, she alone can get a transaction in the ledger that spends the UTXO in question.

So now we have the digital version of physical possession – exclusive information control. This contrasts sharply with the control we have over passwords with banks and other financial services providers. They have centralized databases of our usernames and passwords. When we sign in, they check to ensure that the provided password matches against the correct username in the database. And, then, our balances reflect funds that they possess and manage.

With bitcoin, you can manage your own funds and, to some small extent, be your own bank. It just depends on whether you'd like to secure your own private keys. Your private keys and addresses needn't sit in a centralized database, waiting for the next hack or data leak. All possible private keys already exist, along with their paired addresses. But instead of being stored in data centers, they sit freely available for anyone to pluck from Plato's heaven, like any other numbers. But under industry standards, your private key is safe. There are close to 10^{77} private keys – within striking distance of atoms in the visible universe.[38] The odds of someone stumbling upon your private key before the heat death of the universe are basically zero.

Bitcoin's cryptography has important consequences not just for possession but for claims of possession too. As we mentioned earlier, the very same private key that can unlock a UTXO can also produce a digital signature over any message at all outside the bitcoin network. So if someone claims to be Satoshi Nakamoto, say, they can simply sign a random message like, "I love cheerios" to prove that they have the private key for any one of Satoshi's early addresses. So if someone claims to be Satoshi but hems and haws when asked to provide a digital signature, they're probably full of it.

2.10 We made it up

To avoid trusted parties, bitcoin was built as a decentralized publication system. And if we pay closer attention to what it publishes, we learn some surprising lessons not only about bitcoin but also about money more generally.

With each new block added to the ledger, quantities of bitcoin *move* to new locations. Quantities of bitcoin *divide*, like a rock split in half, and also *combine*, like two cups of beer poured into one. Quantities of bitcoin are also *measurable*, down to eight decimal places at present.[39]

This collection of properties might suggest that bitcoin is like other measurable things that divide into smaller quantities or combine into bigger ones – physical substances like granite, coffee, or oil. Yet as solids and liquids, quantities of this stuff have volume and mass. Quantities of bitcoin lack both. Bitcoin moves but has no physical location. It combines and divides but has no mass. We can see the numerals that signify how much bitcoin anyone receives, but we don't see the bitcoin itself. If you think otherwise, just ask, What color is the bitcoin you received? What shape?

The ledger obviously doesn't represent movements of an external substance. Bitcoin inhabits the ledger. But if bitcoin isn't a physical substance, what is it?

Here's an answer: each quantity of bitcoin in a transaction output is a string of symbols. That sounds plausible. But it's wrong.[40] Transaction outputs denominate bitcoin in *satoshis* – bitcoin's smallest bits.[41] We've simply adopted Satoshi's own convention of treating 100 million satoshis as a single bitcoin. Furthermore, no satoshi, or group of satoshis, is identifiable with a string of symbols. This hypothesis doesn't capture the actual features of the ledger, and it runs afoul of common philosophical sense.

For example, you might think that each satoshi is numbered '0,' '1,' '2,' and so on, and that certain satoshis belong to an address. Wrong. The ledger doesn't tag or mark individual satoshis. Instead, the ledger simply uses numerals to signify the quantities of satoshis sent.

So then you might think that each quantity of satoshis in the ledger is identical to the numeral that signifies it.[42] If this proposal were right, a transaction output with 250000 satoshis would be identical with the numeral '250000.' In philosophy, this is known as a use-mention error. When we *use* the name 'Einstein,' we refer to the man, Einstein. When we *mention* the name, we refer to the name. This happens when we say that 'Einstein' has eight letters (or five, depending on whether you're counting letter tokens or letter types). And Einstein, the man, isn't 'Einstein' the name. We ought not confuse words with the things they signify.

Likewise, we ought not confuse a numeral '250000' with what it signifies in the ledger – 250000 satoshis. Like Einstein and 'Einstein,' numerals and quantities of bitcoin have very different properties. To start, you can send half of your 250000 satoshis without sending the numeral '250000' with half as many digits or pixels. Paying heed to the ledger's actual details reveals that quantities of bitcoin cannot plausibly be identified with any symbols in the ledger.

Let's review our progress. First, transaction outputs signify quantities of bitcoin. Second, these quantities of bitcoin aren't identical with anything inside the ledger or in the physical world. So what else could they be?

Here's an idea: bitcoin is abstract in the way that numbers are abstract. We can write down numerals on paper (e.g., '1,' '2,' '3'), and what we've written has a physical size and location. But most deny that the numbers themselves – 1, 2, 3 – exist in space. Can you kick the number 1, hear the number 2, or taste the number 3? Likewise, we can see the numerals in bitcoin transaction outputs without seeing quantities of bitcoin. So we're in the right neighborhood, at least.

Yet abstract objects like numbers are static. Not only have they always existed, they've never changed. 1 has always come before 2, 2 before 3, and so on. Now the number 4 might capture, and then fail to capture, the number of living Beatles. But the number 4 itself hasn't changed; the world has (sadly) changed in relation to it.

Unlike numbers, bitcoin does change. First, bitcoin presumably hasn't always existed. Satoshi created it; he made it up. Second, bitcoin changes constantly. The supply changes when miners earn new bitcoin. And users fling it around to different addresses. So although bitcoin is abstract, it isn't quite like the numbers.

So at this point in our process of elimination, one plausible category remains. What's abstract but made up by humans? What things change as humans publish text about them? Imagine if shortly after J.K. Rowling completed the Harry Potter series, some fans created a website to write a collaborative story about butterbeer. Fans would register through the website to be assigned a cup within the story. Then with the website organizer's help, any fan could publish a snippet to the story about passing butterbeer from his or her cup to someone else's. On the outside, this looks like a boring, text-based, massively online multiplayer game. Users might eventually value butterbeer and send it to each other, within the game, for real goods and services, outside the game.

How does butterbeer differ from bitcoin? The publication process is different, yes. But in their fundamental natures, can we point to a relevant difference? Whether people value them or pay for them are external matters – much like whether 4 captures the number of Beatles. Neither are physical substances but nonetheless seem to have features like substances (divisibility, ability to be split and combined, etc.). Both originated with human thought. Both evolve as humans publish text about them. Overall, bitcoin walks and talks like a fictional substance – in the same category as butterbeer and kryptonite. So we think bitcoin is likely a fictional substance.[43]

People often react to this news in one of two ways. Bitcoin enthusiasts might say, "No, that can't be right! Bitcoin is real! The ledger has only truths!" And people who dislike bitcoin might say, "Suspicion confirmed – bitcoin is as fake as I thought it was!"

Hold on to those thoughts; there's more to say, and some of it may surprise you.

2.11 Money is strange

If bitcoin is made up, as we've argued, it's tempting to think that bitcoin is a scam – easily manipulable and overvalued. The wall of voices telling you to buy (or not buy) bitcoin probably doesn't help either. But the move from "bitcoin is made up" to "bitcoin is a scam" doesn't hold water for a few reasons.

First, works of fiction, like the ledger, still have truths about them. Even if no detective named "Sherlock Holmes" ever lived in 221b Baker St., it's still true *in the Conan Doyle stories* that Sherlock lives on Baker Street. Similarly, although the ledger is a work of fiction, we can speak truly about what happens in the ledger. It's true *in the current ledger* that address so-and-so has such-and-such bitcoin. In fact, the fictional status of the ledger helps explain why it can't go wrong. Even if we don't realize it, an address has bitcoin just in case, in the current ledger, the address has bitcoin.

Second, works of fiction can resist forgery. In his own time, Dickens alone could write new installments to extend a particular story. But he's gone now, and we have paper trails. Good luck trying to change *Oliver Twist* so that Mr. Grimwig is a disguised wizard hoping to prevent the birth of Lord Voldemort. Similarly, you can't just compose transactions willy-nilly that will appear in the bitcoin ledger. You need the right credential – a digital signature. You need to "be the Dickens" of your own bitcoin addresses. As we've seen, the network's referees and competitive publishers strictly enforce several rules about which submissions eventually appear in the ledger.

Finally, something can be both fictional and valuable. Suppose you have a ten-dollar bill in your fanny pack. You have ten somethings. But what exactly are these somethings? To begin, your ten dollars are ten in number, not one. But the ten-dollar bill itself is a single piece of paper. The ten dollars aren't ten pieces of paper or even ten partitions of paper, like adjacent lots of farmland. Hence, the ten dollars themselves are not the bill in your fanny pack. They must be something else.

Where do the ten dollars reside? Try as you might, you'll not find these ten dollars anywhere. The bill has the numeral '10' written on it several times, as well as 'Ten Dollars' prominently displayed on both sides. All this writing signifies a quantity of dollars. And just like the name 'Einstein' and the man Einstein, this is another case where what's signified (a quantity of dollars) isn't identical with the numerals or words that signify it. So we have a financial instrument, a physical bill, that represents a quantity of something that exists nowhere. Although dollar bills aren't abstract, dollars are. This has long been known. The economist Alfred Mitchell-Innes put it more eloquently over a hundred years ago, back when dollars were backed by precious metals:

> The eye has never seen, nor the hand touched a dollar. All that we can touch or see is a promise to pay or satisfy a debt due for an amount called a dollar. That which we handle may be called a dollar certificate or a dollar note or a dollar coin . . .[44]

And what holds for ten-dollar bills also holds for one dollar bills. I "give you a dollar" by transferring possession of the bill. The dollar itself doesn't literally change hands. If, as Innes says, no hands have ever touched a dollar, then no two hands have ever touched a dollar in succession either. We admit this sounds strange. It's not how we normally speak. Nonetheless, bills, checks, account balances, and so on represent quantities of these abstract units.

The dollar unit is the native measure of the dollar currency, much like a bitcoin is the measure of bitcoin. There was a time when neither existed. And then humans made up the dollar much like one human made up bitcoin. It's useful to have a word for abstract things that humans make up. We'll use *fiction*. Sometimes, a lone person thinks something up – think here of a private story told only to yourself. And sometimes we think something up together – national borders, artificial languages, and corporate or political offices.[45] Dollars, and the currency of which they are units (namely, the dollar), are fictions too.

So bitcoin and the dollar have more in common than we might think. Like bitcoin, the dollar is an abstract substance. Strictly speaking, we can't physically possess them. At best, we control a quantity of either substance by possessing or controlling something that represents it. You can hold a ten-dollar bill, say. Or after signing in to your bank account, you can submit a message that lowers your balance and increases someone else's – much like bitcoin.

The similarity between bitcoin and the dollar doesn't mean that bitcoin is good or bad or that it's money. But it does prompt some interesting questions, which will be the topic of the next chapter. How, exactly, can something *abstract* and *fictional* be money? What kinds of money are there, anyways? And in the landscape of monetary assets, where does bitcoin lie? As we explore these questions about monetary taxonomy and engineering, we will uncover normative questions, too, not just about what money is or might be but also about what it *should* be.

Notes

1. Nakamoto (2008b).
2. Wilcox-O'Hearn (2002).
3. Cohen (2017).
4. Mullan (2014, p. 38).
5. Mullan (2014, p. 43).
6. Stancel (2020).
7. Comiskey (2012).
8. Mullan (2016, p. 108).
9. Mullan (2016, p. 181).
10. As quoted in Mullan (2016, p. 127).
11. Mullan (2016, p. 184).
12. Dai (1998).
13. Back (2002).
14. Narayanan and Clark (2017). See also Van Wirdum (2018).
15. Szabo (2007).
16. We will omit some details here or there. For a more thorough explanation of how bitcoin works keyed to an argument about what bitcoin really is, see Warmke (2021). The most accurate yet accessible technical resources for understanding Bitcoin include Antonopoulos (2024) and Rosenbaum (2019). An even more technical introduction is Song (2019). Lopp (2022) is the best collection of online resources.
17. A fourth category includes those who maintain bitcoin's software. For details about one group of bitcoin software developers, see Lopp (2018).
18. Strictly speaking, bitcoin doesn't move, much in the way that when I deposit a check from you, no money moves anywhere, but rather, my account balance increases and yours decreases the amount of the check. This is in contrast to physical cash, which almost always physically moves when transferred – from one pocket to another, say.
19. This is a unique aspect of bitcoin pointed out by Glazier (ms, 2021).
20. A Lagadonian language – see Lewis (1986, p. 145) – is one where each word names itself. We might say, accordingly, that physical cash uses a Lagadonian *ledger*.
21. Warmke (2021, p. 27).
22. Dashjr (2022).
23. Anyone with internet access can download the software and operate a node. What we're calling a "node" is, more precisely, a *full* node.
24. For a complete list of the relevant rules, see https://en.bitcoin.it/wiki/Protocol_rules#Transactions

25. Strictly speaking, some nodes – the ones that are also miners – do publish blocks. *Mere* nodes, we might say, are those that don't also mine; and mere nodes do not publish new blocks.
26. The scrunching occurs within a Merkle tree.
27. Just 3,281 guesses is child's play compared to the actual numbers. Bitcoin miners together computed around 234,672,704,259,950,000,000 guesses *per second* in September 2022, for example.
28. Walch (2019, p. 9) puts it this way: "You don't get your transaction on the blockchain unless a miner puts it there. . . . They are 'in the middle' and may pose a 'middleman risk'."
29. The argument commits what is sometimes called a "quantifier shift" fallacy. Compare: everyone has some mother. It doesn't follow from this that there is someone who is everyone's mother. There's an army of mothers out there, in fact – enough for all of us to have one, even if there's no one mother of us all.
30. Voskuil (2019).
31. Miners do best when they build atop the chain that will eventually be selected by the network as its canonical ledger. Their competition, then, is a kind of "Keynesian beauty contest," where judges are rewarded for selecting the entry that other judges select.
32. For much more detailed explanations of how proof of work mining makes double-spending infeasible, see Nakamoto (2008a, Section 11) and Antonopoulos (2024, Chapter 12). We've seen no evidence of successful double-spends. But we have seen false rumors of double-spending. See Harper (2021).
33. The function is some kind of elliptic curve cryptography; bitcoin uses secp256k1. For an accessible, non-book-length explanation, see Warmke (2022). For less accessible, book-length expositions, see Antonopoulos (2017) and Song (2019).
34. Bitcoin wallets such as Bither or Electrum make this user-friendly. Initiating a transaction is very much like – and about as easy as – sending an email.
35. Users can also incentivize miners to include their transactions by offering a fee to the winner.
36. For data that changes over time, our data comes from 12:00:00 UTC on August 1, 2023 unless otherwise indicated.
37. You can possess or control something that isn't yours (as when you've stolen it), and you can own something without possessing it (as when it's been stolen from you). On the ownership/possession distinction, its history, and legal status, see Merrill (2015).
38. Antonopolous (2017, Chapter 4).
39. Under the hood, the bitcoin software treats "satoshis" as the base unit, 100,000,000 of which are equal to 1 bitcoin.
40. Warmke (2022).
41. As you might guess, satoshis are so named to honor bitcoin's inventor. But it wasn't Satoshi himself who chose that name; that moniker was coined by one "ribuck." See https://en.bitcoin.it/wiki/Satoshi_(unit)
42. As in Scott (2022, Chapter 11). Scott also conflates numerals (e.g., '10') with the numbers they signify (e.g., the number 10), another use-mention error.
43. For much more on this theory, see Warmke (2021). For a competing view, see Lipman (2023).
44. Innes (1914, 152).
45. The examples are controversial. Not everyone will agree that they involve abstract fictions; if you don't like them, please supply your own. For more on language and money, see Horwitz (2006).

3

WHERE BITCOIN FITS

3.1 What money is

What color are doorstops? What do they smell like, and what are they made of? How hot does a doorstop burn?

These are weird questions. Each sounds like the beginning of a dad joke. After all, just about any old thing can be a doorstop – no matter its color or smell or material constitution. What makes something a doorstop is that it stops doors. Doorstops are what they do.

Money is similar. *Money*, like *doorstop*, is a functional kind.[1] In other words, money is defined by what it does. What color or smell or material characterizes money? None in particular. What makes something money is that it serves as a commonly accepted medium of exchange. Money is whatever does *that*.

Humans created money. Over thousands of years, through a complex web of evolving practices and social contentions, money emerged. Life was, and is, easier when we have a commonly accepted medium of exchange.

Money is more than a functional kind then. It's also a social kind.[2] This doesn't mean that money is unimportant. Nor does it mean that we could have done without money altogether, while holding fixed our material needs and access to scarce resources. For money uniquely enables trade beyond barter, which in turn unlocks all manner of economic and social and political goods.[3]

Let's take up these two key ideas in a little more depth – that money is a social kind and that it solves a problem. They will together unlock a third

DOI: 10.4324/9781003484721-3

insight: whether something is a money – bitcoin included – varies by time and people and place. Monetary status varies across contexts.

3.1.1   Money is a social kind

Philosophers distinguish social kinds from natural kinds. Members of a natural kind share features and seem to do so without human involvement. Wolves resemble each other more than they resemble any dolphin or ferret or any other animal. H_2O molecules resemble each other more than any of them resembles an NaCl molecule. No matter how we might classify them by name or idea, wolves form a natural class. So do H_2O molecules. *Wolf* and *H_2O molecule* are natural kinds. And they'd be natural kinds whether or not human beings existed.

Yet some things form groups, in part, by human intention and interest. For example, consider the group of all countries – Argentina, Belgium, Croatia, and so on. They share important features. But *being a country* is not a natural kind. Countries exist thanks to social facts and human intention. Without humans, no countries would exist at all. *Country* is a social kind.

Bachelor is a social kind too. A bachelor is, by definition, an unmarried male, and marriage is a human institution. *White person* is yet another social kind. Whether a person belongs to the kind *white person* depends on how a particular society at a particular time interprets the person's skin color.[4] Though skin color is itself not socially based, our reactions are. As we descend deep enough down into the sciences – from biology to chemistry to physics – social kinds disappear from lawlike explanations. We see no explanations in physics involving countries or marital status.

The natural sciences have no place for money either. Money is a social kind. Like marriages and countries, monies exist thanks to the minds and behaviors of people. Monies emerge from our collective preferences about what to accept in exchange for goods and services. At bottom, people determine which things serve as money.

Now some might object that gold pre-existed humanity and is, therefore, money without being a social kind. Therefore, the thought goes, money needn't be a social kind. But this is confused. We must distinguish a thing's serving as money from the thing itself. For example, gold is a natural kind. It would exist without us. But whether gold is *money* depends on the mental and social lives of humans. Gold has atomic number 79 and is not a social kind; money is. The history of money is, in part, the history of humanity.

This history teaches that we've used, and then ceased to use, surprisingly many things as money. Gold has been money in many places at many times. It's still money in some places but not most. The US dollar has not been money for long in the grand scheme of things. Perhaps someday it will cease to be money. As society and technology evolve, some things serve better than others as media of exchange. Perhaps we're turning the page to a new chapter. It's happened before. It can happen again.

3.1.2   The problem money solves

Suppose Casey wants Bennett's chair and has nothing but corn to trade. Bennett doesn't want corn; he wants pigs. To get Bennett's chair, then, Casey needs to flip her corn into pigs first. But for her to do that, someone with pigs must want corn or else Casey is out of luck. Trading without money requires a coincidence of wants – a network of people who desire each others' available goods and services. Since what we want to acquire rarely aligns with what our neighbors want to offload, a society that relies on a coincidence of wants for trade won't trade very much.

It's a real problem. Money fixes it.

Money greases the skids of exchange. Without money, trade requires a rare but perfect match of desired goods and services. But if there's something that everyone would trade for – shells, gold, or dollars, say – then our wants coincide after all. Suppose everyone accepts gold, say. Casey would sell her corn for it, and Bennett would sell his chair for it. So Casey can sell her corn for gold, then trade her gold for Bennett's chair. Problem solved. Gold, in this example, serves as a medium of exchange – something that sellers receive for their goods and services.[5]

In enabling exchange, money helps promote our liberty and happiness. Wesley Mitchell explains:

> When money is introduced into the dealings of men, it enlarges their freedom. . . . By virtue of its generalized purchasing power, money emancipates its users from numberless restrictions upon what they do and what they get. As a society learns to use money confidently, it gradually abandons restrictions upon the places people shall live, the occupations they shall follow, the circles they shall serve, the prices they shall charge, and the goods they can buy.[6]

A medium of exchange – this is *what* money is. Enabling commerce and thus expanding our freedom – that is *why* money is.

Money can do other things, of course, just as doorstops can do more than stop doors. For example, monies tend to have a native unit useful for denominating debt, contracts, and accounts. Your bank account, for example, likely denominates in dollars or yuan or some such. Monies also store value.

Yet these other roles – store of value and unit of account – don't define money's essence. First, neither is *necessary* for something to count as a money. Consider hyperinflationary monies, against which nominal prices grow more than 50% per month, typically fueled by excessive money production. They serve poorly as stores of value and units of account. Yet they are still used in exchange and count as money. Second, every durable asset stores value to some extent, including houses, equities, lumber, gold, toilet paper, and so on. Although storing value makes monies more useful, this function has little to do with money's nature.

Monetary economists standardly characterize money as a commonly accepted medium of exchange.[7] We will follow suit. If we don't use something commonly in exchange – not money. If we do – money. The *defining* role of money is being a commonly accepted medium of exchange. But 'commonly' is a wiggle word. Just how commonly is commonly enough?

3.1.3   What money is, in context

If money is what it does, and what money does is serve as a commonly accepted medium of exchange, then a governmental decree that something is money needn't make it so. Decrees don't guarantee obedience.

On July 6, 1785, the Continental Congress chose the dollar as the monetary unit of the newly formed United States. State and foreign currencies had circulated but no national currency. Then in 1792, the Coinage Act formed the US Mint and established the dollar as the official currency of the United States. For large parts of the US post-1792, the US dollar was not commonly accepted and so wasn't money. Just as saying "I declare bankruptcy" doesn't mean you've declared bankruptcy, a government's decree to adopt a currency doesn't thereby make it money. Other examples sharpen the point. Panama has a government-backed currency, the Balboa. But locals use the US dollar instead. Perhaps the Balboa is still money. But not if nobody uses it – regardless of what the government of Panama says.

Furthermore, something can be money without a government's decree. To be sure, governments have often decreed something to be money and subsequently serves as a medium of exchange. But sometimes, a medium of exchange emerges from the bottom up without government oversight. For example, even after the Coinage Act of 1792, gold and private currencies continued to serve as money. And commodities like precious metals, beads, stones, and shells have long been used as money without state sanction.[8]

Thus, government decree is neither necessary nor sufficient for a thing to be money. Instead, whether something is money depends on whether it's a commonly accepted medium of exchange. But which things achieve common acceptance as media of exchange varies across time and place.

What's commonly accepted in Iraq or Peru may differ from what's commonly accepted in Japan or Canada. And what's commonly accepted in places now may not have been a hundred years ago – or may cease to be a hundred years hence.

So when we ask whether something is money, we're asking whether it's money now for someone somewhere. Consider something that only 381,900 people in the world use as money. Is it *commonly* accepted if less than 0.005% of people use it as a medium of exchange? About 381,900 people in the world, pretty much all in Iceland, use the krona. Is it money? It isn't, right now, for Canadians or Germans, unless they're visiting Reykjavik. And until 1885, it wasn't money, even in Iceland. But the krona is money, now, for the people of Iceland.

Something similar is true of bitcoin. It isn't, right now, money for everyone everywhere. Nothing is, not even the mighty US dollar. But bitcoin has more transactions, and more transaction volume, than many currencies. Yes, says the skeptic, but how many transactions, and how much volume, come from trading bitcoin for goods and services? Well, it's hard to tell, given that bitcoin is internet-native and that its fastest-growing payment network, lightning, is more private than the bitcoin network it's built upon. Bitcoin also has low geographic density as measured in transactions per square mile. Its hundreds of millions of users are dispersed worldwide.

Yet many use bitcoin as money; we ourselves often have. It is, therefore, if you like, *a* money – one among many. So who exactly uses bitcoin as money, and how?

3.1.4 Where, and for whom, and how, bitcoin is a money

Bitcoin is money as long as enough people use bitcoin to make it a commonly accepted medium of exchange. So in order to tell whether bitcoin is money, we must look at bitcoin's uses, its users, and its places of use. We can't do this from the armchair. We need facts on the ground about particular people and places and times.[9]

Empirical matters like these are subject to change, and our main focus in this book is not quantitative. So instead of a statistically robust treatment about bitcoin's usage, we'll provide a few stylized facts that will depict, in broad strokes, the who, how, and where of bitcoin's monetary use.[10]

The first group of people are paid in bitcoin by the bitcoin network. Bitcoin miners perform a service – competitive publishing that protects against double-spending and preserves the issuance schedule. And they receive this very issuance in exchange for the service. Miners, then, receive in hand something that they can trade for whatever else they want, just as you do with your own paychecks.[11] They were paid, and the money in which they were paid is bitcoin. It's a curious case, to be sure. But consider the employees of the central bank in charge of interest rates and counterfeit prevention. They receive salaries in the currency they protect, much like bitcoin miners. Although bitcoin mining also resembles farming and precious metal mining, neither farmers nor precious metal miners receive payment by a monetary system they help secure and in the native unit of that system. Miners later exchange their bitcoin for whatever else they want – houseplants, vintage records, iPhones, and often, dollars.

Ordinary merchants, online and in person, also accept bitcoin payments for their wares. Among the more well-known ones: Microsoft, Home Depot, Twitch, Overstock, Whole Foods, and Google Cloud.[12] Indeed, just as an international credit card allows one to spend any currency anywhere (making automatic conversions from your native currency to that used by the merchant), so also various providers make it possible to spend bitcoin nearly anywhere. In these scenarios, note, bitcoin is used only as a medium of exchange. Since prices are still denominated in a local sovereign currency, bitcoin isn't the unit of account.

Some regions and jurisdictions have made bitcoin legal tender – El Salvador and the Central African Republic, for example. In these places, an appreciable fraction of merchants and consumers have access to bitcoin payment infrastructure.[13] This is not to say that these experiments with bitcoin as legal tender have met expectations. They have not.[14] But in those places, some use bitcoin as money.

Bitcoin also enjoys high trading volumes across speculative markets. Most other cryptocurrencies can be traded against bitcoin. In fact, bitcoin is often the most liquid and traded asset in these markets, second only to the dollar or its synthetic substitutes ("stablecoins"). Other assets trade around it like asteroids and planets within the sun's gravitational pull. In these cases, bitcoin solves a problem of coincident wants, not for consumers in search of food but for speculators in search of a profitable trade.

And of course, criminal operators use bitcoin in various ways. You can buy illegal drugs and stolen personal information online using bitcoin. Ransomware attackers hold computer networks and valuable data hostage and then demand payment in bitcoin. Sex work and other legally marginalized enterprises often use bitcoin for payments too.

In the chapters to come, we'll say a lot more about how to think about these cases and more. For now, the lesson is simple: bitcoin is *a* money.[15] Or at the very least, it has as good a claim to be money as many other things we wouldn't hesitate to call money. For the skeptic, we issue a challenge. Try to find a threshold for some metric that meets four conditions. One, meeting the threshold is plausibly required to count as a commonly accepted medium of exchange. Two, every national currency meets it.[16]

Three, bitcoin fails to meet it. And four, the metric can't be that its payments enjoy lower geographic density (in the sense earlier). Bitcoin is internet-native, after all, and is global in its reach, by design, unlike other niche monies aimed at use across only a small geographical region.

We haven't found such a metric and not for lack of trying. And since it's so convenient to call bitcoin *money*, we'll continue to do so for the rest of the book. However, the question of whether bitcoin is money is less interesting than the question about where bitcoin fits among money-like assets. We tackle this latter question by developing a taxonomy of monies. Our main goal is descriptive – to understand bitcoin and where it lies. Clarity here will later help us evaluate bitcoin's overall goodness.

3.2   Varieties of money

We'll orient our own monetary taxonomy around four questions: Who produces the money, at what cost, what (if any) non-monetary uses it has, and who can directly possess it?[17] Answers to these questions will help us situate bitcoin among other traditional monetary offerings.[18]

3.2.1   Who, or what, produces it?

Once we distinguish the things that serve as money from their serving as money, we can also separate two questions: (i) how things come to serve as money and (ii) the origin of the things themselves. For example, shells existed long before humans ever used them as money. How did they come to exist in the first place? This is a question about the origin of shells, not the factors that led to their use as money. These origin stories matter, and different monetary assets have different origin stories. To illustrate these differences, we'll look at three important candidate monies – the dollar, gold, and bitcoin.[19]

The dollar – as opposed to mere claims to dollars – is produced by a government-controlled central bank. Dollar production is, at heart, a permissioned and state-run operation. Creating dollars without the permission of the state or its deputies has a name – counterfeiting. Other sovereign currencies work like this too. Central banks create currencies and then networks of authorized commercial banks create claims on them in digital form.

Gold, by contrast, emerged from supernovae and neutron star collisions. It is a naturally occurring element, distributed widely across Earth's crust. Who made gold? God, perhaps. Or Mother Nature. But we didn't. Across the galaxy, gold existed long before we arrived and will exist long after we disappear. In the interim, humans will have used gold as a commodity money after unearthing it and melting it into coins and bars. Similar remarks apply to other commodity monies – silver, copper, shells, and so on. We didn't make them. But we can make them *money*.

Bitcoin cuts across these categories. Unlike gold but like the dollar, bitcoin is a human creation. Yet like gold but unlike the dollar, a distributed network pulls bitcoin into the economy.[20] A network creates new bitcoin, not just miners, because no miner receives genuine bitcoin in a winning block unless the network endorses the block as an update to the heaviest chain of blocks. Otherwise, a block reward falls outside the official bitcoin story and isn't bitcoin. This remains true even for early bitcoin rewards. The oldest bitcoin *remains* genuine bitcoin so long as the distributed network in the present day continues to endorse it. To borrow a phrase from the medievals, we might say that the network "continuously creates" past bitcoin by conserving the blocks in which it all first appears.[21]

3.2.2 *What does it cost to produce it?*

Making things isn't free. Making things so that they'll serve as money isn't free either. Suppose we want to make more of something to serve as money. Once we've paid some fixed costs to get the operation going, we can calculate the cost of producing an additional monetary unit. This is the *marginal* cost of production, and different monies cost more or less to produce on the margin.

The dollar has no marginal cost of production. Making dollars involves various fixed costs, to be sure. Physical cash requires printing presses, plates, and so on. But the marginal cost of making dollars is zero, or close enough. Printing a hundred-dollar bill instead of a ten-dollar bill requires a simple swap of the plates. Or consider what's required to change a bank balance from a claim for ten dollars to a claim for a hundred – press "0" once more. The dollar is, again, not unique in this respect. Other sovereign currencies, too, have a zero (or near-zero) marginal cost of production.

Gold has a non-zero, and quite significant, marginal cost of production. Gold miners use gigantic machines and industrial chemical processes. The dominant extraction method from ore – gold cyanidation – is costly too. The costs of unearthing an additional ounce of gold come close to the market price of an ounce of gold. Other precious metals are similarly costly; you can't pull more silver or copper from the earth with a keystroke. But to be fair, just as commercial banks create claims on dollars through keystrokes, we can also create claims on gold and other precious metals with a simple keystroke. An IOU, whether dollar- or gold-denominated, costs little to produce.

Overall, bitcoin resembles gold more than the dollar. Remember all those bitcoin miners who together make trillions of hashes per second, all in search of a nonce that will net them some newly minted bitcoin? Hashing requires both capital expenditures on specialized computer hardware and operational expenditures on their maintenance and energy use. Like gold miners, bitcoin miners often pay close to the market price of a unit to mine the next unit. Hence, bitcoin also has a non-zero, and quite significant, marginal cost of production. But, buyer beware, bitcoin IOUs require no hashing. Like gold- and dollar-denominated IOUs that trade digitally, bitcoin IOUs cost little to produce.

3.2.3   What is its use?

Some monetary assets do more than facilitate trade. In prisons, cigarettes facilitate trade. But people can also smoke them. In other words, they have monetary and non-monetary uses.[22] In prison, the price of a cigarette depends not only on its use as a store of value and medium of exchange but also on its use as tobacco. So non-monetary uses may affect the price of a monetary asset. An asset's *monetary premium* is that portion of its price which derives solely from its monetary use.

Dollars have no non-monetary use. As abstract units, they're pure money. Their price is pure monetary premium. People want dollars because those dollars can buy things, not because you can smoke or wear them. Yes, you could sew dollar *bills* into a dress or burn them for heat. But even then, other materials make for cheaper clothing and heat. The dollar itself is pure money – or close enough.

Gold is not pure money. Although ordinary people and nation states both use gold as a store of value, and plenty more used to use it as a medium of exchange, gold also has non-monetary uses that account for a non-negligible portion of its price. In jewelry, gold signals wealth and status. On domes, gold bestows an air of grandeur. But its non-monetary uses go beyond the aesthetic. Gold also has industrial uses, especially in electronics. Thanks to its various physical features, gold has substantial non-monetary uses.

Although bitcoin resembles gold in production costs, its monetary premium resembles the dollar's. Because it is abstract like the dollar, it has little to no non-monetary use.[23] Bitcoin has no physical features. You can't wear bitcoin or physically burn it.[24] Hence, like the dollar, it enjoys a pure monetary premium, or something close enough. Of course, the bitcoin network and its blockchain may undergird a variety of non-monetary uses. We could wear bitcoin jewelry by displaying cryptographically signed messages that prove control over certain UTXOs.[25] Bitcoin's blockchain also provides a publicly verifiable but decentralized time-stamping service. This time-stamping requires a bitcoin transaction, which itself requires a fee paid in bitcoin, the asset. This use case overlaps the monetary and non-monetary given the close tie between the asset (which pays for the use) and the blockchain (the thing being used).[26] So even if time-stamping someday accounted for a significant portion of bitcoin's price, bitcoin's monetary premium would remain unchanged. Pure money doesn't cease to be pure money because some monetary uses (like paying for time-stamping) grow in relation to others.

3.2.4   Who can directly possess it?

We can directly possess physical dollar bills in our pockets, purses, and wallets. But we cannot directly possess the digital claims on dollars in our Chase and PayPal accounts. These digital dollars are inherently mediated.[27] Ownership requires a custodian to maintain a ledger with your registered identity alongside a balance for claims on dollars. Generally, we cannot directly possess the digital money in traditional networks.

We can also possess gold directly. As with physical cash, just put it in your pocket, lock it behind a safe, or hide it in your backyard. You can also own gold in someone else's possession, as when you have a storage certificate or electronic shares of a gold ETF. But gold isn't itself digital or electronic, obviously. Like the dollar, gold's direct possession requires possession of a physical object.

Bitcoin offers something new. Although bitcoin is digital, we can directly possess it. We've already seen how this works. To possess something, recall, is to have certain powers over it – to control where it goes, for example.[28] You have the relevant powers over a quantity of bitcoin when you can spend it, when you can send it to another address. And you can do *that* with access to one or more private keys. Exclusive access to a private key is analogous to having cash in your pocket. Bitcoin can also be possessed indirectly, as when you trust a custodian to look after your private keys for you. But the point is bitcoin enables direct possession, even in the digital sphere.

3.2.5   Putting it all together

We've thus far identified four key questions and showed how different monies implement different answers to them. We summarize the results in a chart that adds one more row to indicate which items are natively digital – born and bred for life on computer networks:

	Physical Dollars	Digital Dollars	Gold	Bitcoin
Centralized makers	✓	✓	✗	✗
Costly production	✗	✗	✓	✓
Non-monetary use	✗	✗	✓	✗
Direct possession	✓	✗	✓	✓
Digitally native	✗	✓	✗	✓

Bitcoin and other monies

As the chart suggests, bitcoin is special. Neither gold nor physical or digital dollars have costly production, enable direct possession, and lack both non-monetary use and a centralized maker. When it comes to these key properties, bitcoin's profile is special. Too often, discussions about bitcoin ignore its monetary properties and instead focus on the technical machinery that underlies them – the cryptography, the miners, and so on. This machinery endows bitcoin with a special profile of monetary properties, but the machinery isn't the profile. And ignorance of the profile has caused many well-meaning and otherwise educated people to miss bitcoin's importance.

For example, many have tried to fit bitcoin into pre-existing categories of monetary assets. But bitcoin's peculiar profile explains why doing so is doomed to fail. Some think of bitcoin as mere digital money. But digital money is nothing new. The vast majority of circulating money these days is digital and has been for a long time. Bitcoin isn't just digital money; it's directly possessable digital money that's costly to produce and lacks central issuers. Some think of bitcoin as a return to commodity money and perhaps to the alleged follies of a gold standard. Commodity monies, of course, are nothing new either; gold and silver and shells have long been used as exchange media. Bitcoin isn't just commodity money; it's commodity money without non-monetary uses.

Bitcoin is better thought of as blending properties characteristic of both fiat monies like the dollar and commodity monies like gold. It is, in its own strange way, something new altogether.[29] It has a non-discretionary supply, like gold, but lacks non-monetary use, like the dollar.

We have dutifully avoided saying much, so far, about other cryptocurrencies. Our goal in this chapter has been to situate bitcoin against more traditional monies. Having done that, we may now turn to bitcoin's more exotic contemporary alternatives.

3.4   Bitcoin stands apart

Esperanto is amazing. It has no irregular verbs. The writing system is phonetic. And pronunciation is easy. It's probably easier to learn than any natural language. But here's the thing: no one gives a shit.

For all its linguistic virtues, virtually no one speaks, or reads, or writes, or understands Esperanto. It may as well be a dead language made up by some guy in his basement.

A living language has two elements. First, a *species*: words and the rules that govern how they can be combined, sounds and letters, and so on. Dead languages have these as well. What they lack is the second element: an active *network*. A language's network is the group of connected people disposed to use the language. Both elements are vital.

Money has a similar structure. First, there's the *species*: cents and dollars, for example, and the rules that govern their use, such as the rule that 100 cents equal a dollar. Second, there's its network: the group of connected people disposed to use a species of money in commerce and denominate their accounts and savings in the money's native unit.

Monies, like languages, are *network goods*. Both grow in usefulness along with their user bases.[30] The internet and the many services that run atop it are also network goods. So are telephones. The first person with a phone benefits little. But the more phone users, the more each user gains by using a phone. Likewise, more language users make a language more useful. Your money, too, grows more useful, with more users.

Although, intrinsically, Esperanto is a great language – well-crafted, thoughtful, elegant – it has no meaningful network. Esperanto may yet come into its own, but it was created more than 130 years ago and enjoys a couple million users.

Bitcoin isn't like this. Conservative estimates number bitcoin users in the tens of millions – after existing for less than two decades. A recent research report from Wells Fargo on cryptocurrencies says that "adoption rates look to be following the path of other earlier advanced technologies, particularly the internet. If this trend continues, cryptocurrencies could soon exit the early adoption phase and enter an inflection point of hyper-adoption."[31]

Bitcoin has a lively and rapidly growing user base, as well as a uniquely inspiring origin story. While Bitcoin's unique profile of monetary properties sets it apart from legacy financial offerings, as we saw in the previous section, its origin story sets it apart from other cryptocurrencies. Depending on who you ask, between 12,000 and 20,000 cryptocurrency tokens exist.[32] Yet bitcoin has enjoyed the top spot in market capitalization among them for its entire existence – some 14 years, so far.[33] The market knows something. What it knows, in our view, is that bitcoin is special. But neither the intrinsic machinery nor its monetary profile fully explains why. Bitcoin is also special because of its founding and network of supporters. In addition to bitcoin's monetary profile, its social profile sets it apart even further.[34]

3.4.1   Founding

Imagine that you wanted to create a new money. The goal would be two-fold: to craft a new monetary species and to nurture its network – to grow the class of people who treated it as money. How would you do it? You might mint a batch of units – magic beans, as it were – and award them all to yourself. Without doing much more, the beans would be less useful than having a personal secret language. At least with your secret language, you could keep your written thoughts private. Somehow, the beans need to circulate among other hands.

So you might instead give them away. That'd assure some distribution. But distribution isn't enough. You also need to get people to value the beans *as money*. And we suspect that few would trade valuable goods and services for magical beans that you minted from thin air and freely gave away.

Perhaps, then, you could sell them, with a discount to friends and family and then later to others. But this strategy also has flaws. Why should anyone want to treat as money these magic beans you created and then distributed to your inner circle? After all, your inner circle could take advantage of their low cost basis and profit enormously by selling them to others. Plus you could always mint and sell more beans and dilute their value. As long as the sell price exceeds the cost to mint, you can continue to make and rake.

The earlier model isn't too different from how shares work for a start-up business. A founder attempts to start a productive enterprise, and investors take on risk by buying shares from the founder that represent partial ownership of the company. But for very good reason, we don't treat shares as money. As the network for a centralized, private money grows, any central authorities become more powerful over its users and more vulnerable to outside forces. Users experience greater risk of surveillance, censorship, and exclusion, as well as policy decisions that benefit insiders at user expense. Instead, we want neutrality in money – more like public market infrastructure than shares in a private firm.

Thus far, we've failed to pinpoint an appealing method for bootstrapping a new money. It's a real pickle, one long studied by monetary economists and historians.[35] The problem is especially pressing for new *private* monies. States can force citizens to pay taxes in a given monetary species, thereby ensuring non-zero demand for that species, no matter its origins or intrinsic technical features. Non-state actors lack the state's coercive power and must find more persuasive tactics to grow their money networks.

Here is how Satoshi grew bitcoin's network from one to millions.

Bitcoin's inventor didn't freely mint money for himself, his friends, or other insiders. There is exactly one way to mint new bitcoin: to complete proofs of work – that is, to burn electricity and processor cycles in the discovery of new blocks and to claim the accompanying reward of newly minted bitcoin. No exceptions – not even for Satoshi himself. He did not make magic beans out of thin air and hawk them at the local market. He bought them from nature, and the price was energy. Minting requires mining. So the marginal cost of production for bitcoin is non-zero, and it's a price anyone must pay if they wish to mine it.

Satoshi had described the mechanism in a whitepaper posted publicly to the internet and answered questions months in advance of starting the network. When he did launch the network in January 2009, the first block in the public ledger contained a news headline to prove that he hadn't pre-mined bitcoin privately for his own benefit. Mining itself has been open to all since the network launched; the software has been free and open-source from day one. Furthermore, Satoshi mined with a recognizable marker to help secure the network. Thanks to the public ledger, we can tell that he never spent his one million bitcoin.

Putting it all together, Satoshi pulled off a transparent launch. Some call it bitcoin's immaculate conception. While the Virgin Mother might like a word, Satoshi did accomplish something magnificent for the first time: he bootstrapped a monetary network without insiders. Did it have early adopters? Yes. But insiders? No. Nobody received special treatment.

Not all cryptocurrencies follow bitcoin's model. Many, in stark contrast to bitcoin, reward their creators and other insiders with more than half of the token supply. For most cryptocurrencies, the marginal cost of production for new monetary units is effectively zero, and early insiders acquire their units under different rules than others. Under so-called "pre-mines" or "pre-sales," creators do not purchase their coins from nature in a free and open competition. Instead, they mint their units for free and sell some to others.

Like C-suite executives, these creators also exert ongoing influence and control over their projects. Their continued presence adds risk. Think about it: would *you* accept some magic internet beans as money if you knew full well that the creator could later alter them, dilute their supply, or push for any number of technical modifications? Like payment processors and banks, creators are also subject to sticks and carrots. So even if you trust a token creator, you might distrust the creator's government – or their spouse, or their worst enemy (if they differ). Anyone with power over the creator can confiscate their assets or coerce them through things like fines, jail time, or blackmail.

Any would-be monetary engineer faces a real bind. You want to make something useful whose usefulness doesn't rely on *you*. Failure on this front risks creating a cult of personality or a legacy monetary institution of the kind we all know well, one that relies on trusted authorities. Unlike most cryptocurrency projects, bitcoin credibly aims to be neutral money without trusted makers, managers, and mediators. However, Satoshi's strategy ironically put the entire project at risk; his early efforts as bitcoin's unselfish creator inspired many to make him king of bitcoin development. How did Satoshi handle this catch-22?

He left.[36]

Without pomp or ceremony, he removed his name from the bitcoin website, handed its keys over to the community of developers, and quietly exited the spotlight. No one can say that Satoshi exerts undue influence over bitcoin development, or monetary policy, or culture. Satoshi exerts no influence over those things – not under the Satoshi name, at any rate.

Overnight, bitcoin became leaderless. It is not a sovereign currency – and yet despite being private in that sense, it is not a company money. It is private in the sense of being a non-state money, and public in the sense of being non-corporate and open to participation by all. Bitcoin's leaderless status has made it more robust and resilient. Its central bankers can't fiddle with its supply. Its CEO cannot, in a drunken haze, accidentally tweet something foolish. Bitcoin, Inc., cannot go bankrupt or have its assets frozen. There is no bitcoin Federal Reserve, no bitcoin CEO, no Bitcoin, Inc.

Charismatic leaders are sometimes cited as an advantage for other cryptocurrencies. Just as Elon Musk or Steve Jobs drive interest in their products, a magnetic or gifted founder can do the same for a certain cryptocurrency. Satoshi might have done something similar for bitcoin. Imagine the accolades. The press. The power! But if Satoshi had stayed, bitcoin would have lost its credibility as neutral money. He seems to have known that bitcoin's success required his departure. He left his project *for* his project. And he's never returned.

Our description of bitcoin's founding may sound lofty and idealistic. But does it have much to do with the real world now? We think so, and we'll cite two examples.

First, bitcoin has been, for the entirety of its existence, the most valued, most studied, most used, and most widely-known cryptocurrency. But bitcoin has plenty of alternatives – over 12,000, recall, including some that have existed for over a decade. Several enjoy easy on-ramps for market participants, as well as effective marketing and business development teams. Yet bitcoin still leads them. We suspect that bitcoin's high ranking among cryptocurrencies reveals a preference for a leaderless cryptocurrency.

Second, we suspect that bitcoin's launch through a worldwide mining competition has led to a unique and healthy coin distribution. For the entirety of its existence, bitcoin's ownership has become more widely distributed. Two metrics, in particular, support this claim.[37] First, we have Supply Equality Ratio (SER) – the ratio of "supply held by addresses with less than one ten-millionth of the current supply of native units to the supply held by the top one percent of addresses."[38] Even among the most widely distributed coins, Bitcoin has a SER around 50% higher than ethereum and 200% higher than litecoin. According to Coinmetrics:

> This is remarkable, since bitcoin is also the primary cryptoasset being custodied by large financial institutions; a trend that increases SER's denominator and puts overall downward pressure on the ratio. The sustained increase in bitcoin's SER shows that, in spite of large institutions entering the space, bitcoin is still very much a grassroots movement."[39]

A second metric is Network Distribution Factor (NDF), which is the "ratio of supply held by addresses with at least one ten-thousandth of the current supply of native units to the current supply."[40] In this case, "a low NDF signifies better distribution as there are fewer entities at the top 0.01%. Conversely, a NDF close to 1 signifies a very low cryptoasset distribution."[41] Bitcoin shines again, with half the NDF as its closest competitors, ethereum and litecoin.

Bitcoin is young and remains a niche money. Fiat currencies like the dollar enjoy a much wider distribution, although the share of US wealth belonging to the top 0.01% is quite high. But more and more people own bitcoin. A network of one – Satoshi – has blossomed into an ecosystem involving millions. The trend suggests that bitcoin is on a path of global adoption.

Bitcoin is special among cryptocurrencies not only for its high ranking in value and use. Its wide distribution also makes it special. And we hypothesize that its distinctive launch and leaderlessness partly explains its wider distribution. It is simply more attractive as a money.

3.4.2 Bootstrapping

For an asset to monetize, people must trade some of their old money for it or other goods or services. Switching monies can incur steep costs. These costs are greater to the degree that the status quo offers stronger monetary network effects. In such a switch, someone trades an overall more useful money for a less useful one, as when someone exchanges US dollars for Turkish lira. The costs might be worth it if you're moving to Turkey, say, where the lira has more local use than the dollar. But otherwise, the costs are prohibitive. As economist William Luther argues, "there is a systemic bias against monetary transition."[42]

Switching from one money to another is one thing. But switching from a useful money to a monetary hopeful involves even steeper costs. As non-money, it's not only less useful than other monies but likely permanently so. Absent governmental degree or other forms of coercion, some perceived benefit must attract new users and outweigh the disadvantage of unplugging capital from a stronger monetary network. And bitcoin shows that despite the costs, something can monetize, or become money, relatively quickly without the threat of coercion.

Bitcoin attracted new users by offering them a chance at wealth. It drew users neither because it *was* money nor because it was *better* money but precisely because it might *become* money. For if it did, the first buyers would enjoy enormous wealth. Bitcoin proponents made this case for bitcoin early and often. Hal Finney, for instance, did so just the day after his now-famous "running bitcoin" tweet – within two days of, and in direct response to, Satoshi's announcement of the initial software release on the cryptography mailing list.[43] Finney writes:

> As an amusing thought experiment, imagine that Bitcoin is success-ful and becomes the dominant payment system in use throughout the world. Then the total value of the currency should be equal to the total value of all the wealth in the world. Current estimates of total world-wide household wealth that I have found range from $100 trillion to $300 trillion. With 20 million coins, that gives each coin a value of about $10 million.
>
> So the possibility of generating coins today with a few cents of com-pute time may be quite a good bet, with a payoff of something like 100 million to 1! Even if the odds of Bitcoin succeeding to this degree are slim, are they really 100 million to one against? Something to think about . . .[44]

Several days later, Satoshi echoes Finney with a bit more subtlety:

> It might make sense just to get some in case it catches on. If enough people think the same way, that becomes a self fulfilling prophecy. Once it gets bootstrapped, there are so many applications if you could

effortlessly pay a few cents to a website as easily as dropping coins in a vending machine.[45]

Translation: anyone can risk a little now for a potentially massive benefit later. These were direct appeals to greed. And they worked.

Greed played a key role in bitcoin's incredible early growth. But greed is only half of the equation. Lots of things *could* succeed and enrich early adopters. And yet people buy some of them more than others. Bitcoin's design itself couldn't push the "buy" button. People did, in ever-increasing numbers.

An ever-increasing number of people bought bitcoin because an ever-increasing number of people thought bitcoin would enrich them because an ever-increasing number of people *heard* that it might. And they heard as much because bitcoin's dramatic price movements drew frequent media coverage. These headline-grabbing price movements owe much to bitcoin's core economic design – namely, the fixed issuance schedule with four-year halvings discussed earlier. These features predictably engendered major price volatility, which, in time, drew more ears and eyeballs.

You might have first heard about bitcoin from a Slashdot article in July 2010.[46] Thanks to the publicity, the price of bitcoin increased tenfold in a matter of days, from $.008 to $.08. Within four months, the price increased another sixfold. The Slashdot article was no lucky accident, however. Two weeks before its publication, Satoshi was scheming with bitcoin users on the bitcointalk forum about how they should label the latest software release to increase the chance of getting a piece about bitcoin on Slashdot.[47] Satoshi cared about publicity – not for himself but for bitcoin.

Publicity furthered bitcoin's adoption. The Slashdot article in 2010 brought a significant number of new users to bitcoin. So did another Slashdot article a year later – this time about bitcoin's price.[48] The second article explained how bitcoin's price had, in two years, reached dollar parity from nothing. The bitcoin.org website buckled under the wave of curious newcomers, many of whom came from Twitter. Within four months, Wikileaks began to accept bitcoin donations to route around their banking blockade. The price catapulted from $1 to $30. So in the span of months, bitcoin buyers caused a newsworthy spike in price ("dollar parity!"), news of which caused another newsworthy spike (to $30).

This led to a newsworthy crash. In June 2011, coverage of bitcoin's price splashed across the websites of the *BBC*, the *Guardian, The Economist, Forbes, Fortune, NPR*, and *Vice*. It was not bitcoin's privacy features, or resistance to censorship, or its acceptance by Wikileaks that had initially drawn the world's attention. Bitcoin's *price* had taken it mainstream.

Note, too, that bitcoin's price has often commanded attention around the time of scheduled halvings. Through three halvings – a tiny sample size, to be sure – bitcoin saw enormous volatility:

- From the first halving, on November 28, 2012, to a year later, the bitcoin price rose from $30 to over $1,150.
- From the second halving on July 9, 2016, the price catapulted from just over $600 to almost $20,000 within 18 months.
- From the third halving, on May 11, 2020, the price rose from under $9,000 to almost $70,000 in about 18 months.

Since earlier halvings involve bigger drop-offs in the bitcoin issued per block, we would also expect earlier halvings to have had more noticeable effects. Bitcoin's price history confirms this hypothesis too.

We suspect that Satoshi favored sudden issuance drop-offs every four years, despite the fact that price stability is nearly universally invoked as a monetary virtue, because he saw four-year halvings as a chance for bitcoin to garner publicity. US presidential elections, the Olympics, the World Cup – these headline events also happen once every four years and draw enormous amounts of media attention. We have four-year cycles for sports and politics, why not for *money*?

As each of the first halvings loomed on the horizon, bitcoin-savvy speculators might have predictably thought demand wouldn't necessarily halve like its issuance would. The probable price increase and the subsequent news about it would likely draw even more buyers, which would cause the price to increase even more dramatically. Therefore, the bitcoin-savvy should buy bitcoin *now*.

This line of thinking makes for a self-fulfilling prophecy, if enough people have it. It also kick-starts a bubble – a self-reinforcing, positive feedback loop that eventually tops out, runs out of steam, and pops. Bitcoin's core economic design seems tailor-made to generate this sort of reflexivity, over and over. In *The Alchemy of Finance*, famed investor George Soros describes this self-reinforcing feature of reflexivity: "Rising prices often attract buyers and vice versa. How could self-reinforcing trends persist if supply and demand curves were independent of market prices?"[49] We grant the point. At *any* time, bitcoin's market price is the equilibrium of supply and demand. But *over* time, price itself affects demand. This feedback loop explains why news-inducing volatility can lead to even more speculative trading.

Perhaps it's no accident that the same person who thought to maximize the media impact from a software label had also designed bitcoin's economics to inspire interest coming in waves. But even if Satoshi didn't purposely design bitcoin's economics to induce media attention, it has reliably hogged media attention for several years, which has led to more speculation and more adoption – even when it lacked a strong monetary network effect.

In summary, Satoshi had clearly hoped that bitcoin would become freedom technology – that was the main purpose for creating it. However, for bitcoin to achieve this goal, it needed to be useful as money. To be useful as money, it would first need to acquire a network of early adopters. When it was not yet money, bitcoin acquired early adopters by attracting speculators. Bitcoin's volatility-inducing design drew speculation. The headlines followed. Headlines drew more speculators in turn, all helping to provide on-ramps and off-ramps for new participants in bitcoin's monetary network.

Bootstrapping phase 1 – accomplished. Bitcoin has attracted an enormous amount of *external liquidity*. Buyers have left behind significant sums of other currencies, including many with significant network effects.[50] Even now, 1 bitcoin will cost you about $25,000. But this doesn't make it money.

Next is phase 2, where bitcoin serves as money. To succeed on this front, the external liquidity which has poured into bitcoin must transform into the *internal liquidity* of a new monetary system. To serve as money, bitcoin needed a network.

3.4.3 Network

Money is what it is in part because of its network. Bitcoin's network has a number of subgroups: users, software developers, node runners, miners, companies, and finally, hedge funds, traders, and venture capitalists.[51] These aren't mutually exclusive – for example, node runners and miners are often users, a hedge fund may run a node, and so on. But the groups often have competing interests. Some of these competing interests relate to bitcoin's history in becoming a credibly neutral money. To become money, bitcoin must grow less through greed and more through need.

To become money, bitcoin needs to do something better than the money it hopes to replace. As noted earlier, switching from one money to another has steep costs. Normally, switching monies would require updating menus, transaction records, ATMs, as well as our own mental accounting system.[52] That's a lot of work and only worth doing if the replacement money is better.

It's easy, at this point, to pinpoint not only the monies that bitcoin might replace but also why it might replace them.

Suppose the value of your money drops precipitously thanks to hyperinflation[53] (see Chapter 5).

Or suppose you'd like to avoid financial surveillance (see Chapter 6).

Or suppose you'd like to avoid financial censorship (see Chapter 7).

Or suppose you lack access to reliable savings vehicles and payment systems (see Chapter 8).

If you live in any of these scenarios, bitcoin offers more than an incremental improvement over the available alternatives. And to monetize, bitcoin needn't immediately be better than *every* available alternative. Instead, it can monetize by picking off the stragglers on some margin or other – the currencies that minimally benefit or even harm the people who use them. As bitcoin picks off the slowest and weakest, it strengthens its network effect, making it more likely to pick off the next slowest and weakest, and so on, until bitcoin boasts a substantial monetary network effect. The currencies that fall to bitcoin then serve as a cautionary tale to the remaining central banks: if you operate poorly, you'll get swallowed up too. If some central banks do behave more responsibly as a result, then the people using their currencies will benefit from bitcoin without ever touching it.

So bitcoin needn't overcome the dollar's network effect to be money. Instead, it can monetize by attracting the billions of people whose currencies hyperinflate, as well as those whose money serves as a conduit for surveillance, censorship, and exclusion. To a significant extent, bitcoin has already helped millions around the globe. This has strengthened bitcoin's network effect.

Bitcoin enjoys its network effects to the degree that it doesn't fracture. One thing that could cause such a fracture is changing bitcoin's consensus rules. If nodes disagree about which rules to endorse, the blockchain could split into two distinct ledgers tracking the movement of two distinct cryptocurrencies. When that happens, the network effects also splinter. They needn't splinter evenly; it may well be that a substantial portion of the network effects go to one of the two chains. But there's always a risk, so it must be a risk worth the cost.

Bitcoin's software developers have a reputation for moving slowly precisely so that they don't break things. Bitcoin's consensus rules (which together settle which chain is the canonical ledger) have changed around 20 times. And these changes occur less frequently as bitcoin ages; only one such change has occurred in the last five years.[54] The software is open-source, available for all to poke and prod. Proposed changes also undergo rigorous testing.[55] Bitcoin's software has a stellar history, especially when we compare it to the hacks, exploits, outages, and unfulfilled promises of other cryptocurrency protocols.[56]

Leading up to 2017, a civil war broke out in the bitcoin community about whether to increase the block size for higher transaction throughput.[57] The "big blockers" – which included some of the biggest miners and bitcoin companies – argued that bigger blocks would hasten adoption by allowing for more transactions in each block, leading to lower competition for block space and thus lower transaction fees.

The "small blockers" argued that more transactions per block would increase the bandwidth and memory requirements for running a node, leading to fewer nodes on the network and more centralization (and, as you'd expect, more revenue for the companies and miners who pushed for bigger blocks). They wanted to preserve bitcoin's decentralization and argued that Visa-level transaction throughput could come later, on a layer built atop bitcoin.

The small blockers won handily and signaled an overwhelming commitment among bitcoin users to network decentralization. Their victory owed, in part, to the commitment from node runners to reject bigger blocks. The 48,000 bitcoin nodes outnumber the 643 nodes of the big-blockers chain that split from bitcoin – bitcoin cash.[58]

It's worth comparing the network effects of bitcoin with that of the second-largest cryptocurrency network – ethereum. The 48,000 bitcoin nodes also outnumber the 5,103 nodes currently sustaining the ethereum network.[59] And the requirements for ethereum nodes are high and increasing, which has led to a substantial proportion of them (67%) being run on centralized servers. AWS alone handles around 40% of ethereum workloads.[60] This makes ethereum more vulnerable to attack, given this central point of failure.

Another contributor to bitcoin's network effect is the commitment of its users to bitcoin's automated issuance schedule. The schedule has never changed in design, though users have had to install updates to ensure that it behaves as intended on their nodes. Bitcoin contrasts starkly with ethereum in this regard. The latter has changed its monetary policy routinely throughout its existence. Although ethereum's changes might have resulted in improvements, each such change restarts the clock on its path to credible neutrality.

For ethereum's ever-changing monetary policy owes, in large part, to pockets of influence within its own community – the presence and continuing involvement of founder Vitalik Buterin, as well as the sway of the Ethereum Foundation, which has had a trademark on the ethereum name since the network originally launched.[61] These pockets of influence have helped ethereum both survive as a network against certain threats and thrive as a hotbed of technical innovation. Maybe in the wake of bitcoin, this is how it had to be done for a project with ethereum's aspirations.

The most famous case is the DAO hard fork of 2016, which left the old network behind (now "ethereum classic") and instituted a new network ("ethereum"), all to undo an exploit that, though permissible within the stated rules, resulted in unexpected and wide losses among DAO participants.[62] In other words, people had played poorly and then lobbied the creators to reboot to a prior level in the game so they could undo their mistakes. The undoing made sense, in part, because ethereum's central planners had hoped to migrate from proof of work to proof of stake, a system whereby one's ownership of the native asset provides one proportional control over aspects of the ledger. Obviously, you don't want a hacker to serve among the wealthy gatekeepers. Now with a culture of hard-forking, a trademark, and influential co-founders who still exert influence over ethereum's direction, it may be years before ethereum enjoys bitcoin's level of decentralization and credible neutrality.

Monies, remember, comprise both a species and a network. Careful attention to bitcoin's social properties and network show that it is not just an unusual money in comparison to the dollar or gold. It also stands apart among the vast sea of cryptocurrency offerings.

3.4.4 Putting it all together again

Earlier in the chapter, we compared and contrasted bitcoin with physical gold and both physical and digital dollars. Now we can compare bitcoin with some representative cryptocurrencies. Ether (ETH) and BNB are the native tokens of the ethereum and Binance Smart Chain networks. Doge and litecoin are clones of bitcoin's code with alternative parameters for supply and time between blocks. At the time of writing, about 60% of the current ether supply was minted at zero marginal cost by centralized entities – created out of thin air by its makers.[63] The remainder was minted in a way much more akin to bitcoin's, with miners completing costly proofs of work or validators receiving rewards for publishing transactions.[64] The entirety of BNB's supply was minted out of thin air by a central entity. Doge and litecoin, by contrast, involve founding stories much more like bitcoin's own, where even their creators had to pay to mint new tokens.

Together, these alternatives represent the dominant approaches to cryptocurrency development outside of bitcoin: make something out of thin air and sell it (BNB), clone bitcoin (doge and litecoin), or mix those two approaches (ether).

We can represent these points, as before, with a chart. We represented the properties of monies, earlier, with Xs and checkmarks. Since ether only *partially* implements features encoded by a given row, we'll use a percent value there instead:

	Ethereum (ETH)	Binance Smart Chain (BNB)	Doge, Litecoin	Bitcoin
Centralized makers	>60%	✓	✗	✗
Costly production	<40%	✗	✓	✓
Non-monetary use	✗	✗	✗	✗
Direct possession	✓	✓	✓	✓

Bitcoin and other cryptocurrencies

Note that all of the surveyed cryptocurrency tokens are digital bearer assets, as bitcoin is; they allow for direct possession. And all lack significant non-monetary use.[65] Doge and litecoin check exactly the boxes that bitcoin does – no surprise, as they are bitcoin clones. But they are not thereby the same as bitcoin. They have different networks. In fact, their networks are much smaller. Doge and litecoin enjoy only a small fraction of bitcoin's market capitalization, trade volume, liquidity, base of developers, payments infrastructure, and more. They are to bitcoin (in this one respect) as Esperanto is to English: a fine shell but without an animating network of activity.

Some readers may have been wondering why this is a bitcoin book and not a cryptocurrency book. Now you know. Bitcoin is special. This doesn't necessarily make it better (or worse). But bitcoin uniquely commands attention and scrutiny.

3.5 Evaluating money

3.5.1 *Apt money*

Money makes the world go 'round. But take a look at some physical cash – a five-dollar bill, say – and a puzzle emerges. It's just a piece of paper with some markings on it. How can *that* make the world go 'round? How do certain things end up as money when most other things don't?

We also care about words. The right ones can heal wounds. The wrong ones start wars. Getting the right words out can be the struggle of a lifetime – as any writer knows. How exactly do particular sounds (or scribbles on paper or marks on screens) get their meanings?

One special word unlocks this mystery about widely used monies and their network effects. Many languages have more or less the same word for mother. Whether it's in Bengali (*maa*), Cantonese (*màmà*), French (*maman*), Icelandic (*mamma*), Russian (*mama*), or Swahili (*mama*), infants around the world somehow vocalize the same few sounds for their mothers. But these languages don't come from a common family. And infants around the world never decided by vote what to call their parents. What explains this global coincidence?

The linguist Roman Jakobson cracked the mystery in the early 1960s: infants simply make sounds that come more easily for them at their stage of development.[66] Early on, infants can more easily annunciate the "ma" and "na" sounds that appear so commonly in words for mothers. So in this special case, certain sounds have gained global adoption for a single use – naming mothers – thanks to both the properties of the youngest among our linguistic communities and the properties of the sounds themselves.

Something similar is true for money. We face a problem of coincident wants. Money is the solution. But more than one party needs to implement a solution. Money is, remember, a social kind. So how do larger social groups happen upon a common medium of exchange? In particular times and places, and given particular practices and conventions, different candidate monies have had properties that make them especially useful for media of exchange.

And generally speaking, some things are better candidates than others to serve us as media of exchange. As some sounds are easier for human mouths and lungs to make, so, also, are some physical or digital items better suited for commonly accepted media of exchange. We never collectively voted for gold. But gold's particular features made it bubble up to the top for millennia as a medium of exchange. The dollar has more recently become the cream of the monetary crop thanks to its own profile of properties.

Esperanto here serves as a cautionary tale. Any newly engineered language may not carry over the lessons from eons of linguistic evolution. For example, in Esperanto, the word for mother is *patrino*; this is not infant friendly. What other evolutionary wisdom has Esperanto left behind? It's hard to know because we often carry such lessons with us unreflectively, from generation to generation. We can draw a similar lesson for money: any newly engineered money, such as bitcoin, better have properties that make it apt to serve as money. Otherwise, it may go the way of Esperanto.

However, the aptness properties of money aren't too difficult to ascertain. Here are some plausible candidates:

Divisibility	Payable in arbitrary amounts
Durability	Preservation through time and change
Fungibility	Unit-to-unit indistinguishability
Portability	Transportability across space

Scalability	Accommodation of more users[67]
Stability	Lack of price volatility
Verifiability	Counterfeit detectability

Having each of these properties to a higher degree makes something a better, more useful, form of money.

Looking at things that lack these properties may help explain why. Electrons are durable and fungible, but they aren't divisible enough. Tulips aren't durable enough. Pieces of art aren't fungible. Skyscrapers? Too heavy – not portable enough. Try putting the Burj Khalifa in your pocket or tipping your waiter with it.

For a non-scalable asset, imagine a digital money that operated only on Osborne computers from the early 1980s. The machines are now too rare, and too slow, to serve at a global or even regional scale. An apt money candidate will also make counterfeiting difficult. Unmarked bills are too easy to counterfeit; bills need special inks and such to prove they're the genuine article.

We skipped one: price stability. As we've seen, bitcoin's price instability helped it to monetize. But this blessing now looks like a curse; much of the world enjoys, and prefers, media of exchange with more price stability. In more privileged countries with a stable currency, who wants to trade a car for $40,000 worth of bitcoin and then, thanks to a price dip, have $25,000 worth of bitcoin just two weeks later? We'll return to bitcoin's price stability in Chapters 5 and 11.

The earlier list doesn't exhaust the apt-making features for money.[68] There are others, too, like security against theft and auditability of the total supply – features that bitcoin has in spades. But you can see how having the earlier properties, and having them to a high degree, would make something well-suited to serve as money. A monetary species is apt to the extent that it enjoys these features.

Is there some ideal money, some species that is supremely apt as a medium of exchange? We suspect not because some of the various features that make for aptness trade off against each other. High durability, like gold's, seems to cut against its portability; and the portability of paper notes cuts against their durability. And some of the most verifiable goods – think of skyscrapers – will fail at fungibility and divisibility precisely because they are so unique.

Monetary species instead come with different aptness profiles, having some features at the expense of others, and to varying degrees. Monies have tradeoffs. So, too, does bitcoin. Bitcoin excels at verifiability (via cryptographic proof), portability (because it's massless), and divisibility (because it's an abstract substance divisible by up to eight decimal places). However, it fares worse on durability (because it depends on the internet), fungibility (because UTXOs are tied to their most recent transaction), and scalability (because of the relative immaturity of bitcoin payments infrastructure).

Bitcoin also fares well as an uncensorable asset – as an asset that few could stop you from using, even with enormous resources. This censorship-resistance owes to its lack of required trusted parties. But bitcoin achieves all this at the expense of price stability. We'll get a better sense of how bitcoin makes these tradeoffs, and what follows from those tradeoffs, in the chapters to come.

3.5.2 Good money

We have identified dimensions of aptness. There are dimensions of goodness too.

Human teeth score surprisingly well for money aptness. They're small and light – easily portable. Made mostly of minerals, they can survive thousands of years. They're admittedly not divisible in the right way; teeth shatter into uneven pieces that resist easy identification as tooth parts. Even so, a tooth could serve as the smallest unit of account. More for molars, of course, since they're larger.

However, something's serving well as money doesn't mean that we should use it as money. Aptness and goodness can come apart – clearly so in the case of teeth. Consider the negative consequences. With tooth money, we'd have incentive to farm children for their pearly whites, to pull our own teeth and each others', and to distrust dentists even more. A widely adopted tooth standard would make the world worse. Tooth fairies on the prowl, everywhere and always, sounds terrifying.

What, then, makes something *good* rather than merely *apt* money? And how should questions like that even be approached? Suppose we wanted to evaluate a money morally beyond an assessment of its aptness. Whose interests should we take into account, and how? And how should we think about our own biases and their influence on our judgments? In the next chapter, we offer a framework for these questions.

Notes

1. Fodor (1974, pp. 103–104). One way to think about "money" is as a term entirely defined by its role in the relevant theories – a technique now known as "Ramsification." See Lewis (1970).
2. Haslanger (1995), Mason (2016), and Zelmanovitz (2016).
3. On conventions in general as solutions to coordination problems – money and language being two central examples – see Lewis (1969). The invocation of barter does not imply the existence of an actual historical moment

during which all trade was barter. It represents, instead, a game-theoretic problem to be solved by technology that facilitates coordination. Money is that technology.

4. Various racial classification systems are notoriously inconsistent and vary considerably across space and time. See Mills (1998) and Ney (2014, Chapter 10, especially pp 269–272).

5. It is generally agreed that money solves a coordination problem along these lines. How this lines up against the actual history of money is a matter of significant controversy, though. See Szabo (2002) and Graeber (2011) for two important but wildly differing approaches.

6. Mitchell (1944).

7. Hazlett and Luther (2020). Some economics textbooks are not so careful here, running together (i) what makes something a money, (ii) typical money roles, and (iii) properties that make something effective in those roles. For a general diagnosis of such confusion and an exceptionally sharp antidote to it, see Selgin (2021).

8. We part ways here with chartalist theories of money, on the limits of which see Febrero (2009). Which things serve as money, from the bottom up, likely depends on the extent to which they have features that make something more effective as money. For different but ultimately complimentary accounts of this sort, see Menger (1892) and Alchian (1977).

9. For various approaches to the question of whether bitcoin is money, see Ammous (2018a), Baur et al. (2018), Bjerg (2015), Kubát (2015), and Yermack (2015). Passinsky (2020) explicitly connects the question of whether bitcoin is money to mainstream literature in social ontology. Moritz and Thiemann (2017) trace bitcoin's growth as a money through various phases. Dick (2020), finally, offers a helpful taxonomy of philosophical approaches to money.

10. On speculative instrument, hedge, or safe-haven asset uses of bitcoin – related to but distinct from purely monetary uses – see, respectively, Baur et al. (2018), Blau et al. (2021), and Bouri et al. (2017).

11. One difference is that miners may take an intermediate step and first exchange their new bitcoin for a local sovereign currency. Scott (2022, Chapter 11) argues that the presence of an intermediate money (as when you spend bitcoin, which is exchanged for dollars, which is then exchanged for a good) renders bitcoin a means of countertrade rather than a money. The "rather than" is where Scott goes wrong; a more penetrating diagnosis of such cases is that they involve using bitcoin as a means of exchange but not a unit of account.

12. Modderman (2022).

13. Raskin (2021), Taylor (2022), and BBC (2022).

14. Renteria (2022).

15. It is also important to note that bitcoin has a sophisticated fast payments layer, itself served by dedicated infrastructure and a host of developers and software programs. Bitcoin is technically oriented towards payments, we might say. Much more on this in later chapters.

16. Remember, bitcoin's global daily volume surpasses that of many state-issued currencies. For data and commentary on this observation, see Hazlett and Luther (2020).

17. These questions, and the distinctions they mark, are not the only useful ways to divide up monies. There is, for example, the distinction between base and broad money and that between credit money and noncredit money. We raise these four distinctions because they are most relevant to the central project of

this chapter: understanding bitcoin's own special place within the monetary landscape.

18. Our work in this section is in obvious debt to pioneering analysis in Selgin (2015). Where Selgin distinguishes between absolute and contingent scarcity, we'll distinguish between zero and non-zero marginal costs of production, and we'll add three additional dimensions along which to map monies. See also Butler (2022).

19. See White (2023) for an economist's inquiry into all three.

20. This was close to Satoshi's view; see Nakamoto (2009a): "It is a global distributed database, with additions to the database by consent of the majority, based on a set of rules. . . . You could say coins are issued by the majority. They are issued in a limited, predetermined amount."

21. Vander Laan (2022).

22. Economists sometimes say things with non-monetary use have *intrinsic* value. This is confusing twice over: first, since 'intrinsic value' is used elsewhere in finance for instruments with cash flow and, second, since 'intrinsic value' is used by philosophers to denote value things have in themselves.

23. For an alternative approach to essentially the same question, see Luther (2018a).

24. You can make some bitcoin provably unspendable, as when you send it to an address for which no one has the private key. This is sometimes called *burning*. But unlike lighting up a ten-dollar bill, this kind of burning generates little heat or light.

25. Ordinals and Inscriptions, overlays built atop the bitcoin protocol, provide a way to view individual UTXOs as marked in certain ways, whether with images or other data. This is analogous to marking dollar bills with political messages or memes or stamping faces on gold coins. Since most Ordinals and Inscriptions haven't been around for most of bitcoin's history, and aren't accessed by the vast majority of bitcoin users, they directly contribute little to the non-monetary value of bitcoin the asset. It is consistent with this observation that Ordinals and Inscriptions significantly contribute to demand for bitcoin block space, something that is true at the time of writing.

26. Bitcoin's blobspace – the segregated signature data – can also harbor NFTs. But bitcoin, the asset, does not harbor them.

27. Though we often *call* commercial bank deposits dollars, they are not. For the dollar, true central bank money takes only two forms: physical cash (banknotes or coins) and deposits in master accounts at the Federal Reserve. Other digital "dollars," such as deposits in a commercial bank or account balances with PayPal, are representations of or claims on dollars. Even central bank digital currencies that display a so-called "distintermediated" structure involve a custodian: the central bank itself.

28. This is, again, distinct from moral or legal ownership, which is a matter of having a moral or legal claim to possession.

29. We are again following Selgin (2015), who characterizes bitcoin as a synthetic commodity money uniquely blending monetary properties. For further discussion, see Bailey (forthcoming).

30. Or a network good is a social system where additional consumption (participation) drives up the utility of consumption (participation).

31. Wells Fargo (2022).

32. For some comparisons among cryptocurrencies and their design tradeoffs, see Bailey et al. (2021a, 2021b).

33. Market capitalization (circulating supply times token spot price), though widely used, can be a misleading measure, especially with highly illiquid and manipulated assets. A slightly more useful measure is realized market capitalization, which sums the spot market prices of all units at the last time they moved. Bitcoin has dominated cryptocurrency markets by this measure, too, for its entire lifetime. For more, see CoinMetrics (2018).
34. Material in this section draws from, updates, and simplifies some arguments given in Bailey and Warmke (2022).
35. Luther (2019) connects general questions about bootstrapping to bitcoin's story in particular.
36. Rizzo (2021).
37. We're following Nuzzi (2020) here in pointing to both of these metrics.
38. https://docs.coinmetrics.io/asset-metrics/supply/ser
39. Nuzzi (2020).
40. https://docs.coinmetrics.io/asset-metrics/supply/ndf
41. Nuzzi (2020).
42. Luther (2016, p. 565).
43. See Finney (2009a).
44. Finney (2009b).
45. Nakamoto (2009b).
46. https://news.slashdot.org/story/10/07/11/1747245/bitcoin-releases-version-03
47. https://bitcointalk.org/index.php?topic=217.0
48. https://news.slashdot.org/story/11/02/10/189246/online-only-currency-bitcoin-reaches-dollar-parity
49. Soros (1988, p. 30).
50. Nair and Cachanosky (2017).
51. On bitcoin's network effects and their role in its bootstrapping story, see Luther (2016).
52. Dowd and Greenaway (1993).
53. Luther (2016, p. 570).
54. BitMex Research (2022).
55. Lopp (2018).
56. For a list of costly exploits, see https://rekt.news/leaderboard/
57. Bier (2021).
58. https://blockchair.com/bitcoin-cash/nodes
59. See https://ethernodes.org/ for the number of active ethereum nodes.
60. See https://ethernodes.org/networkType/Hosting and https://aws.amazon.com/blockchain/
61. https://trademarks.justia.com/866/34/ethereum-86634529.html
62. Shin (2022).
63. During ethereum's so-called "pre-mine," developers minted about 72 million ether tokens at no marginal cost, which currently swim within a circulating supply of about 120 million tokens.
64. A *very* small but increasing portion of ether supply (at the time of writing, less than 0.5%) was created in a rather different way: as a reward given to nodes who locked up ("staked") tokens. Here, what is sacrificed in exchange for the ability to mint new tokens is the opportunity cost of capital, rather than energy. This is how all ether will be created from now on. We'll say more about how this procedure stacks up against bitcoin's proof of work in Chapter 6.
65. Ethereum and Binance Smart Chain are platforms where their native tokens are used to pay for the execution of applications hosted by the network

("smart contracts"). ETH and BNB do not thereby enjoy non-monetary use. For they are still being used as money – as a medium of exchange by which to buy data storage, validation, and computing services from network operators. Similarly, bitcoin's blockchain can be used for non-monetary applications, as when arbitrary data is stashed in blocks via its OP_RETURN codes; the service provided is publication, and the medium of payment for that service is bitcoin, payable to miners in transaction fees.
66. Jakobson (1962).
67. If portability is understood in terms of the costs of transfer, then scalability is not independent of portability. Nor is it independent of divisibility, as divisibility into smaller amounts allows for use in smaller transactions.
68. All of the following, for example, are controversial criteria for monetary aptness: auditability, natural scarcity, non-monetary use, and predictability of supply. For further discussion in historical context, see Alden (2023b, Chapters 1–3).

4

BEHIND THE VEIL

4.1 The lives you've lived

You wake up, but your surroundings are unfamiliar. You peer outside and see Russian signs. In the mirror, you recognize the reflection peering back at you: it's Russian dissident Alexei Navalny. You head out for breakfast and realize that you – Navalny – have no credit or debit cards. Putin's agents monitor you closely and would prevent you from opening a bank account. Having been financially cut off, you've posted a bitcoin address online for donations. Over the ensuing years, you receive millions of dollars in bitcoin from donors worldwide.

Then you awake as a wealthy tech CEO. Life is great. You don't think much about bitcoin. You may have some in your old Coinbase account, but who cares?

Suddenly, you're an Afghan entrepreneur. You're one of the 12% of Afghan women who can read and write, and you've started a small business employing other women. You pay your employees in bitcoin because, otherwise, their husbands and male relatives would control their hard-earned income. One employee saves enough bitcoin to leave her abusive husband.

You blink, and you're the city clerk of Lake City, Florida. For years, you've digitized municipal records that reach back before the twentieth century. It's painstaking work. Or it was. A month ago, hackers locked everyone out of the city's computer networks and demanded a half-million-dollar ransom to be paid in bitcoin. It's the hackers' lucky day. The city chose to pay the ransom. You need a glass of wine.

DOI: 10.4324/9781003484721-4

In a flash, you're in a new room lined with Spanish literature. You're a Venezuelan lawyer, and it's lunchtime. The house has no food, so you look around for cash. No luck. A glance at your phone shows that you own bitcoin, not bolivars. A glance at a different app tells you why: the bolivar inflated 3%. Yesterday. You treat bolivars like hot potatoes: if you hold them, they'll burn you with hyperinflation. You exchange bitcoin for bolivars and quickly buy food before they lose even more value. Inflation has been 1,000,000% year over year. You can't live this life anymore. Armed with a private key that will unlock your bitcoin stash from anywhere in the world, you emigrate.

The sequence of lives continues. One by one, you live as every person in the world. You come to understand their dreams, joys, and struggles. You learn what's important to them, how they flourish, and what impedes their flourishing. You learn important lessons about life in different circumstances.

In the fullness of time, you forget your original self. One of those eight billion lives is your original life, but you can't say which. The experiences meld together in a stew, none more or less important than any other.

4.2 Awakening

And then you awaken in total darkness. A calm voice who identifies herself as The Architect reassures you:

> You might feel disoriented. That's to be expected after living as eight billion different people. But everything is under control. Exactly one of those lives is yours – you just don't remember which. Before your ride on the carousel of lives, you believed, as we do, that each of us would evaluate the world and its institutions more reliably were we unaware of their personal effects on us. The dreamlike sequences have prepared you to answer a question.
>
> You can no longer pinpoint your own history, family, wealth, ethnicity, sex, or anything about the life you lived before. Right now, you can only recall the lives you lived and what you learned about human nature, world history, the distribution of scarce resources, and institutions public and private.
>
> Now, it's decision time. You must choose one of two worlds. In the first, the world continues as is, with bitcoin. The other world continues, but bitcoin has never existed and never will exist. You must decide which world to enter, without knowing which of the eight billion lives in that world is yours. The question is: Do you choose to enter a world with bitcoin, or a world without?

Before proceeding, a few caveats will focus discussion:

First, this is a thought experiment. We know it can't happen. Nonetheless, it can serve as a helpful tool. Insofar as we can imagine ourselves in this situation, gather relevant data, and try to answer the question as best we can, each of us will have a better grip on whether we'd prefer to live in a world with or without bitcoin.

Second, you must take into account all the imperfections and flaws of the world – and of bitcoin itself. You needn't decide whether a utopia would or should include bitcoin. Your job isn't to design the most just form of money, from the ground up. Your task concerns bitcoin as it actually is, for an imperfect world like ours.[1]

Third, and along these lines, no one asked you to evaluate a world with bitcoin as the only money. That's not your job either. As things stand, bitcoin supplements other monies. So the question is whether you'd prefer bitcoin to remain an alternative or disappear from history.

Finally, your task is to decide which world to live in, not knowing who you'd be. You are "behind the veil" because you know nothing about your identity. For example, statistically speaking, you have a 54% chance of living in an autocracy.[2] Presumably, you'd do your best to discover which world would more likely grant you a better life, whoever you happen to be. So you'll need to judge bitcoin's overall effect on the world and get a sense of where that overall effect occurs. That means looking carefully not just at bitcoin's good and bad effects but also their distribution: Who benefits from or is harmed by bitcoin, how, and to what degree?

Several aspects of the thought experiment require some explanation. We'll take them in turn.

4.3 World options

The two scenarios under consideration are what philosophers call *possible worlds*. A possible world is a way the world could have been. The sixteenth-century philosopher G.W.F. Leibniz was the first to develop a robust theory of possible worlds. Since the twentieth century, most philosophers have treated them like numbers; they grant that they exist and mostly argue about their nature and how we know about them. We avoid these more contentious issues. Instead, we simply assume, with most other philosophers, that we can meaningfully describe and contrast ways reality could have been.

Of course, we have to pinpoint the worlds under consideration before we contrast them. We can easily pinpoint the first world; it's our own.[3]

So we know lots about it. We live in it. But specifying the second world is much harder. We've said that the second world is *much like ours, except bitcoin has never existed*. But how much is much enough? And do we really know what the world would be like if bitcoin had never existed? What would reality look like?

We'll stipulate several features of the second world. You might worry that we'll stack the deck in bitcoin's favor by being too pessimistic about the non-bitcoin world. But we'll be fair. Although we won't assume that erasing bitcoin would solve all sorts of societal problems, we also won't assume that without bitcoin, the world would burn. Neither is realistic.

Most of us know what a world without bitcoin looks like because bitcoin is only a teenager; it has played an extremely small role in the world for most of its life. So we will assume that a world where bitcoin is completely erased from existence, and from our memories, would resemble the world we live in. We propose that each reader imagines that the following happens in the second world:

- The world behaves exactly like ours until you read this book.
- Then bitcoin disappears without a trace.
- The rest of the world instantly harmonizes with bitcoin's disappearance. People who had invested in bitcoin now have their money in other assets. Those who had worked for bitcoin companies now work elsewhere. Souvenirs, memories, and other psychological attitudes now instantly mesh. And so on.[4]
- Life then goes on pretty much as normal, and no one rediscovers bitcoin's main design.

Some may balk at two points. First, a global disappearance event would require "small miracles" the world over. But we're not saying that miracles have happened. We're only saying that a counterfactual situation where bitcoin disappears would require events that would violate our actual physical laws. However miraculous, imagining something's disappearance can teach valuable lessons. Exhibit 1a: Alan Weisman's *The World Without Us*, which explains what would happen were humans to disappear.[5] Exhibit 1b: the 2019 movie *Yesterday*, which explores what might happen if The Beatles had been erased except for the memories of a few people. And then there's exhibit 1c: *It's a Wonderful Life*, where one George Bailey is given a chance to see how the world would have unfolded without him.

Second, we haven't described a unique possible world where bitcoin disappears. Infinitely many possible worlds satisfy the description earlier. And that's okay; let's assume that if you choose bitcoin's disappearance, The Architect will pick a run-of-the-mill world among those that satisfy the description. Remember, the set-up is a heuristic. We're putting ourselves in an imaginary position because we think doing so can help us reason better, here and now, about whether we should be glad that bitcoin exists. We won't claim that our set-up is the best possible. But we do think it's good enough.

4.4 How to choose

The question before you, again, is this: Would you choose to enter a world with bitcoin, or a world without it, knowing everything except who you are? So your job is to decide whether the world you step back into has bitcoin or not. But you have no idea who you are. You might be a Venezuelan lawyer, a Silicon Valley tech CEO, or an Indonesian welder.

In both the bitcoin and non-bitcoin worlds, some lives are more pleasant than others. And the average life in one world might be better than the other. So one world might give you a better chance of having a more pleasant life. Your decision involves both uncertainty (you don't know who you'd be) and risk (you could have an unpleasant, indeed horrible, life). Thankfully, we have an entire field devoted to decision-making under uncertainty – decision theory.[6]

Decision theory rests on the twin pillars of probability and utility. To see how, let's first distinguish choices from outcomes. A choice is a decision between options – like staying home to make a salad or grabbing a gas station burrito. Outcomes are what could happen after choosing an option – like feeling healthy or spending extra time in the restroom. To compare options, we look at the probability and utility of their potential outcomes. An outcome's *probability* measures how likely it is that the outcome occurs. And an outcome's *utility* measures how well it satisfies the agent's preferences. From the utility and probability of each option's potential outcomes, then, we can calculate the *expected utility* of each option. An option's *expected utility* is the average utility of its possible outcomes, weighted by their probability. According to orthodox decision theory, you should choose the option with the highest expected utility.

For example, suppose you have two options: flip a coin or not. Flipping has two equally probable outcomes – heads and tails. If you flip heads, you *win* $100. But if you flip tails, you *lose $25*. The other option, not flipping, nets you $10 automatically. What should you do? To find the expected utility for each option, we multiply the probability and utility for each outcome and sum the results. If you choose to flip, there's a 50% chance you add $100 and a 50% chance you subtract $25. So each flip has $37.50 in expected utility. If you choose not to flip, you should expect to add a crisp Hamilton to your wallet for each non-flip. So for each choice, you are, on average, $27.50 better off if you choose to flip. Since flipping has the higher expected utility, decision theory says you should flip the coin – even though sometimes you will lose $25 and could have instead collected a guaranteed $10.

Let's try to apply this apparatus directly to your decision behind the veil. When you choose a world, you have an equal shot at being any of the eight billion people in the world. And in each world, each person in that world has some level of utility; each person has some level to which the life they're living satisfies their preferences. The expected utility for choosing to enter one particular world equals the sum of everyone's utility in that world divided by the total number of people in that world, i.e., the average utility. Decision theory says we should simply choose whichever world has the higher average utility.

Applying decision theory directly to the veil decision doesn't quite work. The biggest problem is that each world's average utility says nothing about how utility spreads over the population.[7] Averages imply nothing about variance. And variance matters; a world can have higher expected utility even though the vast majority have low-utility lives, for example, if there are 1,700 billionaires but 720 million live in extreme poverty. In this case, would you risk a much higher chance of being destitute for a one-in-a-hundred-million shot at being uber-rich? Or would you rather step into a world with a much better chance of being comfortable, even if that meant a much lower shot at being uber-rich? These questions concern more than expected utility. They concern our attitudes towards risk.[8]

Return to the coin flip. Even though decision theory says you should flip, what if you simply hate losing money or don't really have money to lose? What if flipping tails and losing $25 means you don't get to eat today? It might make better sense for you to take the guaranteed money. It depends on your risk attitude. On one side, risk-seekers place a premium on better outcomes. So they're more willing to risk a bad outcome for the possibility of a better outcome. On the other side, the risk-averse prefer a better chance at any positive result; they discount better outcomes and are less willing to risk a bad outcome for the possibility of a better one. Right in the middle, the risk-neutral simply maximize expected utility, just as vanilla decision theory says – no matter how risky the choice is.

Where do you fall? You might be risk-seeking and prefer a chance at a higher ceiling, even at the cost of a lower floor. Or you might be risk-averse and prefer a chance at a higher floor, even at the cost of a lower ceiling.

Remember that behind the veil, you are choosing for everyone, and so your choice behind the veil doesn't affect you alone but the entire world! As long as you're not an egoist concerned only about yourself, you'll also need to consider the risk attitudes of others. Following Lara Buchak, we think that this respect for others will lead most people to adopt a reasonably risk-averse attitude behind the veil.[9] After all, people do generally like to avoid life-defining risky behaviors. We should respect that.

By now, we have several moving parts, and we'd do well to review them. Behind the veil, you must choose one of two worlds: a world with bitcoin or a world in which bitcoin has never existed. Since you don't know who you are, entering into a world is like deciding to be a random person within it. So you'll want to do as best you can to choose the world with the higher risk-adjusted expected utility.

Of course, we can't really assign utilities to every person in the world, let alone all the utilities of every person in a counterfactual situation. We have neither the time nor the cognitive horsepower to fully commit to this task. We probably don't even fully grasp our own risk attitudes, not with any sort of precision anyway. But remember, the veil is a heuristic. Like most thought experiments, it can help guide our thinking, fantastical components notwithstanding.

4.5 Why the veil?

People tend to favor proposals that would satisfy our desires and reject proposals that would make our desires harder to satisfy. Homeowners oppose property taxes more than non-homeowners.[10] Smokers oppose smoking restrictions more than nonsmokers.[11] The poor generally favor more economically liberal policies.[12] More generally, research suggests that people favor policies that they see as favoring themselves.[13]

Those tempted to disagree might consider what the world would be like had the actually poor traded places with the actually rich. Would the wealthy of such a world mostly favor much higher taxes on themselves? Would the poor vote against welfare programs? Or would their respective stations influence their policy preferences?

Lotteries provide a glimpse into such a world since winners often transform overnight from poor to rich. And their attitudes about taxes seem to change predictably. Although many would hesitate to admit it, our stations in society exert a gravitational pull on the policies we favor. Some individuals escape the pull. Sometimes other forces overpower it. But the pull exists nonetheless.[14]

This pull is the bias of self-interest. And it infects opinions about bitcoin much like anything else. Consider us, the authors. We hold bitcoin. We're currently fellows with the Bitcoin Policy Institute. One of us consults for bitcoin companies. We've risked some finances on bitcoin and yoked our reputations to its defense in both popular and academic venues. We stand to benefit financially and socially if bitcoin succeeds. We'd love to think we're special, among the few able to resist the bias of self-interest. But we know we're not.

The bias of self-interest pulls us to favor policies that favor ourselves, and similarly, the bias of self-enhancement pulls us to favor conclusions that flatter and protect our self-image.[15] When we inquire about some topic, we're likely to flatter and protect our self-image in how we gather and evaluate evidence.[16] Humans tend to gather ego-friendly evidence more easily and then weigh it more heavily. And we tend to ignore or discount ego-unfriendly evidence.[17]

We, the authors, have risked our reputations defending bitcoin. We've spent countless hours studying it. What if we've ultimately hitched our wagon to a failure or to a vehicle for evil? How embarrassing! Or at least that's how we'd expect most friends and colleagues to respond. So if we're invested in a positive self-image, it's reasonable to suspect that we'd search for evidence against bitcoin less diligently than we'd search for more friendly evidence. And perhaps we'd weigh evidence for bitcoin more heavily than evidence against it. Truth be told, we might. We're not special.

Nor are bitcoin influencers on social media. A Twitter user going by "PlanB" has amassed almost 2 million followers by tickling the ears of bitcoin enthusiasts with eye-popping price predictions. When a model would begin to fail to predict accurately, he'd explain the failure away and make new predictions. The original models made little sense in the first place; the higher price predictions were based almost entirely on bitcoin's supply schedule and ignored demand – the very thing that raises or lowers prices, given the available supply.[18] So it's no wonder that as late as June 2021, he predicted a "worst case scenario" of $135,000 per bitcoin by December 2021. Instead, bitcoin peaked in November at around $70,000 and has since sunk to as low as $16,000.[19] In December 2020, Willy Woo, with one million Twitter followers, said that "$200k per BTC by end of 2021 looks conservative," with "$300k not out of the question."[20] Max Keiser predicted that we'd see $220,000 per bitcoin in 2021. That didn't work out. So in January 2021, he simply pushed the prediction to 2022.[21] He was wrong again. In 2023, former Coinbase chief technology officer and cryptocurrency enthusiast Balaji Srinavasan predicted, with hyperinflation looming in the United States, a price of $1,000,000 per bitcoin by June 17, 2023.[22] That didn't happen; by Summer 2023, bitcoin was still trading around $25,000, some $975,000 shy of the predicted million. Most famously, antivirus pioneer and self-described outlaw[23] John McAfee predicted in July 2017 that bitcoin would reach $500,000 in 2020 or else he'd consume his own penis on national television.[24] By January 2020, McAfee revealed that his outlandish prediction was "a ruse to onboard new users" and said that "it worked."[25] Before he died in 2021, McAfee had amassed a million Twitter followers too. (As far as we know, he did not follow through on his pledge.) None of these predictions were remotely realistic, and yet bitcoin enthusiasts promoted and retweeted and discussed them, including many otherwise very smart people.

Bitcoin promoters like these have their mirror image in bitcoin critics. But anti-bitcoin bias receives much less, if any, attention by mainstream journalists and researchers.

We'll ease into the issue of anti-bitcoin bias with a little fable from the National Football League. In 2005, the Green Bay Packers drafted quarterback Aaron Rodgers. He would go on to become one of the greatest quarterbacks of all time. But the Packers already had a legendary quarterback – the aging Brett Favre. For three years, the young Rodgers nipped at Favre's heels. According to Favre biographer Jeff Pearlman, Rodgers liked to brag to his teammates that he scored a 35 on the Wonderlic, the NFL's intelligence test. This was a good score. A 20 is average. Pearlman then reports a conversation between the two in front of others:

Rodgers: "Brett, what did you get on it?"
Favre: "I have no idea."
Rodgers: "I do. I looked it up. You got a 22."

We can't report what Favre said next; it's not family friendly. But over those three years, Favre refused to help Rodgers and, at times, apparently bullied him.[26] After Rodgers took over, Favre didn't speak to him for over a year.[27]

Bitcoin now is Aaron Rodgers circa 2008 – the upstart competitor that threatens to expose the weaknesses of the incumbents. As former senior vice president of the Federal Reserve Bank of St. Louis, David Andolfatto said bitcoin is a "threat" that "will discipline the Fed and other central banks to continue to run responsible policies."[28] We naturally like what makes life easier and dislike what makes life harder. So we'd expect the bias of self-interest to affect those whose lives bitcoin might inconvenience – with the bigger the inconvenience, the stronger the bias. Whose lives might bitcoin inconvenience?

Given what we know about bitcoin, we'd expect strong reactions from authoritarian leaders, central banks, and other entities developing their own centralized digital currencies. Bitcoin also stands to take market share from traditional investment vehicles and wrest control away from those in the legacy financial system who profit from transaction fees and customer surveillance. So we'd also expect self-interest to inspire negativity from digital authoritarians and trusted parties raking in fat margins.

Now we can't read anyone's mind. But this negativity is what we'd expect. And it's exactly what we see. We see it in both explicit remarks and revealed preferences.

- Former US President Donald Trump said, "Bitcoin, it just seems like a scam. I don't like it because it's another currency competing against the dollar."[29]
- As inflation soared over 30% in Turkey, President Erdogan declared that "we are in a war against bitcoin." Around this time, Turkey had unveiled a program to incentivize citizens to deposit money in Turkish banks, to try to stem the tide of inflation.[30]
- JP Morgan CEO Jamie Dimon called bitcoin a "decentralized ponzi scheme" before a congressional hearing.[31]
- The Chinese Communist Party has banned bitcoin mining and squashed bitcoin-related companies.[32] They have been developing a central bank digital currency that doubles as a vehicle for financial surveillance and censorship.
- Russia's central bank proposed to ban mining and using bitcoin. The rationale: wider adoption would limit their monetary sovereignty and make it more difficult to respond to inflation.[33]
- Christine Lagarde, President of the European Central Bank, says that crypto assets like bitcoin are "worth nothing."[34] One of the ECB's executive board members dubbed bitcoin the "evil spawn of the financial crisis.[35]
- Consider the Bank of International Settlements, the central bank of central banks. Its general manager, Augustin Carstens, has said that bitcoin is "a combination of a bubble, a Ponzi scheme and an environmental disaster".[36]
- Several central banks have banned bitcoin as they try to tame inflation, including Argentina's and Lebanon's.[37]
- In a February 2022 speech, the Deputy Governor of the Reserve Bank of India said: "More substantially, [cryptocurrencies like bitcoin] can [and if allowed most likely will] wreck the currency system, the monetary authority, the banking system, and in general Government's ability to control the economy. They threaten the financial sovereignty of a country and make it susceptible to strategic manipulation by private corporates creating these currencies or Governments that control them. All these factors lead to the conclusion that banning cryptocurrency is perhaps the most advisable choice open to India."[38]

Overall, people in charge of the world's money haven't taken kindly to bitcoin. If bitcoin is Aaron Rodgers, the upstart competitor, the incumbents look like the proven but anxious Brett Favre.

Much better hidden is the self-enhancement bias among critics. Over the last dozen years, bitcoin has hit wallets as hard as egos. Imagine being an expert in the very fields that overlap bitcoin and getting it wrong not once but continuously over several years in front of large audiences – and costing your family generational wealth along the way. Although bitcoin proponents often carry bias-inducing bags of bitcoin, bitcoin critics often carry much bigger bags of lost opportunity. But unlike bitcoin proponents who can sell bitcoin for fiat currency at any time, bitcoin critics can't unload their opportunity costs. It's too late. They'd have to change the past. Opportunity costs, like diamonds, are forever. We can measure them too.

We could pick on dozens of different journalists, technologists, computer scientists, and economists. We'll single out the Australian economist, John Quiggin: a good economist and someone who has produced a wealth of anti-bitcoin comments since 2013. In the first piece, dated April 16, 2013, Quiggin says that bitcoin is the "most demonstrably valueless financial asset ever created."[39] Bitcoin traded at $68.28 that day. It dipped slightly below that price for just two days in July of that year and hasn't traded below that value since.

This is a cautionary tale for two reasons. First, journalists and researchers often appear to ride the cyclic wave of anti-bitcoin sentiment. When bitcoin goes high, "it's a bubble," and when it's low, "bitcoin is dead" – even though it's often pronounced dead at the very prices it was previously pronounced a bubble. They stick to the script anyway: the market is wrong on the way up and right on the way down. The following meme documents this popular phenomenon:

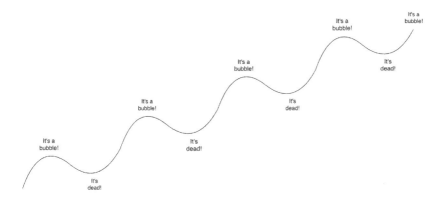

Bitcoin media guide.[40]

The second reason this is a cautionary tale is that Quiggin could have, on the date the first piece was published, bought 15 bitcoin for about $1,000. That'd be roughly $375,000 worth of bitcoin at today's prices. Now those who use bitcoin must disclose that they do so, for reasons of integrity and to give useful context to their remarks. We did, in Chapter 1 and in every piece we write. But as far as we know, prominent bitcoin critics never disclose in their anti-bitcoin pieces their opportunity costs for being wrong; they don't tell us the price of bitcoin on the first day they criticized it. But they should do this, for reasons of integrity and to give useful context to their remarks.[41]

Those disclosures might have been useful to readers when Quiggin doubled down and predicted in January 2015 that bitcoin "should be well below $100 by end of the year, and below $10 not long after that."[42] Bitcoin traded at $212 that day, three times more than the price when he called bitcoin "demonstrably valueless" two years earlier. It has never traded below $100 since, much less below $10.

Then on November 23, 2018, the price began to dip into the low $3,000 range, prompting Quiggin to say that the "2013 claim that Bitcoin has a true value of zero is looking more credible every day."[43] The price was over 50 times higher than it was during that 2013 claim. It has never again been below $3,000.

The point isn't that bitcoin's price always goes up. The point is that prominent bitcoin critics have often doubled, tripled, and quadrupled down on their predictions of bitcoin's demise instead of reconsidering in light of new evidence. They make dire predictions that prove to be wildly incorrect and then make them anew, as if nothing had happened.

Quiggin is in good company. Celebrated economists like Paul Krugman, Nouriel Roubini, and Kenneth Rogoff have said similar things through the years. Krugman's first anti-bitcoin piece appeared in 2011.[44] He called it "evil" in 2013.[45] In 2018, he said he had "cryptofreude" and "took pleasure" in seeing the bitcoin "bubble deflate."[46] In 2021, he continued to dismiss bitcoin as "libertarian derp."[47] And in 2022, he claimed without evidence that "Bitcoin . . . has yet to find any significant real-world uses."[48]

Roubini said in 2014 that bitcoin was "a Ponzi game."[49] In February 2018, he said that it would go "all the way down to ZERO."[50] In March 2018, Rogoff said he thought that "bitcoin would be worth a tiny fraction of what it is now if we're headed out ten years from now."[51] And so on. Of course, these may still turn out to be true. But the evidence suggests they won't. Pronouncements like these look like wishful thinking, much like the outlandish price predictions from bitcoin proponents.

Being wrong about bitcoin's price doesn't mean the critics are wrong about everything else. Krugman's assertion that bitcoin is evil, for example, was not refuted when its price subsequently went up, and stayed up, by many thousands of percent. Sometimes evil things succeed. But if the critics got this one simple thing so badly wrong repeatedly, what else might they have missed in their early dismissals of bitcoin?

Consider longtime bitcoin critic and economist Steve Hanke. He recently coauthored a paper criticizing the law in El Salvador that made bitcoin legal tender.[52] The authors argue that total fees for a bitcoin remittance would exceed 5% of transaction value, a number which includes exchange fees at a bitcoin ATM.

Bizarrely, Hanke and coauthors never mention the lightning network, bitcoin's most popular payments layer. The lightning network boasts transaction fees of less than a penny and played a decisive role in El Salvador's recent decision to make bitcoin legal tender. When you're paid in bitcoin over lightning network, and then pay in bitcoin over lightning network, no ATM exchanges are necessary. The bitcoin experiment in El Salvador may fail. But a fair analysis requires that we consider the facts on the ground.

Bitcoin critics who ignore widely available data are often professionals, with credentials, in high-status positions. In many cases, they could find overwhelming counterevidence to their claims with a simple google search. Why do they make things up instead? We have no privileged access to hearts and minds, of course. But this tiptoe routine around the evidence is a tell-tale sign of motivated reasoning. And in these kinds of cases, it's a likely sign of one kind of motivated reasoning – the bias of self-enhancement.

Most of us would likely dismiss or heavily scrutinize evidence for the "I'm stupid" hypothesis.[53] But evidence for the "I'm smart" hypothesis? We'd likely roll out the welcome mat, give it a hug, and bring it a drink. More generally, we tend to gather ego-friendly evidence more easily and then weigh it more heavily. We also tend to discount or dismiss ego-unfriendly evidence.[54] And what is more ego-unfriendly than something that exposes a prior judgment to have been both wildly wrong, enormously expensive, and in one's very own area of expertise? It's reasonable to suspect that such an expert might discount or neglect evidence of that sort.

Please keep in mind, we're *not* saying that bitcoin critics are more biased than proponents. We're saying we have good reason to believe that critics and proponents are biased in similar ways. They are mirror images of each other, and bias cuts in both directions. Other kinds of biases likely skew judgments in both directions, too, especially political biases. We've pointed some fingers here, yes. But we've done so to expose a real and under-appreciated challenge. People want to "win" for personal, professional, financial, and political reasons. Say "bitcoin" and the fog of bias emerges as those invested in its success fight those invested in its failure.

We offer the veil experiment to help clarify what matters, and what doesn't, in assessing the bitcoin phenomenon. Whoever fully submits to the thought experiment must be open to empirical data about how the world really is – especially whether and to what extent bitcoin actually helps or hurts people. As new data rolls in, we update the decision model. So even if it turns out that, right now, evidence points in one direction, things could change. Maybe the winds have changed once or more already. That's okay. As long as we're wedded to the truth and not to any particular conclusion, we can bob and weave with the evidence instead of with the bias of self-interest, the self-enhancement bias, and other interests and biases. But if someone dismisses or ignores evidence that bears on the question and refuses to correct course, they're not playing the same game. They're trying to win, not understand.

4.6 The plan

Your choice behind the veil has profound consequences for the entire world. It's a big question that requires tools from several academic disciplines. So we break the question into more digestible areas of inquiry. Over the next five chapters, we address bitcoin's relation to the following:

- Monetary policies and institutions
- Privacy
- Censorship
- Financial inclusion
- Monetary security
- Energy consumption and environmental externalities

We also devote an entire chapter to the best objections against bitcoin.

As you read, keep the veil experiment in mind. By the end, you will have learned that bitcoin improves the lives of many. Let's suppose that, from a neutral perspective and with modest risk aversion, by the end of the book you have come to prefer a world with bitcoin over one without. In other words, you wouldn't rid the world of bitcoin if you had the chance.

Even so, it doesn't follow that bitcoin is net good for the world. That's a deeper, more controversial claim. Nor does it follow that you should buy bitcoin, use it as money, or that bitcoin overall benefits you. But we think the exercise is nonetheless instructive. It invites, in particular, an open intellectual stance towards bitcoin.

We can have more or less open stances about an issue. Those with more open stances on an issue welcome the relevant evidence. Those with closed stances find ways to ignore it. Those with open stances weigh counterevidence more fairly. Those with closed stances discount counter-evidence unfairly.

An openness to bitcoin requires welcoming evidence that bears on bit-coin and then weighing it fairly. Such an open stance isn't required, of course. But we designed the veil experiment to inspire this very kind of openness. Since we've taken this path of inquiry, we'd like to guide you through it. Skeptics and critics are especially welcome.[55]

A quick note to skeptics and critics both: we the authors also submit to the veil experiment. We've structured the book around it to invoke restraint and discipline in how we ourselves gather and evaluate evidence. The veil disciplines us the authors, as well as the reader, to consider the evidence that bears on the decision made behind the veil. It disciplines us to get the facts right. And it disciplines us to base our judgments and predictions on solid empirical data and not on flimsy intuitions from the armchair. It forces us to acknowledge tradeoffs and weigh them as best we can. And it requires us to see the world from widely different perspectives – especially from the less privileged. We try our best in what follows. And we hope you will too.

In the chapters to come, we will consider how bitcoin affects people the world over, in very different ways. In doing so, we will equip you to run the veil experiment for yourself.

Notes

1. This is, as philosophers say, an exercise in non-ideal theory. See Jaggar (2019) and Valentini (2012).
2. V-Dem (2020).
3. A world that already exists is clearly possible, and so our world is also a possible world.
4. A similarly pervasive set of small miracles happens in the (2019) movie *Yesterday*, when the world suddenly changes so that The Beatles had never formed as a band.
5. What's more, philosophers routinely assume these "small miracles" when they evaluate certain counterfactual situations. It's fairly standard practice with roots in Lewis (1979).
6. So our veil of ignorance draws direct inspiration from John Harsanyi's work, especially his (1953) and (1955) – not to be confused with a rather different, but perhaps more famous, approach in Rawls (1999). For discussion of Rawls' approach and its connection to central banking, see van 't Klooster (2019).
7. Buchak (2017).
8. Buchak (2013).
9. Buchak (2017, pp. 630–633).
10. Sears and Citrin (1982).
11. Dixon et al. (1991).
12. De La O and Rodden (2008).
13. Chong and Conley (2001).

14. Slothuus and Bisgaard (2021). See also Lewis-Beck et al. (2008) and Rathje et al. (2022).
15. Shepperd et al. (2008, p. 897).
16. Kunda (1990).
17. Gilovich (1991).
18. More precisely, proponents of this "stock to flow" model suggested that it modeled demand, with supply (stock to flow) as the main input. What this approach ignores is the plain fact that demand for bitcoin is a wildly complex phenomenon, and sensitive, even over long periods of time and in aggregate, to all manner of factors well beyond supply.
19. PlanB (2021).
20. Woo (2020).
21. Hodl (2022).
22. Kochkodin (2023).
23. McAfee (2019).
24. McAfee (2017).
25. McAfee (2020).
26. Pearlman (2017, p. 288).
27. Zeigler (2009).
28. Wile (2014).
29. Avan-Nomayo (2021).
30. Michaelson (2022).
31. Bloomberg (2022).
32. Volpecelli (2021).
33. Fabrichnaya and Marrow (2022).
34. Treeck (2022).
35. Jones (2018).
36. Arnold (2018).
37. BCRA (2022), Anderson (2017).
38. Reserve Bank of India (2022).
39. Quiggin (2013).
40. Warmke (2021b).
41. Luther et al. (manuscript). To be fair, Quiggin does come close to doing so in the 2018 piece quoted in the next paragraph, saying that anyone who had bet on those past predictions would have lost money.
42. Quiggin (2015). It is not clear in context whether Quiggin had US or Australian dollars in mind; in either case, the predictions were wildly off mark.
43. Quiggin (2018).
44. Krugman (2011).
45. Ibid.
46. Krugman (2018).
47. Krugman (2021).
48. Krugman (2022).
49. Roubini (2014). In 2023, Roubini launched his own cryptocurrency token, "enabled by AI [Artificial Intelligence], ML [Machine Learning], Climate Technology and Blockchain" (atlastcap.io).
50. Roubini (2018a).
51. Ming (2018).
52. Hanke et al. (2021).
53. Shepperd et al. (2008): 903.
54. Gilovich (1991).
55. On the open epistemic stances here and its use in inquiry, see Manley (2019, Chapter 2).

5

MONEY MACHINE

5.1   To end all wars

In 1618, some disgruntled Protestants threw a few Catholics through a third-story window of the Hradčany Castle. All three survived the 70-foot fall. Catholics cited divine intervention. Protestants later attributed the soft landing to the natural cushioning properties of a dung pile. Either way, the Protestants had been understandably upset. Prior to this so-called Defenestration of Prague, Catholic officials had limited their religious freedoms. And believe it or not, these events jump-started one of the deadliest wars ever. The accurately named Thirty Years' War claimed nearly eight million lives.

In the dispute between Catholics and Protestants, some proposed this solution: everyone should become Catholic. Others proposed this variation: everyone should become Protestant. These proposals did not work.

G.W.F. Leibniz – the polymath who gave us the first theory of possible worlds and who coinvented calculus – was 2 years old when the Thirty Years' War ended. It profoundly influenced his later thinking.[1] He promised a novel way to resolve the tension: everyone should use a calculator, a very special calculator that could put an end to war. He thought that the philosophical and religious disputes that led to war arose from a conceptual tangle. If only we could frame our disputes in a common, formal language and state our reasons rigorously, then we could submit the dispute to a cold-hearted, calculating machine. It would then settle the dispute for us, immune from the biases that prevent us from finding the truth.

DOI: 10.4324/9781003484721-5

It's a strange and intriguing idea. Of course, it couldn't possibly work.

Monetary policy is, like the philosophical and religious disputes that fueled European war, a mess. Interest rates, quantitative easing and tightening, inflation and deflation, floors and corridors, money printing and money burning – these things are hard enough to understand on their own, much less in interaction with broader economic forces. Human biases, furthermore, prevent us from finding and implementing sound policy. Everyone wants monetary policies that benefit *them*. This even holds indirectly for the individual deciders of monetary policy, as you might expect from standard public choice theory.[2] And so we fight over the money:

> Since the invention of money some three thousand years ago, people have quarreled over it. . . . Money was never a quiet, passive tool, and it never stayed long in the same place or in the same hands. For centuries, Western mythology and literature have chronicled the joys and sufferings of people in the process of gaining or losing great amounts of money, but buried beneath those stories lies another and even more important story of the endless struggle between great nations, large institutions, and powerful personalities to control the production and distribution of money itself – to determine even the definition of what constitutes money. . . . Humans have fought over money, not merely because it provides wealth and luxury, but, more importantly, because it confers power on its masters. It is the magic key to raising armies and moving mountains; to building castles and cities, to controlling the land, the water, and the air; to building canals and launching navies; and to gaining and losing power of all sorts over other humans.[3]

But maybe money is not the problem. Perhaps we are. Could replacing people with a machine fix things? Could automating how money is created and distributed somehow mitigate our endless quarrels?

This, too, is a strange and unsettling idea. Perhaps, like Leibniz's calculator, it couldn't possibly work. Yet bitcoin's automated monetary policy helps fix an important problem.

5.2 The problem of monetary luck

Some of us are born into monetary regimes with good policies and wise rulers – central and commercial banks who together enact a stable, useful, and inclusive system. But many of us suffer under poor or poorly run monetary regimes. And we have as little control over which monetary institutions we're born into as we have over the biological mothers who bear us.

If you get a good one, it's not to your credit. And if you get a bad one, it's no fault of your own. Good or bad, it's all just a matter of luck. And bad luck can be very bad indeed. Capricious monetary policies make it hard to plan for the future. Runaway inflation makes everyday life harder to navigate. The problem of monetary luck is that many – perhaps most – people are born into bad monetary regimes through a stroke of bad luck. And they often have little recourse.

Bitcoin, though, may offer recourse. Its monetary policies are fixed and extremely difficult for anyone to change. Its rules are fixed within its protocol rather than set anew each fiscal quarter by a standing body of governors or bureaucrats or elected officials. So bitcoin is, in important ways, predictable. And because bitcoin is opt-in, anyone may freely decide whether or not they would benefit from its own peculiar kind of predictability.

Might some of us benefit from such an alternative, one that replaces rulers with rules and has, instead of money makers, a money machine? Could a money machine help us when legacy monetary offerings falter?

We'll get to all that. But first, a word on how to think about the topics at hand behind the veil.

First, our approach will be non-ideal. Maybe there's a perfect monetary policy. Maybe not. But chasing after it is not our game. We'll look, instead, for improvements on the margin – the ways a world with bitcoin could be better than one without, especially from the neutral perspective granted behind the veil. Second, we'll not assume that bitcoin will become the dominant money. Nor will we argue that it should. Maybe it shouldn't. Maybe it should remain a niche money. Even so, the world might benefit from an opt-in money machine. Finally, we'll pay special attention not just to bitcoin's monetary *policy* (wonky details about interest rates or supply schedule) but also to its monetary *constitution* (the kind of institution it is and its approach to governance).

Remember, you're not designing an ideal money behind the veil. And you aren't designing an ideal money specifically for *yourself* – a money that would make you, in particular, happier. After all, you don't know who you are behind the veil. You must decide, instead, whether you'd want bitcoin to exist, not knowing who you are.

5.3 Monetary policies

Highlighting the invariance in bitcoin's monetary policies reveals little about their nature. To bring those policies into relief, we'll compare and contrast them with the dollar's own. We use the dollar as an exemplar of fiat currencies because it has the strongest network effect. But the main lessons we draw would hold for other fiat currencies too.

5.3.1 Issuance

The Federal Reserve empowers commercial banks to make loans to companies and individuals. Those loans do not involve lending previously deposited money but rather come from nothing, created by the stroke of a pen or click of a computer key. Similarly, the Federal Reserve buys bonds with money that didn't previously exist. With a few keystrokes, new dollars come into being. And of course, the Treasury regularly prints fresh physical bills for distribution through the Federal Reserve.[4]

Bitcoin works differently. Every bitcoin ever issued will have been awarded to a miner for publishing a valid block, and the reward occurs in the very block that the miner creates. Since the publishing competition secures the network against double-spending, it serves both to subsidize network security and to issue all 21 million bitcoin into the wild. Since nodes reject blocks with invalid transactions, nodes thereby audit bitcoin's issuance. They permit miners to reward themselves less than the allowable amount, but nodes reject blocks in which miners try to reward themselves more.

5.3.2 Interest

The Federal Reserve does not directly control how much money is created via commercial bank lending. Instead, it sets a target interest rate and deploys various policy tools to nudge market interest rates towards that target.[5] A lower target results in more lending and more (inside) money creation. A higher target has the opposite effect. Supply and demand ultimately set the purchasing power of the dollar, of course, but monetary authorities have tools to move supply and demand.

Bitcoin has no centrally managed interest rate. You can borrow or lend bitcoin on various platforms, to be sure, and for a price. But here, market forces – supply and demand – set any interest rates. Setting a target interest rate for bitcoin would be difficult to achieve since bitcoin cannot be printed and loaned out at no cost.

5.3.3 Issuance rate and supply cap

Using the tools described earlier, the Federal Reserve and its deputized accomplices may create or destroy however much money they like and whenever they see fit.

Bitcoin, by contrast, has both a deterministic schedule for money creation and a maximum supply cap baked in. We have already described how bitcoin's difficulty adjustment ensures that new blocks arrive, on average, once every ten minutes (see 2.7). In addition, bitcoin's issuance schedule ensures that each block issues, at most, some predetermined number of bitcoin. At the time of writing, each block issues, at most, 6.25 new bitcoin. Since the amount of bitcoin created in each block is cut in half every 210,000 blocks (approximately every four years), the resulting supply schedule imposes an emergent supply cap of just under 21 million bitcoin.[6]

5.3.4   Destruction

Dollars disappear from circulation in several ways. Just as the Federal Reserve can create money by buying bonds, so also it can destroy money by selling them. The Treasury, too, regularly takes old physical notes out of circulation. And ordinary citizens can also burn or tear their physical notes – which we don't recommend. But removal from circulation doesn't require physical destruction. Users can simply put them out of reach, like dropping cash at sea or shooting them to deep space.

Only in this last sense does bitcoin have a similar way to remove bitcoin from circulation. Users can send their bitcoin to addresses for which no one has the private key. When this happens, the UTXOs that represent that bitcoin remain on the ledger for as long as the ledger exists. But no one will ever spend them. This bitcoin has been "burned," in a metaphorical sense.

5.3.5   Goals

By law, the Federal Reserve pursues two main goals: maximum (not necessarily full) employment and price stability. For maximum employment, the Fed aims for the employment of anyone who's able and willing to work, without putting undue pressure on labor markets. And for price stability, the Fed targets a 2% year-over-year inflation rate for consumer goods.[7] The Federal Reserve ultimately decides how to accomplish these goals.

Bitcoin is a monetary institution that aims at predictability and radical disintermediation. It exists not to pursue price stability or full employment but to remove the need for central money makers, mediators, and managers altogether. This is significant. Before we explain why bitcoin's money machine departs so significantly from traditional monetary systems, we must say more about the notions of monetary policy, monetary supply, and price stability.[8]

5.4 Money makers

Bitcoin's design works without trusted parties of various kinds – mediators, managers, and makers. Mediators and managers create risks for their users – confiscation of funds, blocked transactions, leaking of personal information, and so on. We can easily see the rationale for avoiding these risks. But what, exactly, is the problem with trusted makers?

5.4.1 Too much money

Makers mint new units of money and dole them out, whether for free or at a price (interest rate). They can limit the availability of cheap money by boosting interest rates and even destroy money by taking old and wrinkled notes out of circulation. You can see the risks here once you imagine what you might do if you could print money yourself not only with a profit motive but also with the immense social pressure from politicians and the popular press bearing down on you. You might print some. You might spend them. And then you might print some more. Why not? Fiat currencies like the dollar are, on the margin, costless to produce. Not pulling the proverbial money lever would take enormous self-control. And fiat currencies are, of course, the main form of money in use today. So we must trust the lever puller neither to pull too much nor too little.

When the money is free to print, powerful market forces engender the creation of too much of it. If Schrute Bucks have any value at all, Dwight has an incentive to print more. The incentive remains until the value of a Schrute Buck equals the marginal cost of printing a new Schrute Buck.[9] This result holds even if Stanley is also printing Stanley Nickels; competition between issuers is no solution.

George Selgin and Laurence H. White put the point this way:

> the typical paper currency note buys more than the cost of printing it, and does not pay interest. Without some additional constraint, the issuer's profits rise with the volume of notes issued. A profit-motivated issuer of fiat money, public or private, is therefore tempted to expand its volume to the extreme. But extreme expansion will dramatically reduce the purchasing power of the money, imposing sizable losses on its holders. Potential money-holders who anticipate extreme expansion will prefer a different money.[10]

When profit is a motive for money creators, they will print until the point of diminishing marginal utility. Since a state may have motives other than profit, state-issued money may reliably avoid overissuance. So economists generally agree that issuing money is a legitimate state function.[11] A related argument for the wisdom of state issuance of money stems from the idea that the supply of money must respond to facts on the ground. Someone must be able to adjust supply up or down to, say, maintain price stability or ensure optimal employment. And the state is the best institution to respond, the thought goes.[12] Central banks implement this idea through such measures as quantitative easing or adjusting interest rates.[13]

5.4.2   Price (in)stability

However, even the most well-behaved state-issued currencies display considerable price instability, especially when compared to the commodity monies they replaced.[14] Finn E. Kydland and Mark A. Wynne, in a piece published by the Federal Reserve Bank of Dallas, elaborate:

> The classical gold standard, which prevailed in the late nineteenth and early twentieth centuries, can be interpreted as a monetary policy rule that delivered long-run price stability. The fiat monetary standard adopted by countries following the abandonment of gold allows greater discretion on the part of monetary policymakers and has been characterized by greater long-run price instability. . . . The contrast between the price stability that prevailed in most countries under the gold standard and the instability under fiat standards is striking. This reflects the fact that under commodity standards (such as the gold standard), increases in the price level (which were frequently associated with wars) tended to be reversed, resulting in a price level that was stable over long periods. No such tendency is apparent under the fiat standards that most countries have followed since the breakdown of the gold standard between World War I and World War II.[15]

A few charts illustrate these broad trends:

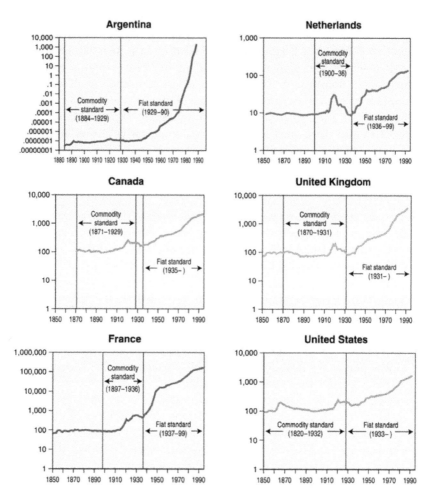

Price levels under commodity and fiat standards.[16]

The point is simple. In theory, discretionary monetary policy can stabilize prices. In practice, however, it often fails to do so. Instead, nominal prices bounce around in the short term and creep – or leap – ever upwards in the long term. Central bankers – the captains at the helm – have thought deeply about all of this, of course. Disputes here draw from various schools of macroeconomic thought and their competing ideas about monetary policy and several related normative issues.[17]

In all this, something of a consensus has emerged in favor of two ideals. First, central banks aim at independence. Since central banks have technocratic rather than political purposes – they have economic goals rather than electoral ones – they must work free from political pressure. Second, central banks aim at positive but low inflation targets.[18] They aim for low inflation to help keep nominal prices growing at a steady clip. They typically target 2% annual inflation, around the annual percentage growth of gold's supply.

Sometimes central bankers get it right. Good for them. And good fortune, for those of us blessed to live under such monetary competence. But they often get it wrong. According to the United Nations, at least two billion people live under double-digit inflation across over 69 economies. Monetary repression, as we might call it, is a global phenomenon:

69 Economies with confirmed double-digit inflation, representing more than 2.1 billion of world population, June 2022 *(Consumer Price Index, change over respective period of previous year)*

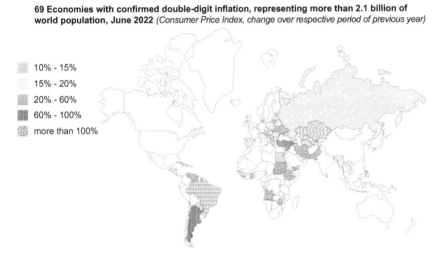

10% - 15%
15% - 20%
20% - 60%
60% - 100%
more than 100%

A global look at monetary repression.[19]

Living in such an environment is not merely inconvenient – it's devastating. And it happens to billions of us. Newborns have a one in four chance of the stork dropping them into a less-than-reliable monetary regime.

A typical economics textbook lists a few standard harms from excessive inflation: menu costs (the inconvenience of updating nominal prices), shoe leather costs (the inconvenience of maintaining our finances under rising prices), and inefficiencies in tax treatment of interest income. But these abstractions hide the more human side of excessive inflation. Not everyone can closely follow central bankers and their latest declarations about policy. Not everyone can reliably hedge against rising prices by buying Treasury bonds indexed to inflation. The wealthy and powerful have *portfolios*, which adjust to the changing times, guided by expert hands. The rest of us have cars or houses. Or maybe just money. When we store value in inflationary money, our worth vaporizes like melting candles.[20]

Inflation of this sort is, as John Maynard Keynes observed, like a covert tax:

> By a continuing process of inflation, governments can confiscate, secretly and unobserved, an important part of the wealth of their citizens.[21]

Keynes further observes that inflation has unequal, and destabilizing, effects:

> By this method they not only confiscate, but they confiscate arbitrarily; and, while the process impoverishes many, it actually enriches some. The sight of this arbitrary rearrangement of riches strikes not only at security but at confidence in the equity of the existing distribution of wealth.
>
> Those to whom the system brings windfalls, beyond their deserts and even beyond their expectations or desires, become "profiteers," who are the object of the hatred of the bourgeoisie, whom the inflationism has impoverished, not less than of the proletariat. As the inflation proceeds and the real value of the currency fluctuates wildly from month to month, all permanent relations between debtors and creditors, which form the ultimate foundation of capitalism, become so utterly disordered as to be almost meaningless; and the process of wealth-getting degenerates into a gamble and a lottery.
>
> Lenin was certainly right. There is no subtler, no surer means of overturning the existing basis of society than to debauch the currency. The process engages all the hidden forces of economic law on the side of destruction, and does it in a manner which not one man in a million is able to diagnose.[22]

Let's consider an example of this redistributive phenomenon – the effect of capricious inflation on asset prices. When dollars flood the system, more dollars chase houses in the market, pumping up the nominal prices of houses. And what's true of houses is true of other assets that are costly to produce on the margin. So the asset-rich get nominally richer. The net effect, however, is often not merely nominal. Monetary policies that lean towards inflation by boosting supply ("loose" or "accommodative," as they're called) are sometimes thought to reduce unemployment and thus benefit those who rely most on labor income. But these two effects – benefiting the asset-rich and the working class – need not and do not balance out. There are net winners and losers. The United States is a useful case study. As a recent research paper from the Federal Reserve reports:

> . . . policy shocks that change asset prices have differential effects on the wealth of black and white households. White households gain more

because they have more financial wealth and hold portfolios that are more concentrated in interest-rate-sensitive assets such as equities. At the same time, monetary policy shocks reduce the gap between black and white unemployment rates and entail larger earnings gains for black households. Bringing the two together, however, leads to a stark finding: the reduction in the earnings gap pales in comparison to the effects on the wealth gap.

Our analysis therefore does not bode well for the suggestion made by politicians and central bankers that a more accommodative monetary policy helps alleviate racial inequalities. With the instruments available – all of which work through effects on asset prices and interest rates – a central bank would not be able to design policies for an income gap reduction objective without increasing wealth inequality. Clearly, this does not mean that achieving racial equity should not be a first-order objective for economic policy. We strongly think it should. But the tools available to central banks might not be the right ones, and could possibly be counter-productive.[23]

And so we all trust our resident makers not to vaporize the value of money too quickly. We also trust them not to increase the value of our money too quickly; this can start a deflationary spiral, as we saw in the Great Depression. We must *trust* that the makers will do their jobs well.[24] In many places and times, they fail. In others, they succeed, sometimes for long stretches. Our births enter us all into a game of monetary roulette. Our luck hangs on when and where we're born, whether we can emigrate, and which monetary assets we can access.

We don't mean to say that central banking shouldn't exist. Nor do we want to dissolve the dollar. Nor do we think that central banks deserve all the blame for our economic woes. Even the most strident monetarists don't go that far, and neither do we.[25] Instead, we simply note that makers within a monetary system create systemic risk. We trust them to navigate this risk. Although central banks aim for price stability, and often succeed, they also frequently fail.

5.4.3 Rulers

What is the problem here, exactly? It is not inflation, exactly. Nor is it deflation. The problem is that decision-making by the few affects the money for all. The few deciders here are humans, of course, and as a species, we have limited cognitive horsepower and serious vulnerabilities. And traditional monetary institutions, by design, require some of us to tinker with levers of great power. Unsurprisingly, then, such institutions often fail or flounder.

People living under the shadow of struggling monetary institutions do have an escape hatch of sorts. No, not bitcoin. The dollar – and physical cash, in particular. Indeed, some have called the physical dollar America's greatest export for this reason: through it, anyone can escape monetary repression, find some semblance of price stability, and save for the future.

Is your local currency dropping in value 30% every month? Do you worry that your wages from this afternoon won't buy groceries or gas next week? If you have access to dollars and merchants accept them, prices will look more reasonable, more stable. If you have access to dollars, you can trade for them and save for the future. They won't last forever, but they'll last longer than your local currency. In saving them, they might just save you.

In this way, the US dollar – one of the better-managed fiat currencies – is a force for good and a check on monetary systems across the globe.[26] Bankers everywhere know it too: if they misbehave, people will simply use dollars instead of the money we produce. So they are incentivized to do it right. That means not printing too much money. That means monitoring inflation carefully and hitting targets as closely as possible. The dollar is a check.

Unfortunately, even the dollar carries the risk that its makers will over- or undershoot in their projections. Even the best technocrats sometimes fail us. What's worse, not everyone can get dollars, physical or otherwise. The escape hatch has limited access.

5.5   Money without makers

Bitcoin has no makers. A maker, by stipulation, has control over an asset's issuance. Makers can change the rate of issuance. Bitcoin does have miners, but miners have negligible amounts of control over the protocol's issuance schedule. Since nodes incentivize miners to play along with, and protect, the issuance schedule, miners aren't makers and don't require the levels of trust we normally place in makers. Fourteen years on, and bitcoin has yet to deviate from its monetary policy.[27] So bitcoin imposes minimal maker risk on its users. But that benefit comes with a cost: uncertainty about its purchasing power.

Throughout its history, bitcoin has shown enormous volatility. Its price swings are notorious – loved by some, feared by others, known by all. The volatility is strange for something that wants to be money because price stability makes money more useful and volatility makes it less useful. But as we'll see, bitcoin's core economic design is tailor-made for dramatic price movements in two places. This is the fundamental tradeoff of the monetary institution bitcoin implements. Without makers to tinker with the issuance schedule, bitcoin's supply is steady and known and not subject to capricious manipulation. But by the same token, there are no trusted makers to tinker away and ensure that its purchasing power remains steady over time.

Let's look closer at bitcoin's sources of volatility.

5.5.1 Inelastic supply

According to neoclassical price theory, equilibrium market price is where demand and supply curves meet. So when demand increases without any increase in supply, price increases. And an increased price incentivizes suppliers to bring more to the market. When more supply comes to market, the price does not rise as much as it otherwise would. Normally, then, increased supply works like a pressure relief valve when increased demand pushes price up.

For traditional markets, the same mechanism also works in reverse. If demand shrinks for loaves of bread, the price will fall, and bread makers will produce fewer loaves. With fewer loaves on the market than there otherwise would have been, the price has a higher floor. Hence, an elastic supply dampens price volatility from both increases and decreases in demand.

Bitcoin's fixed supply exacerbates the normal effects of shifts in demand. The network issues bitcoin on a predetermined schedule and chugs along as planned whether demand goes up, down, or neither. As a result, bitcoin lacks the moderating influence of an elastic supply. With an inelastic supply curve, small changes in demand make for dramatic changes in market price. When demand increases, price increases. Of course, bitcoin holders might bring more bitcoin to market. But since the overall supply *can't* increase in response, the price more easily continues to rise. No pressure relief valve here. And when demand decreases, price decreases; but since supply *can't* decrease in response, price more easily falls.

So bitcoin's price reacts wildly to small changes in demand. When demand goes up, its price can rocket to the moon. When demand goes down, it can plummet to hades.

Now it's untrue that bitcoin has a *perfectly* inelastic supply. When bitcoin quickly increases in price, the mining reward, too, increases in price since it's denominated in bitcoin. This draws miners to flip on more machines and use more electricity. With more computation cycles per second, blocks come more quickly than every ten minutes. Until the next difficulty adjustment to make mining more difficult (remember, the difficulty changes every 2016 blocks), bitcoin's issuance schedule will slightly accelerate. But this elasticity, already quite minimal, has become ever more negligible as the mining difficulty has substantially increased and the block reward itself has substantially decreased. So the issuance schedule is much harder to accelerate, and any such acceleration adds much fewer bitcoin.

5.5.2 Halvings

Bitcoin's halving schedule is another potential locus of volatility. Every four years or so, the mining reward halves. Satoshi embedded a human-friendly geometric series into bitcoin's issuance schedule. Here's how it works: after the first 210,000 blocks, with 50 bitcoin issued per block, 50% of the supply remains. After the next 210,000 blocks, with 25 bitcoin issued apiece, 25% of the supply remains. And so on. As you can see, then, these first halvings involved large changes in issuance measured against the available supply.

In halvings, where the reward drops from 50 to 25 bitcoin and then from 25 bitcoin to 12.5 bitcoin, the amount of new bitcoin coming to market drops substantially and suddenly. With much fewer bitcoin coming to the market, dramatic price movements can come more easily. This doesn't imply that halvings *cause* price movements, however. We simply note that each halving lurches the network closer to what is already expected by rational actors: an ultimately fixed monetary supply. Before a halving, you'd be quite sure, but not necessarily certain, that new supply will dramatically constrict soon. After a halving, there's less guesswork. Now we know. Just as each new block is a tiny discovery (the network is working as planned), so, too, each halving uncovers at least some new information: the supply schedule is working as planned, and there is, accordingly, half as much newly minted bitcoin for sale as there once was.

Satoshi could have easily embedded a more gradual issuance decline.[28] Instead of a sudden drop-off at every 210,000th block, the network might have had a smooth decline, where each block issues slightly less bitcoin than the one before it. But Satoshi chose an issuance schedule with steep drop-offs instead. So it appears that Satoshi endowed bitcoin with the potential, early on, for bitcoin to enjoy more volatility than was strictly necessary.

In sum: these two design choices – fixed issuance and halvings – serve to induce volatility.

5.4.3 No oracles

Bitcoin's supply varies in this sense: each new block creates new bitcoin and will continue to do so for a long while. And yet the rules governing bitcoin's supply are fixed. Its supply *schedule* is non-discretionary and deterministic. No CEO or board member or chief economist can change it, and supply is a function of how many blocks have been produced (itself a measure of internal network time).

You might guess that bitcoin's supply schedule is deterministic because its inventor, users, and proponents agree that such a monetary policy is for the best. That's not quite right. Many proponents do display religious dedication to deterministic supply, for sure. Some bitcoin proponents were goldbugs in another life, for example, precisely because gold supply expands at such a predictable and steady rate. But that's not *why* bitcoin is the way it is.

Instead, bitcoin's supply schedule is deterministic because it had to be.[29] Without a deterministic schedule, the network would have had to issue bitcoin flexibly in response to *something else*, much like central banks respond to various metrics on the economy. Bitcoin itself has no internal metric against which it could reliably issue bitcoin indefinitely. So a non-deterministic schedule would require that bitcoin rely on data external to its blockchain. And this would introduce maker trust – precisely what bitcoin was designed to avoid. Let us explain.

Bitcoin is covered by a one-way, inward-facing window. We can see in; anyone can watch new blocks arrive, audit the total supply of bitcoin, verify signatures, check for double-spending, and so on. We can also observe outside facts, like bitcoin's market price.

However, the bitcoin network itself has no eyes or ears on the outside world.[30] Bitcoin nodes don't know bitcoin's market price. Nor does the blockchain. For the bitcoin network to know these things, it would have to know them indirectly, through someone else's eyes or ears. Using information external to the bitcoin blockchain in order to determine changes in issuance would, in effect, require someone's participation in the moneymaking process – a maker, who might fail. So without a trusted party, bitcoin couldn't achieve purchasing power targets by adjusting the supply up or down in light of market information. Hence, unless bitcoin invoked the aid of a trusted party, bitcoin's issuance would need to run deterministically.[31]

Satoshi chose a deterministic schedule and its attendant price volatility over price stability with a trusted party. Here's why. Imagine a widget factory with just one variable, the rate of widget production, and one goal, for widgets to have a stable price at the local market. The factory manager can stabilize the price of widgets within a local currency by hiring a scribe to visit the market each morning and jot down the local widget price. The factory reduces production when the market price dips below the target price and increases production when the market price flies over the target price. The factory also has no choice but to rely on the scribe's daily reports.

In this scenario, the scribe is a key intermediary in the widget economy, gifted with the power to increase or decrease the supply of widgets, with nothing but a word. You wouldn't want just any old scribe in that job since a bad move could wreck the widget economy. And the scribe is merely the epicenter for influence – others in his orbit have influence too. Widget peddlers might manipulate the market by posting different prices before the scribal visit. They might even collude to form a widget cartel.

Bitcoin avoids these sorts of problems. To do away with makers, along with their associated risks and required trust, bitcoin had to forgo trusted price oracles. To achieve disintermediation, bitcoin was designed as a self-contained, deterministic money machine. The machine issues bitcoin not through rulers but through automated rules.

5.5.4 Volatility forever?

So bitcoin eschews maker trust and instead uses a monetary constitution whose automated rules engender substantial price volatility. In Satoshi's time, and likely still in ours, it had to be this way, with a fundamental tradeoff between price stability (with maker trust) and trust-minimization (with volatility). But volatility doesn't serve everyone, and it surely impedes bitcoin's usefulness as money. Will volatility stay with bitcoin forever? Or like Forrest Gump's leg braces, will it eventually cast off volatility as it races onwards?

Since a quick eyeballing of bitcoin's volatility chart suggests a downward trend, you might simply project that trend forward. Yet despite any secular downward trend, bitcoin's volatility still remains substantially higher than the dollar's own. Also, bitcoin's volatility is itself volatile, careening this way or that in response to market sentiments.

Chart inspection alone will not answer our question.

But armed with some theoretical principles, we can make a few informed guesses about the future. We have already surveyed some of the relevant theoretical principles. Standard price theory itself predicts that an inelastic supply makes for volatility in market price.

No dampening of volatility will come from the supply side of things. So price stability would require the taming of demand. Since demand stems from human decision-making, price stability would, therefore, require the taming of human psychology itself. For volatility to flatline at some non-zero level, then, speculative demand for bitcoin must decrease as another kind of demand for bitcoin emerges and takes priority.

For the last several years, speculators have bought bitcoin with the hope to sell it later for a profit. And they have hoped to reap profits in another money, like dollars. They hope to correctly guess and then front-run the

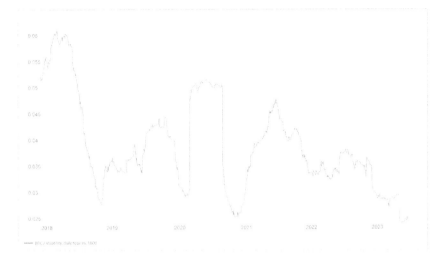

Bitcoin's 180-day volatility since 2018.[32]

behavior of other speculators. This is a Keynesian beauty contest across a multi-asset market, where the winner is the one who correctly guesses which asset other players will select. Finally, speculators are asset-agnostic: they play their games with bitcoin today not because it is resistance money but precisely because it is volatile and because other speculators target bitcoin. As long as these factors persist at scale, bitcoin's current demand profile, and high volatility, will likely persist.

Even so, bitcoin does have realistic possible futures in which its demand becomes less speculative. Many other cryptocurrencies and securities, especially memecoins and memestocks, have more volatility than bitcoin. They might serve as speculative diversions, attracting speculative demand away from bitcoin, much like players in a casino flock towards riskier games with bigger payouts. Diverting this demand wouldn't entirely dampen bitcoin's volatility, of course. It would enhance it in the form of a price crash. That loss of demand must pair with an entry of less speculative capital.

So imagine that along the way, a significant number of market participants took up a bitcoin allocation mandate – doing what it takes to maintain a fixed portfolio allocation to bitcoin – 5%, for example.[33] This would involve selling bitcoin whenever its price rose enough to take the allocation past 5% and buying whenever its price dropped enough to take the allocation below 5%. Market participants have such mandates for other investment vehicles. And such a mandate could arise from the reasonable thought that it'd be wise to have *some* resistance money on hand for emergencies – in case of social cancellation, a sudden need for contraband, uncooperative banks or asset managers, unexpected travel, and so on. In assessing whether to buy or sell bitcoin on the margin, participants of this kind would look not to each other, as speculators do, but to their own portfolio.

In aggregate, these kinds of bitcoin users would dampen price volatility. As market exuberance grows, they'd sell and dampen a price increase. And as market despair spreads, they'd buy and protect bitcoin's downside. This behavior would attract more of the same and drive away speculators looking for more exciting and volatile assets. A virtuous cycle.

We do not predict that this scenario will unfold. Nor do we believe that this is the only route to less volatility.[34] And even if the earlier scenario comes to pass, bitcoin's inflexible supply will likely mean that it remains somewhat volatile for some time. But it and similar scenarios are live possibilities. Many market participants already have a bitcoin allocation mandate. More importantly, our imagined scenario illustrates how, despite a design that engenders volatility, bitcoin's price could find more stability – without central bankers tinkering with supply. The fundamental choice between trust-minimization and relative price stability might only apply to the early stages of bitcoin's monetization.

5.6 Monetary rule of law

Recall the problem of monetary luck. How does bitcoin help?

To begin, note that more policy tinkering doesn't solve the problem. Arguably, tinkering creates the problem in the first place. Tinkering requires policy-makers and policy enforcers. The very existence of these powers impose risk. The fact that someone, or some small group of people, controls the monetary rules is itself a risk.

Milton Friedman commented on this risk long ago, focusing on the American Federal Reserve:

> I have found that few things are harder even for knowledgeable non-experts to accept than the proposition that twelve (or nineteen) people sitting around a table in Washington, subject to neither election nor dismissal nor close administrative or political control, have the power to determine the quantity of money – to permit a reduction by one-third during the Great Depression or a near doubling from 1970 to 1980. That power is too important, too pervasive, to be exercised by a few people, however public-spirited, if there is any feasible alternative. There is no need for such arbitrary power.[35]

Once you see it, you can't unsee it. Traditional fiat monies each involve a small group of people charged with making the money. And people are imperfect; not everyone is well-meaning, especially those under power's spell, and even the well-meaning make mistakes. This is not a "them" problem but an "us" problem. Bitcoin, as an alternative monetary institution, routes around our imperfections. Bitcoin offers a different kind of money system, one without trusted makers. It isn't a bank but a money machine.

Such a money machine fulfills the promise of certain ideas from award-winning economists in the twentieth century. Where others looked for a technically optimal collection of central bank policies, winners of the Nobel Memorial Prize in Economic Sciences such as Friedrich Hayek, Milton Friedman, and James Buchanan recommended, respectively:[36]

- Competitive, privately-issued (i.e., non-state) monies
- Binding and pre-arranged rules or programs that govern policy
- Constitutionalism, an institutional framework designed to keep control of money away from bureaucrats, with built-in checks and balances

Bitcoin combines all three ideas.

"Privately issued." Check. No state issues bitcoin.

"Binding and pre-arranged rules." Check. The rules of bitcoin were advertised well before its launch. And they bind participants through both the software and the incentive system that emerges from it. Network nodes collectively reject blocks that run afoul of the preordained supply schedule.

"Constitutionalism." Check. The rules are baked into its protocol, its digital constitution, and automate away the power of bureaucrats, with built-in checks and balances. Bitcoin does not merely institute an alternative monetary policy; it is a new kind of monetary institution.

Monetary economists have, for years, speculated about a rule-based policy and its benefits over either a commodity money standard or continual technocratic tinkering. The sticking point has always been how to maintain such a rule.[37] Bitcoin has an answer: users themselves enforce the rules through software.

We now arrive at a fundamental question of this chapter: when reasoning behind the veil, is there good reason to prefer a world with bitcoin over one without? Not knowing who you might be in the world, would you like bitcoin to exist as an available option? We would, as we'll explain. For bitcoin offers an opt-in monetary system governed, not by bankers or bureaucrats but by rules. Bitcoin is an institutional solution to the problem of monetary luck.

5.6.1   Rules are good

The rules that govern bitcoin's monetary policy make it an attractive monetary alternative from behind the veil. These rules are *transparent*, *general*, and *predictable*.[38]

As open-source software for a public ledger, bitcoin operates with near complete transparency. Read the code, and you can see both how difficulty adjustment works and how it pairs with the cycle of halvings to forge a maximum supply cap. Plus anyone can audit the bitcoin supply at any time. Just fire up your node, input the relevant command,[39] and it will compute bitcoin's total supply in exacting detail.

Thanks to bitcoin's transparency, we can also see that it has no room for favoritism. Anyone may mint new bitcoin, for example. Just submit some proofs of work to the network, mine a block, and collect your block reward. Entry and exit from bitcoin mining require no permission from authorities. No one has special access. There is no inner circle. The requirement that you can't spend bitcoin without a valid signature applies to all. No exceptions. Anyone can operate a network node. And anyone can contribute to bitcoin software development.

Bitcoin's rules are also predictable. Software development and node operators prize backwards compatibility. So the main consensus rules have remained largely in place since Satoshi launched the network in 2009. Theoretically, the main rules also extend forever – the issuance schedule runs through 2140, for example. You can reasonably estimate exactly how much bitcoin there will be at any given day between now and then.

Because all current state-issued fiat currencies have discretionary monetary policies, they cannot enjoy the same levels of transparency, neutrality, and predictability in supply. That is, "Current monetary arrangements represent not the rule of law, but the rule of central bankers."[40]

Fiat currencies are not transparent. No one knows precisely how many dollars are out there or precisely where they are.

Fiat currencies are not general. Only some people control the levers. Sometimes they use this knowledge and power to benefit themselves or some at the expense of others.

Fiat currencies are unpredictable. How many dollars will there be in 2042? No one knows, not even the chair of the Federal Reserve. What will interest rates be like in 2052? No one knows, not even the chair of the Federal Reserve. Who will be the chair of the Federal Reserve in 2062? No one knows, not even the 2052 chair of the Federal Reserve.

Fiat currencies needn't work this way. We can imagine a state-issued fiat currency that enjoys a high degree of transparency, generality, and predictability. But the chasm between what we could have and what we do have is quite wide. Such a system would work more like bitcoin – a system without centralized makers. Along these dimensions, then, the contrast between bitcoin and state-issued fiat currencies couldn't be more stark. They differ not just with respect to wonky policy details but in their institutional DNA. The dollar is discretionary, and few are the deciders. Bitcoin is a machine.

Better – bitcoin is a machine of machines. And anyone may deploy one by mining or running a node. If we benefit from having transparency, generality, and predictability in the rules that govern us all, then perhaps we can benefit from having at least one monetary institution whose rules have these same features. For those who want a monetary rule of law – money governed by transparent, general, and predictable rules – bitcoin beckons.[41]

Predictable rules enable better markets. They enable participants to plan for likely outcomes. Generality engenders fairness. A system in which only a few can vote, craft rules, or enforce them is less fair than a system in which anyone can. Transparency enjoys both of these features: it makes a system more predictable and more fair. And it has the added benefit of making systemic risks easier to catch: few can hide when anyone can audit the books.

All of this is true, despite local exceptions. It might be expedient, in a given case, for a system to operate a little more capriciously, or opaquely, or nepotistically. But do we always and everywhere trust ourselves and the authorities to make exceptions at all and only the times they're needed? We doubt it. It might be beneficial to have a monetary network that applies the same rules to everyone always, no matter what.

Indeed, invariant rules, despite their tradeoffs, have proven their worth across a variety of domains. Odysseus, tied to the mast, is safe from the Siren calls, even though he might go thirsty. He wouldn't be safe if he could get down so easily. An absolute prohibition on chopping people up for their organs is wise, even though we could put those organs to use. And a love that "alters [not] when it alteration finds" is true love indeed, even when it hurts.[42] Rules prove their worth both when we follow them and when we don't and suffer the consequences – even when it would be nice to carve out exceptions.

5.6.2 Tradeoffs

Let the rules rule even when it hurts. That sounds foreboding, and it is. Bitcoin's deterministic supply schedule has drawbacks. There is a fundamental tradeoff here between two kinds of assurances – *price* and *quantity*.[43]

Central banks promise price stability: they will manipulate supply as required to keep nominal prices stable or perhaps steadily growing at a predictable clip. They can achieve stability in price because they can manipulate the monetary supply, an important variable in determining overall price levels.

Bitcoin promises quantity stability: that monetary supply will predictably unfold according to strict and pre-decided rules. It can achieve stability in quantity because the difficulty adjustment keeps the issuance schedule inelastic. This is simply another kind of systemic stability.

By exhibiting these two different forms of stability, bitcoin and the dollar complement each other by holding firm where the other falters. When bitcoin's price moves up or down too quickly, people who have dollar access can find refuge in its price stability if they need to. When dollars flood the system thanks to miscalculation or political pressure, people can find refuge in bitcoin's stability in supply if they need to. Or people can simply hedge against both forms of instability by holding both dollars and bitcoin.

To voluntarily use bitcoin as money – to save in bitcoin, to spend bitcoin, and to accept bitcoin in exchange for goods or services – is to accept bitcoin's fundamental tradeoff. One relinquishes a price guarantee in exchange for a quantity guarantee. One gives up on technocratic manipulation for predictable automation. Bitcoin offers rule of law and one kind of systemic stability. But it does so at the expense of price stability.

This is a fine bargain for some. And not so for others. If you're one of the two billion people who suffers from bad monetary luck – if the best money you have access to is one of the ones with unpredictable or wildly inflating prices – then there's really no bargain at all. You have, instead, an option. You might rather have bitcoin's stability in quantity rather than no stability at all. And you need no one's permission to exercise this option.

This is where bitcoin shines. As an accessible and permissionless system, those who need it can use it. And those who want to use it, will.

This is not mere theory. Consider, for example, the Bank of Lebanon, an institution riddled with misconduct, poor management, and corruption.[44] Officials embezzled hundreds of millions of dollars, invested in Ponzi schemes, and printed so much money to cover it all up that the Lebanese pound lost 98% of its value against the US dollar. The result was, in the words of a World Bank report, a "Deliberate Depression."[45]

Ordinary Lebanese people paid the price; and for some, their entire life savings, stored in bank accounts, evaporated into nothing. Farhat Farhat, economist and co-founder of Lebanon's Depositors Union, put it this way:

Thousands of professionals and private sector workers entrusted their savings and sometimes entire retirement funds to local banks. But middle-class people have now plummeted into poverty, with retirees unable to afford medication or secure their old-age needs, and forced out of retirement to secure basic necessities.[46]

With this in mind, it is unsurprising that cryptocurrency adoption in Lebanon is unusually strong.[47] When institutions sink, resistance money is a lifeboat. Despite its volatility, bitcoin is a better money for some Lebanese people than any scrip on offer from the banks.

5.6.3 Back to the veil

Behind the veil, you know eight billion lives from the inside out. You don't know which is yours, but you do know that you might be one of the two billion people whose central banks have failed them. In that case, would you want access to an alternative? Might you want the *option* of using a rule-based monetary system without the risks imposed by trusted makers? We would. Perhaps you would too.

Or even if you weren't suffering under a struggling monetary regime, how sure are you that you wouldn't someday live under one? Bad things happen, often unexpectedly. Under political pressure, or in a pandemic, or an economic downturn, will the central bankers pull the lever more than usual to create more money? That's up to them. But if they pull a little too hard and hyperinflation ensues, wouldn't you like to access an asset with no such lever? You might want bitcoin around to hedge, as a form of insurance. We would. But whether you'd want bitcoin around for either resistance or for insurance, you've caught a glimpse of bitcoin's potential as an escape hatch for those trapped in a failing currency.

We began with the story of Leibniz's universal calculator. Let's be realistic; no such thing could actually resolve all our religious and philosophical disputes. No formal language or computer will resolve disputes about such closely held, personal matters. A techno-utopian vision of machines replacing people is not the answer. Yet there is still a place for automation and the assurances it can provide.

Something similar holds for money and for bitcoin. Bitcoin will never resolve all our monetary problems. But for some people, with some problems, bitcoin offers a solution. For many, algorithmically governed money provides the best answer to their problems. They can trust it more than the makers in charge of their local currencies.

In the next three chapters, we'll evaluate how bitcoin enables resistance against surveillance, censorship, and exclusion. The uniting theme is that by eliminating intermediaries, bitcoin empowers individuals to resist increasingly powerful institutions who would spy on, control, or block their money. Given the global prevalence of institutions who do all three, resistance money is choice-worthy behind the veil. If you didn't know who you'd be, you'd want bitcoin around just in case you might need to resist those institutions.

Notes

1. Antognazza (2008).
2. Salter and Luther (2019).
3. Weatherford (1998, pp. 264–265).
4. For a superb guide to how modern fiat monies are created, care of the Bank of England, see McLeay and Thomas (2014).
5. On various corridor and floor systems – the details of which need not concern us here – see Whitesell (2006) and Grossmann-Wirth (2019).
6. Bitcoin's supply schedule is not strictly deterministic with respect to external time (supply is not a function of time). For it's possible for there to be more or less bitcoin at a given time than expected. But when this happens, the difficulty adjustment kicks in and ensures that new blocks still arrive, on average, every time minutes. Bitcoin's supply schedule is strictly deterministic, though, with respect to its own internal clock (block height).
7. Some question whether a dual mandate is necessary – the ECB has just the single mandate of maintaining price stability – and whether dual mandates occasionally push in opposite policy directions.
8. In this chapter, we focus on bitcoin as a monetary institution. It is a distinctive social and political institution as well, on which see Bailey and Warmke (forthcoming) and Kavanagh and Dylan-Ennis (2020).
9. See Friedman (1960, pp. 6–8) and Mafi-Kreft (2003, p. 475).
10. Selgin and White (2005, p. 72), emphasis added.
11. So Klein (1974, p. 423): "Few areas of economic activity can claim as long and unanimous a record of agreement on the appropriateness of governmental intervention as the supply of money. . . . The monetary role of government is agreed to include, at a minimum, the monopolistic supply of a currency, into which all privately supplied demand deposits should be convertible."
12. Skidelsky (2019), especially Chapter 11.
13. The precise relationship between central banks and states is often complicated and displays considerable variation. For details about how this works in the American context, see Federal Reserve Bank of San Francisco (2003).
14. Selgin (2010).
15. Kydland and Wynne (2002, pp. 1, 3).
16. From Kydland and Wynne (2002, p. 3). The figures are in log scale and indicate levels of consumer prices across the listed countries. Footnote 3 from the next page is relevant: "There is some controversy about the exact date of the gold standard's demise. Some authors put it in 1914, at the outset of World War I, since the attempts to resume con- vertibility following the end of hostilities all ended in failure. Others put the date in 1931, when the United States formally abandoned the link between the dollar and gold. And others put it as late as 1971, when the United States stopped redeeming foreign central bank holdings of dollars for gold."
17. For a helpful overview of some of the most important macroeconomic perspectives here and their development over the twentieth century, see De Vroey (2016) and, especially, Eatwell and Milgate (2011).
18. Strikingly, inflation targets around 2% do not enjoy much support among mainstream academic economists. Indeed, if there is a consensus view, it lands somewhere around 0% instead. See Diercks (2017).
19. UNTAD (2022).
20. For a detailed and vivid depiction of these dynamics at play in Weimar Germany, see Fergusson (1975/2010).

21. Keynes (1920, p. 236).
22. Keynes (1920, pp. 236–237).
23. Bartscher et al. (2021/2022).
24. Hence, Nakamoto (2009a): "The root problem with conventional currency is all the trust that's required to make it work. The central bank must be trusted not to debase the currency, but the history of fiat currencies is full of breaches of that trust."
25. Thus, Friedman (1970, p. 24): "Inflation is always and everywhere a monetary phenomenon in the sense that it is and can be produced only by a more rapid increase in the quantity of money than in output." The quantity of money is only one variable here; the other – real output – is not under the direct control of central banks.
26. "Better-managed" does not mean "well-managed." For extensive documentation of the Fed's missteps and resulting price instability, see Selgin et al. (2012).
27. In August 2010, someone exploited the so-called value overflow bug in bitcoin's software and created billions of bitcoin. But a bug, which unintentionally allows a departure from policy, is not a deviation in policy. The bug was quickly fixed and the extra bitcoin orphaned from the blockchain, in line with the original policy.
28. He might have begun with a 1,000 rather than 50 bitcoin block reward, with a total supply of 420 million.
29. Technically, bitcoin's supply schedule could have deployed a random variable, with the reward varying from block to block according to fluctuations in that variable. Designing such a system that didn't require an oracle, that could command network consensus, and that couldn't be gamed is no easy task, however, and serves no obvious purpose. No wonder Satoshi didn't take this path. A non-deterministic supply schedule could have used average block time. After all, the bitcoin network already computes the average block time every 2,016 blocks to determine the mining difficulty for the next two-week period. And mining difficulty has, for most of bitcoin's existence, roughly tracked bitcoin's price. So Satoshi could have used changes in mining difficulty as an imperfect and indirect measure for changes in price. Equipped with this imperfect bridge between the asset internal to the blockchain and its price (external to the blockchain), Satoshi could have chosen to insert a variable block reward at least partly and indirectly determined by changes to bitcoin's price. Notice, though, that even this approach would have no room for discretionary policy or tinkering and would in that vital respect still resemble bitcoin's actual monetary constitution: policy selected by rules, not rulers.
30. The more general phenomenon here is known as the Oracle Problem: How can a given system gather information outside itself? The usual answer, as the name of the problem suggests, is to appeal to an oracle – a trusted party which reliably feeds the system external information.
31. Deterministic supply schedules have something important in common: their supply curve is utterly inelastic – a straight vertical line.
32. There is no one canonical way to measure volatility. The chart given here shows CoinMetrics' "180 day volatility" metric – the standard deviation of the natural log of daily returns over the past 180 days. For discussion of some of the econometric issues at play, see Koning (2019).
33. Nic Carter has made a similar point with respect to *institutional* bitcoin allocation mandates.
34. Another potential route to stability would involve an extremely high market capitalization, high distribution, and an extremely high free float. If these

conditions were met, few, if any, market participants would have enough capital to budge market prices.

35. Friedman (2012, p. 211).
36. Boettke and Smith (2016). See also White (1989, 1999), White et al. (2015), and all the sources cited in Hendrickson and Salter (2018).
37. See, for example, Bordo (1981, p. 17): "A fiduciary money standard based on a monetary rule of a steady and known rate of monetary growth could provide both greater price level and real output stability than a return to the gold standard. The key problem with a fiduciary system, however, is to ensure that such a rule is maintained."
38. The argument of this section is inspired by Boettke et al. (2021).
39. It is, for the record, "gettxoutsetinfo."
40. Boettke et al. (2021, p. 147).
41. If laws essentially involve force – the opposite of consent, one thinks – then "the rule of rules" will be more apt here than "the rule of law," given that participation in bitcoin is by consent.
42. Sonnet 116.
43. See Selgin and White (2005, p. 72).
44. Sabaghi (2023).
45. World Bank (2022, p. 2).
46. Quoted in Sabaghi (2023).
47. Nambiampurath (2023).

6

PRIVACY IN PUBLIC

6.1   What privacy is

Some years ago, Heathrow went to the doctor, who prescribed doxycycline for chlamydia. He bought the medicine right there at the clinic, with cash. Heathrow didn't mind at all that his doctor knew of the infection. After all, he barely knew his doctor and knew that his doctor had seen much worse and that his doctor wouldn't tell anybody. Yet he didn't want any friends to know because he knew them well, they hadn't seen much worse, and they, well, they would tell everyone.

Heathrow's chlamydia diagnosis was private. This isn't to say that it was a secret: Heathrow's doctor knew, after all, and Heathrow knew. Nor is it to say that it was a secret for some people and not others. It's more accurate to say, rather, that Heathrow had control over its disclosure. When Heathrow shares it, it remains private information – so as long as the person with whom he shares it doesn't then share it with others.

Privacy isn't secrecy. Instead, it's a power – the power to selectively disclose oneself to the world.[1] We exercise privacy to the extent that we control our personal information. And someone violates our privacy when they show that they control it, too, by disclosing it without permission.[2] Only-Fans creators don't inspire societal outrage when they post nudes of themselves. But when a stalker posts a nude video of a well-known sportscaster, we welcome news of her $55 million civil lawsuit and celebrate her victory.[3]

Privacy involves consent.

Consent is morally meaningful. It can turn something that would otherwise be inappropriate or wrong into something permissible or even good.[4]

DOI: 10.4324/9781003484721-6

Sometimes we offer consent in response to a request – as when your phone asks to track you and you tap "yes." And sometimes we offer consent without prompting,[5] as when you find the "track me, please" option on your phone and enable it of your own accord.[6] In both cases, consent freely given is a morally transformative expression of permission.

6.2 Privacy is under fire

Your personal information is a hot commodity, whether you consented to share it or not. Indeed, the information you didn't consent to share is often the most useful and, therefore, the most profitable.

Corporations have every reason to extract, analyze, and spread your personal information without your consent. For one, selling things to someone is easier when you know more about them. Baby at home? Diaper ads, coming right up. Homeowner? Paint, sofas, refinancing – surely, you need at least one of these. Vacation to Ireland? Guinness pint glasses and Kerrygold ornaments – just in time for the holidays. Every byte of information helps companies tailor their marketing to you. Once companies have this information, they can do more than use it. They can also turn around and sell it to other companies who would like to use it.[7]

Governments also build digital manila folders of their citizens – and noncitizens. They seek to control and patrol for the safety of all, and payloads of information make that mission ten times easier. Emails, texts, payments, fingerprint and DNA databases, metadata, video feeds from doorbell apps – these enable more efficient investigations into past crimes and more effective prevention of future crimes. And states sell information just as private firms do.

Personal information is often communal information. Whoever finds your personal information often thereby finds the personal information of your friends, relatives, and coworkers. For databases include files not just on individuals but their connections. We exist as nodes in a tangled web of payments – and this web tells many interrelated stories we might like to remain confidential. But we lack control over this information. Our personal financial information isn't private.

Many factors have eroded financial privacy: increased corporate and state surveillance capacity, the rise of credit and corresponding decline of physical cash for everyday consumer transactions, big data, and so on.[8] More eyes vie for personal financial information with fewer constraints on the power to acquire it.[9] Private corporations now collect, analyze, trade, and act on huge swaths of personal financial data, resulting in a "surveillance capitalism" that should concern even those who shrug off government surveillance.[10] Something valuable is under systematic threat.

Now maybe *you* don't care about where your information goes or how it's used.[11] You might choose to disclose yourself to the world in rather profligate ways. Maybe you lifestream (it's what it sounds like – streaming your entire life to an online audience). That's fine, if you freely choose it. But many of us never do. Without our consent, our personal information finds large and sometimes malicious audiences.

6.3   Why privacy matters

Privacy is good in two ways. As an instrumental good, privacy is valuable as a means to other ends. Our relationships are one such end. Consider one of your closest relationships. You know things about each other. Still, they might learn something about you that could either alter the nature of your relationship or even damage it irrevocably. How painful that would be! Privacy is good because it allows us to reveal ourselves on our own terms for the good of the relationship. The value consists not just in the hiding but also in the choice of what to reveal and to whom. Your spouse can reveal private information to you in a way that enhances the relationship. But Visa might even damage or end the relationship if they revealed it instead.

Privacy also helps us preserve various kinds of relationships.[12] Teachers would not, we hope, tell students what they'd tell a lawyer or doctor or lover. Nor would parents, we hope, tell their children what they'd tell therapists or even their own parents. Privacy erects boundaries to help teachers relate to students, parents to children, and therapists and lawyers to their patients and clients, respectively. When others disclose information without consent and tear down these boundaries, everyone stands in every position, as the therapist, lawyer, doctor, and lover. Not a great outcome.

Privacy also serves as a check on public institutions. Many of us enjoy the right against self-incrimination so that prosecutors bear the burden of proving something in court; the accused needn't testify against themselves. The protection against self-incrimination allows a defendant to withhold personal information and shifts the balance of power away from institutions and towards individuals, keeping those institutions in check.

Privacy, like clothing, also reduces unwanted exposure. When your personal information is exposed to the world, you no longer control it. Bad actors can use it to manipulate and do harm. If someone knows both your address and your recent Best Buy purchase for $2,000, they might pay you a special visit.

Or if someone knows your political bent, they might serve you certain information to nudge you towards more extreme views.[13] Or they might try to punish you.[14] This could be explicit and coercive, as with laws that criminalize certain opinions under a truly repressive regime. Or it could be more subtle: edging out you of leadership positions in your work, blocking educational opportunities for your children, spreading unkind rumors about you in church, and so on. When you have the power to disclose at your own discretion, you can cut off would-be censors at the pass. So privacy protects freedom of thought. Freedom of expression is near at hand too.

Pseudonyms and masks also help whistleblowers and activists and those with unpopular opinions to speak freely without fear of reprisal. But this only works as long as their personal connection to a pseudonym or a mask remains hidden. Some abuse pseudonymity, sure. But when *we* reveal what another has clearly chosen to hide – the real-life identity behind a mask – we violate a person's autonomy and discard their rationale for remaining hidden.

Privacy is one kind of freedom of expression: the freedom to disclose oneself to the world. Enabling that freedom enables all the benefits of free expression too.[15] Privacy, then, has significant instrumental value.

Privacy is also a final good: properly valued for its own sake.[16] Privacy is a power of selective disclosure. It's a dual freedom to reveal what we see fit and hide what we do not. And as with other freedoms hailed in the liberal tradition, many value it not instrumentally and only for what other things it produces but as an end in itself. If you think freedom is rubbish, or has mere instrumental value, we direct you instead to the arguments sketched earlier. But in a way, hardly anyone in the liberal tradition, broadly construed, needs an argument here.[17] For this tradition recognizes that freedoms are precious.

We have not claimed that anyone has a right to privacy, absolute or otherwise, or that privacy always trumps other considerations.[18] We think privacy is an instrumental and final good, deserving of full consideration as we weigh the costs and benefits of a monetary system.[19] Nor have we argued for one way of achieving privacy over others. You might trust the state and its army of regulators to be the primary guardians of privacy.[20] Or you might avoid products from corporations with a record of collecting customer data and so retreat to the hermitage. Or you might pull a Tyler Durden rampage, in the hopes of deleting the files "they" have on "us" – using bombs, if necessary. Senator, monk, menace – the familiar approaches.

The cypherpunk way is, instead, to write code. Specifically, the cypherpunks make and protect privacy with cryptography. So Eric Hughes:

> We cannot expect governments, corporations, or other large, faceless organizations to grant us privacy out of their beneficence. It is to their advantage to speak of us, and we should expect that they will speak. To try to prevent their speech is to fight against the realities of information.

Information does not just want to be free, it longs to be free. Information expands to fill the available storage space. Information is Rumor's younger, stronger cousin; Information is fleeter of foot, has more eyes, knows more, and understands less than Rumor.

We must defend our own privacy if we expect to have any. . . . People have been defending their own privacy for centuries with whispers, darkness, envelopes, closed doors, secret handshakes, and couriers. The technologies of the past did not allow for strong privacy, but electronic technologies do.[21]

Cypherpunks don't seek help solely from legacy institutions. Nor do they seek to destroy those institutions or simply retreat from ordinary life. Instead, they help themselves. We'll see how bitcoin fits within the cypherpunk ethos in due course. But first, a few points on *financial* privacy and why it matters.

6.4   Financial privacy and why it matters

Most already value privacy about sexual partnerships, medical conditions, religious practices, dietary needs, and peculiar preferences. We grasp the value and morally transformative power of consent. And much has been written on these matters.

Yet *financial* privacy – the ability to selectively disclose purchases, sales, or stored value – receives comparatively little attention. And it deserves much more.[22] For what we do with our money shows, rather than tells, who we really are.[23] You may claim to be a men's rights activist; but that assertion lacks bite without giving up something of value for the cause – a sizable donation to a suicide prevention hotline for men, say. You may say you care for your own children; but that claim means little if you're behind on child support payments despite having a healthy savings account. In short: if you want to know what someone values, observe not what they say but what they give up. Money, as a medium of exchange, is an altar upon which our sacrifices reveal our values.

Indeed, our monetary behavior doesn't merely express our deepest priorities and desires. It also unearths preferences we didn't even know we had and may well disclose other facts that are otherwise hidden from our own view. Amazon knows when you're depressed long before you go to therapy. The hormones you take, the political books you read, your sex toys and religious icons, and diapers – these say more about us than we might guess. And *buying* them says even more. Someone who knows that you bought something also knows that you believed the thing to be worth its price. And if they know what the price is, as well as when you paid it and where, they can know how much you wanted it, when you wanted it that much, and where.

Money is not just a medium of exchange but a medium of revelation.

Some distinguish various realms of privacy: privacy of the person (e.g., genetics), their behaviors (e.g., sexual preferences), communication, images and data, thoughts and feelings, location, and association.[24] What we do with our money discloses who we are along all of these dimensions. Buying medicine typically used for a congenital condition suggests that you have that condition. Buying coffee at a given café suggests that you were there and when – and so, potentially, who was there with you. Your bank deposits can even reveal hidden conflicts of interest or bias. And so on.[25]

Money talks. Without financial privacy, every transaction is an entry, not just in a ledger but in a potentially public diary.

Unfortunately, we face an uneasy dilemma between convenience and financial privacy. On the one hand, credit cards offer convenience. But leaks and hacks from these services expose our personal information to the whole world.[26] On the other hand, sticking to privacy-enhancing physical cash means forsaking quicker and simpler payment tools, access to credit, and other financial instruments. We would also have to transact in person or through the postal service. Choosing cash is tough in an ever-digitizing world.

Cash has its friends, to be sure. Cash defender, Brett Scott, claims that we must protect the use of cash not only for practical and political purposes but for "the right to be dirty and physical." But Scott acknowledges the inconveniences and says that in our world, using cash amounts to something like "a meditative practice."[27] We admire the passion. But few will take this vow of monetary monasticism. For financial privacy at scale, the privacy of cash must accompany the convenience of credit cards. We need *digital* cash.

6.5   Dimensions of financial privacy

You might now expect an ode to bitcoin's privacy features. But sadly, bitcoin does not automatically provide users with significant financial privacy.[28] The ledger is public, and all amounts, destinations, and sources are available for inspection by all. While the ledger itself does not connect its pseudonymous addresses with real-world identities such as legal names, phone numbers, birth dates, and so on, states and corporations with enough resources regularly draw these connections. They can do so because regulated exchanges require customers to provide identifying information.[29]

To get more precise about bitcoin's potential for financial privacy, let's consider how cash and bitcoin fare along four dimensions of privacy.

6.5.1   Privacy in acquisition

Can you *acquire* money without revealing important personal information?

Cash makes this easy – sell goods or services for cash or use a debit card to get cashback at the local grocery store. In these cases, being physically present might reveal what you look like or even who you are. But a given cash transaction has few eyes on it. And unless you're the focus of a sting operation, the cash itself doesn't carry your personal information. $20 bills aren't like checks; we don't need our names on them. Nor does a database require a recipient's personal information before the transaction occurs. Such a database would also be infeasible to implement; it would require compliance from too many entities who have no incentive to comply.

Bitcoin fares less well on privacy in acquisition. As you might recall from Chapter 2, the vehicle for spending bitcoin is the Unspent Transaction Output (UTXO). Each UTXO is like a single-use digital check that represents some quantity of bitcoin. Spending a UTXO funds a new transaction whose outputs are fresh UTXOs. All these UTXOs appear in a public, globally accessible ledger.

Bitcoin's public ledger limits its privacy assurances, especially given how most people acquire bitcoin. For many years now, most have acquired bitcoin from an online exchange. Exchanges allow users to trade their digital currencies – fiat or crypto – for bitcoin. But popular exchanges require users to cough up their personal information: your full name, a government-issued ID, bank information, address, and maybe even a personal photograph. So when you withdraw your bitcoin, the exchange can tie your unique UTXO to the personal information they've collected.

Some bitcoin users tie personally identifying information to a bitcoin address in full public view.

You might solicit donations for a protest under your legal name by posting a bitcoin address to a website. Or you might sell your wares online for bitcoin, with a public bitcoin address for payment. Any bitcoin you receive is then linkable to your legal identity.

Yet unlike cash, bitcoin doesn't require anyone's physical presence to complete a payment. So you can send or receive bitcoin without showing a face. No masks required.

6.5.2   Forward privacy

Can you receive money without later revealing where it goes?

Suppose you'd like to track the path of a dollar bill. You might install a nano-tracker, give it to a friend, and then sip a glass of wine as you watch its coordinates dance around on your phone. When the dot on the map goes inside the local Taco Bell and then stays, you guess with high probability that your friend fulfilled his desire to Live Más. This would be a failure of *forward privacy*. Forward privacy preserves personal information through later transactions. The less you enjoy forward privacy, the more easily someone can track your future transactions from one earlier on.

Cash lacks nano-trackers, thank goodness, and has excellent assurances for forward privacy. Seeing someone acquire cash provides little clue about how they later spend it, as long as the observer lacks a network of operatives who track serial numbers. Even if someone gives you cash and follows you around, physics can help. Closed doors, for instance, make it hard to spy on a cash transaction.

Bitcoin has much poorer forward privacy. Your nosy neighbor might love to know how you spend your money. So he hatches a plan for you to mow his law for bitcoin. Once he gets your bitcoin address for the payment, he can track future transactions *from* that address.[30] He can also google every address where you send bitcoin. It would sure be nice to throw him off your tracks. Although you could possibly throw him off your tracks, most users would have little clue how to do it. Forward privacy is tough.

6.5.3   Privacy in spending

Can you spend money without revealing important personal information?

When you spend cash, the recipient will know what you look like and perhaps even who you are, unless you've taken more extreme measures like using a drop-off point, wearing a mask, or employing an intermediary. Cash is peer-to-peer, after all. But as long as the spy agencies don't have you on a list, spending a $20 bill needn't expose your personal information; you can even use gloves to avoid fingerprints.

You don't have to be anywhere to spend bitcoin. You can pay anyone anywhere as long as you have internet access. So you needn't leak anything about your looks or behavioral quirks. No masks are necessary. No gloves are necessary either. Since bitcoin is intangible, you needn't worry about fingerprints.

However, spending bitcoin brings other risks. Suppose you have a basket of UTXOs, each unrelated to each other and to your identity. To buy a watch, say, your wallet combines some smaller quantity UTXOs into a single transaction, much like we might combine bills and coins to buy a coffee. Doing so connects previously unrelated UTXOs. Congratulations: now any observer has good reason to believe that a single entity controlled the smaller UTXOs. Every time a bitcoin user combines UTXOs, she telegraphs that the same entity likely controls them, even if the world doesn't yet know who that entity is. This might seem insignificant. But if bitcoin also lacks *backward privacy*, then sleuths might piece together the transaction histories of different UTXOS and discover data you'd like to remain hidden.

6.5.4 Backward privacy

Can you spend an amount of money without revealing where it's been?

Spending cash typically reveals very little about how you acquired it. Suppose you received a $100 bill from stripping on Friday night and a $10 bill from your mother on Saturday morning, then placed both bills in the church offering on Sunday. Ordinarily, the bills themselves wouldn't reveal to the church treasurer that they came from the same person, much less that they came from a single person connected to both Mrs. Smith, respected church lady, and the Polekatz off Highway 20 near Depot Hot Dogs. That's a good thing if you'd like to keep your lifestyle hidden from the church treasurer.

You can fairly easily leak your past transaction history with bitcoin. Spend bitcoin to an address, and anyone can tell exactly where the bitcoin came from. This makes your own transaction history vulnerable to blockchain sleuths. As we'll explain, the sleuths can then decipher, with some probability, the sources of your UTXOs, the sources of those sources, and so on.

It gets worse. Unlike glitter, security footage, DNA, a fingerprint, or the scent of cologne, the bitcoin ledger doesn't fade with time. So even if you meticulously acquired and disposed of bitcoin, a single mistake years later could expose your financial history to the world. Maintaining backward privacy using bitcoin requires consistent future vigilance – and not just by you but also by those with whom you transact.

6.5.5 Cash and bitcoin

Cash enables a remarkable degree of financial privacy with very low effort. Although each bill has a unique and traceable serial number, there's no infrastructure in place to track each bill through the economy or against the identities of the people who use it. (Yet.) Cash also provides enhanced privacy because many people use it. Your banknotes and coins will, quickly enough, get lost in the crowd. With normal use, cash enables you to achieve some level of privacy along all four of the dimensions discussed earlier. Cash is the legacy financial world's main privacy tool. It is low-tech, easy to understand, and easy to use.

Cash has limits and drawbacks, though. By virtue of being physical, cash is ill-suited for transactions with larger amounts and over longer distances. Long distance transactions require travel time and, unless you carry the cash yourself, intermediaries. Bigger amounts are bulky, heavy. Not everyone wants to receive cash, especially for high-value transactions. It's too risky. Bearer assets like cash need to be stored somewhere, and they're much easier to steal. Receiving a big wad of cash can feel like holding a hot potato. Supernotes such as $1,000 bills would help alleviate the burden. But larger bills were discontinued decades ago for fear that they facilitate money laundering.

In small amounts, cash can feel like a burden, too, especially if you don't want to worry about exact change or about jiggling all the way to the restroom at work. Cash also draws no interest rate – a distressing deficiency in an inflationary environment. Put cash in a safe if you like. But its value will slowly melt over time. A dollar's purchasing power in 2023 is 1/7th of what it was in 1971. And as we covered in the previous chapter, billions globally have currencies whose value drops even more steeply.

Cash's physicality means that CCTV monitors can track your movements in the convenience store. Interested observers could match scanned images of your spent bills with your image in the video feed. Serial numbers, while not tracked exhaustively, are tracked more often than we might guess – in automated checkout devices, for example. Overall, cash provides significant but incomplete control over what financial information leaks to counterparties or observers. So while cash is a popular and effective tool for financial privacy, it is imperfect in both its privacy guarantees and its usefulness.

Cash shines brightest in small-to-medium amounts. For anyone hoping to achieve modest financial privacy for modest and in-person transactions, cash is king. In addition to being easy to use and understand, cash is also forgiving. It has no permanent public ledger for all transactions. A single slip doesn't blow your cover forever.

Bitcoin, for now, is none of these things. Despite its cypherpunk roots, bitcoin could become a tool for mass financial surveillance, in the same league as credit cards and digital dollars. This is a problem and not merely in theory.

In 2016, someone stole almost 100,000 bitcoin from Bitfinex, a bitcoin exchange. Five years later, the Department of Justice charged Ilya Lichtenstein and his wife, Heather Morgan – also known as the absurdist rapper, Razzlekahn, the self-described "crocodile of Wall Street." The DOJ confiscated the stolen bitcoin. The story of how they connected the stolen bitcoin with the rapping crocodile and her husband is an object lesson not only to would-be criminals but also to anyone who values financial privacy. Because bitcoin's ledger is transparent, public, and permanent, someone who doesn't track you today might track you several years from now, whether you're a criminal wrongdoer or a saintly whistleblower.

6.6 Finding privacy in a public ledger

Nonetheless, bitcoin does offer financial privacy. It does so on a spectrum, where users can enjoy stronger privacy than they could from traditional payment processors. This sounds paradoxical – that a fully public ledger could enhance financial privacy. But it's true.[31]

Cash enables privacy partly because it is a bearer asset. You can directly possess cash. And you can transfer it without trusted parties. Just hand over the bill, and you're done. Bitcoin enjoys both of these properties. It, too, can be held without the assistance of a manager and transferred without the cooperation of a mediator. So to what extent does bitcoin's cash-likeness extend to its privacy capabilities?

Mark Twain is Samuel Clemens – so we learned in school. Despite all the press about Mark Twain as the author of *Adventures of Huckleberry Finn*, we all know that Samuel Clemens wrote it. Even Clemens's own contemporaries knew it. From this, we draw the obvious lesson that a pseudonym grants privacy only insofar as one's connection to it remains hidden. And so it goes with bitcoin.

The ledger consists of transactions that send bitcoin to addresses. But these addresses bear no automatic link to those who use them. As far as the ledger is concerned, a bitcoin address works like a pseudonym for the person who uses it. Since bitcoin addresses are pseudonymous, the spectrum of privacy in bitcoin largely depends on whether, and to what extent, a user's connection to an address has been revealed. This concerns matters outside the bitcoin ledger.

To acquire bitcoin without revealing your identity – you could earn bitcoin under a pseudonym for a task that takes no special skill – requires you to be in no special place or time so that your employer has no idea about your real identity. Although we could read bitcoin's ledger and see the bitcoin at your address, no one would know that it's *yours*.

Or you could enjoy acquisition privacy by receiving bitcoin in person from strangers. Hand over some cash or goods to your counterparty and receive some bitcoin from them on your phone. No one needs to know anyone's real name. Of course, like cash transactions, higher amounts call for more caution. And you might leak details about your physical appearance.

Or you might use a peer-to-peer exchange of traditional money for bitcoin. Since these services don't custody any funds, the law typically doesn't require them to collect and retain user information. But in both physical and digital peer-to-peer exchanges, your peer might abscond with your money mid-exchange. So you take on counterparty risk.

Acquisition is the easiest privacy problem to overcome with bitcoin. But we need more sophisticated tools for the problems of maintenance, forward, and backward privacy.

Broadly, we can resist online surveillance in two ways: *shielding* as behind a mask and *obscurity* as within a crowd.[32] By shielding, we mean cryptographically secured secrecy. A shielded transaction uses a kind of mathematical armor that prevents third parties from unveiling its financial details. Perhaps the most well-known cryptographic shielding strategy involves *zero-knowledge proofs*.[33] As counterintuitive as it may seem, these allow a user to prove that a given cryptographic claim is true – that a certain transaction is valid, say – without disclosing its contents. Using the cryptocurrency Zcash, for example, users can send and receive value on a public ledger without revealing any information about amounts, destinations, or sources.[34]

Privacy through obscurity provides anonymity within a group. Obscured transactions drive a wedge between users' real-life identities, their place in physical and social space, and the ledger's fully visible financial details.[35] One obscuring strategy – implemented by yet another cryptocurrency, Monero – deploys *ring signatures*. Whereas each Bitcoin transaction determinately claims one or more sources of Bitcoin within a transaction, a Monero transaction involves a ring of possible sources. Under best practices, no one but the originating user knows the true source from within the ring.

Cash achieves its privacy assurances with both shielding and obscuring. When you transact behind closed doors, your transaction is invisible to prying eyes. This is shielding. And when others use cash, too, your banknotes and coins mix with theirs. The larger and more active the crowd, the more easily you can hide your financial activity in plain sight. This is privacy through obscurity.

Financial privacy through shielding and obscurity both benefit from network effects. The more transactions processed in either way, the stronger their privacy.[36] This holds especially for obscurity. The bigger the swarm of indistinguishable transactions (or participants in a ring signature), the more privacy each enjoys. But these swarms raise important questions. Users who participate do not merely secure privacy for themselves; they secure it for others too – both the noble and the nefarious.[37] Double-effect reasoning may apply here. Roughly, subjects avoid moral responsibility for the foreseeable consequences of an action provided that they do not intend those consequences; in this case, helping bad actors conceal their activities.[38]

Bitcoin at present lacks the programmability and technical infrastructure to natively implement either zero-knowledge shielding or ring signatures at its base layer. But its open architecture enables other means for enhancing privacy.

6.6.1 CoinJoin

Imagine a privacy service for PayPal that holds users' money in a single account and forwards their payments wherever and whenever they like.

A lone, privacy-obsessed hacker knows each participant's proportion of the glob of money.

You could get some privacy using this service, even from PayPal's watchful eye. Don't send money directly to the intended recipient. Instead, send it to the glob, and let it sit for a while as money enters and exits the glob. Then instruct the glob to pay someone. Because money that exits the glob comes directly from the glob and not you, neither your recipient nor PayPal could tell it was from *you*. Thus, backward privacy. And when you send your money to the glob, it loses its tie to you and becomes one with the glob, giving onlookers little idea about where it eventually goes: forward privacy.

If only you could later send money back to yourself, in a different account and disconnected from your identity, you could sever your money from its connections to your payments history. But achieving maintenance privacy in this way is not possible, even in this imaginary scheme. You can't make more than one account per person or legal entity.

We run into other problems too. Although a PayPal money glob could be an impressive tool for financial privacy, it cannot work with PayPal or a similar centralized payment service, given the current landscape. PayPal's risk managers would shut down a suspected glob service in a heartbeat. Otherwise, regulators would penalize *them* even faster for facilitating money laundering. Besides, the PayPal glob would require significant amounts of trust. Above all, you'd have to trust its coordinator not to abscond with your funds.

Yet bitcoin enables something like the privacy-enhancing glob. Bitcoin-mixing services worked more or less like the glob imagined earlier. You'd send your bitcoin to the server, and it'd churn for a bit, mixing all the while with bitcoin submitted by other users. And then it would spew out bitcoin to all the intended recipient addresses. When bitcoin entered the mixer, observers couldn't ascertain its destination. And when bitcoin exited, observers couldn't ascertain its source. And since anyone can use as many bitcoin addresses as they please, users could sever their money from their personal transaction histories and enjoy maintenance privacy.

Yet these mixers had the same flaw as our imagined PayPal glob: they involved a central trusted party, the mixing service itself. Predictably, bitcoin mixers have suffered one of two nasty fates. Some operators have been prosecuted by legal authorities, typically for wire fraud, terror financing, money laundering, or operating without a money transmitter license.[39] Others have taken advantage of the trust given to them and absconded with funds, leaving users in the lurch. Variation on a familiar dilemma: fail or jail.

Luckily, bitcoin's open architecture permits the construction of privacy services much like the glob earlier but without a trusted central operator. This reduces the risk of money laundering and theft and enables new possibilities for financial privacy.

A number of protocols can enhance bitcoin privacy, ranging from the purely theoretical to the widely used. They show considerable technical variation, so we will proceed at a high level, describing the core techniques only in broad outline and leaving aside some cryptographic details.[40]

With CoinJoin, multiple users can pool money into glob without trusted parties. They jointly construct a single transaction and then send value back to themselves or others at new addresses. In such a CoinJoin transaction, users sever their identities and histories from old addresses.[41] Furthermore, since a bitcoin transaction's inputs don't map explicitly to any given output, the transaction histories of the bitcoin entering a CoinJoin get smeared across every quantity of bitcoin exiting the transaction.[42] All transactions remain public, but the ledger doesn't say whether the transaction is a true CoinJoin involving many people or just some random user sending Bitcoin from old addresses to new ones.[43] So even if we had known who had which bitcoin at which addresses going in, we wouldn't know who received how much Bitcoin on the other end.[44]

A picture helps. Suppose that Alice, Bob, and Cal together transact as follows:

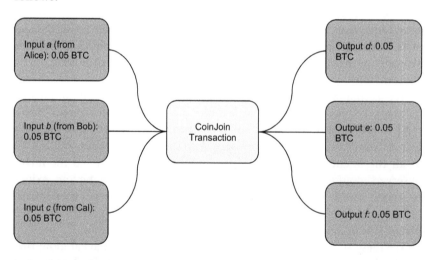

A simple CoinJoin transaction.

There are three inputs and three outputs, all of equal size.[45] And the outputs are each spent to fresh addresses – one each – designated by Alice, Bob, and Cal. The elements are fused into a single transaction and broadcast to the network of nodes.

But now ask, from the perspective of an observer, an observer who already knows that Alice, Bob, and Cal are connected to inputs *a*, *b*, and *c*, respectively: whose is output *d*? The true owner would know. But an outsider to the transaction could only say that d could belong to Alice, Bob, or Cal, perhaps with a probability of one-third for each person (assuming that no other parties are involved, of course).

Let's say d belongs to Cal. He could later spend d, but even the most well-informed observer wouldn't know whether the person who controlled d also controlled a, b, or c. And although Alice and Bob would each know that they didn't control d, neither would know whether the other or Cal controlled it. For them, the probability would be one-half that Cal controlled it. So CoinJoins can sever deterministic links from a UTXO both to its history and to any person connected to its past.

CoinJoins can work without a central operator or custodian. Alice, Bob, and Cal only need compatible wallet software that allows them to find each other and jointly construct the transaction.[46] Well-designed wallets do this under the hood. Alice and Bob and Cal just say how much bitcoin to send and where, and the wallet software automatically performs the CoinJoins. Since no trusted party holds the funds or centrally operates a service, no trusted party can abscond with any funds or serve as the locus of prosecution. Nor can any participant run away with funds from the other participants. CoinJoining, in short, has significant advantages over bitcoin mixers.

And it gets better. The procedure can be iterated. As new rounds of CoinJoining compound, one after another, uncertainty also compounds in the link between inputs and outputs, at least under some common assumptions. To see why, suppose that Cal spends d through another CoinJoin transaction, along these lines:

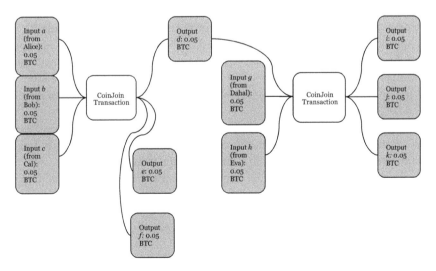

A two-stage CoinJoin transaction.

Imagine how you might discern the provenance of output i. You want to know who spent it and where it came from. You might be able to tell that it came from a CoinJoin transaction.[47] You might even know that two of the inputs to that transaction – g and h, respectively – belong to Dahal and Eva. But which of Alice, Bob, Cal, Dahal, or Eva now controls output i? Under some *highly* idealized assumptions (more on these in a second), you could at most say that there's a one-third chance each that output i is Dahal's or Eva's and a one-ninth chance each that it's Alice's, Bob's, or Cal's.[48] In CoinJoining a second time, Cal has reduced our certainty about what he's been up to from one-third to one-ninth.

Similar remarks apply about tracing the forward fate of output a. You could know for sure that the bitcoin in a might have ended up in $e, f, i, j,$ or k. But you wouldn't know which. For all you know, it has a one-third each chance of being in e or f and a one-ninth chance each of being in $i, j,$ or k.

Successive rounds of CoinJoining smears transaction data of the inputs across all the outputs. Once deterministic links between UTXOs and their histories and fates transform into probabilistic links, each with a low probability.

CoinJoining *can* offer participants significant privacy assurances. In severing the link from a UTXO to its past, it enables acquisition and backward privacy. In severing the link from a UTXO to its future, it enables maintenance and forward privacy. So long as the smearing stands between public behavior on the blockchain and personal financial information, the choice is yours whether or how to disclose the latter. That's privacy.

But CoinJoining faces significant limitations as a privacy tool. First, you'll need enough participants for robust privacy in this age of big data analysis – way more than three. And if you hope to reap the rewards of repeated CoinJoins, you'll need different participants in later rounds.[49]

Second, fellow CoinJoiners will need to front similar amounts of capital. In the examples earlier, transactions involved 0.05 bitcoin, a relatively small amount in today's prices. But CoinJoining in large amounts requires everyone to devote larger amounts. This makes privacy harder to attain for larger amounts.

Third, fellow CoinJoiners must operate on similar timeframes. When your privacy needs are urgent, there's no guarantee that a sufficiently large and diverse crowd will want to CoinJoin at the same time.

Fourth, some counterparties simply refuse transactions that have Coin-Joins in their history. Tough luck for the privacy-minded.

Fifth, CoinJoining doesn't prevent observers from tracking your online activity by monitoring your internet connection and correlating it with public payments on bitcoin's blockchain.

Sixth, user error is always a risk. Forget to CoinJoin, or do it poorly, and you might reveal all sorts of past bitcoin activity and make it forever accessible on the internet.

This last point deserves reflection. Over time, the record of user activity on bitcoin's ledger remains in place; but surveillance techniques, whether from states or corporations, only improve. A single transaction might not make you vulnerable in a month or even a year. But in a decade, it just might.

We'll return to these limitations, shortly. But first, we want to describe another, quite different, privacy tool available to bitcoin users. It is bitcoin's lightning network.[50]

6.6.2 Lightning

Lightning is an open-source, peer-to-peer payment network operating atop the bitcoin blockchain, much in the way that payment services like Visa and PayPal run atop the dollar base layer. Whereas final settlement for Visa and PayPal requires transferring physical cash or digital balances held at the Federal Reserve, final settlement for lightning takes place on the bitcoin blockchain. Lightning nodes (all of which are also bitcoin nodes) stand in a mesh network, with each lightning node connected to some others by way of payment channels.[51] A sender need not have a direct payment channel to a target node. The sender only needs a path of channels to the recipient node.

Each payment channel on the lightning network requires one base-layer transaction to open and, eventually, one base-layer transaction to close. But once the payment channels exist, none of their activities appear on the blockchain. So whereas on-chain bitcoin transactions serve as fair and easy game for financial surveillance, lightning payments require recognition only from the lightning nodes involved in the payment and never appear in the blockchain.

To get a feel for how lightning can be a privacy-enhancing tool, consider a small network of nodes connected to their peers by payment channels:

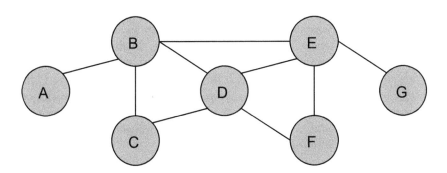

A network of lightning nodes (circles) connected by payment channels (lines).

Suppose that A wants to send some bitcoin to E. A might construct a route that goes from A to B to D and then to E and send payment along that route as follows:

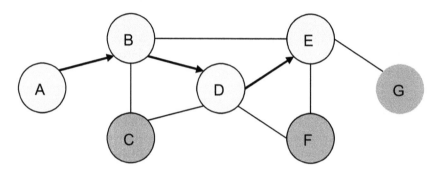

Lightning nodes route payments (arrows).

Think of it this way: A sends B a package, which, when unwrapped, contains a note and a further package. The note says: "please send the smaller package on to D."[52] D opens the package, and it, too, contains a note with a further package intended for E.[53] Payments thus zig-zag across the network, taking the shape and (theoretically) the speed of a lightning bolt. Since payments don't touch the blockchain, constraints on the lightning network's throughput come from things like the speed of light and node connection latency, not the blockchain's intrinsic limits.

A recipient of a lightning payment only knows where the bitcoin came from most directly. So earlier, although E knows that it received bitcoin from D, the trail beyond D goes dark. Intermediate routing nodes are ignorant too. D recognizes B as the source of bitcoin but then the tracks stop. And D itself doesn't know whether E is the ultimate recipient or just another stop along the route.

Routing nodes need not know a payment's ultimate source or destination. This design, in theory, enables some forward and backward privacy. With lightning, you can spend bitcoin without an observer necessarily knowing its source or destination. Links that might be deterministic if observed on bitcoin's public blockchain become, at best, probabilistic. Lightning achieves privacy through both shielding and obscurity. Lightning's swarm of nodes comprise a network – a crowd – within which both senders and receivers of value may find obscurity. And payment information is not broadcast to the entire network or written on a permanent public ledger – a kind of shielding.

Like CoinJoin, the lightning network has significant limitations for privacy. First, we need enough participants. A few nodes are far from enough. For real privacy assurances, we need thousands. At present, there are about 30,000 lightning nodes with public channels. But not all actively route payments.

Second, the network requires capital. Users must lock bitcoin into payment channels for the whole thing to work. To send payments of any real size, then, a lot of bitcoin has to be locked.

Third, you'll need network nodes to be online, ready to route payments, and already connected via channels to the right nodes.

Fourth, the intended recipients of your payments may not use lightning. They may prefer instead to receive bitcoin exclusively through on-chain transactions.

Fifth, lightning payments still generate opportunities for surveillance. An observer can scan the entire network for public information about channel capacities and connections; collecting updated information provides clues for likely payment routes.[54] Indeed, since nodes charge fees for routing payments, and since lightning wallets typically find the shortest and cheapest routes, observers occasionally make educated and accurate guesses about a payment's amount, origin, and destination.[55]

Sixth, your online activity might reveal details about your lightning payments. Someone could conceivably monitor your internet connection and correlate it with activity on the lightning network.

Seventh, there is always the possibility of user error.[56]

These limits resemble several that we encountered not only for CoinJoin but for physical cash too. Privacy is rarely perfect.

6.7   Parity: Cash and bitcoin

We can now unveil a parity thesis: cash and bitcoin create similar opportunities for privacy, with similar drawbacks and limitations. This contention will turn out to have important normative consequences. If the privacy cash offers is desirable, so, too, is the privacy bitcoin offers.

We have already noted the limits of privacy for both cash and bitcoin. Surveillance is possible and can be expensive to avoid. There are liquidity limitations too: just as not everyone who accepts dollars accepts cash, not everyone who accepts bitcoin accepts CoinJoined bitcoin or bitcoin payments over lightning. Both also suffer from severe limitations on transaction size: it's tough to buy a house with physical cash, and it's similarly tough to CoinJoin millions of dollars in bitcoin or send millions in bitcoin through lightning channels. Overall, both cash and bitcoin need a sufficiently large crowd to offer meaningful privacy. As with cash, the more people who use bitcoin privacy tools, the more effective they become.

We can measure a transactor's degree and kind of privacy along several dimensions. We will focus on perhaps the most important.

Suppose that you divulge a secret in a room with five other people. The secret then appears on Twitter through an anonymous account. If you didn't post the secret or tell it to anyone, exactly five candidates remain as the possible source. From your perspective, the *anonymity set*, the crowd of final candidates, has five members. For detectives, the bigger the anonymity set, the harder it is to find the culprit.

We can apply the same idea to cash transactions. A bill's forward anonymity set is the group of its potential direct recipients. So if an observer knows you spent cash in a given neighborhood and that only 30 shops accept cash there, the forward anonymity set has 30 members. A bill's backward anonymity set is the group of its potential sources. When an observer tries to ascertain who spent certain banknotes in the 7-Eleven last Sunday and security cameras show 20 customers that day, the backward anonymity set has 20 members. The bigger the anonymity set, the more privacy one enjoys, at least along this one dimension. You can think of the number of members as providing a privacy score.

With cash, anonymity sets can approach the size of a neighborhood or small city. Across many places and at many times, you can spend cash and achieve forward and backward privacy with anonymity sets ranging from hundreds to perhaps thousands of members.

Bitcoin users can enjoy similarly large anonymity sets, at least when they use CoinJoin or lightning. The forward anonymity set for a lightning payment includes all the indirectly connected nodes with sufficient channel capacity to receive that amount. The backward anonymity set for a lightning payment includes the indirectly connected nodes with sufficient channel capacity to send that amount. Typical lightning payments would have anonymity sets with hundreds if not thousands of members. And the anonymity set for a group of CoinJoin rounds includes its unique participants. At present, a round of CoinJoining can claim hundreds and perhaps thousands of participants. Furthermore, one can engage in successive CoinJoin rounds, as might your fellow CoinJoiners. If everyone CoinJoins in consecutive rounds with new participants, the anonymity score increases exponentially.

Using bitcoin does not guarantee much privacy. But under best practices, bitcoin offers cash-like privacy. Since cash is itself not perfectly private, bitcoin does not offer perfect privacy either, even under best practices. Our earlier arguments in favor of financial privacy would, therefore, seem to tilt the scales in favor of preferring a world in which those who seek financial privacy in the digital sphere can have it – with bitcoin. But privacy also empowers certain kinds of wrongdoing. Perhaps bitcoin's privacy isn't worth whatever good it accomplishes.

6.8   Balancing privacy's benefits

As with knives and hammers, financial privacy can be used for good or bad. And let's admit it, financial privacy enables several sorts of criminal misconduct: tax evasion, human trafficking, the financing of terrorism, bribery and associated corruption, spending of ill-gotten proceeds, and so on. Cash is a privacy technology.[57] Illicit uses account for a significant portion of the significant demand for cash:

> Demand for most advanced-country paper currency notes has been rising steadily for more than two decades. Believe it or not, as of the end of 2015, $1.34 trillion worth of US currency was being held outside banks, or $4,200 floating around for every man, woman, and child in the United States. The orders of magnitude for most advanced-country currencies is broadly similar. Incredibly, the vast bulk of this mass stash of cash is in high-denomination notes, the kind most of us don't carry in our purses and wallets, including the US $100 bill, the 500-euro note (about $570 at present), and the 1,000–Swiss franc note (a little over $1,000). Almost 80% of the US currency supply is in $100 bills.[58]

And what does that underground cash economy amount to? It includes the following:

> . . . a huge range of blatantly illegal activities, for example, the drug trade, extortion, bribes, human trafficking, and money laundering, just to name a few. . . . And it definitely includes small cash-intensive businesses that prefer to get paid in cash so they can underreport revenues to tax authorities. In some countries, like the United States, the underground economy very importantly includes firms that save on costs by hiring illegal immigrants at low wages, enabling them to undercut firms that hire workers legally. . . . Yes, crime will continue with or without cash, but for very good reasons, cash is a medium of exchange highly favored by the underground economy, and the underground economy accounts for a significant share of the demand for cash.[59]

None of this is surprising. Cash is indeed useful for all sorts of nefarious deeds. By offering financial privacy, cash has significant social drawbacks. And it's worth it.

Virtually no serious commentator actually thinks that cash should be abolished, with the exception of the author quoted earlier and the People's Bank of China.[60] It's not just criminals who want cash or the privacy it affords. Privacy is normal. Indeed, a research report from the Federal Reserve Bank of St. Louis notes:

> Privacy in payments is desired not just for illegal transactions, but also for protection from malfeasance or negligence by counterparties or by the payments system provider itself. Proposals to abolish cash take inadequate account of these legitimate demands for privacy.[61]

Despite its drawbacks, many would overwhelmingly prefer a world with cash to one without. Cash is amazing. Not only does it create significant opportunities for privacy, it has somehow found adherents across the political spectrum and users across the world. It is not just for weirdos and deviants. Cash is for anyone. Jerry Brito sums things up nicely:

> Cash – and in an increasingly digital world, electronic cash – is a tool that law abiding private individuals can use to protect their privacy, autonomy, and ultimately their dignity. It should not just be tolerated, but fostered and celebrated. Not only do its benefits outweigh its costs, it is [a] check that individuals may wield over abusive intermediaries. It will help ensure we do not lose our open society.[62]

Cash is a compromise. It balances financial privacy and the felt need for oversight and control. Anyone can use it, but they can't use it just anywhere and for any old purpose. And cash's privacy guarantees are, as we've seen, incomplete.

Bitcoin privacy tools display a similar compromise. Their privacy guarantees are also incomplete and face similar limits. Bitcoin and cash are of a piece in both of these respects. When it comes to privacy, what is true of cash is also true of bitcoin – they're worth the trouble.

That bitcoin and cash enjoy parity of this kind doesn't suggest in the least that bitcoin is redundant or adds little of value to the world. For bitcoin can do something cash cannot: it settles over the internet. In a world where ever more social and economic activity takes place on the internet, bitcoin's native digitality positions it to meet an increasingly important need in ways that cash never can.

You might have hoped for a lengthy argument that bitcoin, suitably enhanced with properly-used privacy tools, is net good for the world, that its benefits outweigh its costs. Such an argument isn't necessary. Cash and its strong analogy to bitcoin already tells us everything we need to know about bitcoin's normative profile in this respect. Traditional financial systems *already* include an element that makes for significant privacy, within limits – which is precisely what bitcoin does as well. Bitcoin does not upset these carefully balanced interests; instead, it imports them into the digital world where they had not yet existed. The core proposal in this chapter is, in a way, pedestrian. Bitcoin is good in this respect, not because it is revolutionary but because it protects the status quo.

Would *you* choose a world with cash behind the veil? We would. Despite its tradeoffs and limitations, physical cash is a vital tool for financial privacy. It's worth the price. And bitcoin is, along just these dimensions, much like cash. So it is similarly worthy of choice behind the veil.

Surveillance is not the only problem with traditional digital money networks. Trusted parties also enable blocking or censorship of payments. Bitcoin privacy tools can help mitigate this threat; it's hard to block what you cannot see without consent. But bitcoin's radical disintermediation provides additional avenues of resistance. We cover these topics in the next chapter.

Notes

1. Hughes (1993).
2. For alternative approaches to defining privacy, see DeCew (2018), Tavani (2007), van den Hoven et al. (2020), and Véliz (2019).
3. Keneally (2016).
4. Alexander (1996).
5. Dougherty (2018).
6. Varon and Peña (2021).
7. Zuboff (2019).
8. Kumar and O'Brien (2019).
9. See Rahn (1999) for a chilling and prescient expression of this trend.
10. Zuboff (2019).
11. It is an unusual person who does not prize their own privacy. There are, for example, constitutional protections for privacy in more than 20 countries. See also Brooke and Véliz (2020): "1107 people responded to the survey. . . . 82% deemed privacy extremely or very important, and only 1% deemed privacy unimportant."
12. Rachels (1975) and Mooradian (2009).
13. Ribeiro et al. (2020) discuss how YouTube does this.
14. Tugend (2015).
15. The *locus classicus* here is Mill (1859/1989).
16. Farrell (2012).
17. Perhaps the most important exception is Mill, cited earlier, who thinks of liberty as having only instrumental value.
18. Moore (2018).
19. Rössler (2005).
20. So Young (1990, p. 119): "The private should be defined . . . as that aspect of his or her life and activity that any person has a right to exclude others from. . . . With the growth of both state and nonstate bureaucracies, the

protection of privacy has become a burning public issue. In welfare capitalist society, the defense of personal privacy has become not merely a matter of keeping the state out of certain affairs, but of calling for positive state regulation to ensure that both its own agencies, and nonstate organizations such as corporations, respect the claims of individuals to privacy."

21. Hughes (1993).
22. Berg (2018).
23. Samuelson (1938, 1948).
24. Finn et al. (2013).
25. Perhaps unsurprisingly, the vital role of privacy – and thus, financial privacy – in self-preservation is especially well-known among historically marginalized communities. See, for example, all of the essays in Lewis (2017).
26. Kahn et al. (2005).
27. Scott (2022, pp. 262–263).
28. Reid and Harrigan (2012) and Bohannon (2016).
29. See Herskind et al. (2020, 54049).
30. For certain pedants – yes, we know that *technically* there are no "from addresses" in bitcoin transactions.
31. Mikerah (2022) is, at the time of writing, one of the most useful, technically accurate, and up-to-date compilations of information on privacy tradeoffs and possibilities on public blockchains. See the "Privacy" section in Lopp (2022) for more resources specific to bitcoin in particular.
32. Compare to Herskind et al. (2020).
33. Li and McMillin (2014) and Androulaki and Karame (2014).
34. Herskind et al. (2020).
35. Matthews (2010).
36. On privacy through obscurity as a public good, see Kwecka et al. (2014). If Kwecka et al. are correct that privacy is a good of this kind, then there is an interesting argument for the conclusion that states have a strong reason to tolerate or even promote privacy tools like cash – or the privacy tools for bitcoin we describe next. Roughly: states have strong reason to promote public goods, privacy is a public good, and those tools themselves promote privacy.
37. On complicity, see Lawson (2013).
38. Dierksmeier and Seele (2018). On double-effect reasoning, see McIntyre (2023).
39. The case of Bitcoin Fog, as discussed in Newman and Greenberg (2022) and De (2021), is representative as is Helix, discussed in Voreacos (2022).
40. For a *very* thorough overview of privacy techniques in bitcoin and their tradeoffs, see Ghesmatia et al. (2021). See also Ficsór et al. (2021).
41. The fundamental technique originates in Maxwell (2013) and is now used across a variety of implementations.
42. Warmke (2022).
43. A CoinJoin transaction on the blockchain: https://blockchair.com/bitcoin/transaction/e4abb15310348edc606e597effc81697bfce4b6de7598347f17c2befd4febf3b
44. Biryukov and Tikhomirov (2019, p. 10).
45. This is all a bit stylized. In reality, there would be fees paid to miners, a point to which we'll return. And CoinJoin implementations differ in how they handle change (as when you spend a 0.5 BTC UTXO and intend to join only 0.25 BTC, keeping the remainder unjoined), how outputs are claimed, and whether inputs or outputs need to all be of equal size.
46. In bitcoin, signatures associated with different inputs can be constructed separately, which in turn enables cooperation without custody. The result includes all the benefits of mixing – but no mixer.

47. Whether this could be deduced is a matter of the precise CoinJoin implementation and its distinctive blockchain signature (whether all users are required to submit inputs of the same size, for example).

48. One-ninth is a lower bound. Somewhat more cautiously, we might say that you'd assign between one-fifth and one-ninth to the hypothesis that output i is Cal's. One-third$_2$ characterizes the probability integrated over the path length for Cal, whereas one-fifth characterizes the probability given that only five people are involved in all relevant CoinJoins.

49. The presence of many participants doesn't just drive down the certainty of observers. It also protects against a flooding attack, as when Alice and Bob conspire to unmask a certain output as Cal's. The main protection against attacks like this is economic: when each round of CoinJoin costs something in fees paid to miners, the bill that'd accrue to any would-be flood attacker starts to accumulate quickly. It is expensive, that is, to unmask participants by flooding CoinJoin transactions with your own inputs and outputs.

50. The standard technical manual for lightning is Antonopoulos et al. (2021).

51. For up-to-date statistics on lightning network nodes and channel capacity, see https://1ml.com.

52. It may also contain a tip for B; many nodes collect fees for their routing work.

53. Crucially, network participants don't actually take custody of the payments they route (this is where the package analogy can be misleading). They can either route the payment or not, but since it isn't addressed to them, as it were, they are cryptographically blocked from seizing it.

54. Such probes cannot detect the existence or capacity of *private* channels between nodes, which are known only to their participants. But there's a tradeoff here between privacy and convenience, for it is public channels that make for the quickest and cheapest routing of payments.

55. Kumble et al. (2021).

56. For a comprehensive and up-to-date overview of privacy on lightning – and its limits – see https://lightningprivacy.com

57. It is important to not exaggerate cash's role in illicit underground activity. For criminals overwhelmingly prefer non-private and noncash financial instruments – bank accounts – for money laundering and such. Danske Bank recently pled guilty, for example, to shuffling billions of dollars through American banking pipes; see DOJ (2022). They didn't use bags of cash – or bitcoin – to do this, just ordinary banking rails.

58. Rogoff (2016, p. 3).

59. Rogoff (2016, p. 58).

60. See Luther (2018b) for a passionate and persuasive reply to Rogoff's anti-cash arguments.

61. Kahn (2018). Intriguingly, Kahn adds this implicit nod to bitcoin: "Therefore the replacement of cash by central bank electronic money is likely to spur demand for alternative means of payments to solve specific privacy problems."

62. Brito (2019).

7

RESISTING CENSORSHIP

7.1 Guarding against the guardians

"I was afraid as shit." That's UFC heavyweight champion Francis Ngannou on his harrowing 14-month journey from Cameroon to France in an interview with Joe Rogan.

During the interview, Ngannou recalls a "game" between migrants and the border guards situated between Cameroon and Nigeria. Here's how the game was played: the migrants had money, and the border guards would try to steal it. He then reveals a winning move:[1]

Ngannou:	Sometimes, we wrap money in the paper and swallow it.
Rogan:	Oof.
Ngannou:	Because you can't cross this zone without . . . getting frisked. So you have to save your money because you have to survive, you have to keep going, you have to eat. . . . They just want to take whatever they can take.
Rogan:	So you'd have to swallow your money?
Ngannou:	Yeah, you swallow your money.
Rogan:	And then find it later.
Ngannou:	"Find it later."
	laughter
Ngannou:	You had to. Like, at this point, it's a matter of surviving. Everything that you can do to survive.
Rogan:	So did you have to wrap it in plastic?

DOI: 10.4324/9781003484721-7

Ngannou: Yeah, you wrap it in plastic to protect it from getting wet and being destroyed.
            laughter
Rogan: Man.

Desperate times call for hidden treasures. But swallowing money isn't just a way to *hide* money. It also protects your money. Even if border guards suspect you're packing pelf in an intestinal vault, what can they do about it? Acquiring your filthy lucre isn't worth their time or trouble.

Yet greedy border guards aren't the only threats to our money worldwide. We're talking, of course, about the mediators and managers in the traditional financial system. In an increasingly cashless world, these digital "border guards" already know where your money is. And they ultimately control it – as 0s and 1s in their databases.

In what follows, we survey these threats and weigh the tradeoffs of censorship-resistant money – money that eludes the grasp of these mediators and managers. For although financial censorship often impedes human flourishing, it is also sometimes a tool for good. International sanctions, for example, use the powers of censorship to make bad behavior costly. So censorship-resistant money has potential downsides; it can provide sanctioned parties a financial escape hatch. Such an escape hatch has also enabled or facilitated new kinds of wrongdoing, such as ransomware.

Before we describe and weigh these tradeoffs, let's look at how financial censorship works.

7.2   Permission and censorship

Censorship blocks the free flow of *expression*. For example, we can prevent certain people from speaking in certain venues, or we can prohibit discussion of certain ideas.[2] Messages are usually digital today – emails, text messages, Tweets, and so on – and most financial transactions occur as glorified digital messages. As expressions, they, too, can be censored. By blocking people from "speaking" freely in the financial world, authorities impede the free flow of *value*. This is financial censorship.

Picture our traditional electronic payment systems as interconnected superhighways. Our transactions are the traffic. Authorities own these superhighways and wield great power over how we access and use them. They are toll roads, with closely monitored and guarded points of entry and exit. For entry, we request permission to open accounts at local banks, apply for credit cards, and tick the box on the terms of service agreement. Authorities then choose whether to grant us access. And even after authorities have granted us access, every transaction travels under their watchful eyes and with their implicit permission, which is revocable at any time, with little warning or rationale. These authorities are the trusted managers and mediators of the financial system.

As both supervisors and gatekeepers of financial traffic, the authorities have various tools to control traffic. Authorities vary in kinds and amounts of power depending on where they operate. But considered as a group, they have four main ways to censor. They can do the following:

- deny an existing customer's requests to open an account
- shut down already opened accounts
- freeze or seize funds from an account
- block transactions, in part or whole

The notion of partial blocking, in the last point, may raise eyebrows. But this happens when mediators extract unnecessarily large or unexpected transaction fees. These extractive emoluments on the financial superhighway qualify as financial censorship because the recipient receives less than the entire message, so to speak.

Authorities have a range of targets when they censor. They might intend to censor particular groups, entities, or kinds of transactions. *Group-centered* censorship targets people with a particular feature, like those who support certain political causes, practice certain religious faiths, or have certain careers. In times of financial distress, a bank might simply censor everyone with money in an account. *Entity-centered* censorship targets a particular person or organization, like the outspoken whistleblower, the non-profit watchdog, or the bigoted influencer. Authorities might also censor more general kinds of transactions. *Transaction-centered* censorship consists in blocking transactions for certain kinds of commerce – like those involving drugs, pornography, or copyright infringement.

Authorities have the power to censor and exercise that power over a range of targets. But financial censorship requires more than control of the superhighways. In many cases, it also requires fine-grained knowledge about the traffic itself. And authorities know quite a lot. Perched atop the superhighways, they see every transaction in great detail – senders, recipients, amounts, times, places, and so on. They keep detailed records too. We've covered several concerns about privacy in the previous chapter. Well, here's one more: the erosion of financial privacy enables troubling forms of financial censorship.

Censorship is a vexing topic. It sounds bad. Few would support censorship under that name. Few in power admit that it happens. Censorship is what dictators and fascists do – not good liberals of sound mind and character. But then again, the very people who say it doesn't happen will sometimes say that it's good. Of course, they really mean that people like *them* don't get censored. Instead, it happens to the bad guys. But the world is a big place, and it would be surprising if censorship everywhere targeted all and only the bad guys. We suspect that once we review some empirical data, most will agree that from a global viewpoint, good guys and gals often get censored too.

The global financial system is designed to enable censorship. Even if you never have your transactions blocked or accounts closed, you might still worry about financial censorship on a global scale. And even if you or people like you aren't censored now, you might be someday. Recent trends suggest that financial censorship is, or will be, on the rise. Behind the veil, we owe it to ourselves and the rest of the world to carefully evaluate the tradeoffs of such a system. Reasoning behind the veil also requires that we consider the lives of real people – any one of which you might be.

7.3   Censorship as it happens

In September 2022, Sali Hafez took her nephew's toy gun and held up a Lebanese bank. Banks around the country had either frozen withdrawals or slowed them to a trickle. Hafez's bank limited withdrawals to $200. But she had $20,000 in her account and needed to pay for her sister's cancer treatment. So Hafez had, in her words, nothing to lose.[3] And she wasn't alone. Lebanese banks closed for a week in September and then, in October, unanimously agreed to shut down indefinitely. Most Lebanese are, as we write, effectively unbanked.[4] The banks also closed for two weeks in 2019. But even before the current banking crisis, Lebanese banks might have simply refused to serve you. For example, in a recent survey of Syrian refugees, most said that banks refused to serve them precisely because they were Syrian.[5]

Nearby, PayPal has refused to serve Palestinians. PayPal offers services to Israelis in Israel and Israelis in Palestine – but not Palestinians in Palestine. Since PayPal is the world's leading e-commerce payment processor, the Palestinian blackout hinders their ability to conduct international business.[6] PayPal isn't the only institution to censor Palestinians. Palestinian banks do too. In 2021, Palestinian banks closed the accounts of 80 NGOs, including some that serve orphans and the poor.[7]

Or consider China, where banks have signs that "explicitly deny service to veiled women and bearded men."[8] The Uyghur minority group faces additional indignities. If you try to remit money to Uyghur relatives in China, they might be arrested and jailed as suspected terrorists. In such cases, the state has also confiscated both the savings and assets of Uyghurs;

in one case, the state confiscated $56,000 of a woman's life savings.[9] Non-Uyghurs, too, face severe difficulties. Four banks in Henan Province, for example, froze accounts for several months in 2022, blocking over 400,000 people from their money.[10]

The Chinese Communist Party also uses transaction data from applications like WeChat and Alipay to calculate "social credit" scores for individual citizens. If you're deemed "untrustworthy," the CCP limits your freedoms; as of July 2019, over 13 million individuals appeared on a blacklist that blocked them from flying, buying high-speed train tickets, and sending their children to private schools.[11] Since people may lose points for interacting with blacklisted individuals, the CCP leverages financial censorship to chill speech and other forms of expression.

Next door, Russia has nested dolls of financial censorship. After Russia's invasion of Ukraine, the international community seized over $300 billion of Russia's central bank funds, as well as $30 billion of assets belonging to Russian oligarchs.[12] Inside the country, Visa and Mastercard had until recently controlled almost 75% of Russian card payments. But post-invasion, the two card companies effectively banned the entire Russian economy. PayPal and American Express suspended service too.[13] Russia is financially censored, and they do plenty of financial censoring themselves.

Well before the invasion, Russia censored activists, journalists, and opposition leaders – and not just by defenestrations and poisonings. In August 2019, Russia froze the bank accounts of two organizations and over 100 individuals and legal entities tied to opposition leader Alexei Navalny.[14] A year later, while Navalny was in the hospital recovering from Novichuk poisoning, Russia froze his accounts again.[15]

Authorities around the world use financial censorship as a weapon to hinder political enemies. A few months before a Nigerian election, banks froze the accounts of the opposition party's vice-presidential candidate.[16] In Venezuela, Juan Guaidó challenged leader Nicolás Maduro and declared himself the interim president. Just a week later, Venezuela's supreme court froze his bank accounts.[17]

Western democracies aren't immune either. Drawing from an anonymous source, the BBC reported that a bank had closed the account of British politician, Nigel Farage, for purely commercial reasons. The BBC later apologized when they discovered that the bank had closed his account after an internal review showed that the bank's risk committee had said his values differed from the bank's own. And what of the anonymous source? This was the bank's own CEO, who not only disclosed a client's private information but had also lied to the BBC about the reasons for closing Farage's account.[18]

Canada does it too. In early 2022, a convoy of truckers converged in Ottawa to protest the government's response to COVID-19. Then in mid-February, Prime Minister Justin Trudeau invoked the Emergencies Act for the first time in history. With these sweeping new powers, the government froze $6 million across over 200 accounts. Trudeau said that he froze the accounts, in part, to block funding meant for protest leaders.[19] In response, the Canadian Civil Liberties Association criticized the government for invoking the act with insufficient reason.[20] Across the border, US-based crowdfunding company, GoFundMe, also censored accounts. At the Canadian government's behest, GoFundMe froze several million dollars in donations for the truckers. The company even intended to redirect the money to charities of its own choosing, which caused a predictable backlash.[21]

GoFundMe isn't an aberration in the US. In the 2010s, a new wave of censorship spread across the country, and the trend looks to continue in the 2020s. As recently as October 2022, PayPal published a new user agreement that gave them "sole discretion" to confiscate up to $2,500 from any user spreading "misinformation" in public. The new policy was carefully crafted in legalese and slated to go live a month later. In response to the public criticism, PayPal said that, actually, they never intended to publish the new user agreement.

We're skeptical, given PayPal's history of financial censorship. In 2021, PayPal froze the account of poker player Lena Evans and, without warning, confiscated her balance of $26,000. She used the account both for her poker business and for a charity that purportedly promotes "female empowerment." Even if PayPal were right that Evans violated the terms of service in using her account for gambling, they could have frozen her account without taking her money. Evans soon joined a class action lawsuit for those whose money had been confiscated by PayPal. The lead attorney on the case estimates that they'll have over 10,000 plaintiffs.[22] Evans replaced fellow poker player Chris Moneymaker as the lead plaintiff; just a year earlier, PayPal had taken $12,000 from his account, funds for a fantasy football league.

PayPal has shut down the accounts of so many people that over 22 rights groups recently sent a joint letter to ask them to stop. The diverse list of signees included the ACLU, the Electronic Frontier Foundation, the Freedom of the Press Foundation, the Tor Project, the Center for LGBTQ Economic Advancement & Research (CLEAR), and The Arab Center for the Advancement of Social Media.[23] The letter accuses PayPal of stalling payments for bail support "during Black-led protests for racial justice," as well as "targeting payments associated with Islam or Arab nationalities or ethnicity." Well before these events, PayPal pressured the indie publisher

Smashwords to stop selling books with adult content (in 2012) and subsequently blocked 100,000 Pornhub models.[24] Visa and Mastercard joined them that time too.

In the very same month that PayPal "accidentally" updated their detailed user agreement, JP Morgan Chase closed down the bank account of Kayne West.[25] This wasn't out of character for JP Morgan; in 2014, the bank terminated the accounts of hundreds in the adult film industry; of course, you wouldn't recognize their names. This came on the heels of Chase refusing to process payments for Lovability, an online condom store. More recently, JP Morgan Chase deplatformed the National Committee for Religious Freedom, a non-profit, nonpartisan interfaith organization. The NCRF apparently never received a rationale and had only had the account for three weeks.[26]

Although several US states now permit the sale of marijuana, dispensaries in these states continue to deal in cash. The federal government still forbids the sale of marijuana. Since electronic payments typically rely on banks, which, in turn, use the Federal Reserve payment system, banks cannot serve marijuana dispensaries without risking stiff penalties, including the loss of FDIC insurance.[27]

These stories might suggest that financial services providers deserve the blame for financial censorship in the US. But the truth is more complex. Please bear with us; what we're about to say makes us sound like conspiracy theorists. But it's all true and in the public record. From 2013–2017, the Department of Justice and the Federal Deposit Insurance Company pressured banks across the country to deplatform individuals and companies engaged in a range of fully legal kinds of business. Government agencies themselves called it *Operation Choke Point* because "it was designed to 'choke out' payday lenders and other 'high risk' businesses."[28]

Banks are particularly sensitive to government pressure. They, like us, dislike fines. So when the DOJ sends a letter to banks saying that certain entities engage in high-risk activity, banks respond by closing down their accounts. And this is exactly what happened for over four years. Targeted merchants included:

- ammunition sales
- ATM operators
- coin dealers
- credit repair services
- dating services
- drug paraphernalia
- escort services
- firearms sales

- fireworks sales
- government grants
- home-based charities
- lifetime guarantees
- lifetime memberships
- lottery sales
- mailing lists/personal info
- money transfer networks
- online gambling
- pawn shops
- payday loans
- pharmaceutical sales
- pornography
- surveillance equipment
- telemarketing
- tobacco sales
- travel clubs

Many of these are lawful. But they had fallen out of favor with the administration. Operation Choke Point met strong disapproval from many in congress, including Democratic Congressman Brad Sherman (a longtime opponent of bitcoin). In a letter to Attorney General Eric Holder, Sherman wrote:

> . . . I've sworn to uphold the U.S. Constitution. Accordingly, I must oppose efforts to "legislate by prosecution" and legislate by "criminal investigation," even if I agree partly or completely with the ultimate substantive aim. . . . Your department should conduct criminal investigations for the purpose of enforcing laws we have – not laws you (and I) might wish we had.[29]

The program finally ended in fall 2017, and data about its extent and lasting effects remain elusive. But many of the US cases cataloged earlier occurred during the program's lifetime.

The US has also pressured companies to deplatform entities outside the US. From 2007–2010, Wikileaks exposed illegal torture programs as well as high civilian death tolls from the wars in Iraq and Afghanistan. The whistleblowing organization also released the Collateral Murder footage of soldiers indiscriminately killing a dozen civilians in Iraq – including two Reuters journalists. Then in mid-2010, Chelsea Manning leaked hundreds of thousands of diplomatic cables to Wikileaks, who then forwarded them to publications like *The New York Times*. In the aftermath, Republican politicians including Sarah Palin and Mike Huckabee called for the assassination of Wikileaks's founder, cypherpunk Julian Assange.

Within ten days of publication, the US government had lobbied payment processors and banks around the world to enact a financial blockade against Wikileaks. Visa, Mastercard, PayPal, Western Union, Bank of America, and all sorts of other institutions banned Wikileaks. On Christmas Day 2010, *The New York Times* condemned the blockade and questioned the motives of those involved. According to the editorial:

> The decisions to bar the organization came after its founder, Julian Assange, said that next year it will release data revealing corruption in the financial industry. In 2009, Mr. Assange said that WikiLeaks had the hard drive of a Bank of America executive.[30]

We could look at many more cases of frozen accounts and confiscated funds worldwide. Alexandra Elbakyan, the communist creator of Sci-Hub, has been blacklisted from financial services in the West. (Sci-Hub opens up tens of millions of research articles to anyone with internet access.) The US has effectively taken billions from Afghanistan's reserves.[31] Banks in Cyprus skimmed $7.5 billion from its citizens' own bank accounts in the wake of the Great Recession.[32] In 2015, Greece closed banks for 20 days, then limited withdrawals to €60, then gradually increased the limit until capital controls were lifted over four years later.[33] In October 2020, the Central Bank of Nigeria froze the bank accounts of 20 prominent activists against police brutality.[34] In December 2022, the same central bank limited daily ATM withdrawals to $45.[35] And so on.

Many of the victims earlier have found recourse in bitcoin, including Russian activist Navalny, Canadian truckers, adult performers, Sci-Hub creator Elbakyan, Wikileaks, and Nigerian protestors.

There is good reason to believe that financial censorship will continue and likely become even more prevalent. First, banks and payment processors suffer reputational and financial risk for serving controversial people and organizations. Serving the controversial is bad for the brand. It makes for a poor marketing pitch: "Come bank with US Central, where all your most-hated enemies bank too!" And if some person or group is also unpopular with the current batch of regulators – see Operation Choke Point – then those regulators may levy penalties on the companies that serve them.

Second, we've become increasingly polarized, at least in the US.[36] With fewer people in the center, those on each end increasingly identify the other side as immoral, even dangerous.[37] So unsurprisingly, each side has become less tolerant and more illiberal with more frequent calls to suppress the freedoms of political opponents.[38] Financial censorship is one way to silence our opponents. So if these trends don't reverse, we should expect particular factions – in the public, in the government – to pressure financial service companies to avoid serving "them."

So we have the necessary ingredients for financial censorship to continue: (a) more pressure to censor, (b) companies vulnerable to that pressure, and (c) a financial system rife with trusted authorities who have the power to censor. And this is just the United States, one of the more liberal societies in the world. Elsewhere, totalitarian leaders, rapacious corporations, and irresponsible banks have the means and motive to censor the flow of value. Capital controls, too, remain across several low-income countries and emerging markets.[39]

At this point, the choice behind the veil might appear like a no-brainer. So much financial censorship makes censorship-resistant money look quite favorite. But still, you might prefer that all money be censorable because financial censorship is such an effective tool against certain kinds of wrongdoing. Perhaps the unfairly censored are the unavoidable collateral damage of a necessary fight against evil.

7.4   Arguments against uncensorable money

In March 2022, Senator Elizabeth Warren and a few other US Senators sent a letter of concern to Janet Yellen, Secretary of the Treasury. The US had sanctioned Russia for invading Ukraine, and they worried that Russia might use bitcoin to evade sanctions.[40] This worry generalizes. Perhaps in the long run, bitcoin could destabilize the international order by making sanctions less effective. And more generally still, you might worry that in the wrong hands, censorship-resistant money like bitcoin could do much further damage.

We take these worries seriously. Let's first look at economic sanctions – how they work and how bitcoin affects them.

7.4.1   Economic sanctions

Even though the US accounts for around 10% of international trade, nearly half of it involves US dollars.[41] Furthermore, about 95% of large-value domestic and international dollar payments funnel through the Clearing House Interbank Payments System – CHIPS.[42] Since every transaction through CHIPS routes through a bank with a branch office situated within US borders and subject to US law, a staggering fraction of international trade falls under US jurisdiction, even when the payer, the payee, and the bank are foreign entities.

The dollar's global reach gives US sanctions a nasty bite. Here's how they work. The Office of Foreign Assets Control (OFAC), an agency of the US Treasury, cultivates a blacklist of Specially Designated Nationals. Those on the list can't use the dollar financial system. And serving someone on the list can lead to severe penalties. Individuals risk up to US $20 million in fines and 30 years in prison, while institutions risk billions of dollars in fines. And with access to payments data via SWIFT (a global financial messaging system) and the European Union, the Treasury can both discern whether foreign entities have traded with sanctioned entities and threaten to separate them from the dollar payments system. Foreign banks typically comply.

The US has the power to sanction those who behave badly on the world stage. Could bitcoin upset this power? US sanctions have had teeth partly because the sanctioned have lacked an accessible alternative. If Specially Designated Nationals can use bitcoin to route around sanctions, then the US loses a key weapon of financial statecraft. So the key question is whether bitcoin offers a *unique* and *effective* detour around international payment rails. For if bitcoin is ineffective for sanctions evasion, then we have little to worry about. If instead bitcoin is effective but not uniquely so, then getting rid of bitcoin wouldn't preserve or enhance the power of US sanctions. Evaders would simply use a close substitute.

In the near term, and on large scales, no one should expect to avoid US sanctions with bitcoin. To see why, let's return to Senator Warren's concern that bitcoin could serve as a financial escape hatch for the Russian state and its oligarchs. Assuming they didn't already have billions of dollars of bitcoin, they'd need to buy it and then sell it undetected. And bitcoin is simply too illiquid and too public to move such large amounts under the radar.[43]

An asset's liquidity measures how much selling or buying affects its price. A highly liquid asset is like an ocean, where a big buy moves its price about as much as dropping a cannonball in the ocean raises sea levels. A highly illiquid asset is like a bathtub, where dropping such a cannonball has much more noticeable effects. Although bitcoin is the most liquid of all cryptocurrencies, it is, in the global financial system, not very liquid. Buying billions of dollars' worth of bitcoin would spike the price – and then selling billions of dollars' worth would sink it. So an evader would risk huge losses in value on both ends. According to Chainalysis, Russian oligarchs held close to $800 billion in offshore assets. But just a single sell order of 1.5 billion dollars' worth of bitcoin would have resulted in a 10% price decrease in bitcoin.[44]

Furthermore, because anyone can inspect the ledger, every spy agency in the world could follow a large hot ball of money through the ledger to see where it's spent. If you wouldn't accept payment from sanctioned entities on a bank's private ledger for fear of reprisal, you also wouldn't take this hot potato on a fully public ledger.

Bitcoin's public ledger even poses a problem for smaller evasion attempts. An evader must take drastic measures to ensure that they leak no personal details when they spend bitcoin in the real world. Bitcoin offers enhanced privacy, but privacy falls on a spectrum. The ability to preserve your privacy depends on who's looking for you and how much they're willing to spend to find you. Many high-profile criminals have failed to realize this simple point. By spending bitcoin and leaking personal information, often much later, they have sunk their own boats. Remember Razzlekhan; in 2022, authorities allegedly caught her with billions worth of bitcoin stolen from the Bitfinex exchange six years earlier.[45]

Despite these caveats, some bitcoin will inevitably sneak through official sanctions. In the case of Russia, and thanks to the public ledgers of most cryptocurrencies, we know that $2.2 million worth of cryptocurrency has been donated to Russian militias during the Russian-Ukraine war.[46] That's not nothing. And Russia would have never received it if bitcoin hadn't existed. It's also likely that some Russian oligarchs protected small percentages of their wealth by buying bitcoin. But we must weigh these potential harms against bitcoin's benefits for Ukrainians.

Since Ukraine solicited cryptocurrency donations through Twitter in early 2022, they've received over $100 million worth in cryptocurrency.[47] And this doesn't even count the volume of payments between Ukrainians and their families abroad. As the banking system ground to a halt under Russian bombs, Ukrainians could use bitcoin and other cryptocurrencies to pay for goods and services. Ukrainian Deputy Minister Alex Bornyakov called them "essential" and said: "In a situation like this where the national bank is not really operating, crypto is helping to perform fast transfers, to make it very quick and get results almost immediately."[48] So overall, bitcoin has helped Ukraine much more than it's hurt. Senator Warren should be quite pleased.

Yet someday, bitcoin might have enough privacy and liquidity that even oligarchs and nation states can use it to avoid US Sanctions. In fact, we fully admit that bitcoin might become *the* tool of choice for sanctions evasion. Whether this counts against bitcoin behind the veil, though, depends on whether bad actors could use something other than bitcoin to evade sanctions. For example, if Russia could just as easily evade sanctions with some vehicle besides bitcoin, then bitcoin itself would not bear much responsibility for making the world worse. And in fact, countries around the world are already developing non-bitcoin rails to avoid US sanctions.

Suppose you're a professional poker player who uses PayPal. Your fellow players and the rest of your circle of activists and adult entertainers routinely have their accounts frozen. Using PayPal is risky; your crew would migrate to another platform as soon as a feasible one surfaces. Many countries find themselves in a similar situation with the global dollar payments system. According to political scientist Daniel McDowell, US economic sanctions reveal the political risk involved in using the dollar payments system. The October 2022 SDN blacklist is almost 2,000 pages long. If you're not next on the chopping block, someone you'd like to trade with might be.

Countries naturally look for an alternative to manage this risk. In 2016, Secretary of the Treasury Jacob Lew noted the same:

> [t]he more we condition use of the dollar and our financial system on adherence to US foreign policy, the more the risk of migration to other currencies and other financial systems in the medium-term grows.[49]

China, Iran, Russia, Saudi Arabia, and several other countries have reduced their exposure to the dollar as they look for alternatives in gold and new central bank digital currencies.[50] In fact, Senator Warren's letter about cryptocurrencies highlights as a major risk the "deployment of a digital ruble that would allow Russia to conduct foreign trade without converting their currency into dollars."[51] A digital ruble wouldn't be a cryptocurrency at all but a central bank digital currency. But Warren and her coauthors confusingly lump them together, echoing a mistake often made by newcomers to cryptocurrency.[52] Beyond the digital ruble, both China and Europe have developed payment rails outside of the SWIFT system, and countries like India and Brazil are also conducting more trade outside of the dollar.[53] Although the dollar's reign is unlikely to end soon, the trend is clear.[54] Plus bitcoin's success would arguably weaken these other centrally controlled currencies, contra Warren.

By the time bitcoin is ever liquid enough for sanctions evasion, countries will have had the time and motive to create alternatives. Indeed, potential alternatives have arrived already, with China's increasingly influential Cross-Border Interbank Payment System (CIPS) and its nascent central bank digital currency.[55] So when it comes to undermining sanctions, bitcoin doesn't and won't make the world substantially worse off. Even if bitcoin were to disappear, several countries would rely on alternatives to avoid sanctions risk anyway.

Senator Warren's letter to the Treasury mentions two other routes for sanctions evasion with cryptocurrencies: (i) hackers who steal on behalf of sanctioned entities, like North Korea, and (ii) miners in sanctioned countries who can use their rewards to bypass sanctions.

First, the North Korean hackers of Lazarus Group have stolen several hundred million dollars' worth of cryptocurrency from exchanges and insecure smart contracts on platforms like ethereum. These ledgers are fully public, so we have detailed information about how Lazaraus Group operates. For instance, they often exchange their stolen cryptocurrencies for bitcoin, which they then launder using the techniques discussed in the previous chapter and exchange for fiat currencies.[56] Without bitcoin, and without the world of cryptocurrency, North Korea would have little to steal. So bitcoin benefits North Korea's totalitarian government. This is bad.

But it gets worse – for the dollar. The UN estimates that between 2%–5% of global GDP is laundered each year – around $800 billion to $2 trillion dollars.[57] And the FinCen files report uncovered $2 trillion dollars' worth of suspicious activity "passing through U.S.-based banks with relatively few impediments" from 1999 through 2017.[58] The files revealed that sanctioned associates of Putin moved over $60 million through Barclays. They also showed that JP Morgan might have helped move more than $1 billion for a Russian mafia boss on the FBI's top ten most wanted list.[59] North Korea loves dollars and has laundered over $2.5 billion of them through the US to pay for its nuclear missile program.[60] And Western banks have themselves paid billions of dollars in fines and settlements for funneling money for drug cartels, terrorism-linked Saudi banks, and notorious criminals like Bernie Madoff and Jeffrey Epstein.[61]

In fact, criminals prefer to transact in fiat currencies through the traditional financial system. Fiat currencies are more liquid. The bank ledgers aren't fully public. And bankers seem to let the money go through. And we haven't even mentioned physical cash. Some estimate that illicit activity accounts for one-third of cash transactions worldwide.[62]

By contrast, in 2022, the illicit share of cryptocurrency transaction volume stood at just .24%, twice the share from 2021 (.12%) but nearly half the 2020 share (.43%).[63] Much but not all of that volume is bitcoin's. In other words, bitcoin hosts less illicit activity than traditional fiat currencies in both absolute and relative terms. And while we can point to kinds of wrongdoing unique to bitcoin, we also have to keep the big picture in mind: bitcoin facilitates less wrongdoing than fiat currencies even on a relative basis.

The Warren letter also mentions mining itself as a potential avenue for sanctions evasion. Suppose you're an oil-rich nation, but you have fewer takers thanks to economic sanctions. Then you can use your oil to mine bitcoin cheaply, effectively selling your oil for bitcoin on the global mining market. Iran has executed this strategy, gaining up to an estimated 7% of bitcoin's global hashrate. But this is not an effective way to avoid sanctions. 7% of hashrate garners around $74 million a year in mining revenue at current prices. This is a lot for individuals but a drop in the bucket for Iran's oil trade. For context, Iran reported $39 billion in oil revenues for the fiscal year ending in March 2022.[64] Bitcoin mining doesn't move the needle for Iran. Iran also recently confiscated 9,400 mining machines across the country and banned bitcoin mining for four months.[65]

Bitcoin does move the needle for smaller and poorer countries. For example, El Salvador can leverage bitcoin's global energy market to sell clean energy from sources that it couldn't previously use. El Salvador is using geothermal heat from volcanoes to mine bitcoin. Anyone in the world with hydroelectric, wind, solar, waste energy, and geothermal can now plop down bitcoin miners nearby and monetize previously untapped sources of energy. Since mining is zero-sum, this has the added benefit of pushing out less profitable miners who use dirtier and more expensive forms of energy. In other words, bitcoin incentivizes countries to green its network for a profit.[66] We'll discuss this in more detail in Chapter 10.

When it comes to evaluating bitcoin's potential role as a vehicle for sanctions evasion, our key question was whether bitcoin offers a *unique* and *effective* detour around international payment rails. For now, bitcoin is not effective in this role. And by the time that it is effective, it likely won't be uniquely so. This last point matters. Our choice behind the veil forces us to consider bitcoin's potential effectiveness compared to whatever countries *would* use were bitcoin unavailable. We call this notion *differential uncensorability*.[67] It concerns whether bitcoin's absence would make a difference for countries who seek to evade sanctions. And this is the central notion for weighing bitcoin's censorship-resistance behind the veil. We should also note that even if countries would fail to converge on a single alternative payments system in bitcoin's absence, they might instead rely on a patchwork of systems as insurance against sanctions.

To conclude, bitcoin's existence likely won't make a substantial difference for sanctions – *even if* it becomes an effective tool of choice for sanctions evasion. In our non-ideal world, countries have already begun developing tools to mitigate the risk of sanctions. Countries would rely on these newer tools if bitcoin were to disappear, tools that likely wouldn't include a fully public ledger. And lest we've forgotten the first half of the chapter, bitcoin would also help many in a way that no other traditional digital currency likely would. For example, even if the digital ruble might later help Russia evade US sanctions, it would likely harm rather than help Russian activists from avoiding state censorship. So bitcoin's disappearance would likely fail to move the needle for sanctions evasion and likely hurt those at risk of persecution.[68]

7.4.2 Ransomware

In each of the last few years, ransomware attacks have hovered between $450 and $770 million. This is a serious problem not only in the value lost and not only in who benefitted but also in the threat to critical infrastructure.[69] According to Chainalysis, ransomware attacks target energy and food providers, schools, hospitals, and financial services companies. Although bitcoin hosts less illicit activity than the traditional financial system in both absolute and relative terms, this is a clear harm that's impossible in a world without bitcoin. The trend is also going the wrong way. From 2019 to 2020, total ransomware payments quadrupled in value. Perhaps bitcoin's benefits won't outweigh the growing costs of ransomware and other bitcoin-enabled harms.

However, for perspective, consider email. Over several decades, email has revolutionized communication. Much like digital money "dematerialized" cash and coin and enabled nearly instantaneous and global financial interactions, email dematerialized stamps and stationery and enabled nearly instantaneous and global communication. But email enabled a new kind of wrongdoing – spam and particularly malicious spam. The number of emails sent and received per day continues to increase each year, with approximately 319 billion per day in 2021.[70] While the percentage of spam has decreased from over 80% to 45% of all email from 2011 to 2021,[71] data from the FBI implies that US losses from cybercrime per year have increased 14-fold over the same time, to $6.9 billion in 2021.[72] Email is the top threat vector.

However, we've not seen a serious political candidate or intellectual suggest that we should erase the internet, or email, because of cybercrime and malicious spam. Although the damage from cybercrime is massive worldwide, most believe the internet's benefits outweigh the costs. We've instead chosen to mitigate the inevitable costs through increased cybersecurity and training. We suspect the same will hold for bitcoin, as it offers a financial life raft for billions suffering from totalitarian regimes, hyperinflation, strict capital controls, and a lack of access to critical financial infrastructure. We support increased bitcoin training.[73]

Efforts to fight against ransomware are also well underway. Most attackers cash out at centralized cryptocurrency businesses. Indeed, since 2020, just six businesses have laundered 56% of funds sent from addresses associated with ransomware.[74] Reflecting on this fact, Chainalysis writes:

> . . . these money laundering trends show how small the ransomware ecosystem really is. That's good news, as it means the strategy for fighting ransomware is likely simpler than it appears at first glance.[75]

As a chain analytics firm who profits from government contracts to fight things like ransomware, Chainalysis has no incentive to underplay the threat. For example, in the Colonial Pipeline ransomware attack in 2021, Chainalysis helped the FBI recoup over half the original ransom payment.[76] Fighting ransomware seems, at this point, easier than fighting email phishing and other scams.

Their recipe for fighting ransomware – beyond tracking and seizing funds – includes tamping down on the businesses that launder funds from ransomware attacks. Without easy access to highly liquid off-ramps into cash, ransomware attacks become less profitable in real terms. This reduces the incentives to attack. OFAC has already blacklisted several entities associated with ransomware. As a result, victims face severe penalties for paying a ransom to these entities. Although this sounds unfair, it's a straightforward instance of the rule not to negotiate with terrorists. By coercing victims not to pay, OFAC further reduces the incentive to attack.

Ransomware is a serious threat, yes. But it's not a serious threat to bitcoin's overall net benefit to the world. For context, ransomware accounted for substantially less than 1% of all reported losses in the US from cybercrime in 2021.[77] And we have serious measures in place to help ensure that ransomware doesn't spiral out of control. Even if criminals demand payment in more private cryptocurrencies like Monero, the most effective measure will likely involve investment in better cybersecurity to prevent attacks in the first place. Many victims thus far have simply had poor security hygiene.

7.6   Two cheers for censorship-resistance

Censorship-resistant money facilitates forms of wrongdoing like ransomware. However, behind the veil, we prefer the world with bitcoin anyway – not as the only money but as a supplement to other monies. It's important to remember that censorship-resistance, like privacy, comes in degrees. In a bit, we'll argue that bitcoin is highly censorship-resistant but far from perfectly so. Yet we won't argue for bitcoin's particular degree of censorship-resistance. Instead, we will overshoot: the world would be better off with perfectly uncensorable money as a supplement to more traditional monetary assets. To the extent that we convince you, you should believe that bitcoin's less-than-perfect uncensorability also improves the world, just to a lesser extent. We have two brief arguments.

7.6.1   Uncensorable money as anti-authoritarian tool

Our first argument is quite simple and rests on three claims about basic freedoms such as freedom of speech and assembly.[78] One, a lack of basic freedoms causes human suffering and hinders human flourishing. Two, in the absence of basic freedoms, access to uncensorable money would limit human suffering and enhance human flourishing. Three, most people worldwide lack basic freedoms. Therefore, a widely accessible uncensorable money would limit human suffering and enhance human flourishing.

Let's first consider a few minimal freedoms and how they figure into human flourishing. Please keep in mind that we don't offer these minimal notions of freedom as ideals. They instead serve an argumentative purpose. Consider your diet, as an analogy. Even if you have a highly restricted diet, food is good, and having none at all would cause great suffering. Similarly, speech may or not require several strong restrictions. Yet we would suffer for having much less freedom of speech or none at all.

Let's focus on speech a bit more. By *freedom of speech*, suppose we just mean the ability to speak openly about what we value and believe to be true without a plausible fear of reprisal. You can build in all sorts of restrictions about the time, place, and manner of speech. You might also prefer restrictions on content, in the case of threats or hate speech. Even if we grant all these restrictions, most would agree that we would be worse off if we also couldn't speak openly about what we believe to be true and about what we love and value. Without this minimal freedom of speech, we would have to hide important facets of ourselves. And we couldn't seek the truth openly as honest inquirers. Minority populations worldwide are especially vulnerable without this freedom.

We adopt a similarly vague and austere notion of *freedom of assembly* – the ability to gather, in person or through an organization, in a way that neither threatens nor causes harm to others. We gather with others to protest wrongdoing, worship, enjoy music and sport, and express support for political causes, among other things. If we can't gather peacefully for these reasons without fear of reprisal, we can't as easily pursue our individual notions of the good life.

And finally, by *freedom of the press*, we mean nothing more than the ability to publish or disseminate information, especially information that holds the powerful to account – again, without a plausible fear of reprisal. Feel free to build in whatever restrictions you deem most plausible. Whatever those restrictions are, we would suffer without the remaining sense of freedom. Without a free press, the powerful can more easily avoid accountability for their actions. And a free press does more than just reveal corruption. By threatening to expose corruption, the mere existence of a free press helps prevent corruption in the first place.

To review, our ability to flourish is limited to the degree that we lack basic freedoms. That's the first claim.

Now, the second claim: in the absence of basic freedoms, access to uncensorable money limits suffering and helps restore the ability to flourish. The rationale for this claim lies in a connection between freedom and commerce: the very exercise of basic freedoms often requires the ability to transact. Microphones, both literal and metaphorical, cost money. We often must pay for something to communicate our ideas to the public – books, pamphlets, websites, computers, and so on. The same applies for journalists and whistleblowers in the press. And to assemble where we'd like, we often must pay to get there. If we stay for any period of time, we must pay for food and lodging too.[79]

Because the ability to transact undergirds our abilities to gather in numbers and speak to wider audiences, those in power can limit basic freedoms by limiting our ability to transact. Fundamentally, this was the rationale behind Operation Choke Point in the US, Canada's exercise of the Emergencies Act, Russian and Nigerian censorship of political activists, and the global financial blockade of Wikileaks. But the point applies much more widely.

According to the Human Rights Foundation, 54% of the world's population lives under an authoritarian regime.[80] Three billion people live under fully authoritarian regimes across 55 countries, "where there are no free and fair elections, no separation of state powers, no independent media, no vibrant civil society, and no civil liberties." An additional 1.2 billion people live under competitive authoritarian regimes across another 41 countries – places where "opposition parties are allowed to exist, but suffer pervasive harassment and judicial persecution." In China alone, 1.4 billion people live under a social credit scoring system that uses the payments system to spy on citizens and calculate their social credit scores. These scores then figure into various forms of financial censorship and thereby function to chill the speech and movement of Chinese citizens. Uncensorable money would provide a way to save and transact outside the control of authoritarians.

Behind the veil, you'd have a greater than one in two chance of living under an authoritarian regime without basic liberties, whichever world you enter back into. Would you really prefer to take this chance without any access to censorship-resistant money?

Many in authoritarian regimes likely rely on bitcoin or close cousins for this express purpose. By pairing the Human Rights Foundation's classification of authoritarian countries with Chainalysis's Global Crypto Adoption Index, we see that both "competitive authoritarian" and "fully authoritarian" regimes appear prominently among the top 15 countries of crypto adoption when indexed for purchasing power parity per capita:

Ranking	Country	Authoritarian Status
1	Vietnam	full
2	Philippines	competitive
3	Ukraine	
4	India	
5	US	
6	Pakistan	competitive
7	Brazil	
8	Thailand	competitive
9	Russia	full
10	China	full
11	Nigeria	full
12	Turkey	full
13	Argentina	
14	Morocco	full
15	Colombia	

Worldwide crypto use and authoritarian rule.

We have no good way to count how many people use cryptocurrencies to route around authoritarian regimes. But the list is suggestive, especially when you factor in Argentina's hyperinflation (in spot 13)[81] and the human rights abuses in Colombia (in spot 15).[82] In spot 3, we find Ukraine, in the shadow of Russian authoritarianism. And there are ongoing disputes about whether countries like Brazil (7) and India (4) have experienced recent surges in authoritarianism. The less free a society is along the dimensions of speech, assembly, and the press, the more its citizenry would benefit from having an uncensorable money to route around authoritarian rulers. We suspect that most readers would prefer to have such a route available were they to find themselves in similar circumstances – even if its existence also enabled things like ransomware.

7.6.2 Disputed territory

We should distinguish the moral from the legal. Whereas the morally permissible is what the rules of morality allow, the legally permissible is what the rule of law allows within some jurisdiction. Although we often disagree about the morality of several actions, we should all agree that the moral and the legal come apart – a lot. What's morally permissible isn't always legally permissible and vice versa. Consider burqas, for example. Several nations have banned burqas as a form of public dress.[83] Others have mandated them.[84] And some have neither banned nor mandated them. So anyone who thinks that it's morally permissible *or* morally impermissible to wear burqas will disagree with the law of the land somewhere. Such conflicts exist not only for what we wear but also for what we buy.

What should we do about these conflicts? In an ideal world, we could use the power of the state to censor all and only those transactions that we know to cause harm. But we don't live in an ideal world. And we have persistent disagreements about what morality permits. Although we might agree to ban transactions involved in terrorism, child pornography, and kidnapping, we disagree about much else. Should we ban financial transactions involved in marijuana sales, abortion, prostitution, or organ markets? What about sex toys, porn subscriptions, armed conflict, or remittances to hated minority groups? Each of these is controversial somewhere, and disagreements will persist. In fact, your next president might be someone who disagrees with *you* about the morality of an action that you deeply value.

This is a reality for many already. Those in power often use financial censorship as a weapon to preserve their power, squash dissent, and inflict punishment on those who disagree with them. You might not now live in such a society. But many do, and – who knows – you might someday too. Let's do it this way. Look at a world map and ask yourself, "Which countries would *never* ban the kinds of transactions involved in my pursuit of a good life?" We suspect that your list will be quite small, maybe empty. Then ask, "What could happen in my country that would result in a ban on the kinds of transactions involved in *my* pursuit of a good life?" This second list might be frighteningly small too – maybe empty as well. And behind the veil, the smaller these lists, the more reason you have to prefer a world with uncensorable money.

You might object: instead of adding uncensorable money to the world, we should simply remove the conditions that make it useful. But this is an unrealistic solution to a pervasive and persistent problem. To make uncensorable money unnecessary, we would likely need to rid the world of corruption and the common impulse to abuse power. But this isn't something we can reasonably do, especially in the short to medium term. And trying to do it would likely result in more abuses of power.

So you might respond that we should simply pass more and better laws to prevent trusted parties from censoring innocent people. Again, this tiptoes around the real problem. A significant portion of the global population has little or no say in the legislative process. They live under the shadow of authoritarianism. And most authoritarians refuse to relinquish one of its best weapons: the power to censor. But replacing the authoritarians isn't easy either. Regime change, building a functional democracy – these can take decades, if they work at all. Meanwhile, bitcoin is already here.

You might object again: if censorship isn't going anywhere, I should do my best to entrench my personal tribe in power and gain control over the financial rails. Setting aside the other problems with this approach, it simply doesn't fly behind the veil. Behind the veil, you don't know who you are or on which "team" you'd be once the veil is lifted. Instead, you have to deal with the fact that you'd have a better chance than not of living in an authoritarian country and a much better chance than not of having little to no political power. Wouldn't you want to have uncensorable money in these circumstances? Will you choose to risk living in those circumstances without it?

We've argued that a perfectly censorable money would have great benefits, especially for those who live under the thumb of irresponsible central banks and authoritarian rule. However, perfectly uncensorable money would also benefit certain kinds of wrongdoers, posing additional challenges on the margins for law enforcement. Bitcoin itself isn't perfectly uncensorable; it can be censored in special circumstances. Hence, compared to wholly uncensorable money, bitcoin may bring fewer harms but also fewer benefits. You might worry, then, not that bitcoin's censorship-resistance helps wrongdoers too much but that it helps everyone else too little. As a result, we must evaluate bitcoin's own censorship-resistance.

7.7   Censoring bitcoin

7.7.1   How bitcoin is vulnerable to censorship

One large and obvious threat to bitcoin users comes from the very kinds of trusted parties that bitcoin was designed to avoid. Famously, "trusted parties are security holes."[85] Because of this, you would think that bitcoin users would avoid trusted parties. And many do. But like sirens, the convenience of trusted parties still attracts them. Currently, few circular economies exist for bitcoin. If you want to spend bitcoin somewhere around town, you'll most likely need an off-ramp from bitcoin to a fiat currency. If you want to acquire bitcoin, you'll first need an on-ramp from fiat currency to bitcoin. Users typically rely on centralized cryptocurrency exchanges to go from fiat currency to bitcoin and from bitcoin to fiat currency. Many people also use centralized exchanges to custody their bitcoin; doing so seems more convenient and less stressful than storing one's own private keys on a fancy USB drive, secret steel plates, and so on. In each of these cases, the user pays for convenience with counterparty risk, and this risk can be expensive.

Users who rely on trusted parties risk losing some or even all of their bitcoin. Centralized services are honeypots that attract hackers and governments alike. Hackers use technical vulnerabilities and social engineering to steal digital assets. State actors take advantage of the fact that centralized custodians operate within their jurisdiction and deploy court orders to seize funds, freeze accounts, or block transactions to certain parties. Some centralized custodians gamble with customer deposits, some seize funds for themselves, and some simply lose them.

Users who rely on trusted parties for custody or transfer also lose any privacy bitcoin might have otherwise afforded them. Custodians are generally required to record each customer's personal information; this information is another honeypot for private or state actors eager to connect identifying information to behavioral patterns.

Trusted custodians sometimes also dilute bitcoin by issuing, in exchange for real dollars, IOUs for bitcoin they don't actually have; the net effect here is muted demand for real bitcoin and suppressed market price. Real bitcoin can be verified in a heartbeat and without trusting anyone else's records. Just look it up on the blockchain; if there's bitcoin at an address you control, it's real and it's yours. Not so with most custodians. You trust but cannot verify.

Do bitcoin users really sign up for the very security holes that bitcoin was designed to avoid? In brief, yes. Bitcoin users reintroduce these security holes when they enlist custodians to store their bitcoin and intermediaries to help transfer it. Earlier, we discussed the example of Canadian truckers. Bitcoin was there. It was used. And it didn't quite work. Now you know why: donors and truckers alike relied on trusted custodians and managers to collect and distribute the donations. This created predictable security risks. And sure enough, authorities took advantage of those risks and clamped down on centralized exchanges used to trade the donated bitcoin for Canadian dollars.[86]

7.7.2 How bitcoin resists censorship

Trusted parties are everywhere in the digital dollar system. Banks, intermediaries, payment processors, and custodians have public faces, reputations, legal presences, and thus, something to lose. By design, trusted parties serve as pressure points. And those who rely on them are vulnerable.

By design, bitcoin lacks makers, managers, and mediators. This doesn't mean bitcoin is censorship-*proof*. But it is censorship-*resistant*. Put another way: when bitcoin is used as designed – without reintroducing intermediaries – it is difficult to censor.

Imagine that you wanted to block the following:

- a certain entity from transacting with bitcoin
- a certain address from sending bitcoin
- a certain address from receiving bitcoin

How might you proceed? When the relevant entities are using centralized services or when the relevant addresses are controlled by those services, you can find those centralized services and call them up. A government agency can tell them the entity has been naughty or that certain addresses are connected to something bad. By continuing to serve the entity, the centralized service might receive threats of legal action, court orders, reputational damage, or a loss of support from advertisers or majority shareholders.

Now imagine that the relevant entities or addresses *aren't* connected to centralized services. There's just someone out there using bitcoin, broadcasting transactions to bitcoin nodes from their own node. How might you put a stop to this? As it turns out, there is no obvious answer here. Though there are possible paths to censoring bitcoin through nodes or miners, all carry a significant price. Bitcoin raises the cost to censor. Let's see how this works by working through a couple of obvious paths.

First, there's no bitcoin CEO, bitcoin foundation, bitcoin representative, or anything else of the sort. And even if some people or entities claimed these titles, they'd be unable to help you. Bitcoin's nodes, users, and miners share transactions and communicate with each other without any attention to legal structures of that sort.

You might try to block your target entity from accessing the internet, and thus, bitcoin. This is tough, unless they're in jail or otherwise under your physical control. Like life, the internet seems to find a way, even in prisons or behind the great firewall of China.

You might try to ban the bitcoin software. This may well be illegal in jurisdictions such as the United States; code is a form of protected speech, guarded by the First Amendment and a host of enthusiastic civil rights attorneys. More importantly, and as copyright holders learned long ago, it is very hard to prevent digital code from spreading. The bitcoin software doesn't take up that much space or require much bandwidth. And there are, already, tens of thousands of bitcoin nodes in operation across the globe, many hidden behind layers of virtual private networks and the like. So this is not a promising route towards censorship.

You might try calling up bitcoin miners and making all of the same threats or pleas as described earlier. "Don't you dare mine any blocks with transactions that have the following features," you might say, "or else!" Good luck with that; bitcoin miners, despite working together in pools, are scattered and unruly. Many are pseudonymous; there's no phone number to call, and while some have CEOs to harass, others have just a few machines mining in a basement. Put one out of business, and others are sure to rise. And convincing just a few of them to censor wouldn't be enough. To reliably stop the target transaction types, you'll need to get the attention and compliance of an appreciable fraction of the network's mining power.

Even then, there's nothing to stop someone else from firing up a new mining operation to publish a block with an offending transaction. Indeed, since transactions have fees attached, all miners have an incentive to include them in blocks, even if you'd rather see them censored. And users themselves can fight against transaction censorship by increasing their fees. Miners who don't include transactions with juicy fees will collect fewer rewards than those that do.[87] Hence, miners who censor as a matter of course might have to close down shop since non-censoring miners can afford to devote more computing power.

Once an offending transaction has made its way into the bitcoin block-chain, there's little you can do to take it back. To do *that*, you'd have to re-mine the block in which it appears, and all those atop it, faster than everyone else is adding to the chain that includes it. The more blocks there are, the more it'll cost you – a topic we'll cover in Chapter 9.

Thus, successful censorship can never be a one-off affair. If you really want to keep a given transaction or transaction-type from appearing on the blockchain, you'll have to keep up your efforts indefinitely. Otherwise, some miner is likely to publish the offending transaction as soon as you've let up.

In the previous chapter, we showed how bitcoin can offer significant financial privacy. Those very features help make bitcoin more censorship-resistant too. It's hard to stop someone from transacting if you don't know how or whether they are. Privacy and censorship-resistance are mutually reinforcing. But the very factors that limit bitcoin's privacy assurances also limit its censorship-resistance. We return to this point shortly.

7.8 Decision update

Consider again how the moral and legal statuses of some activities might coincide or come apart:

	Legally Impermissible	Legally Permissible
Morally Permissible	e.g., protest and dissent in Russia, parading without a permit in Birmingham AL in 1963	e.g., marijuana sales
Morally Impermissible	e.g., ransomware	e.g., buying a gift for one's paramour of whom one's spouse is unaware

In some times and places, the law forbids what's morally permissible or even what's morally praiseworthy. In some of these cases, the laws are *bad* laws. They *should* be resisted.[88] Even if you think that Russian dissidents should face financial censorship for standing up to Vladimir Putin or that Martin Luther King Jr. should have been jailed for marching in Birmingham, we hope you can see the deeper argument. The state censors criminals, yes, but some criminals are, well, good.

In some times and places, private entities censor financial activity associated with legally permissible behavior, whether it's immoral or not. When the behavior is morally permissible – e.g., organizing a fantasy football league or a pro-choice rally – you might have strong moral grounds for routing around financial censorship. When the behavior is, in fact, immoral – e.g., when your neighbor serves as an escort or buys cigars for his tobacco addiction – we might prefer that banks and payment processors stay out of people's business anyway. The particular examples here don't matter; what matters are the categories, however you fill them in.

Financial systems with trusted authorities impose an in-principle risk of censorship. And we should be glad that people can find recourse in resistance money against the threat of government or corporate censorship. Even if you think that *your* jurisdiction and all the corporations in your neighborhood have somehow squared the circle so that financial censorship occurs only against the baddies or against bad transactions, you might recall that over one in two people in the world live under authoritarian regimes.

Admittedly, censorship-resistant money also empowers those who might engage in illegal and immoral behavior. Perhaps this tilts the scales towards preferring a world without censorship-resistant money. But remember, censorship-resistant money does not make someone invincible. Law enforcement often catches those who use bitcoin for illicit purposes like ransomware attacks. Remember, too, that financial censorship often lacks due process. Few cases of financial censorship involve lawful court orders, discovery, or interrogation of witnesses. To echo Congressman Brad Sherman, those who engage in financial censorship often enforce not the laws we actually have but the laws they wish they had.

Now the traditional financial system already has a mechanism for weighing the good in resisting unjust censorship against the good in censoring financial activity associated with immoral and illegal behavior. Physical cash. We saw before that when it comes to privacy, the striking parity between cash and bitcoin gave powerful reason to prefer a world with bitcoin. The same style of reasoning applies to censorship-resistance.

Censorship-resistant money already exists in the form of physical cash. It is hard to prevent a cash transaction from taking place when you're not there and even harder when it happens more privately behind closed doors (shielding) or in a crowd (obscurity). And yet cash has serious limits not just to privacy but also to censorship-resistance. Cash is easy to use in small amounts but a serious burden for larger ones – cumbersome, difficult to hide, and expensive to protect. So cash effectively balances the competing interests at play not just for privacy but also for censorship-resistance. Despite the costs, it is good that cash exists.

Given that bitcoin achieves similar aims and with similar limitations, it is good that bitcoin exists too. Or so we think. But we will rest our case on the following; behind the veil, you have over a one in two chance of living under an authoritarian regime, many with bad laws or poor rule of law. Even in countries like the United States, financial censorship is common. Would you prefer to live in a world without bitcoin's censorship-resistance, if you could be any person in the world? When it comes to the costs and benefits of censorship-resistance alone, we think the answer is clear. But of course, that's not the entire equation.

As we've seen, traditional payment networks censor. They also exclude. Bitcoin helps here as well, and we'll show how in the next chapter.

Notes

1. Rogan (2021).
2. For an up-to-date survey of censorship by non-state actors situated within an ethical framework for evaluation of such, see Messina (2023).
3. Chehayeb (2022).
4. Reuters (2022).
5. de Dinechin et al. (2019).
6. El-Haroun (2021).
7. Jahal (2021).
8. Cook (2017, p. 71).
9. Fifield (2019).
10. Tham and Pollard (2022).
11. Matsakis (2019).
12. Franck (2022).
13. Adams (2022).
14. Osborn (2019).
15. Troianovski (2020).
16. Reuters (2018).
17. Guaidó (2019).
18. Cruise et al. (2023).
19. Platt and Skerritt (2022).
20. GlobalNews CA (2022).
21. Hooper (2022).
22. Hintze (2022).
23. Electronic Frontier Foundation (2021).
24. Manskar (2019).
25. Nolan (2022).

26. Brownback (2022).
27. Baradaran (2020).
28. Keating (2018).
29. EFF (2017).
30. NYT Editorial (2010).
31. Byrd (2022).
32. Joy (2013).
33. Georgiopoulos (2019).
34. Essien (2020).
35. Onu and Osae-Brown (2022). On subsequent adoption of crypto, see Osae-Brown et al. (2022).
36. Dimock and Wike (2021); Abramowitz and Saunders (2008).
37. Koerth and Thomson-DeVeaux (2021).
38. Rothschild (2021).
39. Lorenzoni (2021).
40. Warren (2022).
41. Bertaut et al. (2021).
42. This subsection depends heavily on data in McDowell (2020).
43. Wagner (2022).
44. Chainalysis (2022a).
45. Chow (2022).
46. Chainalysis (2022b).
47. Singh (2022).
48. Chipolina (2022).
49. Lew (2016).
50. Brettell (2022).
51. Warren (2022).
52. Flitter and Yaffe-Bellany (2022).
53. Brettell (2022).
54. Liu and Papa (2022).
55. Greene (2022).
56. These ledgers are fully public, so we have detailed information about how various actors use them, especially those who draw attention to themselves with high-value heists and the like.
57. UNODC (2022).
58. Boland-Rudder and McGoey (2021).
59. BBC (2020).
60. See Choe and Robles (2022) and Mallin (2020).
61. See, for example, Silver-Greenberg (2012), Protess and Silver-Greenberg (2014), and Anand et al. (2023).
62. Luther (2017) discusses this estimate from Rogoff (2016).
63. Chainalysis (2023a).
64. Sinaee (2022).
65. Sinclair (2022).
66. Cross and Bailey (2022).
67. The notion is similar to the notion of *differential privacy* in discussions about data collection in algorithmic training.
68. There's also the risk of "regrettable substitution," when one bad thing is banished, only to be replaced by something worse; see Zimmerman and Anastas (2015). This happens with food and toxic chemicals. And it could happen with money as well, if would-be sanctions evaders turn to even more privacy-focused monetary tools.

69. The data in this subsection comes from Chainalysis (2023a).
70. Statista (2022a).
71. Statista (2022b).
72. Satista (2022c).
73. Bailey and Rettler (2021a, 2021b).
74. Chainalysis (2022c, p. 44).
75. Chainalysis (2022c).
76. Chainalysis (2022c, p. 51).
77. FBI (2021).
78. The core of the argument draws heavily from pseudonymous Twitter personality "6529." See, especially, the thread beginning with 6529 (2022).
79. Though we won't rely on it in our argument here, there's a case to be made for the stronger claim that bitcoin transactions *are* speech. See Wales and Ovelman (2019).
80. Human Rights Foundation (2022): 8.
81. Nicas and Lankes (2022).
82. Human Rights Watch (2022).
83. Jones (2021).
84. Hadid (2022).
85. Szabo (2001).
86. Baydakova and Reynolds (2022) and Bodley (2022).
87. See Voskuil (2019). There are other ways to mount a censorship attack on bitcoin. Some deploy regulatory pressure. Others rely on social engineering. Still, others involve complicated economic attacks, as when taking a short position on bitcoin while attacking the network. And yet others are non-economic (mining empty blocks at a loss, for example). All of these are costly and more costly than censoring a network with trusted parties, which is our main point here. The most comprehensive game-theoretic treatment of bitcoin mining, and various attacks that deploy it, is Warren (2023).
88. Consider Dr. King's distinction between just and unjust laws: "Any law that uplifts human personality is just. Any law that degrades human personality is unjust. . . . An unjust law is a code that a majority inflicts on a minority that is not binding on itself." (1963) There is value in a money that will allow us to financially support protest marches for racial equality, even illegal ones and even ones that would land their participants in jail.

8

MONEY FOR THE MARGINALIZED

8.1   Barriers to entry

When 25-year-old Maria Hassan tried to open a bank account in Lebanon, she was declined.[1] Undaunted, she tried three more banks. But she got the same response each time – no, no, and no. Whether in Lebanon or the US, bank accounts serve as drivers' licenses for the financial superhighway. With no bank account comes no credit cards, no online payments, no checks, and no money transfers.[2] No superhighway for you – access denied. And you can't go very far or very fast on the back roads.

Maria did exactly that, resorting to cash for both savings and payments. We've said before that in many respects, cash is great: it enables self-custody for savings, as well as more private, censorship-resistant payments. But using cash for *everything* is risky and inconvenient. Long distance payments are much slower and require trusted parties. Large stacks of bills are susceptible to both flame and felon. Hyperinflated currencies, like Maria's Lebanese pound, require larger stacks of bills. Then a large stack of bills may suffer rapid depreciation anyway as it becomes a monument to its former purchasing power. So financial exclusion not only locks *out* people from more stable assets, accessible credit, and convenient payments, it also locks *in* people to assets of last resort. Maria is not the only Syrian refugee in Lebanon unable to open an account. The financial exclusion of Syrian refugees is unofficial policy.[3]

Financial censorship and financial exclusion have similar effects, but they differ in at least one important way. Financial censorship afflicts those

DOI: 10.4324/9781003484721-8

who have already gained entry and can involve finely tuned rules that jam or scrutinize only certain kinds of traffic; on the financial superhighway, victims of financial censorship suffer from excessive tolls, lane closures, and forced exits. Financial exclusion, however, occurs when people meet with barriers to entry in the first instance. Whereas censorship typically concerns powers lost, exclusion concerns powers never gained. Hence, while victims of censorship and exclusion may find themselves in the same place – on the outside looking in – exclusion has a distinctive set of causes. It deserves its own treatment.

We have reliable data about both the populations excluded from the financial system and the causes for exclusion, both within the US and without. Since we also know how bitcoin works, we can evaluate whether it might help. As we will argue, bitcoin is by no means a silver bullet for financial exclusion. But it can lessen the harms of exclusion for many worldwide. To some extent, it already does. So behind the veil, you would likely want bitcoin to exist just in case you happened to be one of the world's many financial outsiders.

8.2 Why exclusion happens

8.2.1 Global exclusion

Every few years, the World Bank produces a slick document about financial exclusion. The document, the *Global Findex Database*, summarizes the results of a global survey about the reasons for financial exclusion. The most recent iteration concluded in 2022 and found that 76% of adults worldwide have transaction accounts at regulated institutions, a 50% improvement from a little over a decade ago.[4] Still, by the World Bank's estimates, a total of 1.4 billion adults remain unbanked. And they are not evenly distributed around the world.

Several countries have quite low percentages of banked adults as a share of their total adult population. This includes Afghanistan (10%), Egypt (27%), El Salvador (36%), Iraq (19%), Lebanon (21%), Nigeria (45%), Pakistan (21%), Philippines (51%), South Sudan (6%), and the West Bank and Gaza (34%). And the World Bank produced no data for several African countries likely to have similarly low percentages, including Chad, Ethiopia, Libya, Niger, and Sudan.

Not only do Nigeria and Pakistan have lower percentages of banked adults than unbanked adults, but they also have large populations. So it's no surprise that they also appear among the seven economies which together account for more than half of the world's unbanked adults:

Country	Percent Unbanked	Unbanked Population
India	22%	228,975,136
China	11%	130,272,208
Pakistan	79%	113,770,976
Indonesia	48%	97,735,280
Nigeria	55%	63,703,068
Bangladesh	47%	56,928,864
Egypt, Arab Reb.	73%	49,063,468

Unbanked populations around the globe.

To put this in perspective, a country with only the unbanked adults from India would be the fifth most populous country in the world. A country consisting only of China's unbanked adults would make the top ten.

Of the world's 1.4 billion unbanked adults, the majority are women (54%). They aren't evenly distributed across the globe either. Whereas nearly all US women are banked (97%), several economies have more unbanked than banked women. For contrast, the next chart places the US beside the seven economies with the lowest share of unbanked women.

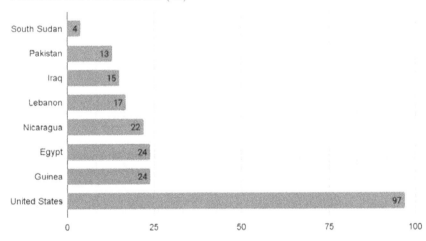

Women with bank accounts.

Significant sex disparities also occur in countries with relatively high populations of banked adults. In Turkey, for example, only a quarter of adults are unbanked. Yet women comprise 71% of unbanked Turkish adults.[5]

The ubiquity of financial exclusion deserves serious attention behind the veil. If you were to become a random person in the world, you'd have a 17% chance of being an unbanked adult and a similar chance of being one of their kids. And if you were an unbanked adult, you would very likely live in Africa or Asia and likely as a less affluent woman.

The underlying causes of financial exclusion also deserve attention behind the veil. In the World Bank survey, the unbanked gave six common reasons for their financial exclusion:

Reasons Cited for Financial Exclusion

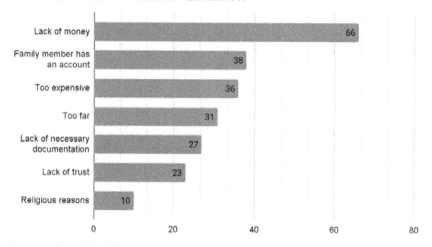

Reasons for global financial exclusion.

Worldwide, 66% of unbanked adults said that they didn't have enough money.[6] No surprise there. But it's telling that only 12% cited this reason alone. Given the other top two cited reasons – too expensive (36%) and too far (31%) – the World Bank inferred that "[t]hese answers suggest that people would open an account if banking costs were lower or if the banks were located more conveniently."[7]

Rounding out the top six reasons, 27% cited a lack of the necessary documentation, 23% cited distrust in the available financial institutions, and 10% cited religious reasons, especially in the Middle East.

As you might guess, these percentages were not uniform across economies.[8]

- Although 31% of respondents overall cited distance as a barrier, this reason garnered 53% in Liberia, 47% in Bolivia, 43% in India, and 41% in Uganda.

- Although 27% of the unbanked reported a lack of necessary documentation to open a financial account, this reason rose to 43% in Colombia and 50% in both Tanzania and Uganda.
- Although 23% of unbanked respondents cited a lack of trust as a reason, about a third cited this reason in Europe, Central Asia, Latin America, and the Caribbean, with higher percentages in Argentina, Bolivia, Bulgaria, Colombia, Jamaica, and Russia. In Ukraine, an eye-popping 54% cited a lack of trust.

The World Bank also collected data about people who had not used their accounts in the last year, not even to send or receive a digital payment.[9] These people are technically banked but effectively bankless. In developing economies, 13% of the "banked" were effectively bankless. Despite having the largest population of *unbanked* adults at just under 230 million, India also had, by far, the largest number of *banked but effectively bankless* adults – adults who had a bank account but couldn't or didn't use it. 35% of the banked adults in India had not sent or received a digital payment over the previous year! Over 280 million adults in India fell into this category. And the top reasons? Distance, lack of institutional trust, and not having a need for an account rounded out the top three, in that order, with rates between 45% and 50%. The fourth most cited reason – lack of money – came in below 40%.

The survey paints a mixed picture of bitcoin's potential impact on financial inclusion. If you simply don't have enough money for an account, switching the denominator from bolivars to bitcoin will not obviously fix your situation; if you have zero bolivars, trading it for bitcoin leaves you with zero bitcoin. But even among those who cited a lack of money as a reason for banklessness, bitcoin might help in smaller ways. Banks often have minimum account balances. Bitcoin does not. Banks often charge fees for both opening accounts and overdrafting them. Bitcoin does neither. So bitcoin provides an alternative to those who are priced out of banking due to fees and minimum balances.

Yet even setting aside everyone who cited a lack of money, whether they cited other reasons or not, still leaves slightly under a half-billion people worldwide. Many of them are unbanked due to distance, a lack of trust, and religious qualms. And this figure doesn't even include the effectively bankless, like the 280 million adults in India with inactive accounts. Of these, remember, nearly 40% cited a lack of money for their inactivity. Once more setting aside those who cite lack of money, we tally another 168 million adults who are effectively unbanked.

Well over 500 million adults worldwide are effectively unbanked for reasons other than that they just don't have enough money to use an account.

We have arrived at this figure of half a billion conservatively, by erring in the direction favorable to skeptical readers who doubt there's much of a problem here or that the problem isn't one that bitcoin can help address. Note, too, that this figure fails to account for the children of the unbanked. How many of *them* are there? Rather than guess and risk overcounting, we will simply not count them at all – a large error that favors the skeptic since we will continue to count children in the world's total population of eight billion people. So we will suppose that half a billion people have money but are effectively unbanked. For our purposes, you have a one in 16 chance of being among them.

8.2.2 Exclusion within the US

Compared to the rest of the world, the US is a haven for financial inclusion. But despite how well the US fares on both relative and absolute metrics for inclusion, all is not well in paradise.

Indeed, for many, the world of US banking feels forbidding indeed. Here's what they've seen: American financial institutions confront prospective customers with blocks and checkpoints at every turn. Attempt to open a bank account, and you'll be ID'd and background checked. Deposit money into your fresh new account, and you might just have to explain where it came from. Make an unusual credit card purchase, and you might just get a call asking what it was for – and if you don't take the call or give a good enough answer, there might just be a chargeback, ruining your reputation with the merchant. Withdraw or deposit too much, and you'll be suspected of money laundering. Withdraw or deposit too little, and you'll be suspected of *structuring* – attempting to hide money laundering. Keep the money in there too long, and you might lose access to it – an abandoned account. Keep it not long enough, and it lacks *seasoning*, and can't be used as a car or home downpayment.

Punishing overdraft fees are always nearby, so watch your balance carefully. If you try to send money to your mother – watch out for fees. If you try to receive money from your brother – watch out for fees. In fact, always and everywhere, watch out for fees. You might even pay fees on your fees, as when a fee sends you into a negative balance, and you get slapped with yet another punishing overdraft fee. Banks structure your debits so that the big ones are taken out first, thus more likely leading to overdraft and causing each subsequent debit to overdraft you again.[10] Banks make about $15.5 billion per year from their own customers overdrafting.[11] About 10% of people with bank accounts pay ten or more overdraft fees per year.

Other than the ID and background check for prospective customers, this sounds like a list of censorious actions rather than exclusion actions.

But that misses the point for two reasons. First, people who are in a group can face actions that attempt to exclude them from a group or that have the effect of kicking them out of the group. To Americans who can just barely afford a bank account, an overdraft fee or a declined transaction at just the wrong time can push them right out. Second, people are well-aware of these banking tactics. So knowledge that they can and do occur is enough to prevent people from trying to get a bank account in the first place. Anticipating these actions and not getting a bank account on that basis can show up as "lack of money," "too expensive," "lack of necessary documentation," and "lack of trust" when cited as a reason.

For many readers, we suspect the earlier paragraphs will sound exaggerated and entirely separated from actual experience. Perhaps none of these things have happened to *you*. But the evidence, to some extent, vindicates this cynical perspective. Let's look at the data more carefully.

Much like the World Bank's *Global Findex Database*, the Federal Deposit Insurance Corporation (FDIC) publishes the *National Survey of Unbanked and Underbanked Households* for the US. They've done so every other year since 2009. In the survey, an "unbanked" household means that "no one in the household had a checking or savings account at a bank or credit union."[12] The most recent survey found that 4.5% of households – about 5.9 million of them – were unbanked.

As you might expect, some subpopulations are overrepresented, especially households which were lower income, less educated, black or Hispanic, and working age with a disability. Here are some concentrated pockets of exclusion:[13]

- Black American households comprise 31.4% of the longer-term unbanked, though they are 12.8% of all households. They also comprise 41.1% of the recently unbanked.
- Hispanic American households comprise 31.1% of the longer-term unbanked, though they are 13.8% of all households. They also comprise 23.9% of the recently unbanked.
- Single-mother households had an unbanked rate of 15.9%.
- Geographically, Mississippi had the highest unbanked rate among states, at 11.1%.

The survey also asked the unbanked about their reasons for not having an account. The most popular main reason for not having an account? Not having enough money to meet minimum balance requirements. 29.2% of the unbanked cited either minimum balance requirements, high fees, or their unpredictability as the main reason. In second and third place of noted reasons: "Don't trust the banks" (13.2%) and "Avoiding a bank gives more privacy" (8.4%). The next chart shows the main reasons given and their corresponding percentages.

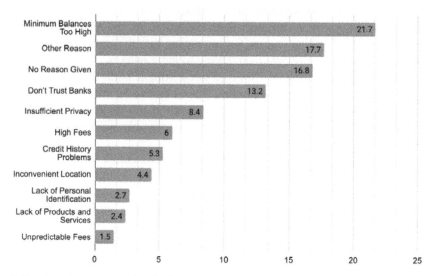

Why Americans are unbanked.[14]

Because in this survey participants cannot cite more than a single "main" reason, we have a fairly reliable picture about the obstacles to financial services and the raw numbers of households affected by them. Let's quickly crunch some numbers then.

By subtracting those who gave no reason (16.8%) and those who cited reasons beyond the FDIC's published list of reasons (17.7%), we're left with 65.5% who gave one of the other eight primary reasons earlier. Therefore, given 5.9 million unbanked households, about 3.9 million households cited one of the other reasons as the primary reason for being unbanked.

The FDIC survey also asked unbanked households about their interest in having an account. Only 27% said that they were very or somewhat interested.[15] So one might think that bitcoin could help at most the 27% of the unbanked who want to be banked. But we shouldn't draw this inference.

Some obstacles to banking are external; they exclude some who would otherwise like to be included. Distance is such an external obstacle. But some other obstacles are internal; some self-exclude from the traditional financial system because it has features they would like to avoid. Concerns about privacy and trust serve as obstacles of this second sort. Crucially, some might desire to save and transfer money electronically in a system without the features that lead them to self-exclude. For some, then, financial inclusion may necessarily involve non-bank alternatives. So when it comes to bitcoin's potential for financial inclusion, we need to ask not only whether bitcoin routes around the obstacles that exclude some from banking but also whether it lacks the features of banking that cause some to exclude themselves.

Now that we've surveyed some main reasons for financial exclusion, both within the US and abroad, let's look more closely at what this exclusion means – and whether bitcoin can help.

8.3 Why exclusion matters

Imagine being stranded – not physically on an island – but linguistically, among a sea of people who speak a foreign tongue. Several years ago, *The New York Times* interviewed a Mexican immigrant in precisely this predicament.[16] Laura spoke no English. This didn't make life easy as an immigrant in New York City. But she barely knew any Spanish either. Instead, she spoke Mixtec, a language indigenous to Mexico that traces back to thousands of years before the arrival of the Spanish conquistadors.

Because Laura couldn't read signs or converse with others around her, she stayed close to home and avoided the subway. "I can't do anything," she said. Her social and economic situation went further downhill when her husband went to prison for domestic assault. This left her and her 2-year-old son fending for themselves – mostly without words. This phenomenon, linguistic isolation, has tremendous social and economic costs. The linguistically isolated face challenges in finding basic information and expressing basic needs.[17] Linguistic isolation makes life much harder than a life of linguistic integration.

For many, financial exclusion makes life harder in similar ways. This is no surprise, given that money is a network good like language (see Chapter 3). If, as the saying goes, money talks, then financial exclusion is just another kind of linguistic isolation. Imagine if everyone but you could send and receive electronic payments. You would likely have a harder time meeting your needs.

Let's reflect on this for a moment. The millions of unbanked individuals we've noted earlier aren't mere abstractions. They're people. Like you, they want various things: Christmas trees, respect from peers, iPhones, sexual fulfillment, housing, job security, food, loving familial relationships, and much more besides. Money is helpful in acquiring all of these goods. Not just amounts of money but the existence of money itself – that there is a commonly accepted medium of exchange is helpful in acquiring these goods.

One could, in principle, lead a fine life without access to money, especially in places or times lacking financial infrastructure. Even in places where financial infrastructure exists, lack of access doesn't necessarily disadvantage individuals, particularly if they already have their needs met or if the infrastructure is subpar.

But the fact remains: money is helpful in living our best lives. In greasing the wheels of mutually beneficial exchange, it promotes human flourishing. Indeed, given the way the world actually works, access to services like electronic payments enables not just access to vital material goods like food or housing but also other freedoms and capacities.

Exercising the freedoms mentioned in the first amendment to the US Constitution often requires money. Freedom of assembly requires financial activity, as when you buy gas and drive to a protest or catch a train to see your friends. Freedom of religion requires financial access since nearly all religions require meeting together somewhere, or owning something, or traveling. Freedom of the press requires financial activity because publishing something on paper or online often requires exchanging money for paper, ink, or web hosting. And so on. People who lack financial access thereby lack powers to exercise these freedoms. Financial exclusion hinders human flourishing. We explored a similar idea that financial liberty is a condition for other important liberties, in more depth in the previous chapter (see Chapter 7.6.1).

The link between financial access and access to other goods isn't complicated. A typical story goes like this: you work and get paid for that work in the form of a check or a direct deposit. You then spend some of that money on stuff you need to get by and live a happy life. You save for the future and, if you're lucky, make investments that grow over time. Throughout, the financial system provides the rails for receiving, saving, and sending money.

To meet our needs and enjoy our basic rights and freedoms, we need access to a monetary system. We need food, clothing, and shelter, as well as access to hygiene and healthcare. We need money to pay for these. We also need money to pursue our visions of the good life. For many faiths, religious practice involves not only a meeting place but also items like prayer mats, icons, books, candles, beads, bells, particular clothing, or incense. The search for truth, or defense of it, requires that we have both the freedom to write and publish in various media and the freedom to access that media. For convenient travel to see and do what we deem necessary or good, we often need modes of transport apart from our own feet. For all this, we need access to a monetary system to ensure that we can flourish as we see fit. Exclusion from any such system would impede efforts to pursue our happiness.

When financial inclusion prevents people from pursuing their vision of the good life, it's a bad thing. On the flip side, financial inclusion is, for the most part, a good thing. It enables the included to pursue their vision of the good and enjoy other basic rights.

8.4   Can bitcoin help?

Legacy financial institutions, by design, have trusted parties. And trusted parties underlie several of the internal and external obstacles to financial inclusion. A monetary network without trusted parties, like bitcoin, can help the excluded overcome obstacles of both sorts.

8.4.1   Bitcoin is open

Traditional financial institutions use gatekeepers to help prevent fraud. If an institution poorly assesses its potential customers for fraud risk, the bottom line suffers. This is why applicants for accounts must submit documents to verify their identities and financial histories. While these checks aim to prevent fraud and comply with the law of the land – good things! – these very checks also impose barriers. Immigrants often lack required documents. The poor often lack the resources to secure them. Cultural norms and prejudices in various jurisdictions may underlie account denials for certain people groups.[18]

The bitcoin network, however, employs no risk management staff. No one needs to submit documents about their identities or financial histories. Since the bitcoin network has no gatekeepers, no one in the network can deny you access. This means convicted felons can use the bitcoin network. But that very feature also provides financial access to the unjustly marginalized.

Bitcoin requires little more than an internet-connected device and a bitcoin private key, along with the address that it generates through elliptic curve multiplication. We don't need certificates or credit histories to multiply numbers. And you don't have to provide documents to bum the WiFi at the local coffee shop. Although some internet service providers may require personal details, accessing the internet requires neither documentation nor the disclosure of personally identifying information, especially with publicly available WiFi. Multiplication isn't prejudiced either. The mathematical realm is universal and unchanging; private keys won't quit working for those from some race, sex, nationality, or what have you. And like the bitcoin network, the internet itself doesn't restrict services based on the users' race, sex, ethnicity, or any other such feature.

Because joining the bitcoin network requires little more than a device that can multiply numbers and access the internet, bitcoin is about as inclusive as the internet itself. The bitcoin network has neither the eyes to collect personal information nor the agency to restrict access based on it. So users also needn't submit information they don't have or would be costly to provide.

8.4.2 Bitcoin is cheap

Financial institutions have bottom lines. And – here's a hard truth – not every potential customer is a net benefit to the bottom line. To sift the wheat from the chaff, financial institutions often require a minimum threshold for funds for opening and maintaining an account. In addition, these same institutions often charge fees to maintain an account as well as penalties for overdrafting an account. Many of us gladly agree to pay these fees because we don't plan on ever being in the situations that would bring them about or because they seem negligible compared to the amounts we sling around. But for many, fees serve as disincentives to opening an account in the first place. If you barely have enough savings, the mere existence of further fees may discourage you from opening an account. Spending significant effort just to stay afloat is unpleasant, both physically and financially.

While bitcoin companies have bottom lines, the bitcoin network itself is not a company and has no bottom line. Granted, the base layer of the bitcoin network has transaction fees. When demand for block space is high, fees reach levels prohibitive for smaller transactions. But bitcoin also has higher layer payment networks with nearly free and instantaneous transactions. The network doesn't allow overdrafts: it's a cash- or commodity-based system, not a credit-based system. You must have the bitcoin you spend. There are also no account maintenance fees; the abstract numbers in Plato's heaven require no maintenance. As long as the bitcoin network remains functional, you can let it sit there for several years without being nickeled and dimed along the way. Of course, if you self-custody, you'll need to protect your private keys; but you can do so cheaply and simply by using old devices or even pieces of paper stored in safe locations. Finally, bitcoin functionally has no minimum balances. The lightning network allows users to transact and store amounts of bitcoin worth less than one cent.

Why is bitcoin so cheap compared to legacy financial institutions? The trick is that bitcoin automates the jobs that normally belong to the managers and mediators of legacy financial institutions. And as history teaches, automation brings efficiency.

8.4.3   *Bitcoin is dumb*

Human beings run the traditional financial system. They sit in positions of influence as makers, managers, and mediators. As managers and mediators, they don't always protect our privacy. And the humans across all three roles don't always appear to deserve our trust. Bitcoin can help those who would rather self-exclude from the traditional financial system than risk their privacy within it or place their trust in the humans who run it.

The intermediaries within financial institutions control the value that flows through them. By controlling the flow, they can also monitor it. In fact, they must monitor it; various laws demand that they do so. These laws aim to protect against fraud, identity theft, money laundering, sanctions evasion, and the financing of terrorism and other illicit activities. But financial institutions also reap profits from collecting our personal financial information. By knowing your identity, location, employment history, income level, transaction history, and financial behavior, institutions can tailor new marketing campaigns and products for you. Collecting our personal information is good for the bottom line. In addition to using our data, they can also sell it to other companies for similar purposes.

Sadly, our collected data is often stolen or leaked. Here are some of the biggest breaches:

- In 2008, Heartland Payment Systems suffered a breach of about 100 million credit and debit cards issued by more than 650 financial services companies.[19]
- In 2014, a breach at JP Morgan Chase compromised accounts belonging to 76 million households and 7 million small businesses.[20]
- In 2019, an Amazon engineer stole information about 100 million Capital One customers.[21]

By collecting, selling, and exposing our financial information to third parties and then the whole world, financial institutions show that we cannot trust them to keep our private information private. The problem, we insist, is not that *they* are uniquely bad at protecting our privacy or that *we* would do better. The problem is *us* – human beings. We lack knowledge. We have imperfect judgment. And we have character flaws. As greed relentlessly nips at the heels, some of us will inevitably succumb. Some of us are bound to fail, especially those in positions of power and influence within the financial system – the makers, mediators, and managers.

In addition to the loss of privacy, banks and other financial institutions sometimes levy hidden charges. These seem exploitative. Employees sometimes engage in unethical practices and insider trading. And of course, we've all seen the headlines about how these institutions fanned the flames of various financial crises, especially the Great Recession of 2007–2009.

Sometimes even the best, brightest, and well-meaning cause severe problems in the financial sector. In late 2020, for example, the Federal Open Market Committee (FOMC) issued forward guidance on future monetary policy. They had projected low interest rates through 2023 but soon began to hike interest rates faster than they had in several decades. Some banks took the FOMC's original guidance at face value and bought long-term government bonds. Then the steep rise in rates caused those bonds to trade at severe discounts, leading several large banks to have an asset-liability mismatch. Several large banks failed as a result.[22] Without an emergency response from FDIC that guaranteed all deposits well beyond the original $250,000, large depositors would have lost many millions, causing further ripple effects throughout the economy.

We have all heard many such stories. So we all understand why some choose to exclude themselves from the financial system.

The traditional financial system has makers; in the US, they sit on the FOMC, and they sometimes make mistakes. Sometimes, they then over-correct. Bitcoin, however, has no makers. So it has no makers who can make mistakes. As a result, those who might self-exclude due to distrust in makers may find a home in the bitcoin network. We should note that within a few days of the first major bank closures – Silicon Valley Bank on March 10, 2023, and Signature Bank on March 12 – bitcoin's price rose from around $20,000 to $24,000. The market seems to have grasped the value of a trust-minimized monetary network in the face of a system that had lost the trust of depositors.

By design, legacy systems also have managers and mediators. They collect and expose our private information, sometimes intentionally and sometimes not. They also sometimes overcharge and exploit. It's hard to blame those who exclude themselves from the financial sector due to a lack of trust or due to privacy concerns, especially outside the US where trusted parties more regularly abuse the trust placed in them. So our point isn't that the financial system is irredeemably untrustworthy or unable to protect our privacy. Instead, we hope to have explained why some might prefer to avoid the traditional financial system.

Those who have these concerns might also find relief within the bit-coin network. Because the bitcoin network employs neither managers nor mediators, ordinary users needn't worry that a trusted party will sell or leak their data, surprise them with a hidden charge, hold their money hostage, or engage in any type of prejudice against them. Because the bit-coin network employs no humans, it can't employ humans with imperfect judgment or character. Bitcoin has fewer vectors for distrust. The bitcoin network, by design, cannot be corrupt, racist, sexist, classist, or just plain incompetent.

8.4.4 Bitcoin is everywhere

A substantial portion of the unbanked cite distance as a key factor in their financial exclusion. They might not have any local bank branches within a reasonable travel distance. Or perhaps they have untrustworthy banks within a reasonable travel radius but no trustworthy ones. Intuitive, frictionless mobile banking isn't available everywhere. And in many places, mobile payments that settle through the banking system are only possible once you've opened up an account at a local brick-and-mortar bank. If your area doesn't have the bricks and mortar to house your trusted parties, you won't have trusted parties to settle and clear your transactions.

By inhabiting the internet, bitcoin is available to anyone with an internet-connected device.[23] This sounds great. But for this very reason, bitcoin is not available to everyone everywhere. In practice, many worldwide lack either the device or the internet connectivity or both.

There are three related worries: the availability of internet coverage, the cost of internet access, and the cost of an internet-capable device. Though these challenges are real, there is some reason for optimism in each case. In 2022, mobile broadband was available in about 95% of the world.[24] And by the end of 2021, about 70% of the adult population worldwide were using the internet on mobile devices.[25] In most low- and middle-income countries, the cost of 1GB of mobile data continues to trend downward and recently dipped below 2% of average monthly income[26]

Yet device affordability remains a sticking point. In low- and middle-income countries, an entry-level internet-enabled device still costs between 9% and 25% of monthly GDP per capita.[27] A mobile phone that can use bitcoin, that is, remains a significant purchase and not one everyone can afford. Of course, people can and do share devices. But sharing devices might reinsert trusted parties into your monetary flow, namely, the other people you're sharing the device with.

Thankfully, we have good news about device affordability. The best evidence we have suggests that an appreciable fraction of the unbanked, globally, have already managed to get an internet-enabled mobile device. It may not have been easy, but they somehow managed. And that positions them well to benefit from emerging payment technologies. Here is how the World Bank Group sums things up:

> The growing presence of mobile phones in developing economies could allow these economies to leapfrog directly to mobile payments

and thereby increase account ownership. . . . In South Asia, for example, 240 million unbanked adults have a mobile phone – that is, more than half of the 430 million unbanked in the region. More specifically, 56 percent of all unbanked adults in the region have a mobile phone, including 51 percent of unbanked adults in India and 55 percent of unbanked adults in Pakistan. In Bangladesh, 69 percent of unbanked adults have a mobile phone; in Nepal, 73 percent. Similarly, in Sub-Saharan Africa 165 million adults without an account (56 percent of the unbanked) have a mobile phone. Although the data show variations from economy to economy, in most Sub-Saharan African economies surveyed, the majority of unbanked adults have mobile phones.[28]

Millions worldwide are unbanked. But given growing mobile device ownership, all is not lost. More people than ever before have what it takes to use bitcoin on their own devices. They can tap into the network and benefit from its inclusive powers.

An important qualification is in order. We have thus far talked only about access to monetary infrastructure – payments and savings. We haven't addressed another significant element of the world of money: finance. Access to credit is important, for quality of life and for building wealth. Most Americans could never afford a home if they had to save up for it; they come to own a home only because they had access to a mortgage.[29] Some of the most appalling stories of financial exclusion, furthermore, often involve credit. In the United States, these stories often involve allegations of racial discrimination, and it's called "banking while black."[30]

Although bitcoin can be used in credit systems by posting it as collateral for a loan, the bitcoin network is not a system of credit. So one doesn't need a credit score, much less a good one, to use bitcoin. But there is no way to get a mortgage for your new home on the bitcoin network either. It is fundamentally a system of money, not finance. There are limits, then, to bitcoin's powers to include. It can't solve every problem of financial exclusion nor should we expect it to.

Bitcoin enjoys yet another advantage as a system not based on credit or debt. The entire electronic payments industry is built on debt. In order to access fast payments, you first need a bank account. And in order to secure a bank account, you technically need to loan the bank money in exchange for interest. And some have qualms about participating in debt-based systems. Remember, 10% of unbanked adults cited religious reasons as a barrier. And those citing religious reasons seem to come disproportionately from economies with large populations of Muslims. Thus, the World Bank: "In the Middle East and North Africa, for example, where adults might prefer Sharia-compliant banking services, 24 percent and 19 percent of the unbanked in Iraq and Morocco, respectively, cited religion as a barrier."[31]

What are Sharia-compliant banking services? This question, as it turns out, is complicated. Since this isn't a book about Islamic monetary theology, we won't pursue those complications here.[32] But one simple point is still in order. Bitcoin does not require its users to loan their funds for interest to access electronic payments. It is, again, not a system of credit at all. In one way, this is a limitation. But it is a limitation that makes bitcoin an attractive alternative to other electronic payment systems that do involve loaning money for interest (as when you deposit dollars to a checking account and earn 0.1% annually). A nontrivial portion of the world's population has ethical and theological qualms with legacy payment networks. And bitcoin, like gold, provides them a non-debt-based alternative.

8.5   Inclusive digital cash

When encountering financial exclusion and its various causes, some will attempt to work within legacy monetary systems. They will try to reform those structures. This is a noble fight. Others will try to burn down the system. Still, others build alternative systems. Bitcoin falls within that third category; it is an alternative system. Its inclusivity stems from the simple but powerful design choice to forgo trusted authorities.

Physical cash is, as we've noted already, terrific monetary technology. It can be traded peer-to-peer, cheaply, easily, and in a private and censorship-resistant way. Cash is, for exactly these reasons, a powerful tool for financial inclusion. And yet cash, precisely because of its connection to permissioned systems, is an imperfect tool to boost inclusion. Many merchants don't accept it, and it won't work for online payments, a damning fact in an increasingly digital world. And perhaps most importantly, there are systematic efforts to block access to cash. Consider, for example, a recent mandate by the Central Bank of Nigeria that no cash withdrawal may exceed 100,000 Nigerian Naira (about $225) and total withdrawals in a week may not exceed 500,000 Nigerian Naira (about $1,125).[33] Any attempts to withdraw more than these limits will face punishing fees of 5% or 10%. The central bank's motives aren't hidden: they want to encourage a cashless society and move ordinary citizens towards controllable digital money.

It sure would be nice, one thinks, to have access to a money without withdrawal limits, where users can spend their own money without the permission of some authority.

Central bank digital currencies (CBDCs) don't help much here either. Indeed, they duplicate some of the very factors we've identified as root problems with traditional systems. Yes, they aren't without benefits. CBDCs would give users direct access to central bank money in digital form as opposed to mere commercial bank deposits. That's all well and good. And they could boost inclusion by solving distance issues, or making banking more affordable, with lower fees and no minimum balances. But by trading lots of small trusted parties for one big trusted party, they'd almost certainly have stricter controls and offer new powers of surveillance to corporate and state entities alike. With a CBDC, there'd be nothing stopping an authority from blocking access on any number of spurious grounds. They are risky, then, in precisely the way that traditional digital money is risky, for they, too, involve trusted authorities.[34] Besides, how many central banks worldwide could responsibly run a CBDC? Even if you think a CBDC in the US could succeed, what about all the countries where most of the excluded currently reside? Many of these economies already suffer under authoritarian governments and high inflation.

Remember, too, some of the other reasons for exclusion. Many don't have bank accounts because they don't trust banks or the government or because they don't want to fork over documentation to get access to payments. A CBDC operated by a central bank and deputized commercial banks would almost certainly command the same kinds of distrust as legacy systems. And if it were closely surveilled, it wouldn't be an attractive alternative for people with privacy concerns. It might scare them even more than extant banking systems, in fact.

Digital cash – not mere digital money – is the solution to these problems of inclusion. And that's what bitcoin is.

Some critics have argued that bitcoin or other cryptocurrencies offer little for the financially excluded. To use bitcoin, they say, you'll first pay on-ramp fees to put fiat money on an exchange, market fees for trading that fiat for bitcoin, a network transaction fee to make a payment, and then off-ramp fees to exchange the bitcoin for fiat money once more. Instead of financial inclusion, bitcoin serves up fees and more friction. Worse, the institutions involved – banks and exchanges – will engage in the very exclusionary practices bitcoin was designed, in part, to avoid.[35]

We grant both points. If bitcoin is used only through a series of intermediary institutions, it is only as inclusive as those institutions. In earlier chapters, we noted limitations on bitcoin's privacy or censorship-resistance. These limitations are most acute when trusted parties are reintroduced into the process. Your ability to transact privately and freely is as robust as trusted parties allow, whether the transactions involve bitcoin or dollars or bolivars.

The same holds for inclusion. The inclusive power of the bitcoin network derives from its lack of trusted parties. Reintroducing trusted parties masks bitcoin's inclusivity and reintroduces the risk of exclusion. The recent situation in Nigeria illustrates how banks can also mask the liberating power of cash. As with cash, so also with bitcoin. Bitcoin is most powerful when users ride the horse rather than watch the rodeo – by receiving, saving, and spending bitcoin through private keys that users themselves control.

8.6   Empowering the unbanked

Behind the veil, you have more than a one in 16 chance of being an unbanked person when you step back into the world. You also have some chance of being the child of an unbanked person, which we haven't factored in. In either case, your life will be much more difficult at best.

We've explained how bitcoin might mitigate financial exclusion in the US and especially abroad. Many factors that cause exclusion in the traditional financial system don't apply as squarely to bitcoin. So bitcoin can help an appreciable portion of the world's financial outsiders. It is an alternative money for them to use, if they see fit.

Many of them likely do. A table below compares the Global Crypto Adoption Index rankings alongside the ranking of the seven economies with the most unbanked individuals.[36]

Suggestive, isn't it? If the countries with the most unbanked adults also happen to have adopted bitcoin and other cryptocurrencies at the highest rates in the world, perhaps we should listen to their revealed preferences. Perhaps we shouldn't wish bitcoin away from behind the veil if we stand a good chance of living in one of their economies.

Unbanked people are better off in the bitcoin world. Given the odds of being such a person, it makes sense to step into the bitcoin world. Even if we suppose that half of the unbanked lack a proper device for using bitcoin, you would still have a roughly one in 32 chance of being helped by

Country	Percent Unbanked	Unbanked Population	Global Crypto Adoption Index
India	22%	228,975,136	1
China	11%	130,272,208	11
Pakistan	79%	113,770,976	8
Indonesia	48%	97,735,280	7
Nigeria	55%	63,703,068	2
Bangladesh	47%	56,928,864	17
Egypt, Arab Reb.	73%	49,063,468	35

Crypto adoption and unbanked populations.

bitcoin now, with a one in 16 chance of being helped by bitcoin in the near future, as devices become increasingly more affordable.

We know what we would do, at least. All else being equal, given the inconveniences and harms of being a financial outsider, and the benefits of making cheap and quick electronic payments at a distance, we would gladly step back into the bitcoin world.

Notes

1. Domat (2016).
2. See Freeman (2017) for a survey of racism in the credit card industry.
3. One reason for exclusion: a series of US executive orders made serving Syrians too risky to be worth a bank's business. If the client happened to sit within a few hops of terrorist organizations, banks could face severe penalties. See Domat (2016).
4. Unless noted otherwise, international data and figures in this section come from Demirgüç-Kunt et al. (2022), the World Bank's *The Global Findex Database 2021*. See also World Bank (2017).
5. Demirgüç-Kunt et al. (2022, p. 34).
6. Demirgüç-Kunt et al. (2022, p. 36).
7. Ibid.
8. The statistics that follow appear in Demirgüç-Kunt et al. (2022, p. 36).
9. Demirgüç-Kunt et al. (2022, p. 111).
10. Touryalai (2013).
11. CFPB (2022).
12. FDIC (2022, p. 13).
13. Data later comes from FDIC (2022, pp. 16–22).
14. This data comes from the Appendix Tables in FDIC (2022).
15. FDIC (2022, p. 18).
16. Semple (2014).
17. Nawyn et al. (2012).
18. Surprisingly, the World Bank's financial inclusion survey mentions neither "racism" nor "sexism" nor "prejudice" nor "bias" a single time.
19. King (2009).
20. Reuters (2014).
21. Bursztynsky (2022).
22. Granja (2023).
23. Technically, the bitcoin network is usable without direct internet access. For you can transact by transferring the data of your bitcoin transaction via radio or satellite to someone else who then will broadcast the data to the internet. But as things stand, these are exercises for tinkerers and hobbyists.
24. Delaporte and Bahia (2022, p. 5).
25. Demirgüç-Kunt et al. (2022, p. 114).
26. Delaporte and Bahia (2022, p. 46).
27. Ibid.
28. Demirgüç-Kunt et al. (2022, p. 39).
29. See Choi (2020).
30. Swarns (2020a, 2020b).
31. Demirgüç-Kunt et al. (2022, p. 36).

32. Instead, we direct readers to Routledge's *Islamic Business and Finance* book series.
33. Benson (2022). Daily withdrawal limits are even tighter – see Onu and Osae-Brown (2022).
34. A complete and full-throated critique of CBDCs goes beyond the aims of this chapter. But for two popular-level articles that lay out some of the main problems, see Bailey and Luther (2022a) and Bailey and Luther (2022b).
35. See, for example, Carmona (2022).
36. See Chainalysis (2023b). For much more on bitcoin and how it serves unbanked or underbanked populations, see Gladstein (2022).

9

SECURITY THROUGH ENERGY

9.1 Protecting Fort Knox

In 1936, on the northern border of Kentucky, the United States built a fortified vault to hold the country's gold – 12,960 metric tons of it. The vault, commonly known as Fort Knox, currently holds 4,580 metric tons of gold, worth about $6 billion.

The gold pooled in Fort Knox is a pirate's dream. Films and stories about Fort Knox involve tales of heists and sabotage. But these tales have remained fiction, largely thanks to the United States Mint Police, which guards Fort Knox. Yet as far as we know, the Mint Police at Fort Knox hasn't stopped a single ounce of gold from being stolen. That isn't to say that someone has pulled off a heist, though. Rather, no one has really tried.

A fool would look at the Fort Knox security budget and declare it wasteful since there haven't been any known theft attempts, much less successful ones. Hundreds of officers get paid to walk around all day to open and close doors, check locks and lights, and watch boring security camera feeds. They attend annual training sessions but never put their training into practice.

Of course, people don't *try* to steal Fort Knox's gold precisely because they'd fail. Mint Police agents would foil any attempted theft. They stand as a deterrent. The principle here – security through deterrence – is well-known. Home security systems and especially their signs are money well spent even if no one tries to break into your house. Many learn martial arts precisely because they don't want to fight.

Bitcoin also uses deterrence as security. Bitcoin miners secure the network. They collect new transactions into blocks and publish them atop

DOI: 10.4324/9781003484721-9

others, burying past transactions farther down in the chain. The farther down the stack they are, the costlier they are to undo, which increases our confidence that the transactions will remain.

Bitcoin's approach to security sets it apart from alternatives. Mining is peculiar and poorly understood. Many claim that mining is bitcoin's greatest liability, largely because of its energy consumption. These critics argue that bitcoin mining is wasteful. But once we distinguish different kinds of security and evaluate how bitcoin and other assets achieve them, we see that the main arguments fail.

9.2   Securing money

9.2.1   Money is built on confidence

Billions of people have confidence in the US dollar. They accept it in exchange for valuable goods or services, price contracts in it, denominate their debts and credits in it, and store their wealth in dollar-denominated bank accounts. Physical cash, in particular, is treasured around the world. It's the USA's finest export. No matter where you are, the dollars in your fanny pack will find willing recipients.

Gold, too, inspires confidence. Millions hoard it under mattresses, within walls, or in vaults. Many around the globe know how to tell false gold from true. No matter where you are, the gold ingots in your coat pocket will find willing recipients.

In both cases, what matters isn't just what people say but what they *do*. By exchanging things of value for gold or dollars, people reveal their confidence in these assets.

That confidence has been earned.

9.2.2   Counterfeiting, false spending, and double-spending

Let's take a look at how this confidence has been earned. The one-word story says that the dollar and gold are *secure*. They enjoy protections against various kinds of fraud or loss. They give their users some peace of mind. This is known, and it is known that it is known. This enables social coordination around each good as a useful money,[1] which then helps resolve the problem of coincident wants (see Chapter 3.1.2) and unlocks exchange beyond barter. Consequently, billions entrust their monetary lives to slips of paper and metal bars.

Bitcoin lacks the expansive monetary network of either the dollar or gold. But it, too, has inspired confidence. At the time of writing, the bitcoin network stores and protects hundreds of billions of dollars in value for tens or perhaps even hundreds of millions of people. Why do so many have confidence in bitcoin? It's the familiar story: bitcoin is *secure*. It, too, provides assurances. And in doing so, it enables social coordination.

How do the dollar and gold command confidence, and how does bitcoin aspire to do the same? To answer these questions, let's distinguish three kinds of monetary insecurity and see how the dollar, gold, and bitcoin protect against them.

First, money may be subject to *counterfeiting*, which occurs when someone makes an imitation convincing enough for someone else to accept in exchange for services or other things of value. Second, money may be subject to *false spending*, which occurs when someone spends your money without your permission. Third, money may be subject to *double-spending*, which occurs when someone spends one and the same unit twice over. A monetary species is vulnerable to any one of these when the costs of executing the attack fall below the benefits.

Though money has a central constitutive role – being a medium of exchange – it often serves other purposes, too, including, crucially, being a store of value. A monetary asset that can be cheaply counterfeited, falsely spent, or double-spent is less apt for storing value. For example, a money that could be easily counterfeited is a rubbish store of value, much like a money subject to hyperinflation. Rather than save it, you would want to spend it as soon as possible.

The three kinds of insecurity help determine the overall integrity of a money. A money's resistance to these vulnerabilities, whether by design or by nature, affects its fittingness not only for its use as a medium of exchange but also for its use as a store of value. So our judgments about the cost-effectiveness of bitcoin's security must factor in its use as both a medium of exchange and a store of value.

9.2.3 How physical dollars and gold are secured

The dollar wards off these threats in two sharply different ways depending on whether we're talking about physical cash or the dollar-denominated claims in bank accounts and payment applications. Let's start with physical cash.

Counterfeiting is discouraged both in the design of physical cash and in the legal framework surrounding it. But the lower the stakes, the less security required. The low face value of physical coins makes producing fakes less lucrative. And their low face value per ounce would make large counterfeiting attempts both burdensome and extremely suspicious; imagine the rolls of fake nickels just to buy a Big Mac, let alone a Mercedez-Bens.

Lower-denomination bills are hardly worth counterfeiting either, though the $5 and $10 now include anti-counterfeiting measures.[2]

It's the $20, $50, and $100 bills with the most extensive anti-counterfeiting features, including colored fibers, linen-blend composition, security threads that glow under black light, watermarks, color-shifting ink, and so on.[3] To counterfeit a hundred-dollar bill convincingly, you'll need an expensive press, fancy cotton paper, special ink, and more. The rise of desktop publishing in recent decades, predictably, led to new security features in US banknotes which have raised the price of forgery.

US banknotes also get an extrinsic boost in security from the legal system. It's a crime to make counterfeit notes, and thousands of Secret Service agents have mandates to catch anyone who'd print fake dollars. They're pretty good at what they do, and if you're caught and convicted, you could face a decade or more in federal prison.[4]

False spending is discouraged in two ways. First, users themselves take measures to protect their cash, such as when they hide it under a mattress or lock it in a safe. In doing so, they raise the price for anyone who'd spend their money. Physics is one potent ally in the war against false spending. The state is another. When enforced, laws against breaking down doors or searching other people's houses for cash raise the expected price of theft.

Finally, double-spending is made unworkable through simple physics. Once a dollar bill has moved from your hands and into a merchant's cash register, spending it again is no easy trick. For in the ordinary course of things, dollar bills do not duplicate *à la* CTRL+C/CTRL+V. Nor do bills inhabit multiple locations. Although science fiction supplies some ideas about how to duplicate objects and their instances, our best physical theories predict that such things are vanishingly improbable. Spending a dollar twice, in an illicit way, likely requires that you first get it back the old-fashioned way – by theft.

Gold's protections are pretty simple and use physics much in the way the physical dollar does.

The Secret Service doesn't need to crack down on alchemy. The laws of physics and chemistry do that just fine. There is no known procedure to turn base metals (or anything else) into gold. It must be extracted from the ground in a well-known mining process. Further, gold has a unique combination of density properties, so one can weigh it and displace water with it and determine whether the numbers check out. Given gold's chemical stability, one can also test putative gold with acid. Overall, gold is difficult to counterfeit. Ordinary physics and the laws of the land together make false spending and double-spending of gold infeasible, just as they do with the physical dollar.

9.2.4   How digital dollars are secured

Compared to gold and physical cash, digital dollars rely less on the laws of physics and more on networks of oversight and trust.

Systems that manage digital dollars are closely guarded. Not just anyone can fire up a database, jot down "Fred" and "$600," and thereby create new dollars or dollar substitutes for Fred. To do that, you need other parties in the digital banking system to acknowledge your database as legitimate. And to do *that*, you need to be a recognized member of the permissioned club of banks, financial institutions, money processors, and so on. If you are, and you follow the relevant rules, the digital dollars or dollar substitutes you mint aren't counterfeits. Break the rules, however, and the network of institutions would judge your database entries to be counterfeit. They would also be right. The digital dollar is, by nature, a creature of trust and permissioned management.

Digital dollars also have simple and effective measures against false spending. The rules that govern these digital dollar databases don't ordinarily let the owner of one account spend dollars associated with someone else's account. And the measures against double-spending work much the same way. Once an account's balance has been spent and marked down accordingly, it cannot again spend the very quantity it just spent without first having the initial transaction reversed.

Could there be software glitches or hacks? Sure. But the cybersecurity measures of commercial and central banks effectively protect against false and double-spending of digital dollars. Permissions to read and write to their databases enjoy close scrutiny. And those with permissions must follow the rules against illicit spending. As before, the legal system complements the software guardrails: break the laws, and you'll face the consequences.

Digital dollars run on trust. Banks and their partner financial institutions trust each other that they are all playing by the rules. Users trust that the Federal Reserve software and commercial bank software and credit card software can't be easily hacked. Everyone trusts that banks and credit card companies and law enforcement will enact penalties against bad actors. Since virtually none of the relevant software is open-source, ordinary users cannot evaluate its security for themselves. They must instead trust that the software and cybersecurity systems don't have bugs or holes that hackers can exploit at low cost. If there is an exploit, users trust that someone up the chain of command will make things right again.

9.2.5   How bitcoin is secured

Bitcoin is software. It might, like other software, have bugs. But it's open-source, so anyone can review the code and fix any bugs. Many world-class programmers are already on the job; some are even reading this book. (Thank you for your service.) Before and even after the core software maintainers push out changes, a larger community of developers vets them in a lengthy process.[5] Then node operators select for themselves which version of the software to run. They often wait to update their software until they have strong evidence that it's safe to do so.

Indeed, bitcoin is among the most scrutinized software ever developed. Finding and exploiting a bug could reap huge rewards and bring the network to its knees. That someone has not created counterfeit bitcoins or killed the network while taking a short position speaks to bitcoin's security.

Dan Kaminsky was a noted security researcher, whose obituary in *The New York Times* hailed as an "Internet security savior" and "digital Paul Revere."[6] *The New Yorker* once captured Kaminsky's thoughts on bitcoin's security:

> "When I first looked at the code, I was sure I was going to be able to break it," Kaminsky said, noting that the programming style was dense and inscrutable. "The way the whole thing was formatted was insane. Only the most paranoid, painstaking coder in the world could avoid making mistakes."
>
> Kaminsky lives in Seattle, but, while visiting family in San Francisco in July, he retreated to the basement of his mother's house to work on his bitcoin attacks. In a windowless room jammed with computers, Kaminsky paced around talking to himself, trying to build a mental picture of the bitcoin network. He quickly identified nine ways to compromise the system and scoured Nakamoto's code for an insertion point for his first attack. But when he found the right spot, there was a message waiting for him. "Attack Removed," it said. The same thing happened over and over, infuriating Kaminsky. "I came up with beautiful bugs," he said. "But every time I went after the code there was a line that addressed the problem."
>
> He was like a burglar who was certain that he could break into a bank by digging a tunnel, drilling through a wall, or climbing down a vent, and on each attempt he discovered a freshly poured cement barrier with a sign telling him to go home. "I've never seen anything like it," Kaminsky said, still in awe.
>
> Kaminsky ticked off the skills Nakamoto would need to pull it off. "He's a world-class programmer, with a deep understanding of the C++ programming language," he said. "He understands economics, cryptography, and peer-to-peer networking."
>
> "Either there's a team of people who worked on this," Kaminsky said, "or this guy is a genius."[7]

More than a decade after the Kaminksy profile, bitcoin is even less likely to suffer a critical exploit. No wonder users entrust hundreds of billions of dollars to the network.

Suppose you tried to spend a non-existent bitcoin UTXO. Such a transaction would create bitcoin out of thin air, outside the ordained supply schedule, which, as you'll recall from Chapter 1, governs the block rewards for miners. Such a transaction would involve counterfeit bitcoin.

Submitting transactions like this to the bitcoin network is both easy and legal. But getting the blockchain to include them is another matter. First, such transactions are invalid. So nodes would reject them and refuse to propagate them. Second, miners would also refuse to put them in any blocks they win. Since miners know that nodes reject blocks with invalid transactions, they don't want to expend energy finding a block that nodes will ultimately reject.

Nodes easily detect departures from the supply schedule. And with the single command "gettxoutsetinfo," a node can audit the entire supply at any time. Since every node has a full copy of the open and trivially auditable ledger, fake bitcoin has nowhere to hide – unlike, say, counterfeit physical cash stashed in an off-grid warehouse.

False spending isn't easy either. To spend someone else's bitcoin, you'll need to submit a valid transaction that spends someone else's bitcoin. This is possible if you gain access to their private key on a device or all the relevant private keys split across several devices. Otherwise, someone would need to crack public key cryptography. Although the private keys that enable users to move bitcoin also generate the bitcoin addresses seen in public, we cannot use those public addresses to reverse engineer their private keys, not under reasonable security practices anyway.

Bitcoin's security against counterfeiting and false spending is relatively cheap and straightforward. Cryptography enables nodes to audit the system at low cost, removing the need for trusted institutions. But its security against double-spending is more recherché.

We have already explained bitcoin's anti-double-spending measures (see Chapter 2, Section 6). To briefly recap: a successful double-spend involves exchanging bitcoin for something of value and then mining a series of blocks that undoes the original transaction and enables one to spend the same bitcoin elsewhere. A successful double-spend provides both the bitcoin you began with and whatever valuable item you had originally exchanged it for. Imagine buying a computer at a store with cash and then leaving with both the computer *and* the cash – an attractive outcome, for sure. Attractive for you, that is. For the store, not so much.

To pull off a double-spend, you must mine a new chain of blocks that branches from the original chain before your original transaction. And the nodes will not endorse your alternative chain unless it becomes the heaviest – the chain with the most accumulated proof of work. Producing such a chain would require both specialized mining hardware and a good deal of energy. Since the costs of hardware and electricity can both vary widely, so, too, can the cost of producing blocks in an attempted double-spend. But we can, with a few assumptions, estimate the cost of a double-spend nonetheless.

To begin, the cost of your double-spend attempt will partly depend on both how many blocks you'll need to mine and the cost to mine each one. Since miners work for the bitcoin reward, the cost of mining each block won't, on average, exceed the block reward.[8] Now, merchants wise in bitcoin's ways know that after receiving your bitcoin, every additional block they wait provides further protection from a double-spend. So they wait a certain number of blocks before completing the exchange. The approximate upper bound for the cost of re-mining those blocks would equal the sum of all their block rewards.

The approximate upper bound cost of mining six blocks with rewards of 6.35 bitcoin per block (0.1 bitcoin in transaction fees plus 6.25 bitcoin in fresh bitcoin, say) would equal 38.1 bitcoin. At the time of writing, where 1 bitcoin commands a market price of around $25,000, the price of 38.1 bitcoin equal around $950,000. So in this scenario, the approximate upper bound cost of double-spending sits around $950,000. That's expensive. Hence, a merchant selling something for more than $950,000 would wisely wait more than six blocks, just in case. This expense will rise or fall with the number of blocks, the price of bitcoin, and each block's reward; as each goes up, so, too, does the cost of double-spending, and as each goes down, double-spending becomes less expensive.[9]

We've spoken of an approximate upper bound. Just how far *actual* mining costs differ from this is, in part, a function of competition. The more perfectly competitive the bitcoin mining industry is, the more we can expect actual block production costs to match block rewards.[10] Bitcoin mining is, at present, *highly* competitive.[11] It is a global and permissionless market that anyone may join. All you need is a computer and some electricity. When a miner in South Africa successfully unearths an ounce of gold, it expands the global supply of gold and can thus make mining elsewhere less profitable. This is ordinary competition at work. Importantly, miners in Alaska can still dig up and sell their new gold too. But competition for bitcoin is more ruthless due to the fixed issuance schedule. In bitcoin land, winning a block in South Africa means no one does anywhere else. About every ten minutes, bitcoin has a worldwide, winner-take-all competition for the available bitcoin. So block rewards, by design, comprise a major component of the cost of double-spending.

We began with a story about Fort Knox. It can teach us something important about bitcoin mining and the security it provides. Security systems, at their best, may appear useless because they fail to stop any attacks. Although security guards at Fort Knox have never stopped an attack, they have surely prevented them. Their presence and activity discourage attacks from happening in the first place. So also with bitcoin miners. Their presence and activity discourage double-spending. And when bitcoin users wait the appropriate amount of time before treating transactions as final, they reward honest miners over those who'd double-spend. Honest miners, like the security guards at Fort Knox, are paid for their trouble.

In sum: we have considered security against counterfeiting, false spending, and double-spending. To secure against counterfeiting and false spending, bitcoin uses cryptography. Nodes can, at very low cost, detect invalid transactions that cheat in either of these ways. They do not trust; they verify. To secure against double-spending, bitcoin uses proof-of-work mining. The fact that mining is expensive, crucially, makes double-spending expensive too.

You may have heard that bitcoin uses both expensive hardware and vast amounts of energy. It's true. And now you know why: to secure the network against double-spending. For bitcoin to be secure against double-spending, mining *has* to be expensive. If mining bitcoin is cheap, double-spending bitcoin is cheap too.

Mining is expensive because it involves a fleet of expensive hardware that requires vast amounts of energy to operate.[12] And therein lies the rub.

9.3   What's the problem?

Many argue against bitcoin from its energy expenditure. We'll begin with the less plausible objections of this sort and work towards the more plausible.

9.3.1   *Energy use*

We've all seen the sensational headlines. In 2017, *Newsweek* blasted out this doozy: "Bitcoin Mining on Track to Consume All of the World's Energy by 2020."[13] It didn't happen. Not even close.[14] Unwittingly or not, the gullible venues that print wild soon-to-be falsified projections about bitcoin's energy use repeat a known pattern. In the internet's earlier days, for example, some claimed that it would use 50% of US electricity by 2010.[15] It didn't – not even close. New technologies throw commentators off balance. Why do real research when you can publish sensational headlines that, to many, *seem* right?

Other breathless headlines steer clear of dubious projections and instead highlight bitcoin's present energy use. By now, this is a recognizable trope: compare the energy use of bitcoin with some small country and call it a day.[16] If bitcoin uses this much energy, the idea goes, we've got a serious problem on our hands.

To be fair, bitcoin mining does use lots of energy. At the time of writing, aggregate power demand for bitcoin mining amounts to around 14.12 GW.[17] That's a lot of gigawatts – about ten nuclear power plants' worth. Annualized, it comes to about 123.82 TWh. That's a lot of terawatt-hours – about the same as Washington State's annual consumption. So among other countries, bitcoin's energy use falls somewhere between that of Finland (population 5.5 million) and the Philippines (population 109 million). This sounds like a lot of energy. And it is. But we should also these numbers into the context of global annual *electricity consumption*, which comes in at about 22,315 TWh. Here, bitcoin's share is about 0.5%. And since global *energy production* is around 167,716 TWh, bitcoin's slice of that pie is about 0.19%.

The mainstream stories about bitcoin's energy use write themselves and often include arresting visual comparisons.[18] In doing so, one can compare bitcoin to other industries or applications and their energy footprints. Bitcoin doesn't top the list, but it's higher up than many might have guessed – at present, somewhere between televisions and fridges in the US.

Some bitcoin advocates recommend a zoom out. "Take these numbers in stride," they might say, "a hundred and twenty terawatt-hours a year sure sounds like a lot, but we must remember that this is something like one half of one percent of annual global electricity use. In the grand scheme of things, that's a rounding error, and may be safely ignored."[20] In our experience, this reply doesn't work – not rhetorically and not on the substance of things either. A closer look is certainly in order.

First, energy use is not, as such, bad. Think of something that people do that is better to do than not: running soup kitchens, raising children, celebrating holidays, protesting fossil fuel subsidies, cultivating crops, holding concerts, traveling, studying philosophy, watching funny videos, washing clothes, you name it. These all use energy. If you disagree with the particulars of the list, please supply your own examples. We're quite sure they'll involve people using energy. We are energy-consuming machines and so are our tools and gadgets. And yet this fact alone does not make any of the listed activities bad or better left undone. No. Indeed, they are better done than not. None of this shows that bitcoin is better done than not, of course. What it shows, instead, is that if there's a problem here, it's not energy use as such.

Nor is there any problem, as such, with using vast quantities of energy. All of the activities named earlier do that. This is one way that human

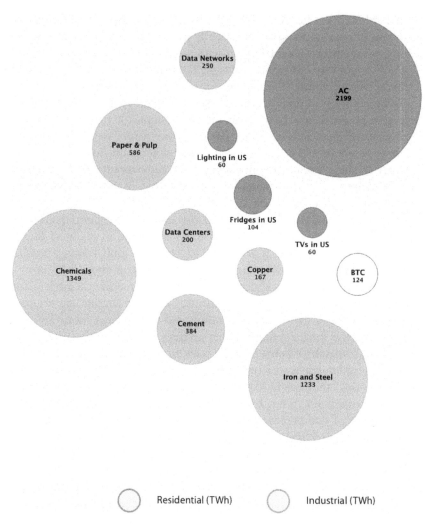

Bitcoin energy use in comparison.[19]

beings show that they value something: they use energy for it. And when they value it a lot, they use a lot of energy for it. Typically, they *pay* for the energy they use; the concert tickets you buy help foot the bill for the overhead lights and PA system, for example. The soup kitchen pays for the gas or electricity for its stoves. Bitcoin is similar. Bitcoin users pay for the energy bitcoin consumes. When a bitcoin user broadcasts a bitcoin transaction with an accompanying fee to miners, for example, the winning miner uses that fee to pay their electricity bill. Block subsidies, which increase supply by minting new bitcoin and awarding it to block publishers, impose another kind of fee on bitcoin holders by diluting their holdings.[21] Either way, bitcoin users themselves, in transacting or holding bitcoin, pay for bitcoin's energy use and for the security that it provides.

So discussions of "bitcoin's" energy use often obscure something important about human agency. Bitcoin doesn't use energy. People do. People express their values – what they find worthwhile and important in life – in how they spend energy. You express your values through energy when you burn calories and walk to your children's day-care center, or when you burn gas by driving to the hospital, or when you purchase electricity to watch silly videos on the internet. As with money, what we do with energy shows what we value.

As it turns out, one thing that millions of people across the world value is transacting with or holding bitcoin. Bitcoiners collectively pay miners to help secure bitcoin's monetary system, and those miners buy electricity with their earnings. In return, miners provide important security assurances, especially against double-spending. Do bitcoiners err in paying miners as much as they do?

Let's find out.

9.3.2   Energy waste

Different people value different things. And so people use energy in different ways. People who don't like to do certain things, furthermore, have a long history of objecting when other people do those things. Religious vegans don't see much sense in the enormous energy footprint of factory farms. Principled bikers sneer at automobiles. Pacifists look askance at warplanes and battleships. Apolitical centrists sneer at raucous political rallies and militant atheists at churches. Anti-intellectuals pour over state school budgets and angrily highlight spending on books or libraries. The common refrain is, *what a waste!*

And then there's bitcoin and its energy use. What a waste!

These objections aren't very good, of course. Wastefulness emerges not from using energy but from using too much energy. And something can use too much energy either by using much more than it needs to, in itself, or by using more than an effective alternative. So bitcoin's energy use would be wasteful if it weren't worth what it provided or if some alternative could serve equally well for much less energy. We'll organize our thoughts on these matters around two key questions: *How* are claims about bitcoin's alleged waste to be evaluated, and *who* gets to decide?

Thus far, we've explained how and why bitcoin users pay for energy use – for security against double-spending attacks, which, in turn, enhances user confidence in the system's capacity to store and transmit value. That confidence, in turn, helps make bitcoin useful money. What remains, then, is an assessment of bitcoin's efficiency: Do users, in paying for bitcoin's security, get their money's worth?

The *total value protected* by a monetary network, let us say, is the number of base monetary units in circulation times the value of each.[22] Total value protected is a snapshot datum; we also need data about value protected over time, over many snapshots. So we also look at average figures (average total value protected in a year, say). A network's *security expenditure* for a year is whatever is spent in a year to prevent counterfeiting, false spending, and double-spending.[23] We can then define the *annual security fee* of a network as total security expenditure in a year divided by average total value protected for that year.

Lower security fees aren't always better. But provided that the total security expenditure provides sufficient assurances (whether absolutely or relative to the total value protected), lower is better. To see why this qualifier is necessary, imagine what would happen if credit card companies fired their compliance officers and network security technicians. Cheaper security costs but bad move! We want lower security costs, if possible. But we don't want to pay so little that we suffer for it.

Bitcoin miners provide security for users. They protect the network against one class of attacks. And over the course of a year, bitcoin users pay them for that service. This is bitcoin's annual security fee. In what follows, we'll report this fee as an annual percentage. And thanks to bitcoin's transparency, we can easily calculate it.

Bitcoin's total value protected, at the time of writing, comes to around $500 billion. Nodes protect against false and counterfeit spending; miners protect against double-spending. Bitcoin's security expenditure, accordingly, is equal to the operational cost of all nodes plus mining revenue. Nodes are, by design, exceedingly cheap to run. The tens of thousands of full nodes currently operating almost certainly cost less than $20 million a year to operate.[24] That's a drop in the bucket compared to mining, so we'll ignore nodes from now on. The vast majority of bitcoin's security expenditure goes not towards preventing false or counterfeit spending but towards securing the integrity of bitcoin's ledger against double-spending.

How much bitcoin users pay miners for protection against double-spending, and how that stacks up against the total value protected, varies considerably over time. So we will use data from several years and then measure it against two different approximations of bitcoin's total value protected – an end-of-year market cap figure as well as a 365-day moving average.[25]

The data says that for the last five years, bitcoin has managed to secure hundreds of billions of dollar value for about $5 billion to $15 billion per

	EOY Market Cap (in billions of USD)	Annual Miner Revenue (in billions of USD)	EOY Security Fee	Average Market Cap (in billions of USD)	Average Security Fee
2018	64.36	5.45	8.46%	128.36	4.24%
2019	129.97	5.19	3.99%	131.41	3.84%
2020	539.43	5.04	0.934%	205.52	2.45%
2021	876.85	16.71	1.90%	889.81	1.87%
2022	322.67	10.33	3.20%	537.147	1.92%

Bitcoin value protected and mining revenue, 2018–2022.[26]

year. The end-of-year data show security fees between 1% and 9%. And the averages show security fees between 1% and 5%. Bitcoin users, in aggregate, pay between $1 to $10 per year for every hundred dollars in value secured during that year.[27]

Bitcoin miners are not trusted parties. They do not custody funds for the ordinary transactions they publish. Users don't need permission from any single miner to transact. And miners prove rather than simply report the work they've done.[28] Yet we can compare their work to that of a trusted money manager – someone you pay to look after your money for you. Some managers charge a modest fee – just 0.4% per year, say. Others charge far more, with lavish promises of high returns or safe management. Others hide their fees, routing transactions through expensive channels while extracting kickbacks.

The entire bitcoin network is like a money manager who babysits your money on your behalf but without being a trusted party. Miners are, together, a money manager who can't steal from you. They protect funds from double-spending. In return, you pay a variable fee – somewhere between 1% and 10%, per year, of assets under management. And all of this is transparent. The price of using bitcoin – fees paid to miners and dilution of holdings in the form of newly minted bitcoin – is public and plain for all to see. The security achieved is also public.

To bring bitcoin's efficiency into relief, let's return to the dollar, in both digital and physical form. Comparing security expenditures with the dollar isn't easy. In fact, the obscurity of the dollar's security costs makes bitcoin's transparency something of a public relations liability. The decor inside the glass house will attract the most criticism. But with some napkin math about the dollar's security costs, we will make some progress in evaluating the charge that bitcoin's security model is wasteful.

How much value do various agents extract from securing the dollar's vast network of networks? We can't say for sure. We're not sure anyone else can either. But consider this beginning move: the dollar's total security expenditure is equal to all relevant measures to prevent counterfeit, false, or double-spending taken by commercial banks, the Federal Reserve, the Office of the Comptroller of the Currency (and some other arms of the US Treasury), the Secret Service, and all other relevant federal, state, and local agencies. But this raises more questions than it answers. No one, so far as we know, tracks all this information reliably in a way that doesn't double count and that distinguishes security measures in our target sense from other activities all these agents perform. Commercial banks do far more than just block false spending, for example.

The dollar's security costs are a black box. We aren't even sure how much total value is protected. In the case of bitcoin, we defined total value protected as base money. We could do something similar for the dollar and look at just M0 – currency in circulation plus commercial bank reserves held in central bank accounts.[29] This would be a mistake, though. The security measures banks and state agencies use to secure the dollar's monetary base also help secure claims to dollars, dollar-denominated accounts of other kinds, and so on. They do more than just secure base money, that is. It is by no means obvious that we can disaggregate the resources deployed to secure dollar base money from those deployed to secure some expanded measure.

How does bitcoin stack up against the dollar, then, in terms of its security fee? Is bitcoin, from this perspective, a waste? Some critics say so. We have three points in reply.

First, serious assessment here is *hard*. Have critics actually crunched the numbers? Have they compared bitcoin to alternatives? As far as we can tell, none have. The dollar's opaque security costs make comparison difficult. Critics often point to a number or two, like the billions of dollars per year paid to miners; those dollars then buy as much electricity as the residents of Washington State. But then critics conclude that bitcoin is wasteful. This is approximately as insightful as pointing to the Ohio State University's $8.2 billion dollar budget and yelling, "waste!"[30]

Have we gone astray? We began discussing energy use, and now we're rambling about security expenditures. We've gone from terawatt-hours to dollars. But spending tracks energy use. Money spent on securing the dollar buys electricity or gas, powers buildings, sends employees on trips, and feeds calories to hardworking humans. We can expect that the dollar's security expenditure will buy a significant amount of energy. But more importantly, remember the original charge: bitcoin is *wasteful*. To know that bitcoin is wasteful, we'd need to know, in part, whether bitcoin's security fee returns less in security than the security fees of other monetary networks like the dollar. In spending *money* to get *security* through the use of *energy*, bitcoin and the dollar differ less than they might appear.[31]

Second, a glance at what we *do* know suggests that bitcoin is not obviously wasteful. We agree with the critics that it *looks* clownish for magic internet money to cost billions of dollars per year to purchase terawatt-hour upon terawatt-hour of electricity as security against double-spending. But looks can be deceiving, and in this case, they are. Some people pay a few percent per year to their money managers to look after things for them. Bitcoin is like that. Some people choose to use bitcoin and they pay accordingly. Sometimes that price is 1% per year, sometimes higher. That's their choice.

We have now the contours of a challenge for any argument that alleges bitcoin's energy use is wasteful. Waste, remember, is comparative, both in relation to what is achieved and in relation to alternatives. So we issue this challenge to the critics: compare bitcoin to its alternatives and see how they stack up against each other. Find some real numbers. Disaggregate the security component of banking and regulator budgets. Distinguish base money from other measures. See how much it costs to block false, counterfeit, or double-spending of dollars. Then compare all that to bitcoin's own security expenditure. Without solid numbers here, there can be no convincing case for wastefulness.

There is a principled reason to think that this case will be very difficult to mount. Bitcoin is unusually transparent about its security expenditure. We can estimate this quite precisely by simply looking at miner revenue, along with the assumption that miners don't generally spend more on securing bitcoin than they earn for doing so. The dollar is far more opaque. Its security expenses are spread across thousands of actors, both public and private. So we're not at all sanguine that, even after running such numbers as we have, we'll find a reliable and precise comparison on which bitcoin's security fee is significantly worse than the dollars. The dollar simply isn't transparent enough for that.

And now we arrive at a third and much deeper point. We do not think that critics who call bitcoin a waste because of its security model or energy use have properly understood their own critique. Their problem with bitcoin is not really that it's *wasteful*. It is that it's not *useful*. We have implicitly addressed this problem at some length already, for we've argued that bitcoin is useful as resistance money on dimensions ranging from privacy to financial exclusion and more.

So, sure, bitcoin's security costs something. It may even cost more to secure than its alternatives – an order of magnitude more than the dollar, say. But it is *worth it* because it does things that those alternatives cannot do. Gold and physical cash can't teleport; bitcoin is gold with wings.[32] Digital dollars can't resist authoritarians; bitcoin does.

Bitcoin is resistance money, and resistance money makes the world better. All things that make the world better come at a price, and bitcoin is no exception. But it is worth that price. For a few billion dollars a year, all paid voluntarily, and for less than half of 1% of global electricity use – far less than is used for global tobacco production, mind you, or American clothes dryers or any number of other things – bitcoin provides a monetary lifeline to billions. Worth it.

Unsurprisingly, making a new global money is expensive, especially when that money can do things few others can. Bootstrapping new technologies can be tough, especially when it's managed by no centralized corporation, much less by a powerful state. But the bitcoin network manages your money without being a trusted money manager. In return, you pay higher fees. For those who need resistance money – worth it.

This "it's worth it" response depends on some controversial claims about what's valuable and how various goods stack up against each other. It depends on the soundness of the arguments given in the previous chapters, or arguments like them. It requires that bitcoin is indeed resistance money and that the existence of resistance money has made our world – the messy and imperfect world we inhabit – better. What shall we say to those who disagree about those values and goods? What about those who reject all of the reasons given in Chapters 5 through 8?

We say this: we can disagree about what's valuable and about how we want to use energy. Those who find bitcoin wasteful may avoid it. Non-users pay nothing towards bitcoin's energy use and security. This is good.[33] But those who find bitcoin useful may, of their own free will, pay miners to secure the network through energy. Behind the veil, this arrangement is exactly what you'd want. Not knowing whether bitcoin would be useful for you, you'd likely want to have the option to use it and thus the option to pay miners to secure it, by transacting or holding.

Who gets to decide whether bitcoin is wasteful? You do. And so do we. Ideally, everyone does. We each decide for ourselves whether to use bitcoin. We each decide, that is, whether to pay bitcoin miners to purchase energy and use it to provide network security. We do *not* get to decide for others whether they ought to think bitcoin is wasteful and whether they get to decide whether to pay bitcoin miners to use energy to secure it. That is how a free society works, and it is the world one would want behind the veil.

Bitcoin is far from unique in this respect. People often disagree about the allocation of resources. Some people think that mosques are a waste because of their intricate designs and all the effort and energy to create them. Others disagree. Who gets to decide? You do. And so do we. Ideally, everyone does. We each decide for ourselves whether to support a local mosque or not. We each decide, that is, whether to give our time and attention and money to a local mosque or simply leave them alone. That is how a free society works, and it is the world one would want behind the veil.

Autocrats and despots and paternalists, of course, disagree. They believe that they are especially well-suited at detecting what is truly valuable. They believe that they deserve special control over energy use. Aspiring autocrats should, again, heed the veil argument. When you wake up, you stand a good chance of being one of the 2.6 billion people living under authoritarian rule, in need of resistance money. The wise stance to adopt behind the veil is one of openness to bitcoin with a standing preference for a world in which individuals can choose whether or not to use it and pay for its energy costs.

We have presumed thus far that bitcoin users pay for the energy bitcoin uses. And they do, in the sense explained earlier – through fees and dilution of holdings. But using energy isn't neutral. Bitcoin's energy use changes the world beyond bitcoin, in both good and bad ways.

9.3.3   Energy externalities

It is time to present and evaluate by far the most impressive objection to bitcoin's approach to security through energy. This objection says that bitcoin users don't pay the most important costs for its energy use; the rest of us do, at least in part. Energy use has externalities. Carbon emissions from burning fossil fuels, most importantly, spur on climate change. A voracious appetite for electricity can put pressure on power grids and drive up prices for other consumers.[34] And the e-waste resulting from outdated and discarded mining rigs creates another kind of environmental harm, that of junk piled higher and deeper.[35] So, the objection goes, users accrue the benefits and everyone else pays for the negative externalities.

Focusing on bitcoin's energy use as such or its use of large amounts – these are red herrings. Critics who fixate on these objections have lost sight of a much deeper problem. For if bitcoin distributes benefits to users and costs to everyone else, it is a pollutant. So even if bitcoin's aggregate benefits outweighed its aggregate costs, it might still be unfair. And then it wouldn't matter so much that everyone can choose to use bitcoin or leave it alone. When the makeup factory down the street is dumping toxic sludge and glitter into your water supply, it's little consolation that you can choose not to buy their products.

So if bitcoin's approach to security faces a problem, it resides in the externalities of its energy use. Behind the veil, this is what we'd want to know: Do the negative externalities of bitcoin's energy use negate all the benefits we've claimed for it in previous chapters?

Let's find out.

Notes

1. Gold and the dollar are, in game-theoretic terms, Schelling points.
2. Treasury (1999).
3. Cornell University Police (2022).
4. For a fascinating tour of the history of counterfeiting, some more recent cases, and challenges money makers face in fighting off forged money, see Christin et al. (2008).
5. Lopp (2018).
6. Perlroth (2021).
7. Davis (2013).
8. The reward for any block is the sum of its fees (paid by transactors) and subsidies (newly minted bitcoin awarded to the winning miner).
9. A point to which we'll return in Chapter 11: if one or more of these variables is too low, bitcoin's measures against double-spending will be less credible. This paragraph describes things only at the level of a block. For present purposes, this broad approach will do. More fine-grained measurements will look at the cost of rolling back a particular transaction or the cost of double-spending a particular UTXO. See Shinobi (2021b).
10. The idea here isn't complicated; assuming it doesn't cost as much to mine a block as you'd get in rewards, there's an incentive for new miners to enter the industry and spend more on mining than you do. An equilibrium outcome, where that incentive disappears, is where the cost of production approaches rewards. And this is exactly what is happening; see Das and Dutta (2020) and McCook (2023).
11. In addition to standard economic principles and the outcomes they predict (see the previous footnote), two lines of empirical evidence support this claim. First, bitcoin miners often go bankrupt, which is evidence of thin margins. Second, some bitcoin miners are publicly traded firms, and their financial reports also indicate razor-thin margins. For more on the economics of mining, see Valfells and Egilsson (2016), Ciaian et al. (2021), Cross and Bailey (2023), Section 3, and McCook (2023).
12. This observation is compatible with the further claim that all this hardware is expensive because bitcoin is itself expensive. That bitcoin has a non-zero price, in other words, is what motivates miners to spend all that money on hardware and energy.
13. Cuthbertson (2017).
14. To their credit, *Newsweek* has since published a much more informed take on bitcoin mining; see Carter (2022).
15. Some even guessed that iPhones use as much electricity as two refrigerators each (they don't). For extensive documentation of alarmist stories along these lines, and lessons for future research about the energy footprint of new technologies, see Koomey (2017) and Koomey and Masanet (2021).
16. For incisive methodological commentary on and citations to nearly every extant study of bitcoin's energy use up to the time of publication, see Lei et al. (2021).

17. Our numbers about energy use and emissions derive from the Cambridge Bitcoin Electricity Consumption Index (2023). This is an independent and academic source, maintained by reputable and independent scholars at the Cambridge Centre for Alternative Finance. Precise and reliable estimates of bitcoin mining's energy use are hard to find. The lower bound for the Cambridge estimate is 8.47 GW; the upper bound is 25.05 GW; so there is more uncertainty in these numbers than what a quick glance might suggest. There are other attempts to measure bitcoin's energy use and associated carbon emissions. One is from a graduate student and Dutch central bank employee (formerly known as "Dogeconomist"), who now moonlights as "Digiconomist," a bitcoin pundit and energy hobbyist; see Digiconomist (2014) and Digiconomist (2022). His numbers tend to be inflated. Another comes from the Bitcoin Mining Council, an industry coalition that mostly represents North American mining operations; see Bitcoin Mining Council (2022a) and one of their sample quarterly reports, Bitcoin Mining Council (2022b). Their numbers are, unsurprisingly, on the low side. In what follows, we'll rely on neither of these sources and generally favor the numbers from Cambridge. The Cambridge methodology is best, in our view, at giving ballpark figures for bitcoin's energy use but less reliable at estimating its energy mix and associated carbon emissions – more on that in the next chapter.
18. See, for example, Huang et al. (2021).
19. https://ccaf.io/cbeci/index/comparisons
20. See, for example, Throuvalas (2022) or Void and Alper (2022).
21. Marginal buyers of bitcoin help pay miners to use energy. They discount for further dilution when acquiring bitcoin, of course, since bitcoin's supply schedule is known in advance, rule-based, deterministic, and ultimately capped. Someone buying one bitcoin, for example, is expressing what she thinks 1/21,000,000 of bitcoin's ultimate supply is worth. Holders, furthermore, remove bitcoin from markets that would otherwise be for sale, and so prop up its price, indirectly paying miners by enhancing the value of mining rewards.
22. Base money, in the case of the bitcoin monetary network, would just be all on-chain bitcoin UTXOs and would exclude off-chain claims to bitcoin, bitcoin-denominated credit, or bitcoin IOUs. See Hügli (2022). One reason we stick to base money here is that there is no standard way of measuring non-base money in the case of bitcoin. What's worse, off-chain claims to bitcoin often involve fraudulent or wildly nontransparent trusted parties, making reliable measurement even more difficult.
23. This is sometimes called bitcoin's *security budget*, following McKinney (2018). We prefer *expenditure* since what's in view is actual spending on security, rather than allotments towards that aim that may or may not be spent, as in ordinary budgeting.
24. About 48,000 full bitcoin nodes currently operate; see Dashjr (2022). Operation costs vary widely but clock in at less than $400 per year each; see Braiins (2022), including hardware. A safe upper bound for total node operation costs, then, is $19.2 million per year.
25. Market capitalization (circulating supply times token spot price), though widely used, can be a misleading measure, especially for highly illiquid and manipulated assets. A slightly more useful measure is realized market capitalization, which sums the spot market prices of all units at the last time they moved; see CoinMetrics (2018). Deploying this alternative measure here boosts total value protected and reduces the resulting security fee. Realized

market cap at EOY 2022, for example, was $383.22 billion, yielding an EOY security fee of 2.69% instead of 3.20%.

26. All data here are drawn from CoinMetrics.

27. Song and Aste (2020) take a rather different route to results that differ from ours but not by orders of magnitude: "in order to keep the Blockchain system secure from double spending attacks, the proof of work must cost a sizable fraction of the value that can be transferred through the network. We estimate that in the Bitcoin network this fraction is of the order of 1%." Where our approaches differ is this: we compare miner revenue to overall monetary value on the assumption that assurances against double-spending enhance user confidence in the network as a whole, whereas Song and Aste compare miner revenue in an interval to value transferred in that interval. Our approach has the advantage of being able to account for miner activity even when no value is transferred at all (empty or nearly-empty blocks). For further analysis, see Alden (2023a).

28. For more details, see Chapter 2, Section 2.5.

29. https://fred.stlouisfed.org/series/BOGMBASE

30. OSU's budget taken from https://busfin.osu.edu/university-business/financial-planning-analysis/university-operating-budget.

31. There have been few direct attempts to measure the banking sector's electricity footprint. In one industry-sponsored report, Rybarczyk et al. (2021) estimate that annually the global banking system uses 264 TWh.

32. As Alex Thorn has said.

33. We do not assert any principle here that holds with absolute generality – such a principle would risk ruling out, for example, any taxation at all (as when some people use the force of law to require others to pay for energy use they'd rather not bankroll). Our point is that for *this* use of energy, it is best to let everyone decide for themselves.

34. As it turns out, the excess power demand from bitcoin mining has counter-intuitively positive effects on electric grids and prices; see Section 10.3.2 for discussion.

35. Concerns about bitcoin e-waste are founded on gross misinformation and can be safely set aside. One influential estimate – Digiconomist (2021) – begins with the assumption that bitcoin mining rigs are useless after just 18 months and then discarded. Bitmain S9 ASICs manufactured in 2017, in truth, still command a positive resale price at the time of writing – strong evidence that they are not in fact useless. Why Digiconomist did not bother to look up the market facts, but instead stuck with a theoretical model, is a mystery we'll not solve here. In the main text of the following chapter, accordingly, we'll focus entirely on environmental concerns that center around bitcoin's emissions.

10

THE PRICE OF ENERGY

10.1   Dirty coin bad

As recently as the 1930s, inexpensive but effective insecticides were poisonous. And not just to insects – they would poison you too. Then a Swiss chemist saw insects cause both a famine in his home country and a major typhus epidemic in Russia. In an Edison-like story of repeated failure, Paul Hermann Müller hunted four years for a poison that would kill bugs but not babies. In 1939, he found an astounding insecticide which earned him a Nobel Prize not ten years later. In 1970, the National Academy of Sciences estimated that Müller's insecticide had prevented 500 million deaths from malaria alone.[1]

Then in 1972, the US Environmental Protection Agency banned the chemical for agricultural use. The world followed suit in 2004. The chemical, dichlorodiphenyltrichloroethane, commonly known as *DDT*, still enjoys limited use as an insecticide to prevent disease. But since the 1970s, dozens of countries have levied total bans. It thins the eggshells of birds of prey and has been linked to animal deformities and various ailments and diseases among human beings, including lymphoma, leukemia, and pancreatic cancer. Despite its benefits, DDT was not worth its environmental price.

Perhaps Satoshi, like Paul Hermann Müller, provided a tool for humanity that would serve its purpose well – for a time and place. But in an era of growing concerns about climate change, journalists and environmentalists claim bitcoin uses too much energy and emits too much carbon dioxide. No matter bitcoin's potential benefits as resistance money, critics argue, we

DOI: 10.4324/9781003484721-10

cannot justify its environmental costs. Perhaps we need something like the 1972 EPA ban on DDT – for bitcoin.

The previous chapter laid the groundwork for a deeper and more difficult discussion about bitcoin's negative externalities – carbon emissions, in particular. The big question is whether bitcoin's negative environmental externalities undermine the case for bitcoin behind the veil. Sadly, much of the most-cited research on the topic is not very good. At the same time, bitcoin users have incentives to trivialize bitcoin's climate impact; many outspoken bitcoin proponents reject the framing entirely, some even labeling climate change a hoax. It can be hard to know who to believe.

We will give you the real story. It lies somewhere between the apocalyptic predictions of naysayers and the casual idealism of popular bitcoin advocates. Many who paint a depressing picture of bitcoin's climate impact also argue that it doesn't need to be this way. They say that bitcoin can serve its purpose without energy-guzzling miners completing proofs of work. This is false. We will show that changing bitcoin's security model would hinder its ability to serve as resistance money.

10.2 Emissions, present and future

Using energy is how we get stuff done. But producing energy has consequences, some of which are diffuse, non-obvious, and harmful. Chief among them are carbon emissions that result from burning fossil fuels. CO_2 drifts up into the atmosphere and serves as a greenhouse gas, absorbing energy from the sun and preventing its escape from the Earth. The result is significant and human-caused global climate change. It is already here and will worsen without a solution. Climate change also stands to harm the least well off among us globally. So this is a species-level problem with unfair consequences.

This is not a book about atmospheric chemistry or environmental economics. We will not argue that global climate change is real, significant, human-caused, bad, or unfair. We take these for granted. This chapter is primarily for those concerned about climate change and bitcoin's relation to it. Even so, readers who lack these concerns may still benefit from seeing how environmentalists *should* evaluate bitcoin's carbon footprint, given their assumptions.

Bitcoin mining uses electricity, and most electricity still comes from burning fossil fuels. So bitcoin mining involves carbon emissions. We'll sometimes refer to these as "bitcoin emissions" or "emissions from bitcoin mining." To be clear, bitcoin mining rigs do not have exhaust pipes that emit CO_2. But like data centers, they use electricity, much of which does come from processes that emit CO_2.[2]

Bitcoin's emissions raise important and genuine concerns. In some scenarios, its emissions could pose real problems. But if you stick with us as we nail down numbers and trends and cover some counterintuitive ideas, you'll see that environmentalists can embrace bitcoin without betraying their values.

10.2.1 Snapshots

Greenhouse gasses aren't equally harmful; methane, for example, is a far more potent greenhouse gas than carbon dioxide. But CO_2 is the base case against which others are measured. Bitcoin mining, at present, results in something like 63.53 megatons of CO_2 equivalent ($MtCO_2e$) annually.[3]

As with energy, we can compare bitcoin to other industries or applications and their emissions footprints. Bitcoin doesn't top the list, but it's higher up than many might have guessed – about five times as much as YouTube and half as much as gold mining.

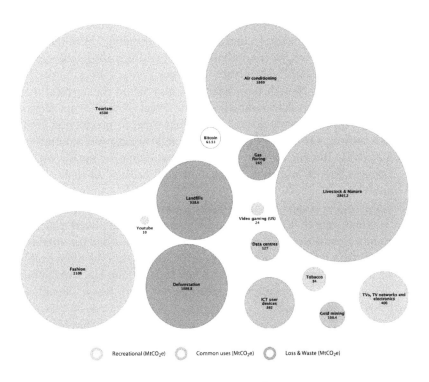

Bitcoin emissions by comparison, in $MtCO_2e$.[4]

Comparison to US states – or to entire countries – is irresistible. At present, for example, bitcoin-associated emissions fall somewhere between those of the Central African Republic (population 5.78 million) and Ireland (population 5.05 million).

Finally, total global emissions clock in at around 49,758.23 $MtCO_2e$ annually; bitcoin's share of that is about 0.13%. The astute reader will note that bitcoin's share of total emissions (about 0.13%) falls short of its share of total electricity consumption (0.5%). Bitcoin's energy mix is, on average, cleaner – that is, less carbon intensive – than the global average. For reasons that we'll explain later, bitcoin miners tend to rely less on fossil fuels and other carbon-belching energy sources than do other industries.

Comparisons can paint either positive or negative pictures of bitcoin's emissions. On the one hand, you may stack bitcoin against something that emits less than bitcoin. Bitcoin doesn't look so good then. "Why in the world," one wonders, "do we allow bitcoin to do more harm to our planet than YouTube, video games, or Switzerland? Someone really oughta do something about this ridiculous outcome." It seems like a fair point.

On the other hand, you may stack bitcoin against something that emits more than bitcoin. "Bitcoin emits far less than tobacco production, data centers, or gold mining – not to mention air conditioning," goes the idea, "and we don't seem too worried about emissions from *those* sources. Is bitcoin really all that bad?" That, too, seems fair.

Fair or reasonable though these reactions may be on the surface, they don't get us far. Favorable comparisons might reveal a critic's ignorance or hypocrisy. Perhaps the critic doesn't know that tobacco production emits more than bitcoin. Or perhaps she does and rails against bitcoin and not tobacco anyway. But such a flaw in our critic wouldn't get bitcoin off the hook. Perhaps bitcoin and tobacco are *both* bad because of their associated emissions.

The unfavorable comparisons are shallow too. They often hide substantive value judgments that deserve elucidation and scrutiny. Even if bitcoin produces more emissions than video games, so what? Is it bad for anything to emit more than video games? Or is the critic who makes the unfavorable comparison sneaking in the claim that it's *bad* for anything less worthwhile than video games to emit more than video games – you know, something less worthwhile, like bitcoin?

Let's consider what critics might mean when they suggest that bitcoin is bad for having more emissions than video games. Sometimes "bad" means "bad in some respect, but not necessarily overall."[5] Physical exercise, for example, is bad in some respects. It involves pain and risk of injury, which are certainly not good. But being bad in some respect is consistent with being overall good and being *worth it*. Physical exercise is like that – worth it despite the pain and risk of injury.

Sometimes, though, "bad" means "more bad than good," or "bad overall," or "all things considered, bad." Smoking is bad overall. Even though it can foster community and enhance memory, the costs outweigh the benefits. Notice that even things that are bad overall can have *some* redeeming features.

We can combine the different ways of understanding "bad" and the different claims about the relationship between bitcoin emissions and video game emissions to get a number of different claims. We might be saying that everything that emits more than video games is bad overall. Or that everything that emits more than video games is bad *in some respect*. Or that everything less worthwhile than video games *with more emissions than video games* is bad in some respect. Or that everything that's less worthwhile than video gaming but emits more than video games is *bad overall*.

No one who's given an emissions-based argument against bitcoin says which claim they're using. But these four claims differ in important ways. Some are true and some false. The true claims don't support an emissions-based case against bitcoin. And the claims which would support an emissions-based case against bitcoin are false.

Consider first the claim that anything which emits more than video games is bad overall. Since bitcoin does emit more than video games, we could conclude that bitcoin is bad overall. A decisive blow, if the claim is true. But it's not true, by almost anyone's lights. It would imply that tourism, televisions, fashion, air conditioning, national defense, agriculture, and the internet are all overall bad. A great many non-bad things have a bigger emissions footprint than video games.

Each of the remaining three claims about bitcoin's energy use, even if they're true, do not preclude bitcoin from being good overall. This is clearly so with the claim that it's bad in some respect for something to emit more than video games. If this claim is true, then bitcoin is, in some respect, bad. We agree: it *is* a strike against bitcoin that it emits more than video gaming. The same point can be made about the claim that it's bad in some respect to do something that's less worthwhile than video gaming but emits more than video games. Something can be bad in one respect, less worthwhile than video gaming, and still good overall. So these claims do not threaten an overall positive assessment of bitcoin.

Finally, consider the claim that it's bad overall to do something less worthwhile than video gaming but with more emissions than video gaming. If we *also* assume that bitcoin is less worthwhile than video games, then we could infer that bitcoin is overall bad. But we cannot simply assume that bitcoin is less worthwhile than video games. This is a substantive claim. We must argue for it. And so far as we know, critics have not done so. Given the arguments of the previous chapters, critics have some serious work to do to build their case. They would need to show that video gaming is more valuable than a tool for global financial inclusion, for resisting censorship, for enhancing financial privacy, and so on. We return, then, to a familiar point: some negative environmental judgments about bitcoin don't concern the environment at all. They really concern bitcoin's usefulness.

The broader lesson is a familiar one. Bitcoin's emissions do not count against it, in and of themselves. A stronger argument would pair claims about bitcoin's emissions with claims about its lack of value for the world. In doing so, the critic would need to address the uses we've covered in previous chapters. Bitcoin might not exist in a utopia, but it nonetheless does great good for our nonutopian world. Therefore, critics of bitcoin's energy use must argue either that bitcoin doesn't do nearly as much good as we've claimed for it or that the emissions are so bad that bitcoin's benefits aren't worth the price. Both routes seem unpromising.

Bitcoin isn't yet off the hook. Quite apart from whether bitcoin is a net good or net bad, it still has emissions. And carbon emissions are bad no matter the cost. We should mitigate or eliminate them when possible. What can we do about bitcoin's emissions?

10.2.2 Projections

Carbon emissions differ from the more obvious pollutants. They don't reek to high heaven. They're invisible. And their atmospheric effects run on a delay. As with good or bad habits, the effects of carbon emissions build over time. So trends matter. Let's consider those trends and where some experts project they'll take us.

We have already encountered some wildly off-the-mark predictions about bitcoin's energy use. Bitcoin's emissions have received similar treatment. One would think that our best peer-reviewed scientific venues would hold bitcoin research to a high standard. But this hasn't always been the case. Take, for example, a note led by oceanographer Camilo Mora and drafted by a group of undergraduate students in connection with their research seminar.[6] It eventually appeared as a Comment in *Nature Climate Change*.[7] The title is gripping: "Bitcoin emissions alone could push global warming above 2°C."

Their model takes the total amount of emissions from bitcoin mining and divides by the number of transactions. Then it projects that bitcoin's use follows the trajectory of other technologies – a steep adoption curve that ends with billions of users, that is – and assumes that in such a scenario, billions of additional transactions would take place on bitcoin's blockchain. The result is alarming: a world-historical spike in bitcoin-related emissions and a resulting spike in global warming.

The model fails some initial sniff tests. First, the bitcoin blockchain can't accommodate billions of transactions due to the difficulty adjustment and blocksize cap. Second, the emissions projections would also require bitcoin users to pay miners hundreds of billions of dollars a year, hundreds or thousands of times more than they do now. Their projections should have raised red flags – for their own model.

Indeed, Mora et al. suffered withering refutations in the very venue in which it initially appeared.[8] The responses identified several major problems. First, transactions do not drive bitcoin emissions; block subsidies, being the lion's share of miner revenue, do that. Independent experts accordingly reject per-transaction energy or emissions statistics as unhelpful and misleading.[9] Second, Moral et al. chose dubious adoption curves without comment or justification as to why bitcoin adoption should follow one path rather than another. Third, the model ignores bitcoin's halving cycles, which dramatically decrease miner revenue in the absence of dramatic price increases. Assuming static or growing miner revenue across such halvings amounts to assuming that bitcoin's price will skyrocket upwards or that miners will find other sources of revenue (higher transaction fees or sale of excess industrial heat from mining rigs, for example).[10] Fourth, the model assumes that "the portfolio of fuel types used to generate electricity remains fixed at today's values"[11] – i.e., that bitcoin's energy mix will remain static. And finally, the model ignores how bitcoin actually scales (in layers, which remove transactions from the blockchain, and hence, from miners)[12] in favor of a fantasy, in which all transactions appear on the blockchain in ever-expanded blocks.[13]

Yet the fundamental error in Mora et al. is the assumption that bitcoin emissions scale with use. They do not. Blithely projecting from one to the other is nonsensical and betrays a poor understanding of bitcoin and the economics of mining.

Now that some years have passed since the paper's publication, we observe another major problem: the model has been empirically falsified and decisively so. In 2018, Mora et al. projected that by 2020, cumulative CO_2 emissions from bitcoin mining would reach the 500 Mt range and catapult from there.[14] 2020 has come and gone. This didn't happen. In reality, cumulative bitcoin emissions were 102.25 $MtCO_2e$ by 2020 and barely topped 200 $MtCO_2e$ by 2022. No special knowledge or understanding of bitcoin, bitcoin mining, or the economics of mining is required to recognize the model's failure. We know now that the model was off by a factor of at least two.

Despite being soundly refuted thrice over in the very journal in which it appeared, and despite being empirically falsified, Mora et al. enjoys hundreds of academic citations and thousands of mainstream ones. It lies within the "99th percentile [ranked 18th] of the 349,688 tracked articles of a similar age in all journals and the 98th percentile [ranked 2nd] of the 77 tracked articles of a similar age in *Nature Climate Change*."[15] It's even been cited in a report from the White House on bitcoin mining and the environment.[16] Virtually none of the mainstream reporting that draws on the paper shows any awareness of its poor methodology or the justifiably scathing pushback from the scholarly community. Mora et al. is a spring, and from it flows a torrent of misinformation about bitcoin emissions. We can safely say that nearly every scandalous headline you've ever read about bitcoin emissions lies downstream from Mora et al.'s intellectual pollution.

This is a travesty twice over. First, it has set bitcoin climate research back years and impeded genuine understanding of bitcoin's climate impact. Second, it fuels hostile campaigns against bitcoin – all based on error. Bitcoin can survive in a hostile environment. It is, after all, resistance money. But we nonetheless mourn how this poor science has pushed many away from bitcoin by masquerading as scholarly consensus.

Fortunately, Mora et al.'s errors can guide future research. We propose these guidelines for future modeling of bitcoin emissions or climate effects:[17]

1. In the short term, look to bitcoin's block subsidy as the primary driver of mining activity, not on-chain transactions.
2. In the longer term, take into account bitcoin's halving cycle, the associated exponential decline in block subsidy, and its effects on the incentive to mine.
3. Remember bitcoin's difficulty adjustment. When hashrate increases, mining gets harder. More hashrate does not cause faster blocks or more blocks or more transactions. Nor does higher demand for block space equal faster blocks, more blocks, or more transactions.
4. When modeling mining incentives, take into account its dollar value and thus, bitcoin's price. The way to do this is to include various projections linked to various possible price paths (bitcoin price going up, going way up, staying as it is, going down, going way down, etc.).
5. Do not assume a fixed energy mix.
6. Take into account layers built on bitcoin and do not assume that increased transaction volumes associated with adoption will take place directly on bitcoin's blockchain.

Models that follow these guidelines may still fail. But at least they will avoid duplicating the errors in Mora et al.

One such attempt comes from Ross Stevens and Nic Carter, who model bitcoin's electricity use and carbon emissions under a range of possible price scenarios (meeting point 4 earlier).[18] Their model takes into account expectations about future grid energy mix and emissions associated with future use of grid energy (point 5). The fundamental dynamics include bitcoin's exponentially declining block subsidy (points 1 and 2) and global grid decarbonization (point 5).[19] Thus far, the Carter-Stevens model has been more accurate than Mora et al. It predicted bitcoin emissions of 20–60 $MtCO_2$ in 2022 and 20–120 $MtCO_2$ in 2023; the actual numbers were 53.01 and 63.53 $MtCO_2$. Looking forward, the Carter-Stevens model projects that bitcoin's share of global emissions will peak within the decade, at around 0.9%, and decline thereafter.

With an honest look at the data, and a sober knowledge of how bitcoin works, we can hold two claims in tension. On the one hand, like most other industries, bitcoin mining uses electricity and, therefore, contributes to climate change. But on the other hand, it does not significantly contribute to climate change, and our best available evidence indicates that it will not significantly contribute to climate change in the future either. Doomsday predictions, whether from journalists or academics, do not reflect the real world.

Thus far, we have downplayed neither bitcoin's emissions nor the importance of rectifying them. In fact, we would like to rectify them. And we have some ideas about how to do that.

10.3   What to do about bitcoin's emissions

10.3.1   Harm reduction for policy-makers and users

It would be better if bitcoin had fewer carbon emissions. With that in mind, we turn to the question of harm reduction. We have suggestions for both policy-makers and bitcoin users. We'll first propose some rough guiding principles and then apply them.

The main principle is to respond *proportionally* – cater responses to an activity's level of emissions. Activities that contribute to the lion's share of emissions, like gas-powered transportation, deserve the lion's share of our focus. And activities with fewer emissions deserve less focus. Disproportionate focus incurs an unacceptable opportunity cost, like a student who devotes more energy to insignificant assignments than to the term paper that largely determines the course grade.

From the proportionality principle, we infer two more principles.

First, since some activities have less carbon-intensive energy mixes, some activities can use more energy than others but deserve weaker responses. Energy mix matters. The global low-carbon or zero-emissions mix is somewhere between 16% and 20%, for reference.[20] Harm reduction should prioritize activities to the extent that they fall below this average.

Second, proportionality demands neutrality.[21] Targeting specific uses of energy from subjective opinions about their worth will tend to produce disproportionate and, therefore, inefficient responses.[22] Those in power typically lack the necessary insight to judge the value of certain activities, especially when they involve new technologies. Because non-neutral responses are almost always disproportionate, they lay bare a mismatch with the public goal of emissions reduction. So beyond the risk of unnecessarily impinging on our freedoms, non-neutral responses stand to erode public trust and heighten political polarization. A non-neutral response motivates opponents to respond in kind when they later come to power. It's best to stay off the political teeter-totter in the first place.

We recommend these principles because they direct action to actual harm. We do not recommend them out of special pleading for or against bitcoin. They are themselves neutral. Policy-makers should act to reduce the carbon intensity of *all* electricity generation. Climate action at this level will mitigate emissions not just from bitcoin but also the remaining 99.91% of emissions as well. It will, furthermore, have the largest effect, especially on those industries with worse energy mixes. Neutrality underlies a pragmatic approach towards actual harm reduction.

We could also eliminate subsidies for carbon-intensive energy generation. Across the world, governments heavily subsidize the generation of energy from fossil fuels. The International Monetary Fund reports, for example, that "Globally, fossil fuel subsidies were $5.9 trillion or 6.8 percent of GDP in 2020 and are expected to increase to 7.4 percent of GDP in 2025."[23] By removing subsidies and allowing markets to price fossil fuels more naturally, we would likely see positive effects in the fight against global climate change. The same IMF report notes:

> Raising fuel prices to their fully efficient levels reduces projected global fossil fuel CO2 emissions 36 percent below baseline levels in 2025 – or 32 percent below 2018 emissions. This reduction is in line with the 25–50 percent reduction in global GHGs below 2018 levels needed by 2030 to be on track with containing global warming to the Paris goal of 1.5–2C.[24]

If policy-makers are serious about cleaning up bitcoin, they'll clean up the grid. Doing this would also clean up bitcoin's 0.13% share of global emissions and much of the remaining 99.87% as well. For this isn't a bit-coin problem. It's an energy production problem.

Our proposal has two potential problems. The first is political. We suspect that globally, lawmakers lack the will to eliminate subsidies for fossil fuels and for all the usual reasons – lobbyists, campaign finance structures, kick-backs, public choice theory, and so on. The second is distributive. Eliminat-ing subsidies will increase the market price of fossil fuels, and some of that burden will fall on the shoulders of the least well off. These two problems could be resolved in tandem by redirecting subsidies for the production of fossil fuels towards renewables instead, bringing down their market prices.

We're under no delusions that politicians will save us from global climate change. They helped create this mess, after all, and often fail us. When polit-ical institutions flounder, cypherpunks take things into their own hands. As it turns out, bitcoin's design uniquely enables direct climate action.

Investments in green bitcoin mining – mining that uses electricity from carbon-neutral sources – can precisely offset any incentive to mine cre-ated by holding bitcoin. When such investments are made in proportion to holdings, bitcoiners can "green" their portion of the network, entirely eliminating any emissions that result from their use of bitcoin. The idea, proposed by Troy Cross and Andrew M. Bailey, has a few moving parts. Due to bitcoin's fixed issuance and difficulty adjustment, adding more hashrate nets a bigger share of the fixed rewards compared to those who fail to add a proportional amount of hashrate. Those who don't add as much hashrate lose revenue. Since certain investments in green mining can make green mining more profitable, in total, compared to non-green min-ing, investing in green mining can thereby increase the overall proportion of bitcoin's green mining to non-green mining.[25]

Notably, bitcoin's energy mix is already impressive – somewhere between 37% and 50% of the electricity that miners use is zero-emissions, compared to the global average of 16%–20%. If bitcoiners do their part to green the network in the way suggested earlier, that number will see a significant boost.

El Salvador is leading the way.[26] The country holds bitcoin. It mines bit-coin, too, using zero-emissions energy. Their share of bitcoin's total mining accounts for a greater proportion of global hashrate than their proportion of holdings, which means they are doing more than their fair share. Other entities should follow suit and take direct climate action in this way.

10.3.2 Positive environmental externalities

Bitcoin's physical footprint also opens the door for positive environmental externalities. Though critics tend to fixate only on the negative ones, we should also factor in any positive environmental externalities in any over-all evaluation.[27]

To bring them to the fore, let's begin with bitcoin's unique electricity demand signature. Miners are unusually portable and interruptible. You can mine bitcoin anywhere, anytime, as long as you have an energy source that you can parlay into electricity – like waste energy or stranded energy. You can stop and start at will without lost progress that requires a do-over. Profit margins, furthermore, are razor-thin. Mining is a highly competitive and global race to find a winning hash. It is also zero-sum since block rewards are fixed no matter how many miners enter the race. When one miner successfully produces a new block and nets its reward, every other miner fails. This makes bitcoin mining extremely price sensitive.[28]

Other consumers of electricity are generally less portable, less interruptible, and less competitive. Factories, once built, stay there, usually fairly close to population centers for labor and transportation. If you stop mid-widget, you might lose your progress and have to start all over again. We can put traditional data centers further out in the boonies. But they need 100% uptime or close to it. Aluminum smelting is slightly more flexible and tends to happen far from population centers. But it still needs to be near bauxite deposits, or at least with easy access to cheap transportation to those deposits. And a smelting operation that produces a ton of aluminum doesn't thereby block another from doing the same. Virtually no other consumer of electricity is as ruthlessly competitive yet as geographically flexible as bitcoin mining.

When bitcoin's market price is in the middle of a wild upswing, it is profitable to mine even with expensive electricity. Mining is viable on grid power in these special circumstances, perhaps even in the middle of a bustling city.[29] But this is far from the norm and simply cannot remain the case for long due to bitcoin's intrinsic features. High prices drive new miners to enter the race, which increases hashrate and decreases profit margins for all. Only those with the cheapest energy survive long. In equilibrium, then, miners are pushed to the spatial and temporal corners of energy markets. And unlike other industries, they can actually go to those corners.

The spatial and temporal corners of energy markets increasingly rely on our least carbon-intensive energy sources. Among these are off-grid renewables like wind and solar, which have few other buyers. And for good reason – electricity sourced from wind and solar is intermittent and distant. So without partnering alongside a different kind of energy consumer, renewable energy seems ill-suited for serving human civilization.[30]

Now you know why bitcoin's energy mix is far less carbon-intensive than the global average. Bitcoin is, as some have said, the dung beetle of energy consumption. The economics of mining drive hashrate to the margins, which tend to be served by energy sources that few others want or can even use. These happen to be *renewable* sources of energy. Bitcoin is, as a result, *inherently* self-decarbonizing. It decarbonizes without policy interventions or direct climate action from its users.

It gets better. A sustainable future is carbon-neutral. A happy future is energy-rich. To get both futures together, we must, first, electrify everything. Doing so would replace gas engines with electric motors, gas furnaces with electric resistance heaters, and so on. But electrifying everything does nothing if all this electricity comes from burning fossil fuels anyway. So second, we need a massive buildout of renewable energy sources. Otherwise, we simply push the emissions bubble somewhere else under the carpet.

Bitcoin helps here too.

We need thousands of new wind and solar farms. Many will be out in the middle of nowhere, generating electricity when and where no one wants it. To match supply with demand, we must radically overbuild intermittent sources so that people have enough electricity even when the sources suddenly generate much less electricity. Someone has to pay for this massive infrastructure buildout.

Bitcoin users are already footing the bill. They pay miners, remember. And miners, in scrounging for electricity on the margins, subsidize the development of renewable energy. When bitcoin mining increases, so does clean energy generation.[31] Bitcoin is the partner we need to drive the buildout of renewable energy sources. Bitcoin miners are always willing to pay something for excess energy. They mitigate a central barrier to overbuilding – costs.[32] The economics predicts all this, and the empirical data show that it's happening. One recent survey put it this way:

> Bitcoin mining proved profitable in all of the examined planned installations, and by adopting this approach, investors could generate economic returns from otherwise unutilized assets. Simultaneously, this strategy could address the climate impact of conventional bitcoin mining operations, which rely on fossil-dominant grids. Therefore, integrating bitcoin mining with planned renewable installations could enhance the economic potential of renewable projects during their precommercial operation phase and correspondingly mitigate the climate challenges tied to traditional mining practices.[33]

Bitcoin mining doesn't just help with balancing intermittent sources of renewable energy. It also helps balance grids themselves. Power plants conduct a very delicate balancing act, making sure that energy creation matches demand. Often this means producing less energy than they could produce; this is known as "curtailment." Without curtailment, plants would produce energy with no buyers.[34] But when demand spikes, like when Texans need to heat their homes in an ice storm, the grid needs enough power to provide what's needed. When there's not enough power to go around, there's an outage.

Bitcoin's unique demand profile helps. When power is cheap and demand is low, bitcoin miners operate at full capacity. By adding demand in times of low demand, bitcoin miners help ensure that there's enough power to go around in times of high demand. For when other sources of demand spike – and with it, power price – bitcoin miners power down.[35] Given their extraordinarily thin margins, energy costs would exceed their block rewards.[36] By providing demand during periods of low demand and powering down in periods of high demand, bitcoin miners provide the grid with a power cushion. In times of high demand, like a Texas ice storm, residents can pick up the slack of available power that miners have left behind.

Miners play a unique role in methane capture too. Methane is a potent greenhouse gas – between 28 and 85 times more potent than carbon dioxide. Since burning methane produces carbon dioxide, doing so is one of the more effective strategies for slowing down global climate change.[37] Carbon dioxide isn't great, of course, but methane is far worse. Methane is, furthermore, one of the byproducts of oil drilling. Sometimes this methane is flared – burned day and night in an open flame. Sometimes it is vented. And that is a problem.[38] Oil fields across the planet, many far from major population centers, need a turbine atop every methane vent, burning that methane and turning it into useful electricity. Who will pay for these turbines? Who will supervise the safe burning of methane? What industry is so location agnostic and scalable as to plop electricity demand atop every would-be vent in every oil field? You know the answer.[39] Bitcoin mining for this use is expanding rapidly, turning an extremely dangerous greenhouse gas into a much less dangerous one.[40]

10.3.3 Positive social externalities

A complete assessment of bitcoin's effects on the world must take into account all of its externalities. We've been focusing on environmental ones – positive and negative – but some externalities are social. The preceding chapters basically argue that bitcoin's social externalities are net positive.

Bitcoin does not just benefit its users as individuals. We are all connected. In truth, *everyone* benefits from the wide availability of resistance money. Resisting autocrats and their attempts to surveil and control the money makes the rest of us better off. Enabling inclusion of people on the margins isn't just good for them; it's good for the world, as it expands the web of beneficial economic activity.

To see this clearly, consider an analogy to freedom of speech. Does this freedom benefit only those who speak? Of course not. Does every speaker benefit everyone? Quite the contrary. Freedom of speech nonetheless improves our institutions, keeps our leaders accountable, inspires listeners, helps us hone our ideas, and more besides. So also for resistance money. It's not just a tool for its users. And not every bitcoin user benefits everyone. Quite the contrary. But its very existence improves the world.

Many fixate on bitcoin's distinctively environmental externalities and the negative ones at that. But this is a mistake. The environmental externalities are not as bad as the headlines suggest. The trends are promising. And bitcoin has a unique role to play as an incentivizer of renewable energy, grid balancer, and methane mitigator. It can also be fully greened through voluntary investment. And again, this says nothing of the positive *social* externalities.

10.3.4   Would removing bitcoin help?

Bitcoin mining has some negative environmental externalities. It does not follow from this that a world without bitcoin is a world without those externalities. For that to follow, it would have to also be the case that the portion of energy used by bitcoin that has significant associated externalities would otherwise go unused. There is little reason to accept this assumption. We can see why by looking more closely at two sources of energy used in bitcoin mining.

Some of the energy deployed in bitcoin mining, as we've seen, is non-rivalrous and lies on the spatial and temporal margins of energy grids. As Hass McCook explains: "they would all remain wasted, stranded and curtailed if there were no electrical loads as dynamic and flexible as Bitcoin. These are non-rival energy sources, meaning that Bitcoin miners are not competing with other customers to obtain this power."[41] Removing bitcoin from the picture would indeed remove this kind of energy use from the picture; bitcoin is the only buyer in town, at those locations and times and at those prices. But note that this kind of energy is precisely the kind that is more likely to derive from sustainable sources and thus, to have fewer negative environmental externalities. Think, for example, of a hydropower facility built atop a dam far from any city or solar farms on a desolate plain hours from civilization; they supply clean and cheap energy, for sure, but not necessarily when and where people want it the most. So this portion of bitcoin's energy would not move the needle of bitcoin's negative externalities if we simply removed bitcoin.

Turn, then, to the other portion of bitcoin's energy used – bitcoin's rivalrous energy use. Here, bitcoin miners are indeed competing with other users for energy from the grid. Much of that grid energy will involve negative externalities. But if bitcoin were not to exist, the current losers would win the competition and use that energy. Precisely because energy markets involve competition, removing bitcoin from the picture would not remove the externalities associated with this portion of bitcoin's energy.

The critic may reply that it is still harmful for any energy at all to be deployed in securing bitcoin since bitcoin is pointless or otherwise without benefit. To say this, though, is to retreat from an environmental critique of bitcoin to allegations of waste, allegations which we addressed in the previous chapter. The environmental critique of bitcoin is more powerful precisely because it avoids value judgments about bitcoin's utility. In its most potent form, it says we can remove those externalities by removing bitcoin. But if that just isn't true, the critique fails.

10.4   Doing without proof of work

Some pundits say bitcoin's benefits could be captured without any of its environmental costs, if only bitcoin transitioned from proof of work to some other consensus mechanism like proof of stake.[42] They are wrong.

Traditional voting systems use trusted authorities to prevent fraudulent votes from swaying outcomes. If we put the bitcoin ledger to a simple vote, without trusted parties, it would predictably buckle under a phenomenon much like fraudulent voting. In a so-called sybil attack, swarms of cheap nodes would spam the network with their own favored versions of the ledger. To combat sybils, decentralized consensus procedures must make block production costly. Bitcoin makes block production costly through computation, which requires both energy and hardware. Proof of stake networks make block production costly through staking, which requires devoting capital to the network in the form of its native tokens.

Proof of stake networks pair a staking requirement, their anti-sybill mechanism, with a protocol for agreeing on the state of the ledger. Instead of bitcoin's heaviest chain rule, proof of stake networks rely on one among many weighted voting systems. These networks randomly pick an eligible validator, weighted usually by the amount staked, to propose the chain's next block. By pairing staking requirements with a stake-based consensus rule, proof of stake networks protect against double-spending without proofs of work and so without a significant energy footprint.

In bitcoin, miners compete, and doing the most computational work provides the best chance for publishing the next block. In a proof of stake network, validators also compete. But here, staking the most tokens provides the best chance for publishing the next block. Whereas bitcoin's price of security is energy, the price of security for a proof of stake network is the opportunity cost of capital. What is staked cannot be deployed elsewhere.[43] Publishing blocks is costly in both, but the costs differ.

Although mining brings security to bitcoin, proof of stake systems use less energy and have fewer associated emissions. So why hasn't bitcoin switched to a proof of stake system?[44] Proponents of alternative cryptocurrencies have begun to ask this question in the public arena. One of them has even paid Greenpeace USA millions of dollars to campaign for a change in bitcoin's code.[45] The campaign is unlikely to succeed, and this is for the best.

Bitcoin is resistance money. The whole point is to remove the need for trust in and permission from central authorities. Bitcoin enables anyone to save, receive, and transmit value without being subject to the whims of a trusted party. In the ordinary course of things, many have no need for resistance money. Regular money – compliance money – serves them well enough. But resistance money is for edge cases, for those on the margins and those who might someday find themselves there. For people on the margins, compliance money simply will not do since it subjects them to the whims of monetary authorities who lack the will or the ability to help them.

Proof of stake networks are vulnerable to centralization and involve trust. For this reason, bitcoin would risk becoming a less resistant form of resistance money if it were to transition to proof of stake. Notice, then, that we don't claim that proof of stake networks are worthless. They have served as centers of experimentation and innovation – in decentralized exchange, borrowing, and lending, for example. In operating 24/7/365 globally, without requiring documentation, the most liquid proof of stake networks greatly improve on the nine-to-five, Monday through Friday, permissioned, surveilled, and non-global financial services companies. Even so, bitcoin would lose something precious were it to replace proof of work with proof of stake.

In changing to proof of stake, bitcoin would first risk a loss in decentralization over time. Three different features of proof of stake engender this risk. First, proof of stake has inherent rich-get-richer effects. Those who stake more tokens receive a higher proportion of block rewards. Those who re-stake their rewards then enjoy the beauty of compounding interest. Certain technical schemes can mitigate these effects. But the rich-get-richer effects still remain because networks dangle rewards proportionally to the amount of funds staked.

Second, proof of stake bestows power in proportion to wealth. Validators publish blocks in proportion to the size of their stake. As a result, the bigger the stake, the more power one has to censor certain kinds of transactions. In proof of stake, affluence affords influence.

Third, the influence that owes to staking resists the forces of entropy. The main ingredients in bitcoin mining – hardware and energy – create a continuous churn in influence over block production. Miners come and go thanks to the sheer physicality of block production – as with cars, use wears bitcoin mining rigs down. In addition, declining energy prices force some miners out of business. Miners are forced to renew their stock of hardware and buy new energy by selling their newly minted bitcoin. But in a proof of stake network, control over abstract coins enables those who stake them to retain influence indefinitely. Proof of stake validators can simply tread water. Their operations are capital intensive but have close to no ongoing operating expenses.

Put these three pieces together. With proof of stake, bitcoin would be more vulnerable to centralization because the bitcoin rich could capture an increasingly large share of power over block production and more easily retain that power. The more control they have over block production, the more control they have over which transactions are included in the blockchain. And for this validating service, they're paid in coins which, if re-staked, would confer more control over block production, which rewards them with more coins, which confers more control, and so on – a vicious cycle. This risks turning validators into mediators. And it's a risk that isn't worth taking, given bitcoin's goal of being resistance money without makers, mediators, or managers.

In addition to putting bitcoin's decentralization at risk, moving to proof of stake would also reinsert the very trust it was designed to eliminate. Imagine connecting your node to the bitcoin network just as someone tries to double-spend. As they produce an alternative chain with a different history, your node will, in short order, see both candidate chains. One will include a block with the original transaction. The other will have a different series of blocks from then on, without the original transaction. Which history will your node endorse? Bitcoin nodes choose on the basis of the candidate histories themselves – no trusted party required. Your node will choose the chain with the most accumulated proven work.

Imagine instead connecting your node to a proof of stake network, just as someone tries to double-spend. As before, your node sees two inconsistent transaction histories and must choose between them. Both chains embed proofs that a validator with the requisite tokens had attested to the transactions they contain.[46] But the chains alone don't say which includes the original transaction and which includes the double-spending attempt. Nor can they endorse one or the other based on accumulated proof of work, without trusted parties. Proof of stake networks must rely on trust.

To decide which chain to build on, you find a trusted node – perhaps run by a programmer everyone respects or the foundation that runs most of the research and development for the network. You ask that node for a "checkpoint," a cryptographic snapshot of the state of the chain regarded by the queried node as canonical, at some past time. The original transaction will show up here, but the attempted double-spend will not. Your node endorses the chain endorsed by the trusted party and rejects the other. So in such cases, proof of stake networks achieve consensus through trust.[47]

Trust carries risk. Trusted parties – from individuals to foundations – can be compromised or influenced or controlled by corporate or state authorities. Relying on them introduces vulnerabilities bitcoin was designed to avoid. It makes resistance more difficult and compliance more likely.[48] Trusted parties are checkpoints, and checkpoints all too easily become chokepoints.

These worries involve edge cases. But edge cases are where we most need resistance money. This is where bitcoin shines and where proof of stake networks may falter. Central authorities and trust serve us well – until they don't. And when they don't, there is bitcoin.

Finally, many bitcoin users are aware of all this; they like proof of work and what it does. Thus, an attempt to change the bitcoin code along these lines would not be universally accepted. Some reasonably high percentage of nodes would continue to run the bitcoin code that used proof of work. The result would be a chain split. And as we discussed in Chapter 3, chain splits diminish bitcoin's network effects and its usefulness.

Again, our point is not that proof of stake networks are bad.[49] Rather, the point is that bitcoin's goals are best achieved with proof of work instead. To change the code would be to compromise the mission. It would be to replace resistance money with resistance money *lite*. If much of what we've said so far is true, we better not risk our best shot at having resistance money from misplaced or disproportionate concerns about bitcoin's emissions.

10.5 Energy behind the veil

These last two chapters have addressed the most powerful set of concerns about bitcoin. Since we've been through some twists and turns, let's recap the main points.

Like other monies, bitcoin deploys significant resources for security. Billions are spent every year to protect the dollar. The same is true for bitcoin. Bitcoin users pay miners, in particular, to prevent double-spending. Miners use electricity: about 0.5% of global consumption. In paying for so much electricity, bitcoin users express their values: they evince a preference for resistance money secured against double-spending despite its tradeoffs.

The deeper problem is not energy use but carbon emissions. Bitcoin's carbon emissions are real: about 0.13% of global emissions. Much of the public discussion around this number and its likely trajectory stems from bad science. Better models, which take into account how bitcoin actually works and broader trends in energy, predict that this share of emissions will peak within the next decade and then decline.

The best way to manage bitcoin's emissions, from a perspective of harm reduction, is to proportion climate action to share of emissions. The best way to do that, from a policy perspective, is to clean up energy grids by repealing fossil fuel subsidies. Bitcoin users, too, can help by investing in green bitcoin mining operations in proportion to their holdings. Bitcoin's positive social and environmental externalities, furthermore, help tip the scale in bitcoin's direction. So despite its emissions, bitcoin still deserves an overall positive evaluation.

Importantly, removing bitcoin from the picture would likely not thereby remove associated emissions. For some of bitcoin's energy footprint, other users of energy would simply step in and use the energy currently deployed in bitcoin mining. Other portions of bitcoin's energy footprint involve no competing for energy at all; here, bitcoin is a unique buyer from renewable sources on the spatial and temporal margins of energy grids. This non-rival portion of bitcoin's energy footprint has few associated emissions. So in either case, deleting bitcoin from the world is not a reliable route towards deleting associated externalities.

Paid propaganda campaigns that urge bitcoin users to "change the code" and switch to a proof of stake model are misguided. In adopting proof of stake, bitcoin would risk becoming less resistant resistance money. With proof of stake, bitcoin could very well become highly centralized and reliant on trusted authorities. Compliance money, hello.

These points are useful behind the veil in evaluating bitcoin and its approach to security. We have already argued at some length that if you didn't know who you'd be, you'd want a world with bitcoin; that's Chapters 5–8. Bitcoin's emissions do not give us reason to change this basic stance. Not only are bitcoin emissions already likely to peak and fall but there are also concrete steps we can take to accelerate that decarbonization. Behind the veil, whoever you turn out to be can both benefit from bitcoin and help mitigate or remove any negative externalities. Bitcoin remains a net good for the world. And from behind the veil, we should likely choose it.

Notes

1. National Academy of Sciences, Committee on Research in the Life Sciences of the Committee on Science and Public Policy, The Life Sciences: Recent

Progress and Application to Human Affairs, The World of Biological Research, Requirements for the Future (Washington, DC: GPO, 1970), 432.

2. Such are bitcoin mining's so-called "Scope 2" emissions – secondary effects following not from an activity itself but from the production of the energy it uses.

3. We will, as noted before, rely on the Cambridge numbers about bitcoin energy use and associated emissions. There is some reason to think that their methodology overstates bitcoin's emissions. It relies on a "top-down" approach, moving from electricity use and grid energy mix to conclusions about emissions. Since bitcoin mining takes place, increasingly, with zero-emissions energy sources that are off-grid, a "bottom-up" approach can yield both more reliable and more favorable numbers. On the Cambridge model and some recent changes to it, see Neumueller (2023). For some very recent discussion by an industry analyst, see Batten (2022).

4. https://ccaf.io/cbeci/ghg/comparisons

5. Philosophers might here say, "*Pro tanto* bad."

6. Harmon (2022) tells the fascinating story of how this now-notorious paper made its way from an undergraduate research methods seminar into the pages of a peer-reviewed scientific journal.

7. Mora et al. (2018).

8. See Houy (2019), Dittmar and Praktiknjo (2019), and especially Masanet et al. (2019).

9. Here's how the Cambridge Centre for Alternative Finance puts the point (2021): "The popular 'energy cost per transaction' metric is regularly featured in the media and other academic studies despite having multiple issues. First, transaction throughput [i.e. the number of transactions that the system can process] is independent of the network's electricity consumption. Adding more mining equipment and thus increasing electricity consumption will have no impact on the number of processed transactions. Second, a single Bitcoin transaction can contain hidden semantics that may not be immediately visible nor intelligible to observers. For instance, one transaction can include hundreds of payments to individual addresses, settle second-layer network payments [e.g. opening and closing channels in the Lightning network], or potentially represent billions of timestamped data points using open protocols such as OpenTimestamps."

10. Read (2022): Chapter 8. See also Hutabarat (2023): Chapter 2.

11. Mora et al. (2018, p. 932).

12. This is an unfortunately common mistake. Two recent examples of the same error are Hinzen et al. (2022) and Malik et al. (2022). We discuss their shortcomings in more detail in Bailey et al. (ms).

13. Indeed, bitcoin's blocksize cap is one of its most hardened properties; see Bier (2021).

14. See Mora et al. (2018, p. 932), figure 1c, "Cumulative emissions from Bitcoin usage." We are assuming that the use of "Gt" in the chart is a typo and that "Mt" is intended. If not, the projection is off by a factor of more than 1,000 and implies that by 2020, cumulative bitcoin mining emissions would have matched those of all of human civilization from 1860 to 2014 (a historical emissions factoid cited on the first page of the paper). Another interpretive option has it that figure 1c concerns not cumulative emissions from bitcoin (as the title suggests) but rather bitcoin's additions to global cumulative emissions. For discussion of further interpretive difficulties and inconsistencies in figure 1c, see the supplement to Masanet et al. (2019, p. 654).

15. Nature Climate Change (2022).
16. OSTP (2022).
17. For more criteria ("best practices") for responsible research on bitcoin's energy use and associated emissions, see Lei et al. (2021), who argue that every extant study falls short of the mark on at least one dimension. According to their view, the Cambridge index comes closest to being satisfactory, despite the fact that it's not constructed in a ground-up way. We concur. For other criteria for sound bitcoin research and a bevy of open questions, see Rudd (2022).
18. There is a catch. Though not derived from an undergraduate research seminar, the Carter and Stevens model we discuss was developed by analysts from within the bitcoin industry. Some will think that, for this reason, it should be taken with a massive grain of salt. We have some sympathy with that reaction. The key thing to pick up is not some specific projection about future bitcoin emissions but rather, the general shape of results from more responsible methods.
19. "The global share of electricity generated from renewables – which includes hydro, solar, wind, geothermal, biomass and marine energy – increased from 20 percent in 2010 to 27 percent in 2019. This rise was driven by declining costs, especially of solar and wind energy, plus growing demand resulting from increasing environmental concerns. . . . Using renewable sources instead of fossil fuels significantly lowers the carbon emissions associated with electricity generation. Renewables are expected to grow rapidly in the future, as their costs continue to decline, and environmental concerns persist. This trend may ultimately lead to the decarbonization of electricity grids. In the IEA 2020 Sustainable Development Scenario, renewables reach a share of 52 percent in 2030 and 72 percent in 2040, as coal, gas, and oil are gradually phased out" Carter and Stevens (2021, p. 20).
20. https://ourworldindata.org/electricity-mix
21. There is a lively debate in policy circles about use neutrality and a closely related stance of renewable energy technology neutrality (as between wind or solar, for example). Much of it revolves around whether there are principled economic reasons to remain neutral (to avoid distorting market price signals, for example) or whether moral principles require as much. Our case is different and much simpler and pragmatic in spirit: use-neutral policy is better for reducing actual harm. For critical discussion and citations, see Azar and Sandén (2011).
22. Given the economics of bitcoin mining, some attempts to single out bitcoin emissions via legislation are bound to backfire; see Cross and Bailey (2023).
23. www.imf.org/en/Topics/climate-change/energy-subsidies
24. www.imf.org/en/Topics/climate-change/energy-subsidies
25. Cross and Bailey (2021, p. 7) note that the strategy has several unexpected benefits. They put it this way: "Bitcoin's difficulty adjustment and fixed issuance allow investors to precisely balance their price-based incentive to mine with an equal and opposite difficulty-based disincentive, simply by mining sustainably themselves. Broad adoption of this practice would further strengthen bitcoin's settlement and security assurances, improve not only bitcoin's environmental reputation but its actual environmental record, and unlock capital currently bound by either ESG mandates or individual conscience. In sum, we see no real tension, or tradeoff, between an enthusiasm for bitcoin and a thoroughgoing commitment to a low-carbon future. Rather, we see the possibility for a win for bitcoin, and for the world." See the full whitepaper for a complete explanation of how this works and the relevant math.

26. For a full case study of El Salvador in the context of sovereign adoption of bitcoin, see Cross and Bailey (2023).
27. For a more careful description of the mechanisms at play and extensive documentation of how bitcoin is helping build an energy-rich and carbon-neutral grid, see Paez and Cross (2022). Of all research on bitcoin and the environment, theirs is among the most reliable and nuanced, and we follow it closely. See also Rudd (2023) and Consolvo and Caron (2023).
28. An important factor here is specialized hardware – the main capital expense for mining. For discussion, see Carter and Stevens (2021).
29. This is why stories about bitcoin mining reviving an otherwise unprofitable coal plant happen only during bull markets; see, for example, Milman (2022).
30. Bastian-Pinto et al. (2021).
31. Dogan et al. (2022).
32. Ibañez et al. (2023).
33. Lal et al. (2023).
34. Niaz et al. (2022).
35. For a robust and up-to-date analysis of flexible loads from mining and their effect on power markets, see Menati et al. (2023).
36. For a recent example of bitcoin's role as flexible demand, see Gkritsi (2022b). For useful treatment of data centers with flexible demand as vital companions to renewable energy buildout, see Fridgen et al. (2021).
37. See Jackson et al. (2019).
38. See, for example, Tabuchi (2020).
39. And so does a recent report from the US White House; see OSTP (2022, pp. 23–24).
40. It is a matter of some controversy whether to call this kind of operation deserves the title "net carbon negative." One key factor is whether the relevant counterfactual is one in which methane that is actually burned to mine bitcoin is simply vented. If so, then the title seems apt, with the caveat that mining with methane is not strictly *carbon*-negative but is, rather, *carbon-equivalent*-negative. For discussion and extensive analysis, see CoinShares (2022).
41. McCook (2023, p. 24).
42. See, for example, Kaplan (2022).
43. See, though, Dale (2021).
44. Hinsdale (2022), for example.
45. Gkritsi (2022a). Greenpeace USA does not ordinarily take on corporate sponsors. For Chris Larsen, co-founder of Ripple Labs (creator of the XRP token), they made an exception and accepted $5 million to launch a campaign against bitcoin mining.
46. Since chain histories can include cryptographic proof that tokens have been staked by a validator, they are not entirely subjective. But choosing between them, for a node that is coming online, does require some trust, and so the condition proof of stake networks fall under has become known by their proponents as "weak subjectivity." See Buterin (2014).
47. Here's how one proponent of proof of stake describes the procedure: "new nodes joining the network, and nodes that appear online after a very long time, would not have the consensus algorithm reliably protecting them. Fortunately, for them, the solution is simple: the first time they sign up, and every time they stay offline for a very very long time, they need only get a recent block hash from a friend, a blockchain explorer, or simply their software provider, and paste it into their blockchain client as a 'checkpoint.' They will then be able to securely update their view of the current state from there" Buterin

(2014). Though proof of stake protocols have added bells and whistles since 2014, their fundamental approach remains the same. For updated and more comprehensive thinking about proof of stake and the limits of blockchains with weak subjectivity in edge cases like these, see Buterin (2022).

48. There is a fix of sorts. It requires, perhaps ironically, that bitcoin continue to exist and not operate through proof of stake. The idea: stash checkpoints for a proof of stake network, not with trusted nodes but rather within the bitcoin blockchain itself. Since the bitcoin blockchain is extraordinarily expensive to roll back, and operates without trust, these can reliably indicate tampering with chain history, as when double-spending. Backstopped by bitcoin's security, proof of stake networks could host genuine resistance money, at least when it comes to trust. For discussion and technical details, see the Babylon protocol as in Tas et al. (2022) and the Pikachu protocol as in Azouvi and Vukolić (2022).

49. At least one of us has grave ethical misgivings about proof of stake networks and their tendency towards enriching the already rich. But our argument in this section makes no use of that conviction.

11
AGAINST BITCOIN

11.1 Let the hate flow through you

Many are skeptical about bitcoin. It's understandable; bitcoin is strange and new and deserves some skepticism. But some positively *hate* bitcoin. Here's Charlie Munger, longtime friend and business partner of Warren Buffett: "I never considered for one second having anything to do with it. I detested it the moment it was raised. . . . It's just disgusting. Bitcoin is noxious poison."[1]

Years later, he doubled down:

> Of course I hate the bitcoin success. I don't welcome a currency that's so useful to kidnappers and extortionists and so forth. Nor do I like just shuffling out of your extra billions of billions of dollars to somebody who just invented a new financial product out of thin air. I think I should say modestly that the whole damn development is disgusting and contrary to the interests of civilization.[2]

When it comes to criticism of one of his own investments, however, Munger insists that "we ought to have a law . . . people shouldn't be allowed to cite the defects without citing the advantage. It's immature and stupid."[3] And yet Munger doesn't follow his own advice; he has never cited bitcoin's advantages. For whatever reason, bitcoin ruffles his feathers. And he isn't alone. Bitcoin arouses passion, for and against. Studied indifference is rare.[4] And despite bitcoin's size and youth, objections abound.

DOI: 10.4324/9781003484721-11

Some deny that bitcoin improves the world or that it has any reason to exist. Others go further, claiming that bitcoin worsens it. We have implicitly addressed objections of both kinds in the preceding chapters:

- Bitcoin has no point (Chapters 1 and 2)
- Bitcoin isn't money or pales in comparison to other cryptocurrencies (Chapter 3)
- Bitcoin proponents are biased (Chapter 4)
- Bitcoin's monetary policies are silly (Chapter 5)
- Bitcoin is too volatile to be money (Chapter 5)
- Bitcoin isn't private enough or perhaps too private (Chapter 6)
- Bitcoin enables too much crime (Chapters 7 and 8)
- Bitcoin's security model is wasteful or pointless (Chapter 9)
- Bitcoin has negative environmental externalities (Chapter 10)

Other objections remain. We can't cover every single one; bitcoin seemingly inspires new objections every day, some quite shabby. Instead, we'll address objections to our main thesis – that bitcoin, as resistance money, makes the world better. We'll divide objections into which of three constituent elements of our main thesis they target: (i) that bitcoin is apt money, (ii) that it is useful for resistance, and (iii) that it makes the world better. In some cases, we'll show that the objections fail. Others suggest areas of ongoing research rather than decisive reasons for or against a pro-bitcoin stance. None, we'll argue, give any real reason to doubt our main thesis or its three elements.

Some of these objections will, again, prove to be rather shabby. But we promise the reader this: every single one of them has been proposed, in full seriousness, by someone or other. So we will take them seriously as well, steelman them insofar as we are able, and assess them in a measured and informed way.

11.2 Is bitcoin apt money?

We've argued that bitcoin is an apt money, suitable for use as a commonly accepted medium of exchange. This claim is partly empirical; bitcoin is a money for some people in some places (see the data presented in Chapter 3, Section 3.1). But bitcoin isn't like other monies. Its unique blend of properties – or, if you like, its sheer *weirdness* – invites theoretical objections that purport to show it isn't a useful money. Here are a few.

11.2.1 Bitcoin might be hacked

Bitcoin has critical cryptographic scaffolding. If someone could find a vulnerability here or there and exploit it, bitcoin might come crashing down like a Jenga tower. The cryptography in bitcoin is crucial in two places: mining and transacting.[5] Cracking the cryptography in either place would undermine bitcoin's claim to being apt money.

Someone who cracked bitcoin's mining algorithm could complete proofs of work without working much. Such a hacker could "outwork" all the other miners without spending a nickel on energy or hardware. They could also roll back the chain at will, mine empty blocks, or censor transactions. With any such attack on the mining algorithm, users would at least temporarily lose confidence in bitcoin's ledger.

Or imagine if banks hung the keys outside to all their safety deposit boxes. Anyone could grab keys and gain access to customer valuables. Nobody would use them for anything of value. Bitcoin might suffer a similar fate if someone cracked the cryptography involved in protecting and spending it. By cracking private keys or a digital signature algorithm, someone could spend someone else's bitcoin. Without an immediate remedy, an attack could cause a massive loss in trust.

However, both attacks are incredibly unlikely. Worries about bitcoin's cryptographic primitives often ignore that they're among the most battle-tested and well-understood digital building blocks in the world. They are open-source and contain few mysteries. For several years, the world's best hackers have failed to win a multibillion-dollar bug bounty program – by hacking the network itself and cashing out. Bitcoin's private keys also have built-in redundancy. Cracking them would likely require breaking not one algorithm but two. And cracking bitcoin's mining or signature algorithms would pose enormous problems for the internet overall, not just bitcoin. Finally, bitcoin's design is intentionally modular; in cases of emergency, one primitive could be swapped out for another.

In sum: bitcoin's cryptographic scaffolding is sturdy and provides no reason to think that it cannot serve as a money.

11.2.2   Bitcoin is insecure

Whereas some worry that bitcoin uses too much energy, bitcoin experts more often worry that in the long run, bitcoin will use *too little*.

Miners earn bitcoin for protecting the ledger against double-spending attacks. The less valuable the reward, the less energy miners will devote to earning it. Less valuable rewards would mean that blocks come more cheaply. If they come cheaply enough, someone could roll back the blockchain and double-spend or carry out other attacks.[6] Bitcoin would garner less trust. And with less trust, bitcoin would depreciate, as would the miner reward, making blocks even cheaper to produce. Thus begins the doom loop. Miners and users would race for the exits, leaving behind an unused and then unusable network. Bitcoin would not be money, not resistance money, and not much of anything at all.

Recall that the miner reward has two elements: (1) the subsidy – bitcoin's issuance – which began in 2009 at 50 bitcoin per block and halves every four years and (2) transaction fees. Satoshi had hoped that fees would eventually comprise a larger portion of the mining reward as the subsidy decreases. This has yet to happen consistently. Fees currently remain a small fraction of miner rewards – typically less than 1%. But miner rewards have remained strong thanks to bitcoin's price appreciation. Security through bitcoin appreciation is not a sustainable strategy, however. To sustain bitcoin's current security expenditure without additional fees across the next ten halvings, its current purchasing power of around $25,000 per bitcoin must double, double again, and then double eight more times – to over $25 million per bitcoin. Bitcoin's price will someday cease to double as the subsidy continues to halve. This raises significant questions about its long-term security model.

For bitcoin to work as money, it must offer users sufficient assurances that double-spending would prove too expensive. While bitcoin has successfully resisted double-spending attacks, its history does not show that the present security expenditure, whether in absolute terms or considered as a ratio against total value protected, is *just enough*. So we have little empirical reason to think that miner revenues must maintain current levels for sufficient security assurances.[7] For all we know, Bitcoin might remain secure with reduced miner revenues. But we don't know where the revenue floor might be either. We could try to find it; just let miner revenues dwindle until a successful attack occurs. But this could jeopardize bitcoin's future.

Concerns about a potential doom loop due to decreasing block subsidies have persisted since Bitcoin's inception.[8] Someday, bitcoin's price will cease to double every four years even as the subsidy continues to halve. We simply don't know whether transaction fees will pay miners enough to secure the network. While we recognize the concern as legitimate, we can also envision some more optimistic scenarios.

In the most optimistic scenario, bitcoin enjoys high transaction fees through user demand for block space. Users hope the ledger will include their transactions. Since block space is a scarce resource, users outbid one another with higher transaction fees to have miners include *their* transactions over others'. Increased demand for block space, then, could drive up fees. What, though, might ultimately boost block space demand?

A potential catalyst is state crackdown. As governments push central bank digital currencies on or pull cash out of circulation, private and censorship-resistant payments will become more difficult, and more costly, to achieve. As these costs rise, so does bitcoin's appeal.[9]

Layer 2 payment networks like lightning might also increase demand for block space even though they might initially appear to undermine demand for bitcoin's block space. While lightning payments are off-chain and fee-free to miners, they make block space more efficient, akin to adding lanes to a highway. The Jevons paradox says that increasing a resource's efficiency *induces* rather than reduces demand.[10] Just as adding lanes to roads in cities like Atlanta and Austin can lead to more traffic, a payments network that increases bitcoin's block space efficiency might induce more demand for block space.[11] Because lightning ultimately settles to bitcoin's ledger, more lightning usage might indirectly boost demand for block space. So Jevons paradox suggests that layer 2 payment networks might boost both base layer traffic and transaction fees.

Relatedly, bitcoin's capabilities could expand to include features present in other networks, such as enhanced privacy (like Zcash or Monero) or advanced smart contracts (like ethereum). Market participants reveal a preference for these extra features by paying for them. Compared to bitcoin users, for example, ethereum users paid ten to 100 times more in transaction fees on a weekly basis through 2022.[12] Paul Sztorc has developed an idea to bring these capabilities to bitcoin through "sidechains" – alternative blockchains that plug into bitcoin's ledger and piggyback on some of its security assurances.[13] The main idea – Drivechain – introduces trust-reduced, two-way bridges between bitcoin's main network and new alternative networks. These networks enable new uses for bitcoin and pay miners additional revenue.

The result could be a win-win-win situation. First, bitcoin users who want more functionality from bitcoin get it. Second, since the sidechains pay fees to miners, bitcoin users who want a sustainable long-term security model might get it. And third, the sidechain users themselves benefit from bitcoin's security assurances; their chains approach bitcoin's own level of tamper resistance without having to spin up a new global network of miners.

Maybe Drivechain will happen; maybe it won't. The broader point is that bitcoin users may themselves take steps to drive up miner revenue from fees. Network security depends on people and their choices. Guessing what will happen must take into account not just the possibility of a doom spiral but also ways bitcoiners might coordinate action, with the explicit aim of avoiding that spiral. It is not obvious that they will do nothing to stave off doom. Indeed, the more invested they are in the network, whether literally or otherwise, the more implausible it is to suppose bitcoin users will stand idly by as a crisis brews.

Another optimistic scenario involves a subtle upending of miner economics as we know them and goes back to an old idea of Satoshi's.[14] At present, total miner revenue equals block rewards and approximates block production costs. But mining, like other industries, produces byproducts – heat, most importantly. Profitably harnessing these byproducts would break the aforementioned equality. Miner revenue could, inclusive of profit from byproducts, exceed block rewards. Thus, despite declining block rewards, incentives to mine could remain static – or even grow.

How would this work? First, note that specialized mining chips are, from the point of view of physics, strictly equivalent to resistance heaters. Running electricity through them generates exactly as much heat as would be generated by running the same amount of electricity through an electric space heater. Indeed, mining chips, from that perspective, just are resistance heaters. It doesn't follow that resistance heaters or mining chips are the most economically efficient way to, say, raise the temperature of a room. Thanks to heat pumps, they aren't. But for any heating task where space heaters are apt, mining chips are no less apt, in terms of how much heat is generated per watt. Second, remember that bitcoin mining is, to a greater degree than perhaps any other use of energy, geographically and temporally agnostic. It can happen anywhere and at any time. In theory, then, just about any industrial application that used resistance heaters – greenhouses, drying facilities, water purification, and so on – could replace them with bitcoin miners without any loss of efficiency. What matters most of all here is the cost of specialized mining hardware. If the hardware is sufficiently cheap, rational actors in need of additional heating will use bitcoin miners on account of the extra revenue that mining would create in the form of even very low fees. In this scenario, mining machines double as subsidized heaters.

Mining for heat has just begun.[15] And the use may not grow enough, or fast enough, to make up for declining block rewards. But critics have, almost universally, ignored it and other scenarios like it. This is unwise for anyone hoping to predict bitcoin's future monetary use.

Another range of scenarios involves what we'll call *defensive mining*, an idea Satoshi mentions in the initial software announcement in January 2009. There, he says that "there will probably always be nodes willing to process transactions for free."[16] In the software at the time, a "node" was also a miner; these jobs had not yet been differentiated. So Satoshi here speculates that some people might mine for free. The idea isn't crazy. For value protection, an entity that holds several billion dollars' worth of bitcoin might mine unprofitably for themselves or pay a small "security" fee for others to mine. Nations might also mine unprofitably to ensure that foreign entities never gain too much control over the bitcoin network, especially if they use bitcoin for international trade or their citizens hold wealth in bitcoin. We can imagine "hash treaties," too, where nations agree not to limit weaponry to end an arms race but to limit power over financial settlement to end a race for hashrate. More liberal nations like the United States might also support the bitcoin network to counter the influence of more authoritarian countries; although bitcoin isn't the dollar, it's not the digital yuan either.[17] In these scenarios, bitcoin's security remains high even if transaction fees fail to pay for most of it.

In other scenarios, bitcoin fails to thrive as resistance money but at least survives. Perhaps bitcoin scrapes by with a lower security expenditure. It could still serve as a niche but useful resistance money.

Here's how. In the absence of defensive miners, lower mining revenue enables cheaper attacks. With lower levels of security, users must now endure longer wait times before considering a transaction to be safe from double-spending. They would have to wait until the transaction is buried beneath a chain of blocks long enough that would make rollbacks and other attacks sufficiently expensive.[18] To be safe, users may need to wait hundreds of blocks (days) instead of the more typical six blocks (an hour).[19] This would not be ideal. But bitcoin would still bring its users significant benefits when it came to privacy, censorship-resistance, and so on. They would just have to wait. Not all people on the margins can afford to wait, of course. So we note that even in such a scenario, users needn't suffer these wait times on the lightning network given assumptions about the age and liquidity of certain open channels. Lightning payments would still occur instantly. And since they are non-revocable, users with sufficient outbound liquidity could send bitcoin on as soon as they received it, blocking clawbacks.

In other survival scenarios, bitcoin sacrifices one or more core features. Bitcoin users might agree to run node software that breaks the sacred supply cap and introduces tail emissions – say 0.1 bitcoin per block in perpetuity. This would set a precedent for changing bitcoin's monetary policy and would ruin its appeal as a predictable monetary asset. Issuance schedules are like Pringles – popping leads not to stopping.

Instead of changing monetary policy, some might push to redistribute Satoshi's roughly 1 million bitcoin to miners to buy more time for fees to gain traction. Redistribution at a rate of .1 bitcoin per block could grant bitcoin around 50 extra years of leeway. But such a strategy would at least partly undermine bitcoin's censorship-resistance. Once the network decides to confiscate the funds of its own creator, why not confiscate the funds of thieves or of those perceived to be bad actors? Sometimes, slopes are indeed slippery.

Finally, instead of increasing miner revenue, the network could decrease bitcoin's security costs. As a last resort, users could replace proof of work with some version of proof of stake. Block production would then require users to pledge bitcoin to earn fees. Bitcoin might survive but, for reasons explained in Chapter 9, not without a hit to its status as resistance money.

Bitcoin's future security expenditure merits concern. But the concern provides insufficient reason to think that bitcoin will ultimately fail as resistance money. If pressed, we would guess that one or more of the optimistic scenarios will come to fruition. And if they don't, one or more of the survival scenarios will. But our position is far from certain – as the critics' should be too. Whatever the case may be, bitcoin's security expenditure remains an open research question. The correct stance requires openness to new evidence, not dogmatic insistence on any one outcome.

11.2.3 Bitcoin is too divisible

1 bitcoin equals 100,000,000 satoshis (sats). And at present, one sat has the purchasing power of about $0.00025 – small enough for very small payments. Satoshi himself imagined that bitcoin could enable micropayments and unlock previously impossible forms of commerce.[20] But if bitcoin significantly appreciates, micropayments may become infeasible once again. Even mundane payments for things like candy bars and coffee might prove difficult if the exchange rate for a sat exceeds a penny. We should note that at this point, bitcoin would have already become a wild success in terms of purchasing power, trading at $1 million per bitcoin.

But suppose that bitcoin has succeeded so wildly that micropayments have become infeasible. For bitcoin to fulfill Satoshi's hope for micropayments, or even just small payments and transaction fees, the network would need to subdivide bitcoin even further.[21] Doing so would require a hard fork – the kind of rule change that could cause the network to fracture between nodes that run the new software and nodes that don't.[22] It would not be an easy protocol change to implement, in other words.[23] But it would not be impossible.[24] And bitcoin users eager to access micropayment opportunities themselves would have good reason to coordinate and implement it.[25]

Some notable bitcoin critics have alleged that making bitcoin more divisible would ruin its scarcity. They think that creating smaller denominations would increase the overall amount of bitcoin, as if dividing a pizza into smaller pieces would result in more pizza. More *pieces*, yes, but not more *pizza* – not when we measure by mass, say. Similarly, adding a new denomination like a tenth of a sat would result in more pieces of bitcoin but not more bitcoin. Bitcoin would remain capped under 21 million. This cap is what bitcoin proponents have in mind when they tout its "scarcity."[26] Bitcoin's scarcity would remain intact, even with increased divisibility.

11.2.4   Bitcoin's throughput is too small

The Visa network processes around 1,700 transactions per second and could process up to many times more.[27] Bitcoin's ten-minute blocks, by contrast, have data limits. As a result, the bitcoin network maxes out at roughly seven transactions per second, 1/240th of Visa's own throughput. So, concludes the objection, bitcoin is doomed as a payments network; it can't handle more than a small fraction of payments from a single credit card company. Only a very small portion of humanity could use it as money.

However, the Visa-Bitcoin comparison is apples-to-oranges.[28] Unlike bitcoin, Visa isn't a final settlement layer. Visa transactions settle instead through commercial inter-bank settlement networks and, ultimately, through master accounts with central banks. One such settlement network, Fedwire, handled 204,490,893 transactions in 2021.[29] That amounts to 6.5 transactions per second – not far from bitcoin's own maximum throughput. Bitcoin is a decentralized Fedwire.

Visa is a payments layer built atop the Federal Reserve. And in much the same way, bitcoin has its own payment layers built atop it. So we should instead compare Visa to one of these, the most important being the lightning network (recall our description of lightning in Chapter 6, Section 6.6.2). Users on the lightning network enjoy the security of bitcoin's ledger to send and receive bitcoin nearly instantaneously and at very low cost.[30] Transactions currently cost less than a penny.[31] And its theoretical throughput matches or exceeds Visa's own. Here's why. For an on-chain bitcoin transaction to settle, the entire network must recognize it as valid. For a lightning transaction to settle, only the lightning nodes involved must agree. Each payment channel on the lightning network requires one base-layer transaction to open and one base-layer transaction to close. But once the payment channels exist, there is no technical constraint on the lightning network's transaction rate beyond familiar limits that restrict all internet traffic – the speed of light, latency and throughput for node connections, and so on.

Amazingly, lightning accomplishes this feat without trusted intermediaries. So apples to apples and oranges to oranges, bitcoin is to Fedwire as lightning is to Visa.[32] The main difference in each case is that the bitcoin side works without trusted intermediaries. The original worry about bitcoin's throughput almost always results from ignorance about how bitcoin scales in layers – just like the USD.

Critics might counter with a dilemma. If the lightning network gains little adoption, bitcoin will remain, at best, niche money for the few. If on the other hand, lightning gains widespread adoption, it does so at bitcoin's expense. Lightning payments aren't bitcoin payments, goes the thought; lightning transfers, instead, bitcoin IOUs.

The dilemma rests on a misunderstanding. The lightning network doesn't transfer IOUs; unlike Visa, it is a scaling layer without credit. It consists of a complex web of two-party payment channels, where each party has posted bitcoin. A payment from Barry to Fred over lightning begins with Barry pushing some bitcoin into Fred's direction. This begins a series of pushes, from channel to channel, until Fred receives the final push from someone with which he's connected. The "pushings" themselves don't appear in the ledger; each requires a signed bitcoin transaction that remains off-chain. Then when a payment channel closes, both parties submit to the latest account balances over lightning and update their addresses with an on-chain transaction. Bitcoin on lightning, then, is less like an IOU and more like cash jointly held in escrow – but with no trusted party.

11.2.5   Bitcoin is not backed

Money is a social kind. Money is also real. Squaring these two truths isn't always easy. Social kinds are things that we made up, after all, and it is very tempting to contrast made up things with real things. Santa, for example, is made up – and thus, not quite real.

But again, money is real. It is so real that you might think it, therefore, requires special ties to things that aren't made up. Money, so the thought goes, is *grounded in* or *backed up* or made *substantial* by those ties. Bitcoin has no formal ties to vaults of gold or centralized issuers. And indeed, we have argued that it is a fictional substance. So it is tempting to think that it is unusually imaginary and unfit for monetary duty.

We can make the worry more useful by distinguishing various ways that something might be "backed" and thus, sufficiently tied to reality:

- *Reality*: as when an item is not fictional
- *Representation*: as when an item stands for some physical good (or is that physical good)
- *Rights*: as when an item entitles its holder to redeem it for some physical good
- *Recognition*: as when an item is endorsed by a state as being legal tender
- *Requirement*: as when merchants or creditors are, as a matter of law, obligated to accept an item in exchange for goods or to pay off debts

None of these conditions, as a matter of fact, are necessary for something to be a money.

Look at the dollar. It is fictional, or at least non-physical, but this hasn't stopped the dollar from being money. Dollar banknotes and digital ledger entries are physical, of course, but the dollar quantities they represent aren't (Chapter 2, Section 2.11). So money can be non-physical. So also with bitcoin and its UTXOs. Bitcoin UTXOs aren't physical either, but neither are the quantities of bitcoin they represent.

It was once the case that dollars represented physical goods. The word "dollar" began its life as a unit of gold or silver, after all. Dollar certificates, accordingly, once stood for amounts of gold or silver stored in the vaults of public or private issuers. Sometimes those certificates gave their holders legal claims to those vault contents and could be redeemed for them. There's just one problem. The dollar hasn't involved rights of this kind since 1933. And it hasn't represented a physical good since 1971 or so. This has not, again, stopped the dollar from being money. So money needn't stand for some physical good or be able to be redeemed for some physical good.

Historical examples of commodity money show that money needn't be recognized by a state as legal tender nor must merchants be legally required to accept something in order for it to be money. Gold, for example, has been widely used as money across space and time without any legal structures granting it official status or requiring merchants to accept it.[33] Local niche monies, like cigarettes in a prison, further tell against the need for state recognition and legal compulsion to accept.

On these specifications of "backing," bitcoin isn't backed, and neither are other familiar monies. Here's an understanding of "backing" on which bitcoin is backed, though. Consider the familiar idea that the dollar is backed by the entire US economy. Backing, in this sense, is what happens when people buy and sell using something as a money; it's a relation uniting those real goods and services with some medium of exchange. On this understanding of the term, bitcoin turns out to be backed after all, for there are people who accept bitcoin in exchange for real goods and services. If the dollar is backed by the US economy, then bitcoin is backed by the bitcoin economy.

There's one sense of "backed" in which the dollar is backed and bitcoin isn't. Consider the oft-quoted saying that the dollar is backed by the "full faith and credit" of the US government. Usually applied to treasury securities, this might be another way of saying that the US will take measures to support the dollar and its price stability. Bitcoin lacks an issuer, or any central authority to support bitcoin and protect its price stability. This is, in part, why bitcoin has been much more volatile than the dollar. What bitcoin does have to support its price is some number of people who stand ready to buy bitcoin when price goes low enough. We'd also remind the reader that many currencies have backers, in the current sense, with poor track records.

Money is defined by, and only by, its role. Something is money if and only if it is a commonly accepted medium of exchange. That's it. No more, no less. Since this role can be satisfied by just about anything regardless of its ties to the physical world, money doesn't ultimately have a "backing" requirement.[34]

11.2.6   Bitcoin is a Ponzi

Some say that bitcoin is a Ponzi scheme, or otherwise pyramid-shaped.[35] A closely related critique claims that bitcoin is at best a zero- or negative-sum financial game. The conclusions thought to follow from these premises may include that (i) bitcoin is, therefore, a bad investment; (ii) bitcoin, therefore, couldn't be money; or (iii) bitcoin, therefore, cannot create net benefits for the world.

Critics of this kind seem to picture bitcoin as a machine where you put dollars in and hope to get more dollars out. Early investors buy bitcoin and cash out at a tidy dollar-denominated profit, thanks to the fact that later investors are willing to pay more. These later investors would be foolish, the idea goes, because they pay more for their bitcoin despite the fact that bitcoin is not a productive enterprise and has created no real goods or value. Such a game would be zero-sum, at best, because you can't take dollars out of the machine without others putting them in. It might even be negative-sum because, along the way, miners and exchanges have skimmed off the top in the form of fees and such and burned real resources along the way.

If bitcoin only offered the world these profit-seeking games, bitcoin would indeed be Ponzi-like or pyramid-shaped. We say "-like" and "-shaped" because bitcoin does not satisfy the recognized definition for Ponzi and pyramid schemes. Ponzi schemes are a form of fraud where someone deceives others into investing in a non-existent enterprise and pretends to pay investors from its profits. Behind the scenes, though, earlier investors simply receive money from later investors. But bitcoin involves no such fraud or deception. Its ledger is transparent, and its rules are open-source. Bitcoin also has no CEO to cook the books in secret.

In a pyramid scheme, members receive profit from those they've recruited to sell their products, who receive profit from those they've recruited, and so on. Bitcoin, by contrast, is a monetary asset. It has no non-monetary uses, no hierarchical organizational structure, no product. It is no more a pyramid scheme than any other asset traders and speculators and early adopters can use to amass more value.

However, perhaps bitcoin does involve a greater fool scenario.[36] Greater fool scenarios unfold when an asset can only be sold for a profit when someone comes around who is willing to pay more for it and when that higher price is *more than it is worth*. The judgment that price exceeds actual value is crucial here. For bitcoin, this would mean that its market price exceeds its worth and that later investors will fundamentally overpay.

The greater fool critique discounts the worth of a rule-governed, private, censorship-resistant, and inclusive money. We have argued that resistance money is indeed valuable for its users and for the world. Though bitcoin has no non-monetary use, its monetary uses set it apart from other monies. It can do things that they cannot.

The greater fool critique furthermore assumes that bitcoin's worth has not kept pace with its adoption. This flies in the face of what we know about monetary networks; they become more useful as they grow. Bitcoin really has become *more* useful over time as its network has expanded; it is easier than ever to receive, store, or send value using bitcoin. So we find it neither foolish nor surprising that users are willing to pay more for bitcoin now than they did in 2009. People pay more for bitcoin now, in part, because they can do more with bitcoin now.

Our point is not that bitcoin is a good investment, much less that you should buy some. Nor do we claim that it's a bad investment. Remember the provisos in Chapter 1; we don't pretend to be price prophets or investment advisors. We claim, rather, that none of these observations about the structure of bitcoin investment or speculation support the conclusions that it couldn't be money or that it doesn't overall benefit the world.

11.3   Is bitcoin resistance money?

We have made a positive case for the claim that bitcoin is not just a money but resistance money. In sum, bitcoin is a lifeline to people across the world in need of a private, censorship-resistant, or inclusive monetary institution.[37] The point isn't theoretical. In a recent letter to Congress, for example, 21 human rights advocates from 20 countries write:

> We can personally attest – as do the enclosed reports from top global media outlets – that when currency catastrophes struck Cuba, Afghanistan, and Venezuela, bitcoin gave our compatriots refuge. When crackdowns on civil liberties befell Nigeria, Belarus, and Hong Kong, bitcoin helped keep the fight against authoritarianism afloat. After Russia

invaded Ukraine, these technologies (which the critics allege are "not built for purpose") played a role in sustaining democratic resistance – especially in the first few days, when legacy financial systems faltered.[38]

Despite bitcoin's actual use as resistance money, some objections suggest that it will not continue to serve in this way or that it is not nearly so resistant to autocratic intrusions as its proponents imagine.

11.3.1 Governments will crack down

Skeptics have long warned that state-led bans on bitcoin are just around the corner. They are not totally wrong. In the US, Senator Joe Manchin introduced a bill to ban bitcoin in 2014.[39] It didn't get anywhere. But at least 17 countries – Algeria, Bangladesh, Bolivia, China, Ecuador, Egypt, Ghana, Iceland, Indonesia, Kyrgyzstan, Mexico, Nepal, Nigeria, Russia, Thailand, Turkey, and Vietnam – have at one time or another attempted partial or full bans.[40] These measures have targeted mining, buying, selling, custody, or spending of bitcoin. Apart from direct bans on bitcoin, some countries may impose stringent regulation that might hinder bitcoin: bans on new fossil-fuel power plants for bitcoin mining,[41] burdensome requirements on sending bitcoin from an exchange to a noncustodial wallet,[42] and so on.

Do such bans or restrictions have their intended effects? It is surprisingly difficult to say, in part because it's hard to know counterfactuals like the number of people in Russia that would have used bitcoin had it not been banned. In some places, the banning of bitcoin seems to drive increased adoption.[43] As Reuters puts it, "the clampdown has highlighted the benefits of using currencies outside the central bank's control."[44] When a person distrustful of a government sees that the government is threatened by something, they tend to look at the thing a bit more closely. So perhaps government action against bitcoin will not only fail to hinder the adoption of bitcoin as resistance money but facilitate it.

Instead of asking whether governments will ban bitcoin, we suggest a different question: Why have attempted bans failed?[45] With traditional financial systems and their many intermediaries, censorship is cheap. With bitcoin, it is not. Bitcoin significantly *raises the price* of such interference (see Chapter 7, Section 7.7). Bans have little hope without an extremely intrusive response that uses significant resources. But even these sorts of responses may fail.

States that hope to disincentivize bitcoin adoption will vary in their overall enforcement ability and the degree of punitive measures they're willing to take.[46] Though large and effective governments might find that their rules are readily followed with only a light touch, small governments' attempts might be similarly successful only if they are willing to mete out very harsh punishments. But such draconian measures may discourage use of bitcoin at the price of state credibility and might even backfire.

For any state, though, outright bans are expensive to execute. As states see the light, they might turn to more subtle measures. States could perhaps undermine bitcoin most effectively by improving their own monetary institutions.[47] More responsible monetary policy, less restrictive and more private digital payment channels, more usable cash, fewer draconian pushes towards central bank digital currencies, and so on. If these reforms crushed the demand for bitcoin, its failure in this case would count as a success.

For all this, though, states also have incentives to adopt bitcoin – to acquire it, mine it, trade in it, and support its ongoing use as money. El Salvador, for example, has done all of these things. But the country has thus far inspired few imitators.[48] Should others eventually follow suit, though, dire predictions that governments will successfully ban bitcoin will require significant qualification.

11.3.2 Developers are authorities

Software developers and the companies that employ them often enjoy enormous power. Big tech firms can, at the whim of an executive, surveil or block all sorts of messages. The networks these companies operate have authorities, and they sometimes exercise their powers in disquieting ways. Could bitcoin be captured in this way? Is it likely that its developers could be persuaded or cajoled into breaking bitcoin somehow or building chokepoints into its core protocol? Is bitcoin helpless against such attacks? By looking at how bitcoin's software differs from the products of a tech firm, we see that the answer to all these questions is "no."

Bitcoin is neither owned nor controlled by any company. There is no bitcoin CEO or bitcoin foundation. Bitcoin is free and open-source software. Anyone may inspect its code or modify it and run the modified code as they please. There are, therefore, no "official" bitcoin developers, for there is no officer to confer on them that status.

Anyone may interact with the bitcoin network, furthermore, using any software they like. There is, however, one implementation that many bitcoin users deploy, sometimes called "Bitcoin Core." And there is a group of software developers who've contributed to Core over the years.[49] Since there is no bitcoin foundation to pay them and since bitcoin can't be printed for free, many rely on charity to fund their work on Core. Individual donations are part of their income stream. Corporate sponsors include Blockstream, BitMEX, Lightning Labs, Block, Chaincode, and more. Other sponsors include MIT's Digital Currency Initiative and the

Human Rights Foundation, both 501(c)(3) non-profit organizations. And though some Core developers are pseudonymous, as Satoshi was, many work under their own real names.

These facts – that one bitcoin client dominates use, that its Core developers are supported by a small group of organizations, and that many work under real-world identities – suggest a possible attack vector. Target the funding organizations, or the developers themselves, and pressure them to merge certain nefarious changes to Core.

Attacks along these lines could happen to software run by big tech firms. Their applications are typically closed-source, and users have no options about whether to use the official version or not, if they wish to interact with the relevant network. If Facebook makes a change to their software, for example, there is no guarantee that any users will know of it. Nor can users access the Facebook network using an alternative client without the change. It's Facebook's way or the highway.

Bitcoin, by contrast, is highly resistant to such attacks. Changes to the software cannot be hidden from users. Bitcoin is, as we saw in Chapter 9, Section 9.2.5, both open-source and some of the most scrutinized software in the world. Given the sheer number of eyes on the thing, it would be next to impossible to hide a change that broke bitcoin's fundamental design. And even if Core were to break in that way, no one could coerce bitcoin users to run it. They'd simply run an older version or create a "fork" of their own that doesn't include the censorship measures.

So despite bitcoin's funding model and the fact that many users execute just one version of its software which is maintained by an identifiable group of developers, they are not authorities in the relevant sense. They have no special power to block transactions on the network itself or make any changes at all to bitcoin without user consent. The fact that bitcoin is opt-in and open-source means, furthermore, that there is no realistic path towards a future in which they acquire such powers. Could bitcoin users eventually coordinate at a sufficient scale and agree to switch over to versions of the software that enable censorship? This is possible, of course. But critics who think it likely have much to learn, we suspect, about bitcoin users and their priorities.

11.3.3 Miners are authorities

Another objection suggests that bitcoin's miners are its true authorities. We'll consider two variations. The first says that miners are intermediaries. The second says that it's mining pools.

Bitcoin is designed to do without makers, mediators, and managers. But, say some, it has failed in this task, for its miners are mediators after all.[50] Miners include transactions in blocks and can block any transactions they want. Even if they never do, the very fact that they can means, according to these critics, that they are intermediaries. And they could begin blocking transactions at any time. Bitcoin was designed to be peer-to-peer and eliminate intermediaries, but it failed. So claims the objection.

This version of the objection is mistaken for reasons we've given in Chapter 2, Section 2.5. In brief: no individual miner is an intermediary. Unlike the Federal Reserve, which is an unavoidable hub in the dollar's network around which no bank can route, it is relatively easy to route around any particular bitcoin miner. Though a transaction can't get published without the cooperation of some miner or other, no single miner is necessary to get the job done. Miners, unlike traditional intermediaries, take no custody of funds. And new miners may enter freely, should old ones fail at their tasks.

A slightly more sophisticated version of the objection notes the risk posed by mining *pools*. Though no individual miner is an intermediary, miners who work together using these pools *could together* become an intermediary or authority with the power to censor. At present, no pool has this power. Even the largest mining pool, a union of hundreds or thousands of individual miners, only controls around 30% of the hash rate.

Miner / Pool	Block Mined
● Foundry USA Pool	29.0
● AntPool	27.1
F2Pool	11.9
● ViaBTC	11.4
Binance	7.3
MARA Pool	3.9
Luxor	3.2
● BTC.com	1.7
● SBI Crypto Pool	1.6
● Braiins Pool	1.1
● Poolin	1.1

Bitcoin's hashrate distribution across mining pools, from mid-October to mid-November 2023.

So if you submit a transaction and every member of the very largest pool has decided not to include your transactions, there's a 30% chance your transaction won't get in the next block and then a 30% chance it won't get into a block after that and so on.[51] So there's a 70% chance it gets through right away, a 91% chance it gets through in two blocks, a 97.3% chance it gets through in three blocks, and so on. If you're willing to wait, this isn't a serious concern. If you want to censor bitcoin transactions, you'll need to do more than mine a block here or there; you'll need to command over half the hashpower. And that is expensive indeed.

Perhaps, then, certain pools might collude to block transactions. For most of bitcoin's history, very few pools have had enough hashrate to collude in this way. There is even a tradition of avoiding such high hashrates for fear of devaluing bitcoin and their large expenditures on specialized mining hardware.[52]

More importantly, the objection misunderstands how pools work.[53] Miners enter and exit pools regularly and at no cost. There is nothing keeping them in a pool that requires its participants to censor or block certain kinds of transactions. And provided that the transactions have fees attached, it will be more profitable to publish them and thus claim their fees. Ongoing technical developments, finally, promise to allow miners to choose for themselves which transactions to include as pool participants.[54] Since mining is itself highly distributed, this is another bulwark against pool capture.

11.3.4   Lightning hubs are authorities

Anyone can send value to anyone else over bitcoin's lightning network, provided that a path connects them with sufficient liquidity. Lightning is most usable when there are short paths from any node to another with high capacity and low fees. These conditions, however, lead to an increasingly centralized network structure, where large and well-connected nodes serve as centers through which other users route their payments. Modeled by diagram, they resemble hubs with radiating spokes. Though this hub and spoke model makes for fast and cheap payments, goes the objection, it comes at a price: hub nodes serve as de facto mediators and could conceivably censor transactions. They would have outsized power in the system and increase network fragility. And if most people were to use bitcoin via lightning, lightning's own fragility would affect bitcoin too.

A hub-and-spoke model is perfectly adequate for a wide range of ordinary payments. For payments that authorities would permit anyway, users will likely prioritize speed and cost and gladly opt to route through hubs.

And there will likely be many interoperable hubs. Hubs compete with each other for payments, after all. With this in mind, the economics isn't that different from mining. Just as miners will always have reason to publish any transaction at all (to collect fees), so also hubs will have reason to route any transaction at all (to collect fees).

Although anonymous hubs operating under the cloak of things like Tor will not perfectly shield users from scrutiny or censorship, they would be *expensive* to stop. What's more, entry or exit from the payment routing game is, like mining, voluntary. No hub can monopolize payment flow or block others from joining the game. So users who need censorship-resistance the most can use other payment layers or even resort to bitcoin's more expensive base layer.

11.3.5   Bitcoin is vulnerable to semantic takeover

Suppose you find an abundant and easily accessible kind of rock. Wouldn't it be a neat trick to get everyone in the world to refer to the rock as "gold" and gold as the rock and then, as a result, inspire everyone to treat the rock as gold and the gold as the rock? This is a semantic attack on gold. Were it to succeed, the price of genuine gold would drop precipitously and the price of fool's gold would rise. If, for some reason, you wanted to sink the demand for gold, this could help.

A semantic attack on bitcoin would usurp the bitcoin label and apply it to another asset, namely, one without the features that make bitcoin resistance money. Such an attack would succeed insofar as the non-bitcoin asset eats into the use and valuation of the real bitcoin. The fool's bitcoin could improve on bitcoin's privacy, say, and still, in our view, make the world worse off. But a more malicious attack might try to neuter bitcoin by propping up a replacement without bitcoin's resistance-making properties.

One kind of semantic attack would involve custodians. When someone else holds your bitcoin for you, you don't possess it. An app calls the thing you have "bitcoin," but you really have a bitcoin IOU. Since you don't have the private keys, you can't actually spend it without the permission of your custodian. For you, it is not resistance money. You have compliance money parading with the name of resistance money. What if most users traded their resistance money for compliance money? A state might try to pass laws banning self-custody. Or users might simply opt-in over time for the convenience that custodians offer.

Another kind of semantic attack involves modifications to bitcoin. Suppose there are latent fault lines among bitcoin users, with each group favoring different design tradeoffs. Each group modifies the bitcoin software *they* run in a way that they think improves upon bitcoin. They also insist on calling their new coin "bitcoin." One possibility – factions issue competing claims for the brand and splinter the developers and the network itself. Another possibility – a faction with neutered bitcoin wins.

These attacks aren't purely theoretical.

In 2015–2017, a conflict over the proper size of blocks threatened to tear the community apart.[55] Its subject might appear to be purely technical and even a bit boring: Should blocks be around 1 megabyte each? Or perhaps 2, or even 4? The conflict put bitcoin's heart on the line: Would its blockchain be small enough for everyone to run their own node? Or would node operation eventually belong to larger entities like corporate exchanges? The so-called "big blockers" who favored an increasingly bloated ledger hoped that its native asset would gain traction as "bitcoin." They tried to persuade others that their software preserved the *real* bitcoin. Had these big blockers won the war for "bitcoin," developer energies and user enthusiasm might well have gone to a version of the software that would, in time, prevent bitcoin from enjoying a widely distributed network of nodes.

Small blockers won the blocksize war. They kept the big block version of bitcoin from claiming bitcoin's brand, network effects, and developer community. The big block version is known as "bitcoin cash." The bitcoin brand is intact and attached to a version of the software that nearly anyone can run and that has to this day a flourishing network of nodes.

Paradoxically, institutional blowups in the cryptocurrency space serve some good, in the long run. When custodians abscond with customer funds, for example, they teach everyone the value of bitcoin self-custody. The message to those with ears to hear is simple: self-custody or else. Every time an FTX or Celsius or whatnot absconds with user coins, people everywhere hear this message. And some listen. (For more on these custodial blowups and their implications for bitcoin, see Section 11.4.4, next.)

So although bitcoin has indeed suffered semantic attacks, it has continued to thrive. History suggests that its layer zero – bitcoin users – have grown resilient from attempts to co-opt the bitcoin brand. Trends suggest that enough bitcoin users will continue to have the wisdom to discern bitcoin from fool's bitcoin.

11.4   Is bitcoin good money?

We have argued that because bitcoin is resistance money, it is good money. This is not merely the claim that bitcoin is good at being money but that it is good. Bitcoin makes the world better when it's used as money. Let's consider some objections to this claim.

11.4.1 Bitcoin disarms the state

Some worry that bitcoin will disarm the state. The objection concedes that bitcoin is resistant – all too resistant – and concludes from there that it weakens or even dismantles governments to the detriment of all. In the most extreme case, bitcoin inaugurates a new era of chaotic anarchy.

Here are two scenarios. In the first, bitcoin makes taxation difficult or impossible, by making surveillance or control of payment flows difficult or impossible. It is harder to collect taxes when you don't know who has what money and when you can't easily confiscate it upon noncompliance. In the second, bitcoin makes state spending difficult or impossible; the assumption here is that states must be able to print money in order to spend. In a world where bitcoin is the dominant or only money, state spending couldn't be funded in this way; no one can print bitcoin for free, after all. These scenarios could unfold in tandem and together undermine state spending power across the board. Principled pacifists and anarchists rejoice. For the rest of us, though, these scenarios seem quite bad.

Both scenarios significantly overstate bitcoin's likely impact. In our view, it is highly improbable that bitcoin will be the dominant or only money, a scenario called *hyperbitcoinization*. The most probable paths to hyperbitcoinization, furthermore, go by way of early and aggressive government *adoption* of bitcoin, which would enable rather than block future state spending. Were the Federal Reserve to regularly make large purchases of bitcoin, for example, that would certainly spur on hyperbitcoinization and a bump in bitcoin's purchasing power. But that bump would enrich the US government and enable future spending.

Without the assumption of hyperbitcoinization, the first scenario makes little sense either. Provided that people still use ordinary bank accounts and dollars, governments will find a way to tax them. The existence of physical cash – which is a kind of resistance money, after all – didn't disarm the state, so there's little reason to think that bitcoin will either.

A final problem for this objection is its assumption that states spend money well. Our view is more measured; sometimes they do and sometimes not. Limiting state spending capacity would likely have mixed effects then.

11.4.2 Satoshi could return

Satoshi controls about a million bitcoin that have never moved – about 5% of the total supply. Satoshi's identity is not generally known. He might be dead. He might be alive. He might still have the private keys to those bitcoin – or maybe not. We just don't know. For now, he's gone.

Satoshi might come back, though. He might spend his coins or unveil his real identity. He could dump them all on the open market and tank bitcoin's price – for a time, at least. He could turn out to be a criminal, or an off-putting extremist, or even a fan of some alternative cryptocurrency. In any number of scenarios in which Satoshi returns, the idea goes, bitcoin faces a significant public relations problem.

In our view, these scenarios are either unlikely given what we know or not so dire after all.

Satoshi last communicated with the world about bitcoin in early 2011. He didn't spend his coins in those early years and hasn't spent them since. Satoshi took meticulous steps, furthermore, to maintain pseudonymity. The publicly available evidence indicates that Satoshi preferred to be a quiet creator and early guardian but never a lasting figurehead.

Bitcoin works without makers, mediators, and managers. It has no place for a lasting figurehead. It has no CEO and no board who can elect one. Even someone armed with Satoshi's private keys would have no more authority in the network than any other user. The most they could do is to either spend Satoshi's bitcoin or exert social influence. Neither of these things are obviously bad. Spending Satoshi's bitcoin would distribute bitcoin more widely than it is now – not obviously a bad thing. Counterintuitively, it would also, in the long run, remove uncertainty about whether the coins might be spent. Most importantly, the network has grown well beyond its early days when a single voice could exert overwhelming influence over its direction. Satoshi could speak, but bitcoin users might not obey – all to the good.

11.4.3 Bitcoin is unfairly distributed and isn't universally accessible

We've argued (see Chapter 8) that legacy monetary systems exclude many.[56] We've also shown that bitcoin's design serves to include many of the excluded. Yet not everyone has bitcoin, and not everyone has access to bitcoin's network. According to some estimates, approximately 114 million people in the world own bitcoin. That leaves 7.9 billion or so without bitcoin. Even if that estimate is low, it's unlikely that more than 1 billion people own bitcoin, leaving 7 billion out. Some people also have *a lot* of bitcoin.[57]

We would be very happy to see bitcoin more widely distributed. We wonder, however, whether the critics agree. Critics who complain that bitcoin's distribution is too concentrated tend to discourage newcomers from acquiring bitcoin. It's a curious stance, rather like complaining that not enough people have been vaccinated while also warning against getting a shot. So here's some free advice to critics: if you are actually worried about bitcoin's distribution, then perhaps you can help even things out by encouraging people without any bitcoin to get some.

In Chapter 3, we discussed bitcoin's Supply Equity Ratio and Network Distribution Factor. There, we compared bitcoin's score on these metrics to other cryptocurrencies and noted that bitcoin is the best. But in the present context, we're not comparing. The objector simply believes that bitcoin isn't good enough along these dimensions. It would be nice to compare to a money that the objector supports, like the US dollar, to see whether the number really is so terrible. But as far we know, there is no Supply Equity Ratio or Network Distribution Factor for the dollar. So we must simply note that for all we know, the dollar's SER and NDF – and the SER and NDF of every other government-backed currency – are even worse than bitcoin's and request that the objector give us reasons to think it isn't.

We also believe that trends and structure are more important than snapshots. A money with an unjust structure will tend towards injustice. Bitcoin started off in the hands of one person – Satoshi. Then Hal Finney started running bitcoin. Then Dustin Trammell. And so on. As more people acquired bitcoin, the Gini coefficient trended downward. In 2018, Nouriel Roubini said that bitcoin's Gini coefficient was 0.88,[58] citing data from seven years earlier when bitcoin was two years old.[59] As of June 2021, a peer-reviewed paper estimated bitcoin's Gini coefficient of 0.47.[60] This is a substantial move in the direction of equitable distribution. Meanwhile, the US dollar is moving in the opposite direction.[61] And remember, many if not most of the people who have become wealthy from bitcoin ownership would not have become nearly as wealthy without bitcoin. So bitcoin might have already played a small but meaningful role in leveling out inequalities in the wider global economy, even if we concentrate on its largest holders.

A disquieting problem remains, however. For there are non-negligible technical, social, and technological barriers to access. The wealthy have more money to buy bitcoin. They also have identity documents or bank accounts that enable access to financial services, including on-ramps to bitcoin. This was an important theme in Chapter 8.

But here, again, trends matter more than snapshots. To access bitcoin, all a person needs is a cell phone or laptop. And phones are becoming ever more ubiquitous and always getting cheaper. For example, in Indonesia, which is 114th in the world in per capita GDP, there are more mobile phones than people.[62] 85% of Americans own a smartphone and that number has steadily increased; ten years ago, the number was 39%.[63]

The internet was once a niche tool. In its earliest years, it was accessed only by university researchers. Then came along other technically adept or curious people with money to spend on modems and other gizmos. And then we were off to the races. Bitcoin is similar. It used to be used only by researchers and technically adept weirdos. Now books are written about it, and millions use the network. This is an encouraging trend indeed. It does not mean that bitcoin proponents should be complacent in their efforts to expand access to bitcoin tools, but it does show that there is little reason yet for alarm.

11.4.4 Bitcoin suffers from extrinsic blowups

Bitcoin is one element within a broader cryptocurrency world.[64] For better or for worse, it is affected by that world. We've argued that bitcoin stands apart (see Chapter 3, Section 3.4). It would be nice to think that bitcoin stands alone too – unaffected by what occurs in the rest of the cryptocurrency space. But this has not been the case.

Recent calamities have caused immense disruption, with effects on both the price and public perception of bitcoin.

Celsius promised its users a steady yield, in exchange for taking custody of their bitcoin and other crypto tokens. Then they lost it all in leveraged trading games.[65] Three Arrows Capital had $10 billion in assets under management and then went bankrupt almost overnight.[66] Terra ran a stablecoin – supposedly pegged to the US dollar – that had a market cap of $18 billion on May 8, 2022, and had a market cap of $100 million on June 8, 2022, as the price of the "stable" coin had fallen to just under a penny.[67] FTX, one of the largest cryptocurrency trading platforms, reportedly lost billions of dollars in customer funds by playing the market with those funds, in direct violation of their own terms and conditions.[68]

And this was just 2022.

During this time, the market cap of bitcoin went from a high of $1.2 trillion to a low of $300 billion, and the bitcoin price went from over $60,000 to just under $16,000. Many suspect that Celsius, Three Arrows Capital, FTX affiliates, and others had leveraged their assets to buy bitcoin, and when they had to sell that bitcoin, the price crashed.

Similarly, some argue that the current price of bitcoin is still being supported by suspicious entities. Many cite Tether, a stablecoin with a $65 billion market cap, and point out that it has had serious issues in proving that its tokens are backed by real assets.[69] Even if bitcoin intrinsically has no serious problems, it is surrounded by a culture rife with scams. And bitcoin is inevitably affected.

We concede that these crypto calamities show that factors well outside bitcoin's own network limit its capacity to enrich its users. And in some cases, they can lead to the impoverishment of bitcoin's users by leading to crashes in its purchasing power.

Bitcoin users can mitigate or eliminate some of these risks by accessing bitcoin directly – that means avoiding exchanges, hedge fund counterparties, custody platforms, and so on. Bitcoin's magic lies in eliminating trusted parties; the magic disappears when users welcome trusted parties back into the mix. But strict use of bitcoin itself doesn't protect users from crashes in its purchasing power caused by extrinsic institutional implosions (or the volatility induced by bitcoin's own design – recall Chapter 5).

So there is no easy solution here.

Yet bitcoin plods along. Despite these massive obstacles, people use it as resistance money. Recall the quotation from human rights advocates at the start of Section 11.3: bitcoin is a liberating force in the real world despite price crashes and the like.

Here is a pessimistic scenario. Bitcoin continues to plod along, and its users are occasionally harmed by crypto blowups. This is the world in which we live. Here is a more optimistic scenario: cryptocurrency users increasingly distinguish bitcoin from its alternatives, and bitcoin becomes increasingly insulated from the effects of fraudulent or foolish crypto projects. Is one of these scenarios more likely than the other, given what we now know? We can't say. Perhaps no one can. Yet even in the pessimistic scenario, bitcoin still plays a vital role as resistance money. At most, then, this objection shows that due to crypto shenanigans, bitcoin won't realize its full potential for improving the world.

11.4.5 Bitcoin is associated with extremist politics

Some allege that bitcoin's origin makes it a tool for the hard political right.[70] Anyone who does not hail from the hard political right could take this as an argument that bitcoin, therefore, makes the world worse.

The critics admittedly have gobs of ammo. Founding cypherpunk Timothy May once said that he "will not be sorry to see assassination markets used to deal with [politicians]" – or as he called them, "Congressrodents." May also supported capital punishment for theft. Over the next two years, cypherpunk Jim Bell defended assassination markets across a ten-part essay. Early bitcoiners said and did outrageous things too. For example, Mircea Popescu committed, at a minimum, two outrageous crimes. He not only put a bounty on the life of bitcoin developer Peter Wuille but also claimed to be the "world's greatest erotica writer."[71]

Although bitcoin didn't exactly sprout from pristine soil, critics miss a few things. First, they apply unrealistic standards to bitcoin. Second, they overlook the viewpoint diversity among cypherpunks and early bitcoiners.

And third, they ignore the values that actually united these otherwise diverse thinkers.

First, unrealistic standards. Some argue that bitcoin encodes antisemitic conspiracy theories because some antisemites and some bitcoiners would both like to end the Federal Reserve.[72] This is a simple guilt-by-association fallacy. We could play the same awful game: one "bitcoin-is-right-wing" critic praises the Fed, an institution whose structure and existence owes to William Gibbs McAdoo, a top-tier racist. While McAdoo was Secretary of the Treasury, he became the first chairman of the Federal Reserve. He was also a segregationist and ordered the implementation of Jim Crow laws in all Treasury facilities – even in the North.[73] The critics draw lines all over the chalkboard to tie bitcoin to racism but ignore explicit racism at the founding of an institution they praise.

Some might say that pro-bitcoin sentiment doesn't merely accompany bad beliefs in people's minds. Rather, many support bitcoin *from* those bad beliefs. Even so, people have supported all sorts of things for bad or ugly reasons. Early champions of abortion like Margaret Sanger fought for abortion access to further eugenicist ideals.[74] Henry Ford, a notorious antisemite, funded square-dancing initiatives across the country to counter jazz's growing popularity – in his mind, a Jewish conspiracy.[75] But we doubt we'll see critics sign petitions against Planned Parenthood or picket seniors' night at the Do Si Do. Since precious few things meet the standards that these critics apply to bitcoin, they apply those standards inconsistently.

Second, the cypherpunks had a good deal of ideological and political diversity. What united them was opposition to digital authoritarianism. But they were divided in other important ways.[76] While some, like Timothy May, hoped that cryptography might help cripple government institutions, others, like Julian Assange, thought cryptography could reform them and serve as a check against both government and corporate overreach.[77] According to Robert Manne, the cypherpunks:

> . . . formed a house of many rooms. The only thing they all shared was an understanding of the political significance of cryptography and the willingness to fight for privacy and unfettered freedom in cyberspace.[78]

May himself estimated that around half the cypherpunk mailing list were strongly libertarian or anarchist, around a fifth were liberal or leftist, and that they also had "anarcho-syndicalists, . . . Neo-Pagans, Christian Fundamentalists, and maybe even a few unreconstructed Communists."[79]

Researchers found an eerily similar breakdown in the early bitcoin community – around half in the dataset self-identified as libertarian, a third identified as either progressive (17%) or socialist (9%) or green (7%), and then a fifth as either centrist (8%), anarchist (7%), or conservative (5%).[80] A study on google search trends around the same time found little or no evidence that libertarian ideology drove interest in bitcoin. The cypherpunks and early bitcoiners had more ideological diversity than critics admit.[81]

Yet the critics get something importantly right. Bitcoin has cypherpunk DNA. Its creator cited cypherpunks, incorporated cypherpunk ideas into the design, and first shared the discovery with cypherpunks. Its earliest and most influential supporter – Hal Finney – was a cypherpunk, who had previously made real progress on digital cash. Several other cypherpunks have also supported bitcoin through the years, including Adam Back and Nick Szabo. It's no surprise why. The very thing that unites cypherpunks to each other also unites the cypherpunks to bitcoin – anti-authoritarianism.[82]

Here's the thing. Authoritarians exist on the right and the left, within governments and within corporations. These authoritarians often collude in nefarious ways too. So anti-authoritarianism doesn't neatly fit into our partisan divisions. Most can see that in a digital age, *physical* cash defends against authoritarians, whether they be right or left, government or corporate. But the same point applies to digital cash too.

Physical cash routes around regimes of digital surveillance and control.[83] So if *physical* cash isn't essentially right-wing, why would *digitizing* cash serve primarily right-wing purposes? If bitcoin is truly digital cash, then it doesn't "literally encode" an "extreme rightist" vision.[84] Bitcoin is neither anarchic, nor conservative, nor libertarian. By design, bitcoin is anti-authoritarian. And that would be true even if, contrary to fact, all the cypherpunks were on the hard political right.

11.5 The objection from other objections

For all that, you might suspect we are more like Charlie Munger than we care to admit – mired in bias and unwilling to consider lines of reasoning that are unfriendly to bitcoin.

It's a good worry.

We have three main things to say in reply. First, fair enough. Don't take our word for it. We are not asking you to believe that bitcoin is net good for the world based on our say-so. We could have done that in a tweet. Instead, we wrote a book. The book contains arguments. The arguments have premises that we think you believe or should believe based on good reasons, and those premises entail conclusions that we think you might not have realized. So consider the arguments on their own merits. Reason behind the veil, think about people living in authoritarian regimes or households, think about what could happen in the future in your own country, and consider whether it's good that bitcoin is around.

Second, the worry cuts both ways. It is not only those who are pro-bitcoin who are invested in the truth of their claims. People who are anti-bitcoin – like Charlie Munger – are invested in their positions too. For some, it's because they work for entities that bitcoin disrupts, like central banks, pawn shops, payday lenders, money transmitters, credit card companies, commercial banks, and so on. For some, it's because they criticized bitcoin early on or predicted its demise, and its ongoing existence and flourishing is an embarrassment. So this isn't an objection that tells one way or another. The only thing to do is to evaluate the arguments for and against bitcoin on their own merits.

Third, as an act of good faith, we're now going to give our own novel objection. We think it's got some bite.

In the first ten chapters of this book, we implicitly discussed at least ten objections to bitcoin. In this chapter, we've discussed 15 more. Some of them we've answered. Others we've speculated about possible answers to. Yet others require more research. We don't consider any of them decisive reasons to think that a world without bitcoin is better than a world with bitcoin. But by now, the reader might be thinking, "Yeah, individually, the responses to the objections seemed pretty good. But there are so many objections! It's likely that at least one of them is right."

Perhaps so. It's much easier to be sure that just one objection is wrong than that all 25 are wrong. Even if each objection looks shabby on its own, they can together appear impressive indeed.

This line of reasoning can be strengthened. In its strongest form, it focuses not on the soundness of the objections but rather, the public perception of them. There are so very many objections to bitcoin, and they're very well known. Even if none of them actually succeeds, people don't know that. People are aware of the objections but not the responses. So most people will remain against bitcoin. The ubiquity of the objections will be a permanent barrier to bitcoin use and adoption and growth. Bitcoin is a network good. As with languages and other network goods, it's most useful when used and even more so when used by many.

The objection from the perception of many objections shows this then: all those people who say nasty things about bitcoin have the power to make at least some of them come true. They can, simply by spreading objections, reduce bitcoin's capacity to improve the world.

To this objection, we have no decisive reply. It is plainly true that some people have a very poor opinion of bitcoin. And perhaps most won't ever change their minds. Nevertheless, we're hopeful. People change. Minds expand. Maybe the arguments of this book will help. Maybe you will too.

In the meantime, bitcoin is still resistance money. It is good for the world despite widespread suspicion. And that's good enough for us.

Notes

1. Kollewe (2018).
2. La Roche (2021).
3. Imbert (2016). Munger was defending his favorite sugar-water stock, despite acknowledging the negative externalities of its main product and the obesity crisis it has helped spread.
4. For extensive documentation of other extremely negative – and sometimes amusing – receptions of bitcoin in the popular imagination, see Chowdhury (2020).
5. SHA-256 is a hashing algorithm used in both address construction and mining. RIPEMD-160, another hashing algorithm, is also used in address construction. ECDSA is used in signatures.
6. Mining empty blocks to censor transactions, for example. Or arbitrarily rolling back the blockchain in non-economic "zig-zag" attacks to undermine network credibility. The cheaper it is to mine blocks, the easier these strategies are to execute. On other concerns about bitcoin's long-term security model and its response to strategic mining, see *inter alia*, Arnosti and Weinberg (2018), Bonneau (2017), Budish (2018), Carlsten et al. (2016), Eyal and Sirer (2013), Gervais et al. (2015), Messias et al. (2021), Moroz et al. (2020), Motlagh et al. (2021), Negy et al. (2019), Romiti et al. (2019), Saad et al. (2019), and Tsabary and Eyal (2018).
7. For useful discussion, see Carter (2019).
8. Many of these conversations have unfolded on bitcointalk.org, for example. One influential and semiformal expression of the worry is Hasu et al. (2019).
9. See Luther (2022).
10. Polimeni et al. (2008).
11. Bergeron (2017).
12. www.theblock.co/data/on-chain-metrics/comparison-bitcoin-ethereum
13. www.drivechain.info/
14. Nakamoto (2010).
15. See, for example, Hall (2022a, 2022b). See Cross (2022) for further discussion.
16. Nakamoto (2009c).
17. Pines (2022).
18. The reasoning here applies only to attackers who command less than half of the mining network's hashpower. See Nakamoto (2008a: Section 11). For nuanced and skeptical discussion well beyond what we offer in the text, see Kelly (2021a, 2021b).
19. See Carter (2019). There are technical details here that go well beyond the scope of the present discussion. One factor, for example, is the degree to which miners attempting a strategic attack can collect fees, which would subsidize their attacks. This will, in turn, depend on the kind of attack at play and on the structure of transactions being rolled back (whether they are independent, for example, or build atop other transactions being rolled back). For extensive and technically adept discussion, see Warren (2023).
20. Nakamoto (2008a, p. 1).
21. Coppola (2021).

22. A technical challenge is that, under the hood, bitcoin is measured in integers, not decimals; satoshis, not bitcoin, are the base unit. Subdivision involves more than just "moving the decimal point a few spots over," then, and indeed requires significant overhaul of bitcoin itself as well as other programs that interact with it – wallets, exchanges, lighting nodes, and so on.
23. See Murch (2022).
24. Another option is to use fractions of sats in payment layers that sit atop bit. coin's main settlement network. Such measures are already in place in bitcoin's lightning network, with this limitation: settlement to the main chain is still strictly a matter of whole satoshis.
25. For further discussion, see Bitcoin Stack Exchange (2020).
26. This is different from how economists use the term to denote demand outstripping supply.
27. Visa (2022).
28. Bailey and Warmke (2023).
29. Fedwire (2022).
30. Poon and Dryja (2016) first described the network. See Antonopoulos et al. (2021) for a book-length technical guide.
31. https://1ml.com/statistics
32. This, too, is imperfect because Visa settles through banks on both the cardholder side and merchant side. Lightning is probably then more akin to these banks. Better payment solutions will likely be built on top of something like lightning. So a true apples-to-apples and oranges-to-oranges comparison would pair Visa with payments solutions that have yet to be built. For further discussion of lightning – and its limits – see Bailey et al. (ms).
33. Indeed, US merchants are not required to accept the US dollars in all its forms. See Federal Reserve FAQ (2022).
34. We've interpreted the objection as descriptive – as a claim about what it takes for something to, in fact, be money. Perhaps the objection is normative instead – a claim about what it takes for something to be *good* money. The objection would then amount to the claim that, since bitcoin is unbacked, it is not *good* money. Some of the same replies we've given before would apply to this objection too. The dollar has been a good-enough money and so has gold. We do not claim that bitcoin is ideal money or the most apt money, furthermore, and thus have no quarrel with arguments purporting to show that some other money is better than it. Indeed, and as we argued in Chapter 3 (Section 3.5), there are ineliminable tradeoffs here, leaving some monies as better in some ways and others better in others but without any overall victor.
35. For a representative sample, see McCauley (2021).
36. "Cashing in these early coins involves pumping up the price and then selling to later adopters, particularly during the bubbles. Thus, Bitcoin was not a Ponzi or pyramid scheme, but a pump-and-dump. Anyone who bought in after the earliest days is functionally the sucker in the relationship." This from a long-time bitcoin critic Gerard (2017, p. 30).
37. Gladstein (2018).
38. Financial Inclusion Tech (2022).
39. Manchin (2014).
40. See Hendrickson and Luther (2017): footnote 5, Orji (2022), and Quiroz-Gutierrez (2022).
41. Gronewold (2022).
42. European Parliament (2022).
43. Ohuocha and George (2021).

44. Ref_363_FILE150326860BM1Ibid.
45. For discussion of this question tied to specific attempts at banning bitcoin, see Gladstein (2021).
46. Hendrickson and Luther (2017).
47. Ammous (2018b, pp. 249–251).
48. For discussion, see Cross and Bailey (2022).
49. See Lopp (2018) for some of the details about the internal politics of Core development.
50. See, e.g., Auer et al. (2022) and Walch (2019).
51. We've made some simplifying assumptions about your transaction's fee (competitive) and the length of the queue (short).
52. See, for example, the case of Bitfury, as detailed in Popper (2015: 299).
53. Shinobi (2021a).
54. See, e.g., https://stratumprotocol.org.
55. Bier (2021).
56. For one particularly compelling example, see Baradaran (2018).
57. See, for example, Makarov and Schoar (2021) and Partz (2021).
58. Roubini (2018b).
59. https://bitcointalk.org/index.php?topic=51011.msg608239#msg608239
60. Sai et al. (2021).
61. Collins (2021) and Collins (2022).
62. Balea (2016).
63. Pew Research Center (2021).
64. Many use the word "ecosystem." We deliberately do not because ecosystems involve spontaneous order, not foundations that sponsor projects with tokens printed out of thin air. See Farrell (2022) for more.
65. Laurent (2022).
66. Wieczner (2022).
67. Sandor and Genç (2022).
68. Berwick (2022).
69. Debevoise and Plimpton (2022) and Griffin and Shams (2020). For critical replies, see Lyons and Viswanath-Natraj (2022) and Kristoufek (2020).
70. Golumbia (2016). For documentation of the economic and historical errors that riddle that book, see Luther (2019). For further discussion of bitcoin's capacious politics, see also Bailey et al. (2022).
71. Popescu (2015, 2019).
72. Golumbia (2016, pp. 23, 61).
73. Packard (2003, p. 124).
74. See Stewart (2020).
75. See American Experience (2017).
76. Beltramini (2021). For a cautionary note and expanded historical context, see also Anderson (2021).
77. Manne (2011) argues that Assange, in particular, was left-leaning and, though a radical in several ways, saw corporate overreach as a serious threat to personal privacy and autonomy.
78. Manne (2011).
79. May (1994).
80. Bohr and Bashir (2014).
81. Jarvis (2021).
82. Beltramini (2021).
83. Scott (2022).
84. Golumbia (2016).

12

SCORECARD

12.1 The Architect returns

You may have forgotten about The Architect from Chapter 4. But she hasn't forgotten about you. She's back, and she wants answers. In a calm voice, she speaks:

> You might feel disoriented. That's to be expected after reading a book of this length. The good news is that you're nearly done.
>
> In Chapter 4, you forgot your own history, family, wealth, ethnicity, sex, and everything else about yourself. This empowered you to evaluate the evidence about bitcoin in an unbiased way as you considered whether you'd prefer to live in a world with or without bitcoin.
>
> You've set aside your own circumstances and reflected on how bitcoin might help or hurt each of the world's 8 billion people. Since then, you've uncovered who benefits or suffers from bitcoin, and to what degree.
>
> Now, it's decision time. Soon, you will set this book down and remember who you are. But you must first choose which of two worlds to enter. One world continues with bitcoin and the other world continues without. You must decide which world to enter without knowing which of the eight billion lives is yours.
>
> Which world shall it be?

This is not an idle question, even though it occurs in a fanciful thought experiment. Your reaction to the thought experiment can guide your

DOI: 10.4324/9781003484721-12

beliefs and actions in the here and now. If, behind the veil, you'd rather step into the non-bitcoin world, you might try to make our world more like that world. You might, accordingly, discourage your friends' interest in bitcoin, lobby governments to limit its use, or write anti-bitcoin op-eds. But if, behind the veil, you'd rather step back into the bitcoin world, then you have reason to be glad that it exists and reason to encourage its success as resistance money.

The choice is yours.

12.2 Evaluating from behind the veil

This book has offered a framework for judging bitcoin's merits. We've also used that framework. If you've followed along, so have you.

We've considered where bitcoin stands along various dimensions – monetary institutions, privacy, censorship-resistance, financial inclusion, and security. In each case, we've identified factors that support bitcoin. Some face serious limitations. And some objections to bitcoin do reveal genuine risks and downsides. We've covered several such objections along the way, especially in the prior chapter. It's now time to look at the whole picture.

An overall evaluation involves comparing potentially incommensurable goods – goods that cannot easily be stacked up against each other. For example, which is better: feeding a starving robin or recording data about a distant star? Some will answer quickly, as if the answer is obvious. But others will hesitate, as if we've asked them to compare apples and oranges. Bitcoin's costs and benefits may seem like this. How do we weigh the good of accessible remittances within a dysfunctional country versus the bad of ransomware? Yet if we wish to evaluate bitcoin overall, we must do our best.

Bitcoin is a special kind of money. It is money without trusted makers, managers, and mediators. It has a non-zero marginal cost of production but no non-monetary uses. In blending various features of traditional fiat currencies and gold, bitcoin invites new reflection on which kind of monies we'd want there to be, if we didn't know who we'd be. Its unique monetary profile also merits special attention and scrutiny. Bitcoin stands apart and beckons the open-minded and intellectually curious.

Those who opt in to bitcoin encounter a new set of tradeoffs. To choose bitcoin is to choose rules over rulers. We do not say this choice is wise for everyone. Bitcoin provides stable rules but makes no guarantees of nominal price stability. But we do think that behind the veil, you'd want to have this option available. You might suffer from monetary bad luck with a poor or poorly managed local currency. So you'd likely want a functional alternative, just in case. To reject a world with bitcoin is to remove a possible lifeline for billions of people, any one of which might be you.

Considerations about monetary institutions, then, favor bitcoin.

Financial privacy is both precious and under fire. Despite operating on a public ledger, bitcoin offers users new ways to control their sensitive personal information. In doing this, bitcoin enables privacy across all sorts of activity, from the ordinary to the nefarious to the saintly. And yet the privacy it affords is not without limits. It is very difficult to hide criminal activity on bitcoin at any real scale, for example. This limits the potential downsides to bitcoin's privacy.

Anyone can benefit from financial privacy. Indeed, the most precarious stand to benefit the most. Consider those who might suffer for having certain of their payments revealed to the world – payments for hormones or medicines, abortions or medical treatments, political causes, religious icons, or diapers. Since you don't know who you'd be, choosing a world without private money would involve great risk. Furthermore, bitcoin's drawbacks compare favorably with its legacy financial cousin, physical cash. Even considering those drawbacks, financial privacy concerns weigh in favor of bitcoin. So it's better, we say, to choose a world with bitcoin and its privacy features.

Bitcoin's privacy features, on balance, count in its favor when reasoning behind the veil.

Authorities pepper the financial landscape, often for good. But some act as monetary censors. Although they often block payments associated with legally or morally impermissible activity, they also block payments associated with legally and morally permissible activity. Is there some reason to think that resistance money – free of authorities with the power to block – could make the world better without excessively enabling nefarious activity? We think so. Resistance money is a vital check against the rising threat of authoritarian rule, a condition under which billions already suffer today. Resistance money also helps those whose vision of morality differs from those in power and those in the majority.

Money without intermediaries – and thus without censorship – carries some downsides. Compared to physical cash, bitcoin enables some wrongdoing more easily over longer distances. But the data suggests that our world does not, and will not, pay too high a price for this wrongdoing. For bitcoin's existence does not substantially increase things like money laundering or sanctions evasion. And effective countermeasures already exist for the ransomware that it enables.

As noted, billions suffer under authoritarian rule. Behind the veil, then, there is a very high chance that you'd want access to money outside of authoritarian control. Bitcoin enables censorship-resistant donations, remittances, and commerce where authoritarians and capital controls have limited the freedom of billions worldwide. Your moral views also stand a good chance of differing from those around you – that you are more enthusiastic about travel clubs, tobacco, pornography, pro-choice charities, pro-life charities, firearms, dating services, or any number of other kinds of censored financial activity. Without bitcoin, you have a high risk of suffering from financial censorship without much recourse. An extra option for resistance would appear extremely attractive behind the veil – especially given the mitigated downsides.

Censorship considerations also weigh heavily in favor of bitcoin.

Hundreds of millions suffer from financial exclusion. They lack access to banking. And so they lack access to digital payment platforms built on top of the banking system. Many lack access because trusted authorities exclude them. They face discrimination. Some lack the right documents. Many self-exclude because they distrust the authorities who demand trust. And many others self-exclude for financial or religious reasons.

Bitcoin is not built on top of the banking system. Those who distrust banks can place their trust in bitcoin. It doesn't require documentation. The network is everywhere open to anyone with an internet connected device, 24/7/365. It doesn't – and can't – discriminate on the basis of race, ethnicity, sex, politics, religion, sexual orientation, criminal history, credit history, family history, vocation, income, social standing, or beauty. It doesn't have high minimum balances or charge exorbitant fees for overdrafting or account maintenance. And for those with religious qualms, users needn't participate in usury. Bitcoin is the most inclusive monetary network in the world.

Wealthy and otherwise privileged people typically have adequate access to financial systems. But we should think beyond the wealthy from behind the veil. A reasonably risk-averse stance would prioritize the plight of the less privileged, both because of how many there are and how much harm they endure. You'd at least want them to have the *option* of using a monetary system that does not exclude them. After all, you might very well be one of them. And you'd want the option to save, receive, and send value without the permission of the privileged.

Financial inclusion considerations weigh heavily in favor of bitcoin, with no significant drawbacks.

Let's put it all together, from considerations about monetary institutions to considerations about privacy, censorship-resistance, and inclusion. We have argued that bitcoin is most useful for those who suffer under monetary policies that beget high inflation, autocratic rather than democratic rule, or financial exclusion. A quick look at the relevant data (see Table) vindicates that hypothesis. The people who would most benefit from bitcoin also seem to have adopted bitcoin at the highest rates. Cryptocurrencies – bitcoin chief among them – are most widely used in places without healthy democratic institutions, with poor rates of financial inclusion, or that languish under bad inflation or incompetent monetary rulers.

Our case for bitcoin's desirability isn't mere theory. It's vindicated by the facts.

Here's where things stand. Along four dimensions – monetary institutions, financial privacy, censorship, and inclusion – we've argued that bitcoin offers significant benefits, even lifelines. In each case, the reasons to select a world with bitcoin outweigh those against. Each of these four reasons, then, is an independent argument for the central contention of this book: bitcoin, as resistance money, is choice-worthy behind the veil.

All these considerations individually weigh in favor of bitcoin. And combined, they weigh strongly in favor of bitcoin. Throughout the book, we've compared bitcoin to cash. Physical cash, too, is a kind of resistance money. Though it does not involve a novel kind of monetary institution like bitcoin does, it still enables significant financial privacy, resists censorship, and makes for significant financial inclusion. Yet its powers are limited. It isn't quite as useful for crime as it is for more ordinary purposes. For these reasons, cash is choice-worthy behind the veil. Bitcoin is digital cash. It, too, provides significant benefits to its users without too many unacceptable downsides. Bitcoin is choice-worthy behind the veil largely for the same reasons that cash is.

Country	Adoption[1] (out of 146)	Democracy[2] (out of 176)	Inclusion[3] (out of 142)	Inflation[4] (out of 181)
Vietnam	1	145	92	18
Philippines	2	112	98	44
Ukraine	3	92	48	164
India	4	85	110	73
USA	5	36	31	92
Pakistan	6	123	137	139
Brazil	7	75	56	115
Thailand	8	135	33	59
Russia	9	144	41	147
China	10	172	45	4
Nigeria	11	100	113	164
Turkey	12	137	61	178
Argentina	13	44	67	179
Morocco	14	105	118	55
Colombia	15	84	79	120

Crypto adoption and democracy, inclusion, and inflation.

What of the many objections to bitcoin? Some seemed formidable, and we have answered them across the various chapters of this book. Some objections suggest reasons to not buy bitcoin. Others suggest that bitcoin will remain a niche money. With a lone exception, none detract from our fundamental thesis that, since bitcoin is resistance money, it is choice-worthy behind the veil.

Negative externalities loom especially large behind the veil. If bitcoin has significant negative externalities, then you don't get to choose whether to suffer under them. You pay the price no matter who you are, especially in the case of highly diffused externalities like carbon emissions. These harm everyone. You pay the price even if you don't benefit from opting to use bitcoin yourself. Any spillover effects that harm non-users must also factor into our rough calculation.

Considering bitcoin's negative externalities is especially important behind the veil. Bitcoin does involve significant carbon emissions. These are bad. But that's not the whole story. A pragmatic approach to bitcoin tunes our response to its share of total emissions – that means neither downplaying nor exaggerating them. Not only are bitcoin's emissions lower than they initially seem, our best evidence shows that bitcoin's carbon emissions are *already* trending in the right direction. Moreover, policymakers and users can take steps to mitigate these emissions, both by decarbonizing the grid itself and by investing in green bitcoin mining. Bitcoin's *positive* social and environmental externalities, furthermore, tip the scale back in its direction.

We conclude that bitcoin's negative externalities should not upend an overall positive evaluation. Bitcoin's enabling of financial privacy, its resistance to censorship, its lack of monetary authorities, and its radical inclusion outweigh its negative externalities.

People can reasonably disagree about how much risk-weighted utility accrues to bitcoin along these dimensions. Some, especially those with a broadly anti-authoritarian mind, will find financial censorship extremely alarming and judge that the power to resist it is even more weighty than we think it is, for example. Readers especially concerned with the least well-off and the systems that exclude them might think bitcoin is even better than we do because of its inclusiveness and its inability to exclude. And of course, those with an especially active environmental conscience might be inclined to weigh even more heavily bitcoin's significant (though declining) emissions or, conversely, its positive environmental externalities.

How should we assess all of these factors together? Along which dimensions is bitcoin most impressive, and where does it falter? We shouldn't ask and answer these questions as the people we actually are; doing so would invite undue bias. So we've suggested a different frame of reference. From a personally neutral perspective – not knowing which of eight billion lives you'd live and with a modest risk aversion – would you prefer a world with bitcoin or one without? Would you rid the world of bitcoin if you had the chance? Tally up the points and find out for yourself where the truth might lie.

If you like charts, you might make one. You can use numbers to represent precise quantities of risk-weighted utility or perhaps just pluses or minuses. These numbers or pluses or minuses would represent bitcoin's net comparative value against a world without bitcoin along each dimension. A positive mark suggests that bitcoin improves the world along that dimension, and a negative mark suggests that bitcoin makes it worse.

Before reading this book, you might have had an overall feeling about bitcoin – pro, con, or otherwise. Now that you've read the book, you can be more precise. You can attend to bitcoin's positive and negative attributes. You can now imagine situations in which you'd need bitcoin and consider the stories of others who've needed bitcoin. You're now aware of the tradeoffs.

We won't tell you how to weigh each factor against each other. The important thing is to consider them holistically. Those who merely focus on bitcoin's use to combat inflation in Argentina, for example, but ignore its ransomware and carbon emissions, miss crucial parts of the calculation. The same goes for those who criticize bitcoin's energy use and ignore its uses for anti-authoritarianism and financial inclusion. When evaluating bitcoin, we must attend to all the factors before assigning a positive score (bitcoin benefits the world on net) or a negative score (bitcoin harms the world on net).

A negative total score for bitcoin would mean at least one of two things: we've either exaggerated bitcoin's benefits or greatly undersold its negative externalities. So if a critic disagrees with our evaluation, we invite them to explain why one or both of these is true. And where applicable, please use reliable empirical data to overturn the empirical data that we ourselves have relied on.

12.3 Practicum

We're philosophers. Although this book spans a number of disciplines, we aim primarily to evaluate bitcoin rather than make practical recommendations. But we have some of those too.

First, we categorically do not say that you should buy bitcoin. Sometimes friends ask whether, or when, they should "buy" bitcoin. They see it as a speculative investment rather than a money. We do not offer investment advice. So we don't recommend against buying bitcoin either;

that, too, would be investment advice. Few, if any, ever ask how to *use* bitcoin. But like any money, using bitcoin requires having some. If you wish to send value using dollars, you must first acquire some dollars. If you are connected to the right kind of bank, perhaps you can even make dollars. But otherwise, you'll have to buy them, or earn them, or steal them, or whatever. So also with bitcoin, if you wish to send value using the bitcoin network, you must first come to possess its native token by buying, earning, stealing, or some other means. But like gold, you could also mine it – not out of the ground, of course, but from Plato's heaven.

So we recommend the following: if you could imagine yourself ever being in a position that you'd need resistance money or you'd need to teach someone else how to use resistance money, it would be wise to learn how to use bitcoin. The best way to learn is by experience and, in particular, low-stakes experimentation towards understanding what it can and cannot do for you. Should you ever find yourself or a friend or family member at risk of surveillance, cancellation, censorship, wildly unstable monetary rules, or exclusion, bitcoin might help. As with insurance or home maintenance, it's wise to prepare *before* disaster strikes. You don't want to be stuck researching bitcoin wallets or exchanges *after* discovering you need illegal medical care, for example – or after having your bank accounts closed because of an ill-advised tweet.

Second, do not impede. Perhaps you have no use for bitcoin. That's fine. Plenty of other people do, though. And they deserve the option of using bitcoin, if our arguments are largely correct. And if they are, you might even feel compelled to help bitcoin succeed as resistance money. Resist draconian legislation that would ban bitcoin mining, hinder financial privacy, or burden those who custody their own bitcoin. Denounce corporate and state overreach in legacy monetary networks. Vote for officials and perhaps support companies who will take steps to decarbonize energy and remove bitcoin's negative externalities. Vote against autocrats who'd implement central bank digital currencies or other novel systems of monetary surveillance and control.

Third, reflect on physical cash and what it can do for you. Cash is bitcoin's legacy cousin. It, too, is a resistance money. Use it. Strength in numbers. And when you use privacy technology like cash, you don't just protect your own personal information. You grow the crowd into which others may recede and there find safety. Promote privacy by obscurity.

Fourth, and this is for bitcoin users, think about how you can help make bitcoin more effective resistance money. Tools of state and corporate surveillance grow ever more potent. If bitcoin is to keep pace, it must evolve too.

For bitcoin users who accept all of the arguments thus far, especially those who desire even greater financial privacy, we share this practical recommendation. Seek out proposed privacy improvements in bitcoin.[5] Analyze them. And when you deem the tradeoffs are worth it, do your part to enact privacy upgrades in your own node software. To date, other cryptocurrencies – like Zcash and Monero, as discussed earlier – are better for privacy than bitcoin. This needn't be the case forever. But it might. The future here is in the collective hands of bitcoin's users.

12.4 Cypherpunks

We began this book with the cypherpunks. Where others turn to the state for help, or resort to violence, or retreat entirely, cypherpunks are software activists.

Some of us lack the luxury of waiting for institutions to resolve the problems they've created. Recall Judith Milhon's motto: "girls need modems." Were she alive today, we imagine St. Jude might say as well: "girls need bitcoin." It is the cypherpunk way. Cypherpunks build programs to empower individuals and to protect their freedom:

> Cypherpunks write code. . . . Our code is free for all to use, worldwide. We don't much care if you don't approve of the software we write. We know that software can't be destroyed and that a widely dispersed system can't be shut down.[6]

Cypherpunk code empowers individuals. But, with money, writing code is not enough. For money is, as we've seen, a network good. Bitcoin isn't DIY money – do it yourself. It is, instead, DIT money – do it together. Using bitcoin means joining users in supporting resistance money for those who need it, with or without the permission or cooperation of authorities.

Cypherpunks have been writing code for 30 years. This is bitcoin's past. What of its future?

No one knows for sure where bitcoin will go. But we'll chart a few possible paths and comment on what they mean for human flourishing in an increasingly digital world.

Bitcoin might live on and grow in usefulness and strength. It might continue to be a refuge for the marginalized and money for those rejected by legacy financial institutions. It might even discipline these institutions into better behavior or replace those that fail to reform. The arguments of this book do not establish that this will happen, but they show that it would be a fine outcome indeed.

Bitcoin might die. Death would mean that price and use both going to zero or close to it. No users. No nodes. No miners. No resistance. Critics have been predicting or even proclaiming bitcoin's death for well over a decade. So far, the obituaries have been wildly wrong.[7] But there is no guarantee that bitcoin will live forever. Monies, like languages, live and die. The dollar may fail within our own lifetimes too.

The death of bitcoin needn't be an entirely depressing affair, though. The toothpaste has left the tube. No matter what happens to bitcoin, Satoshi's discoveries will remain. We now know how to make digital cash, what it's good for, and its tradeoffs. So we'll go out on a limb and make this guess: even if bitcoin dies, it will have spiritual successors for years to come, some of which will build on techniques discovered or perfected by Satoshi. As long as autocrats hope to use computers to surveil or control the rest of us, cypherpunks will find a way to bring resistance money to the world.

They'll write code.

12.5 Epilogue

The central claims of this book – that bitcoin is resistance money and that from behind the veil we'd prefer to live in a world with it rather than without it – may seem theoretical or abstract. We'll conclude with something more concrete.

Let's revisit Roya Mahboob, who we briefly met in the introduction to this book. Roya was born in Afghanistan in 1987. Life there wasn't always easy – for women like Roya or for anyone else. But then Roya discovered computers and the internet. She founded her own IT firm, often working with international clients who wanted to make their payments digitally. Most of the engineers that worked for Roya were women. Many were, whether socially or legally, blocked from traditional banking systems. Would-be patriarchs don't always take kindly to women managing their own money – no surprise there. So how was Roya supposed to pay her staff?

It would be heartless, and in willful opposition to reality, to expect Roya Mahboob to petition banks in Afghanistan for better financial inclusion and to politely linger until they gave her permission to start a business. Roya would need to take matters into her own hands, just as St. Jude did years ago.

For Roya, bitcoin was the answer. Without trusted mediators to say "no," Roya could pay her engineers in bitcoin. And without any managers to say "no," they could save some of that bitcoin for a rainy day. And without any trusted makers, they could trust that they'd keep a consistent share of all bitcoin in existence. For them, bitcoin was resistance money. And for some, it was salvation too. According to journalist Laura Shin:

> one woman whose husband beat her and confiscated her money was able to save her money once she began earning bitcoins, because her

husband could no longer take the money. She eventually saved enough to file for divorce.[8]

If you had been Roya or one of her engineers, would you want to receive and save your earnings without the permission of your husband or some bank manager?

Hold that thought.

Let's revisit Alexei Navalny. In 2011, Navalny was arrested for alleging election fraud on the part of Vladimir Putin. When he was released from jail, he began calling on Russians to unite against Putin. Since then, he has been jailed multiple times, surveilled, poisoned, and is now facing an indefinite prison sentence for "fraud and contempt of court."

Navalny chiefly lives on the donations of others; they fund his fight. But Putin's government blocks and closes down bank accounts. According to Navalny's campaign manager, Leonid Volkov, bitcoin has provided a lifeline:

> We use bitcoin because it's a good legal means of payment. The fact that we have bitcoin payments as an alternative helps to defend us from the Russian authorities. They see if they close down other more traditional channels, we will still have bitcoin. It's like insurance.[9]

The Russians are trying to crack down on Navalny's bitcoin donations as well,[10] but so far, Navalny has raised more than 658 bitcoin to support his work.[11] When you step out from behind the veil, you could be him.

Our final story is about Alina. That's not her real name. You'll never know it, and neither does the bitcoin network. But we can tell you a few things about her. Alina is a Ukrainian refugee who fled Kyiv with her children in early 2022. Alina's family stored their wealth in two ways. They had a house, and they had bitcoin. At the time of writing, Alina doesn't know how that family home is doing; she hasn't been there for over a year. And there was, of course, no time to sell the home before leaving nor any obvious buyer.

In times of tumult and war, bank deposits are unreliable. Gold would have been too heavy. Paper currency – too vulnerable. But the family bitcoin is just fine. When Alina crossed the border into Slovakia, the bitcoin came with her. Its private keys were stored in a small piece of paper, disguised as a bookmark and protected by a further passphrase. Alina doesn't know when she'll get to go home. But until then, she can dip into the family savings, and no war can stop her from doing so. For Alina, bitcoin is resistance money.

When you step out from behind the veil, you could be Alina. Or Navalny. Or Roya. And if you're not, someone else is.

Stories like these number in the thousands. We don't know them all, and even if we did, we wouldn't have the space to tell them. But when financial privacy has been eroded, when transactions have been censored, when monetary policy can change on a whim, when rapid inflation has threatened, and when the financial system has been closed to some, people have found refuge in bitcoin. As you step out from behind the veil, remember that you could have been any one of them.

We began with the claim that bitcoin is for criminals. And that's right. Bitcoin *is* for criminals – both good and bad.

But the deeper truth is that bitcoin is for whomever you might turn out to be.

Bitcoin is for anyone.

Notes

1. Chainalysis (2023b). Here and in other columns, one is best.
2. From www.democracymatrix.com/ranking
3. Rank by percentage of people who made or received digital payments, World Bank Findex Database, 2021.
4. From https://wisevoter.com/country-rankings/inflation-by-country/
5. Seth for Privacy (2022).
6. Hughes (1993).
7. https://99bitcoins.com/bitcoin-obituaries/
8. Shin (2017).
9. Zverev and Belton (2021).
10. Berwick and Wilson (2022).
11. Zverev and Belton (2021).

REFERENCES

6529. (2022). [Tweet]. https://mobile.twitter.com/punk6529/status/14944446246 30403083

Abramowitz, A., & Saunders, K. (2008). Is polarization a myth? *The Journal of Politics*, 70(2), 542–555.

Adams, D. (2022, July 22). These payment companies are cutting off Russia. *American Banker*. www.americanbanker.com/payments/list/these-payment-companies-are-cutting-off-russia

Alchian, A. A. (1977). Why money? *Journal of Money, Credit and Banking*, 9(1), 133–140. https://doi.org/10.2307/1992014

Alden, L. (2023a). *Bitcoin's energy usage isn't a problem*. www.lynalden.com/bitcoin-energy/

Alden, L. (2023b). *Broken money*. Timestamp Press.

Alexander, L. (1996). The magic of moral consent. *Legal Theory*, 2, 165–174.

American Experience. (2017). Ford's anti-semitism. *PBS*. www.pbs.org/wgbh/americanexperience/features/henryford-antisemitism/

Ammous, S. (2018a). Can cryptocurrencies fulfil the functions of money? *The Quarterly Review of Economics*, 70, 38–51.

Ammous, S. (2018b). *The bitcoin standard*. Wiley.

Anand, N., Nguyen, L., Cohen, L., & Stempel, J. (2023). JPMorgan settles with Jeffrey Epstein victims for $290 million. *Reuters*. www.reuters.com/legal/jpmorgan-agrees-settle-with-epstein-victim-class-action-suit-2023-06-12/

Anderson, M. (2017, December 13). Lebanon Central Bank to launch digital currency. *Zawya*. www.zawya.com/en/economy/lebanon-central-bank-to-launch-digital-currency-fm7gclzf

Anderson, P. D. (2021). *Prolegomena to any future historiography of the cypherpunk movement*. https://wikileaksbibliography.org/blog/prolegomena-to-any-future-historiography-of-the-cypherpunk-movement/

Androulaki, E., & Karame, G. O. (2014). Hiding transaction amounts and balances in bitcoin. In T. Holz & S. Ioannidis (Eds.), *Trust and trustworthy computing* (pp. 161–178). Springer.

Antognazza, M. R. (2008). *Leibniz: An intellectual biography*. Cambridge University Press.

Antonopoulos, A. M., & Harding, D. (2024). *Mastering bitcoin* (3rd ed.). O'Reilly.

Antonopoulos, A. M., Osuntokun, O., & Pickhardt, R. (2021). *Mastering the lightning network: A second layer blockchain protocol for instant bitcoin payments* (1st ed.). O'Reilly.

Arnold, M. (2018). Cryptocurrencies' underlying technology is here to stay. *Financial Times*. www.ft.com/content/47127c32-0b35-11e8-839d-41ca06376bf2

Arnosti, A., & Weinberg, S. (2018). *Bitcoin: A natural oligopoly*. https://arxiv.org/pdf/1811.08572.pdf

Auer, R., Frost, J., & María Vidal Pastor, J. (2022). Miners as intermediaries: Extractable value and market manipulation in crypto and DeFi. *BIS Bulletin, 58*. www.bis.org/publ/bisbull58.htm

Avan-Nomayo, O. (2021, April 22). Trump calls bitcoin a scam, advocates for dollar hegemony. *Cointelegraph*. https://cointelegraph.com/news/trump-calls-bitcoin-a-scam-advocates-for-dollar-hegemony

Azar, C., & Sandén, B. A. (2011). The elusive quest for technology-neutral policies. *Environmental Innovation and Societal Transitions, 1*, 135–139. www.semanticscholar.org/paper/The-elusive-quest-for-technology-neutral-policies-Azar-Sandén/9a3b838da2c622ceb6b33a0469c1d2b4faad33ea

Azouvi, S., & Vukolić, M. (2022). *Pikachu: Securing PoS blockchains from long-range attacks by checkpointing into bitcoin PoW using taproot*. https://arxiv.org/pdf/2208.05408.pdf

Back, A. (2002). *Hashcash – a denial of service counter-measure*. www.hashcash.org/hashcash.pdf

Bailey, A. M. (forthcoming). *Digital value*. Philosophy & Digitality.

Bailey, A. M., Cross, T., Hendrickson, J., Luther, W., Rettler, B., & Warmke, C. (ms). Bitcoin works in practice, but does it work in theory?

Bailey, A. M., & Luther, W. (2022a). The U.S. needs digital cash, not just digital currency. *Barron's*. www.barrons.com/articles/the-u-s-needs-digital-cash-not-just-digital-currency-51646431864?refsec=commentary

Bailey, A. M., & Luther, W. (2022b). If the Fed starts a digital currency, it had better guarantee privacy. *RealClearPolicy*. www.realclearpolicy.com/articles/2022/04/04/if_the_fed_starts_a_digital_currency_it_had_better_guarantee_privacy_825155.html

Bailey, A. M., & Rettler, B. (2021a). Bitcoin: An orange new deal. *Bitcoin Magazine*. https://bitcoinmagazine.com/culture/bitcoin-an-orange-new-deal

Bailey, A. M., & Rettler, B. (2021b). Governments should invest in the bitcoin network. *Newsweek*. www.newsweek.com/governments-should-invest-bitcoin-network-opinion-1623331

Bailey, A. M., Rettler, B., & Warmke, C. (2021a). Philosophy, politics, and economics of cryptocurrency I: Money without state. *Philosophy Compass, 16*(11).

Bailey, A. M., Rettler, B., & Warmke, C. (2021b). Philosophy, politics, and economics of cryptocurrency II: The moral landscape of monetary design. *Philosophy Compass, 16*(11).

Bailey, A. M., Rettler, B., & Warmke, C. (2022, January 28). Bitcoin isn't a right-wing plot. It's inclusive by design despite what critics say. *USA Today*. https://www.usatoday.com/story/opinion/2022/01/28/bitcoin-helps-low-income-americans/9225120002/

Bailey, A. M., & Warmke, C. (2023). Bitcoin is king. In J. Liebowitz (Ed.), *Cryptocurrency: Concepts, technology, and issues*. Taylor & Francis.

Bailey, A. M., & Warmke, C. (forthcoming). What Satoshi did. In T. Demeester & N. Smolenski (Eds.), *The Satoshi papers*. Texas Bitcoin Foundation.

Balea, J. (2016). The latest stats in web and mobile in Indonesia. *Tech in Asia*. www.techinasia.com/indonesia-web-mobile-statistics-we-are-social

Ballantyne, N. (2019a). Epistemic trespassing. *Mind, 128*(510), 367–395.

Ballantyne, N. (2019b). *Knowing our limits*. Oxford University Press.

Baradaran, M. (2018). *How the other half banks: Exclusion, exploitation, and the threat to democracy*. Harvard University Press.

Baradaran, M. (2020). Banking on democracy. *Washington University Law Review*, 98(2), 353–418. https://openscholarship.wustl.edu/cgi/viewcontent.cgi?article=6427&context=law_lawreview

Bartlett, J. (2016). Cypherpunks write code. *American Scientist, 104*(2), 120+.

Bartscher, D., Brown, M., Hryshko, D., Schuh, S., & Weinberg, J. (2022). The role of the private sector in the U.S. payment system. *Federal Reserve Bank of New York Staff Reports, 959*. www.newyorkfed.org/medialibrary/media/research/staff_reports/sr959.pdf (Original work published 2021)

Bastian-Pinto, C. L., Araujo, F. V. D. S., Brandão, L. E., & Gomes, L. L. (2021). Hedging renewable energy investments with bitcoin mining. *Renewable and Sustainable Energy Reviews, 138*. https://doi.org/10.1016/j.rser.2020.110520.

Batten, D. (2022). *A more complete picture of bitcoin's energy use*. https://batcoinz.com/a-more-complete-picture-of-bitcoins-energy-usage/

Baur, D. G., Hong, K., & Lee, A. D. (2018). Bitcoin: Medium of exchange or speculative asset? *Journal of International Financial Markets, Institutions and Money, 54*, 177–189.

Baydakova, A., & Reynolds, M. (2022). Frozen bitcoin tied to Canadian protests lands at Coinbase. *Nasdaq*. www.nasdaq.com/articles/frozen-bitcoin-tied-to-canadian-protests-lands-at-coinbase-crypto.com

BBC. (2020, September 21). Who leaked the FinCEN files and why? *BBC News*. www.bbc.com/news/uk-54225572

BBC. (2022). Bitcoin becomes official currency in Central African Republic. *BBC News*. www.bbc.com/news/world-africa-61248809

BCRA. (2022). *BCRA desalienta oferta de criptoactivos en el sistema financiero*. www.bcra.gob.ar/Noticias/BCRA-desalienta-oferta-criptoactivos-sistema-financiero.asp

Beltramini, E. (2021). Against technocratic authoritarianism. A short intellectual history of the cypherpunk movement. *Internet Histories, 5*, 101–118.

Benson, J. (2022). CBN reduces over-the-counter withdrawals to N100k/N500k per week for individuals, companies. *Nairametrics*. https://nairametrics.com/2022/12/06/breaking-cbn-reduces-over-the-counter-withdrawals-to-n100k-n500k-per-week-for-individuals-companies/

Berg, C. (2018). *"Financial privacy." The classical liberal case for privacy in a world of surveillance and technological change*. Palgrave Macmillan.

Bergeron, A. (2017). *The lightning paradox*. https://bitcoinwords.github.io/the-lightning-paradox

Bertaut, C., von Beschwitz, K., & Curcuru, S. (2021). The international role of the U.S. dollar. *Federal Reserve Bank of Boston*. www.federalreserve.gov/econres/notes/feds-notes/the-international-role-of-the-u-s-dollar-20211006.html

Berwick, A. (2022). Exclusive: At least $1 billion of client funds missing at failed crypto firm FTX. *Reuters*. www.reuters.com/markets/currencies/exclusive-least-1-billion-client-funds-missing-failed-crypto-firm-ftx-sources-2022-11-12/

Berwick, A., & Wilson, T. (2022). Special report: How crypto giant Binance built ties to a Russian FSB-linked agency. *Reuters*. www.reuters.com/technology/how-crypto-giant-binance-built-ties-russian-fsb-linked-agency-2022-04-22/

Bier, J. (2021). *The Blocksize War: The battle over who controls bitcoin's protocol rules*. https://blog.bitmex.com/the-blocksize-war-chapter-1-first-strike/

Biryukov, A., & Tikhomirov, S. (2019). Security and privacy of mobile wallet users in Bitcoin, Dash, Monero, and Zcash. *Pervasive and Mobile Computing*, *59*, 1–11.

Bitcoin Mining Council. (2022a). [website]. https://bitcoinminingcouncil.com

Bitcoin Mining Council. (2022b). *2022.10.13 BMC presentation Q3 22 presentation*. https://bitcoinminingcouncil.com/wp-content/uploads/2022/10/2022.10.13-BMC-Presentation-Q3-22-Presentation.pdf

Bitcoin Stack Exchange. (2020). https://bitcoin.stackexchange.com/questions/122/will-we-ever-need-smaller-amounts-of-bitcoin-than-a-satoshi

BitMex Research. (2022). *A complete history of bitcoin's consensus forks – 2022 update*. https://blog.bitmex.com/a-complete-history-of-bitcoins-consensus-forks-2022-update/

Bjerg, O. (2015). How is bitcoin money? *Theory, Culture and Society*, *33*, 53–72.

Blau, B. M., Griffith, T. G., & Whitby, R. J. (2021). Inflation and bitcoin: A descriptive time-series analysis. *Economics Letters*, *203*, 109848.

Bloomberg (Producer). (2022, September 22). Jamie Dimon calls crypto "decentralized ponzi schemes" [Video file]. *Bloomberg News*. www.bloomberg.com/news/videos/2022-09-22/jamie-dimon-calls-crypto-decentralized-ponzi-schemes

Bodley, J. (2022). Government crypto powers in spotlight after Canadian trucker protest is disbanded. *Blockworks*. https://blockworks.co/news/government-crypto-powers-in-spotlight-after-canadian-trucker-protest-is-disbanded

Boettke, P., Salter, A., & Smith, D. (2021). Money and the rule of law. In *Money and the rule of law: Generality and predictability in monetary institutions* (pp. 146–166). Cambridge University Press. https://doi.org/10.1017/9781108806787.007

Boettke, P., & Smith, D. (2016). Introduction to the economics of institutions and organizations. In *Economics of institutions and organizations: An introductory text* (pp. 1–26). Springer.

Bohannon, J. (2016). The bitcoin busts. *Science Magazine*, *351*, 1144–1146.

Bohr, J., & Bashir, M. (2014). Who uses bitcoin? An exploration of the bitcoin community. In *Twelfth Annual International Conference on Privacy, Security and Trust*. https://doi.org/10.1109/pst.2014.6890928

Boland-Rudder, A., & McGoey, L. (2021, September 20). As reforms sparked by 'FinCEN Files' roll out, a key source is behind bars. *International Consortium of Investigative Journalists*. www.icij.org/investigations/fincen-files/as-reforms-sparked-by-fincen-files-roll-out-a-year-on-key-source-is-behind-bars/

Bonneau, J. (2017). *Hostile blockchain takeovers*. https://fc18.ifca.ai/bitcoin/papers/bitcoin18-final17.pdf

Bordo, M. D. (1981). The classical gold standard: Some lessons for today. *Federal Reserve Bank of St. Louis Review, 63*(5), 2–16.

Bouri, E., Molnár, P., Azzi, G., Roubaud, D., & Hagfors, L. I. (2017). On the hedge and safe haven properties of Bitcoin: Is it really more than a diversifier? *Finance Research Letters, 20*, 192–198.

Braiins. (2022). Bitcoin nodes vs. miners: Demystified. *Braiins.* https://braiins.com/blog/bitcoin-nodes-vs-miners-demystified

Brettell, A. (2022, March 29). Sanctions weaponize the U.S. dollar, but some Treasury buyers could fall back. *Reuters.* www.reuters.com/business/finance/sanctions-weaponize-us-dollar-some-dollar-some-treasury-buyers-could-fall-back-2022–03–29/

Brito, J. (2019). The case for electronic cash. *Coin Center.* www.coincenter.org/the-case-for-electronic-cash/

Brooke, S., & Véliz, C. (2020, March). *Views on privacy: A survey. Data, privacy, and the individual.* https://docs.ie.edu/cgc/research/data-privacy/CGC-Data-Privacy-and-the-Individual-Report.pdf

Brownback, S. (2022). Are big banks chasing away religious organizations? *Washington Examiner.* www.washingtonexaminer.com/restoring-america/faith-freedom-self-reliance/are-big-banks-chasing-away-religious-organizations

Brunton, F. (2020). *Digital cash: The unknown history of the anarchists, utopians, and technologists who created cryptocurrency.* Princeton University Press.

Buchak, L. (2013). *Risk and rationality.* Oxford University Press.

Buchak, L. (2017). Taking risks behind the veil of ignorance. *Ethics, 127*(3), 610–644.

Budish, E. (2018). *The economic limits of bitcoin and anonymous, decentralized trust on the blockchain.* https://ericbudish.org/wp-content/uploads/2018/06/Economic-Limits-Bitcoin-Blockchain-June-2022.pdf

Bursztynsky, J. (2022). Former Amazon employee convicted in Capital One hack. *CNBC.* www.cnbc.com/2022/06/18/former-amazon-employee-convicted-in-capital-one-hack.html

Buterin, V. (2014). *Proof of stake: How I learned to love weak subjectivity.* https://blog.ethereum.org/2014/11/25/proof-stake-learned-love-weak-subjectivity

Buterin, V. (2022). *Proof of stake: The making of ethereum and the philosophy of blockchains.* Seven Stories Press.

Butler, S. (2022). The philosophy of bitcoin and the question of money. *Theory, Culture & Society, 39*(5), 81–102.

Byrd, M. (2022). US moves to transfer Afghanistan's frozen central bank reserves to a new Swiss fund. *United States Institute of Peace.* www.usip.org/publications/2022/09/us-move-afghanistans-frozen-central-bank-reserves-new-swiss-fund

Cambridge Centre for Alternative Finance. (2021). https://web.archive.org/web/20210504080905/https://cbeci.org/faq/

Cambridge Centre for Alternative Finance. (2023). *Cambridge bitcoin electricity consumption index.* https://ccaf.io/cbnsi/cbeci

Carlsten, M., Kalodner, H., Weinberg, M., & Narayanan, A. (2016). *On the instability of bitcoin without the block reward.* https://dl.acm.org/doi/10.1145/2976749.2978408

Carmona, T. (2022). Debunking the narratives about cryptocurrency and financial inclusion. *Brookings.* www.brookings.edu/research/debunking-the-narratives-about-cryptocurrency-and-financial-inclusion/

Carter, N. (2019). It's the settlement assurances, stupid. https://medium.com/@nic__carter/its-the-settlement-assurances-stupid-5dcd1c3f4e41

Carter, N. (2022). Bitcoin mining is America's most misunderstood industry. *Newsweek*. www.newsweek.com/bitcoin-mining-americas-most-misunderstood-industry-opinion-1669892

Carter, N., & Stevens, R. (2021). Bitcoin net zero. *NYDIG*. https://assets-global.website-files.com/614e11536f66309636c98688/616dbaa0e7aa2af652d58983_NYDIG-BitcoinNetZero_SML.pdf

Chainalysis. (2022a). Cryptocurrency liquidity and Russia sanctions. *Chainalysis Blog*. https://blog.chainalysis.com/reports/cryptocurrency-liquidity-russia-sanctions/

Chainalysis. (2022b). Pro-Russian crypto donations and the war in Ukraine. *Chainalysis Blog*. https://blog.chainalysis.com/reports/pro-russian-crypto-donations-war-in-ukraine/

Chainalysis. (2022c). Crypto crime report 2022. *Chainalysis*. https://go.chainalysis.com/2022-Crypto-Crime-Report.html

Chainalysis. (2023a). Crypto crime report 2023. *Chainalysis*. https://go.chainalysis.com/2023-Crypto-Crime-Report.html

Chainalysis. (2023b). The 2023 geography of cryptocurrency report. *Chainalysis*. https://go.chainalysis.com/geography-of-cryptocurrency-2023.html

Chaum, D. (1982). Blind signature for untraceable payments. In D. Chaum, R. L. Rivest, & A. T. Sherman (Eds.), *Republished in advances in cryptology proceedings of crypto 82* (pp. 199–203). Plenum. https://chaum.com/wp-content/uploads/2022/01/Chaum-blind-signatures.pdf

Cheah, E., & Fry, J. (2016). Speculative bubbles in Bitcoin markets? An empirical investigation into the fundamental value of bitcoin. *Journal of Monetary Economics*, 79, 47–60. https://doi.org/10.1016/j.jmoneco.2016.05.003

Chehayeb, K. (2022, October 7). *Lebanese banks close again after depositor hold-ups, bankers say*. Associated Press. https://apnews.com/article/middle-east-lebanon-beirut-0eef8f1fbe90ea77ce4284b410dd0e83

Chipolina, A. (2022). Crypto helping Ukraine in face of Russia invasion, says deputy minister. *Decrypt*. https://decrypt.co/94712/crypto-helping-ukraine-russia-invasion-deputy-minister

Choe, S.-H., & Robles, P. (2022). North Korea wants dollars. It's a sign of trouble. *New York Times*. www.nytimes.com/interactive/2022/12/09/world/asia/north-korea-promises.html

Choi, H. (2020). Breaking down the Black-white homeownership gap. *Urban Institute*. www.urban.org/urban-wire/breaking-down-black-white-homeownership-gap

Chong, D., Citrin, J., & Conley, P. (2001). When self-interest matters. *Political Psychology*, 22, 541–570.

Chow, C. (2022). Cryptocurrency laundering: How Bitfinex hack led to a lack of transparency in the crypto world. *Time*. https://time.com/6146749/cryptocurrency-laundering-bitfinex-hack/

Chowdhury, N. (2020). *Inside blockchain, bitcoin and cryptocurrencies*. CRC Press.

Christin, N., Androulaki, E., & Kim, J. (2008). Traveling the silk road: A measurement analysis of a large anonymous online marketplace. *Carnegie Mellon University*. www.andrew.cmu.edu/user/nicolasc/publications/CAPP-IS.pdf

Ciaian, P., Kancs, D., & Rajcaniova, M. (2021). The economic dependency of bitcoin security. *Applied Economics*, 53(49), 5738–5755. https://doi.org/10.1080/00036846.2021.1931003

Cohen, B. (2017). [Tweet]. https://twitter.com/bramcohen/status/892495105206083584

CoinMetrics. (2018). *Introducing realized capitalization*. https://coinmetrics.io/realized-capitalization/

CoinShares. (2022). *The bitcoin mining network: Energy and carbon impact*. https://coinshares.com/research/bitcoin-mining-network-2022

Collins, C. (2021). A year of billionaire pandemic gains: Who are the ten biggest pandemic profiteers? *Institute for Policy Studies*. https://ips-dc.org/a-year-of-billionaire-pandemic-gains/

Collins, C. (2022). Updates: Billionaire wealth, U.S. job losses and pandemic profiteers. *Inequality.org*. https://inequality.org/great-divide/updates-billionaire-pandemic/

Comiskey, D. S. (2012). The bizarre story of the liberty dollar. *Indianapolis Monthly*. www.indianapolismonthly.com/news-and-opinion/business/mad-money

Consolvo, B., & Caron, K. (2023). Bitcoin's role in the ESG imperative. *KPMG*. https://kpmg.com/us/en/articles/2023/bitcoin-role-esg-imperative.html

Consumer Financial Protection Bureau. (2022). CFPB research shows banks' deep dependence on overdraft fees. *Consumerfinance.gov*. www.consumerfinance.gov/about-us/newsroom/cfpb-research-shows-banks-deep-dependence-on-overdraft-fees

Cook, S. (2017, February). The battle for China's spirit: Religious revival, repression, and resistance under Xi Jinping. *Freedom House*. https://freedomhouse.org/report/special-report/2017/battle-chinas-spirit

Coppola, F. (2021). Why bitcoin should be priced in sats (and why it has a divisibility dilemma). *Coindesk*. www.coindesk.com/tech/2021/05/12/why-bitcoin-should-be-priced-in-sats-and-why-it-has-a-divisibility-dilemma/

Cornell University Police. (2022). Detecting and avoiding counterfeit currency. *Cornell University*. www.dfa.cornell.edu/sites/default/files/detect-counterfeit.pdf

Cross, T. (2022). Fighting the bitcoin mining FUD. *What Bitcoin Did* (podcast). www.youtube.com/watch?v=1vROP40L9Bg

Cross, T., & Bailey, A. (2021). *Greening bitcoin*. https://www.resistance.money/green/

Cross, T., & Bailey, A. (2023). Carbon neutral bitcoin adoption for nation states. In S. Matsuo, L. Gudgeon, A. Klages-Mundt, D. Hernandez, S. Werner, T. Haines, A. Essex, A. Bracciali, & M. Sala (Eds.), *Financial cryptography and data security. FC 2022 international workshops*. Springer. https://doi.org/10.1007/978-3-031-32415-4_4

Cruise, S., Withers, I., & White, L. (2023). UK banks back in political crosshairs after Farage fiasco. *Reuters*. https://www.reuters.com/business/finance/uk-banks-back-political-crosshairs-after-farage-fiasco-2023-07-28/

Cuthbertson, A. (2017). Bitcoin mining to consume all the world's energy by 2020. *Newsweek*. www.newsweek.com/bitcoin-mining-track-consume-worlds-energy-2020-744036

Dai, W. (1998). *b-money*. www.weidai.com/bmoney.txt

Dale, B. (2021). Lido protocol does Eth 2.0 staking but with a DeFi twist. *CoinDesk*. www.coindesk.com/lido-protocol-does-eth-2-0-staking-but-with-a-defi-twist

Das, D., & Dutta, D. (2020). Bitcoin's energy consumption: Is it the Achilles heel to miner's revenue? *Economics Letters*, *186*. https://doi.org/10.1016/j.econlet.2019.108530

Dashjr, L. (2022). *Bitcoin node count.* https://luke.dashjr.org/programs/bitcoin/files/charts/historical.html

Davis, J. (2013). The crypto-currency: Bitcoin and its mysterious inventor. *The New Yorker*. www.newyorker.com/magazine/2011/10/10/the-crypto-currency

De, N. (2021). State of crypto: The bitcoin fog indictment shows the permanence of user data. *CoinDesk*. www.coindesk.com/policy/2021/05/04/state-of-crypto-the-bitcoin-fog-indictment-shows-the-permanence-of-user-data/

Debevoise & Plimpton. (2022). *Re: In re tether and bitfinex crypto asset litigation, no. 19 Civ. 9236 (S.D.N.Y.). Memo to the Honorable Katherine Polk Failla.* https://storage.courtlistener.com/recap/gov.uscourts.nysd.524076/gov.uscourts.nysd.524076.247.0.pdf

DeCew, J. (2018). Privacy. In E. N. Zalta (Ed.), *The Stanford encyclopedia of philosophy* (Spring 2018 ed.). https://plato.stanford.edu/archives/spr2018/entries/privacy/

de Dinechin, E., Duhaut, S., Teffo, C., & Reynolds, O. (2019). Financial lives of Lebanese and Syrian refugees in Lebanon. *Findev Gateway*. www.findevgateway.org/sites/default/files/publications/files/financial_lives_of_lebanese_and_syrian_refugees_in_lebanon.pdf

De La O, A. L., & Rodden, J. A. (2008). Does religion distract the poor?: Income and issue voting around the world. *Comparative Political Studies*, *41*(4–5), 437–476.

Delaporte, A., & Bahia, K. (2022). *The state of internet mobile connectivity 2022.* www.gsma.com/r/wp-content/uploads/2022/12/The-State-of-Mobile-Internet-Connectivity-Report-2022.pdf

Demirgüç-Kunt, A., Klapper, L., Singer, D., & Ansar, S. (2022). *The global findex database 2021: Financial inclusion, digital payments, and resilience in the age of COVID-19.* World Bank Publications.

De Vroey, M. (2016). *A history of macroeconomics from Keynes to Lucas and beyond.* Cambridge University Press.

Dick, D. G. (2020). What money is and ought to be. *Journal of Social Ontology*, *6*(3), 371–380. https://doi.org/10.1515/jso-2020-0033

Diercks, E. (2017). The impact of digital innovation on the payment industry and its regulation. *Social Science Research Network*. https://papers.ssrn.com/sol3/papers.cfm?abstract_id=2989237

Dierksmeier, C., & Seele, P. (2018). Cryptocurrencies and business ethics. *Journal of Business Ethics*, *152*(1), 1–14.

Digiconomist. (2014). Dogeconomist rebranding to Digiconomist. https://digiconomist.net/dogeconomist_rebranding_to_digiconomist/

Digiconomist. (2021). Bitcoin electronic waste monitor. https://digiconomist.net/bitcoin-electronic-waste-monitor/

Digiconomist. (2022). Bitcoin energy consumption. https://digiconomist.net/bitcoin-energy-consumption

Dimock, M., & Wike, R. (2021). America is exceptional in its political divide. *Pew Research Center*. www.pewtrusts.org/en/trust/archive/winter-2021/america-is-exceptional-in-its-political-divide

Dittmar, L., & Praktiknjo, A. (2019). Could Bitcoin emissions push global warming above 2°C? *Nature Climate Change, 9, 656–657.* www.nature.com/articles/s41558-019-0534-5

Dixon, R. D., Lowery, R. C., Levy, D. E., & Ferraro, K. F. (1991). Self-interest and public opinion toward smoking policies: A replication and extension. *Public Opinion Quarterly, 55,* 241–254.

Dogan, E., Majeed, M. T., & Luni, T. (2022). Are clean energy and carbon emission allowances caused by bitcoin? A novel time-varying method. *Journal of Cleaner Production, 347.* https://doi.org/10.1016/j.jclepro.2022.131089

DOJ. (2022). Danske Bank pleads guilty to fraud on U.S. banks in multi-billion dollar scheme to access U.S. financial system. *U.S. Department of Justice.* www.justice.gov/opa/pr/danske-bank-pleads-guilty-fraud-us-banks-multi-billion-dollar-scheme-access-us-financial

Domat, C. (2016). Show me the money! No bank accounts for many Syrians in Lebanon. *Middle East Eye.* www.middleeasteye.net/features/show-me-money-no-bank-accounts-many-syrians-lebanon

Dougherty, T. (2018). Affirmative consent and due diligence. *Philosophy and Public Affairs, 46,* 90–112.

Dowd, K., & Greenaway, D. (1993). Currency competition, network externalities, and switching costs: Towards an alternative view of optimum currency areas. *The Economic Journal, 103*(420), 1180–1189.

Eatwell, J., & Milgate, M. (2011). *The fall and rise of Keynesian economics.* Oxford University Press.

Edstrom, A. (2019). *Why buy bitcoin?* Countercycle Media.

EFF. (2017). Documents about financial censorship under Operation Choke Point concern Congress. *Electronic Frontier Foundation.* www.eff.org/deeplinks/2017/02/documents-about-financial-censorship-under-operation-choke-point-concern-congress

Electronic Frontier Foundation. (2021). Letter to PayPal and Venmo: EFF and others. *Electronic Frontier Foundation.* www.eff.org/document/letter-paypal-and-venmo-eff-and-others

El-Haroun, R. (2021, October 21). Palestinians urge PayPal to offer services in West Bank, Gaza. *Reuters.* www.reuters.com/world/middle-east/palestinians-urge-paypal-offer-services-west-bank-gaza-2021-10-21/

Essien, E. (2020). Exclusive: Court documents confirm CBN froze bank accounts of Rinu Pamilerin, Gatefield, 17 other #EndSARS champions. *The Gazette Nigeria.* https://gazettengr.com/exclusive-court-documents-confirm-cbn-froze-bank-accounts-of-rinu-pamilerin-gatefield-17-other-endsars-champions/

European Parliament. (2022). Crypto assets: Deal on new rules to stop illicit flows in the EU. *Press Release.* www.europarl.europa.eu/news/en/press-room/20220627IPR33919/crypto-assets-deal-on-new-rules-to-stop-illicit-flows-in-the-eu

Eyal, I., & Sirer, E. G. (2013). *Majority is not enough: Bitcoin mining is vulnerable.* www.cs.cornell.edu/~ie53/publications/btcProcFC.pdf

Fabrichnaya, E., & Marrow, H. (2022). Russian c.bank proposes banning cryptocurrencies, crypto mining. *Reuters.* www.reuters.com/business/finance/russian-cbank-proposes-banning-cryptocurrencies-crypto-mining-2022-01-20/

Farrell, J. (2012). Can privacy be just another good? *Journal on Telecommunications and High Technology Law, 10,* 251–265.

Farrell, M. (2022). Your platform is not an ecosystem. *Crooked Timber Blog.* https://crookedtimber.org/2022/12/08/your-platform-is-not-an-ecosystem/

FBI. (2021). *Federal Bureau of Investigation. Internet crime report 2021.* www.ic3.gov/Media/PDF/AnnualReport/2021_IC3Report.pdf

Febrero, E. (2009). Three difficulties with neo-chartalism. *Journal of Post Keynesian Economics, 31*(3), 523–541.

Federal Deposit Insurance Corporation (FDIC). (2022). *FDIC: National survey of unbanked and underbanked households.* www.fdic.gov/analysis/household-survey/index.html

Federal Reserve Bank of San Francisco. (2003). *Private and public corporation. The Doctor of Economics.* www.frbsf.org/education/publications/doctor-econ/2003/september/private-public-corporation/

Federal Reserve FAQ. (2022). www.federalreserve.gov/faqs/currency_12772.htm

Fedwire. (2022). Fedwire funds service – annual statistics. *Fedwire.com.* www.frbservices.org/resources/financial-services/wires/volume-value-stats/annual-stats.html

Fergusson, A. (2010). *When money dies: The nightmare of deficit spending, devaluation, and hyperinflation in Weimar Germany.* PublicAffairs.

Ficsór, Á., Kogman, Y., Ontivero, L., & Seres, I. A. (2021). W*abiSabi: Centrally coordinated CoinJoins with variable amounts.* https://eprint.iacr.org/2021/206.pdf

Fifield, A. (2019, September 19). For China's embattled Uighurs, a bank transfer abroad can become a terrorism ordeal. *The Washington Post.* www.washingtonpost.com/world/asia_pacific/for-chinas-embattled-uighurs-a-bank-transfer-abroad-can-become-a-terrorism-ordeal/2019/09/19/eb6a8b1e-c3dd-11e9-b5e4-54aa56d5b7ce_story.html

Financial Inclusion Tech. (2022). *Open letter.* www.financialinclusion.tech/

Finn, R. L., Wright, D., & Friedewald, M. (2013). Seven types of privacy. In S. Gutwirth, R. Leenes, P. de Hert, & Y. Poullet (Eds.), *European data protection: Coming of age.* Springer. https://doi.org/10.1007/978-94-007-5170-5_1

Finney, H. (2009a). [Tweet]. https://twitter.com/halfin/status/1110302988

Finney, H. (2009b). Re: Bitcoin v0.1 released. *Email.* www.mail-archive.com/cryptography@metzdowd.com/msg10152.html

Flitter, E., & Yaffe-Bellany, D. (2022, February 23). Russia sanctions turn to cryptocurrency. *The New York Times.* www.nytimes.com/2022/02/23/business/russia-sanctions-cryptocurrency.html

Fodor, J. (1974). Special sciences (Or: The disunity of science as a working hypothesis). *Synthese, 28,* 97–115.

Franck, E. (2022, June 29). DOJ says allies have frozen $30 billion of Russian oligarch assets. *CNBC.* www.cnbc.com/2022/06/29/doj-says-allies-have-frozen-30-billion-of-russian-oligarch-assets.html

Freeman, A. (2017). Racism in the credit card industry. *North Carolina Law Review, 95,* 1071. https://ssrn.com/abstract=2976471

Fridgen, G., Körner, M. F., Walters, S., & Weibelzahl, M. (2021). Not all doom and gloom: How Energy-intensive and temporally flexible data center applications may actually promote renewable energy sources. *Business & Information Systems Engineering*, 63, 243–256. https://doi.org/10.1007/s12599-021-00686-z

Friedman, M. (1960). *A program for monetary stability*. Fordham University Press.

Friedman, M. (1970). Counter-revolution in monetary theory. Wincott Memorial Lecture, Institute of Economic Affairs, occasional paper 33.

Friedman, M. (2012). *The indispensable Milton Friedman: Essays on politics and economics*. Alan O. Ebenstein.

Frisby, D. (2014). *Bitcoin: The future of money?* Unbound.

Georgiopoulos, L. (2019). Greece to fully lift capital controls imposed during bailout chaos. *Reuters*. www.reuters.com/article/us-greece-economy-capital-controls/greece-to-fully-lift-capital-controls-imposed-during-bailout-chaos-idUSKCN1VG148

Gerard, D. (2017). *Attack of the 50 foot blockchain: Bitcoin, blockchain, ethereum & smart contracts*. CreateSpace Independent Publishing Platform.

Gervais, A., Karame, G. O., Wüst, K., Glykantzis, V., Ritzdorf, H., & Capkun, S. (2015). *Tampering with the delivery of blocks and transactions in bitcoin*. https://eprint.iacr.org/2015/578.pdf

Ghesmatia, S., Fdhila, W., & Weippl, E. (2021). *SoK: How private is bitcoin? Classification and evaluation of bitcoin mixing techniques*. https://eprint.iacr.org/2021/629.pdf

Gilovich, T. (1991). *How we know what isn't so: The fallibility of human reason in everyday life*. Free Press.

Gkritsi, E. (2022a). Bitcoin miners powered off as winter storm battered North America. *Coindesk*. www.coindesk.com/business/2022/12/26/bitcoin-miners-powered-off-as-winter-storm-battered-north-america/

Gkritsi, E. (2022b). Bitcoiners Scoff at Chris Larsen's $5M campaign to force a BTC code change. *Coindesk*. www.coindesk.com/tech/2022/03/29/bitcoiners-scoff-at-chris-larsens-5m-campaign-to-force-a-btc-code-change/

Gladstein, A. (2018). Why bitcoin matters for freedom. *Time*. https://time.com/5486673/bitcoin-venezuela-authoritarian/

Gladstein, A. (2021). Can governments stop bitcoin? *RealClearPolicy*. www.realclearpolicy.com/2021/02/25/can_governments_stop_bitcoin_661635.html

Gladstein, A. (2022). *Check your financial privilege*. BTC Media, LLC.

Glazier, M. (2021). Enterprise blockchain doesn't work because it's about the real world. *CoinDesk*. https://www.coindesk.com/markets/2021/03/31/enterprise-blockchain-doesnt-work-because-its-about-the-real-world/

Glazier, M. (ms). In blockchain we trust?

GlobalNews CA. (2022). CCLA calls for emergency legislation to protect democracy and civil liberties. *Global News*. https://globalnews.ca/news/8620547/ccla-emergency-legislation-democracy-civil-liberties/

Golumbia, D. (2016). *The politics of bitcoin: Software as right-wing extremism*. University of Minnesota Press.

Graeber, D. (2011). *Debt: The first 500 years*. Melville House.

Granja, J. (2023). *Bank fragility and reclassification of securities into HTM*. University of Chicago, Becker Friedman Institute for Economics Working Paper.

Greene, R. (2022, August 22). Southeast Asia's growing interest in non-dollar financial channels and renminbi's potential role. *Carnegie Endowment for*

International Peace. https://carnegieendowment.org/2022/08/22/southeast-asia-s-growing-interest-in-non-dollar-financial-channels-and-renminbi-s-potential-role-pub-87731

Griffin, J., & Shams, A. (2020). Is bitcoin really untethered? *The Journal of Finance, 75*(4), 1913–1964.

Gronewold, A. (2022). Hochul signs partial cryptocurrency mining ban into New York law. *Politico.* www.politico.com/news/2022/11/22/cryptocurrency-mining-ban-new-york-00070613

Grossmann-Wirth, V. (2019). What monetary policy operational frameworks in the new financial environment? A comparison of the US fed and the eurosystem perspectives, 2007–2019. *International Journal of Political Economy, 48*(4), 336–352.

Guaidó, J. (2019). Venezuela's Juan Guaidó faces investigation. *The Guardian.* www.theguardian.com/world/2019/jan/29/venezuela-juan-guaido-tarek-saab-investigation

Hadid, D. (2022). Taliban women and the burqa decree. *NPR.* www.npr.org/2022/05/07/1097382550/taliban-women-burqa-decree

Hall, J. (2022a). Flower powered: Bitcoin miner heats greenhouses in the Netherlands. *Cointelegraph.* https://cointelegraph.com/news/flower-powered-bitcoin-miner-heats-greenhouses-in-the-netherlands

Hall, J. (2022b). Sustainable bitcoin miner uses waste heat to dry wood. *Cointelegraph.* https://cointelegraph.com/news/sustainable-bitcoin-miner-uses-waste-heat-to-dry-wood

Halvorson, M. J. (2021). Judith Milhon: Hacking on the edges of polite computing society. https://halvormj.medium.com/judith-milhon-hacking-on-the-edges-of-polite-computing-society-5128e03ee141

Hanke, S. H., Klingaman, E. D., & Kwok, A. C. (2021). Why cryptocurrencies are not the future of money. *Journal of Housing and the Built Environment, 36*(1), 1–24. https://doi.org/10.1007/s10901-021-09824-8

Harmon, N. (2022). Bitcoin, energy, and the environment. *Podcast.* https://anchor.fm/troy-cross0/episodes/Nathaniel-Harmon-e1gl1t4

Harper, C. (2021). The bitcoin double-spend that never happened. *CoinDesk.* www.coindesk.com/tech/2021/01/21/the-bitcoin-double-spend-that-never-happened/

Harsanyi, J. C. (1953). Cardinal utility in welfare economics and in the theory of risk-taking. *Journal of Political Economy, 61*(5), 434–435.

Harsanyi, J. C. (1955). Cardinal welfare, individualistic ethics, and interpersonal comparisons of utility. *Journal of Political Economy, 63*(4), 309–321.

Haslanger, S. (1995). Ontology and social construction. *Philosophical Topics, 23*(2), 95–125.

Hasu, J. P., & Curtis, B. (2019). *A model for Bitcoin's security and the declining block subsidy.* https://uncommoncore.co/wp-content/uploads/2019/10/A-model-for-Bitcoins-security-and-the-declining-block-subsidy-v1.06.pdf

Hazlett, P. K., & Luther, W. (2020). Is bitcoin money? And what that means. *Quarterly Review of Economics and Finance, 77*, 144–149.

Hendrickson, J., & Luther, W. (2017). Banning bitcoin. *Journal of Economic Behavior & Organization, 141*, 188–195.

Hendrickson, J. R., & Salter, A. W. (2018). Going beyond monetary constitutions: The congruence of money and finance. *The Quarterly Review of Economics and Finance, 69*, 22–28.

Herskind, L., Katsikouli, P., & Dragoni, N. (2020). Privacy and cryptocurrencies – a systematic literature review. *IEEE Access, 8*, 54044–54059.

Hinsdale, J. (2022). *Cryptocurrency's dirty secret: Energy consumption.* https://news.climate.columbia.edu/2022/05/04/cryptocurrency-energy/

Hintze, J. (2022). Moneymaker lawsuit vs. PayPal filed in Singapore; Amazon added as second defendant. *Poker.org.* www.poker.org/updated-moneymaker-lawsuit-vs-paypal-filed-in-singapore-amazon-added-as-second-defendant/

Hinzen, F. J., Kose, J., & Saleh, F. (2022). Bitcoin's limited adoption problem. *Journal of Financial Economics, 144*, 347–369.

Hodl. (2022). Bitcoin bull Max Keiser updates $220,000 BTC prediction: Here's his timeline. *Daily Hodl.* https://dailyhodl.com/2022/01/17/bitcoin-bull-max-keiser-updates-220000-btc-prediction-heres-his-timeline/

Hooper, D. (2022). Canada freedom convoy fundraiser draws Republicans. *Politico.* www.politico.com/news/2022/02/08/canada-freedom-convoy-fundraiser-republicans-00007007

Horwitz, S. (2006). Language, monetary exchange, and the structure of the economic universe: An Austrian–Searlean synthesis. In B. Montero & M. D. White (Eds.), *Economics and the mind.* Routledge.

Houy, N. (2019). Rational mining limits bitcoin emissions. *Nature Climate Change, 9*, 655. www.nature.com/articles/s41558-019-0533-6

Huang, C., O'Neill, B. D., & Hiroko, K. (2021). Bitcoin's heavy hand: The power of cryptocurrency is consuming as much electricity as all of Argentina. *The New York Times.* www.nytimes.com/interactive/2021/09/03/climate/bitcoin-carbon-footprint-electricity.html

Hughes, E. (1993). *A cypherpunk's manifesto.* www.activism.net/cypherpunk/manifesto.html

Hügli, P. (2022). Bitcoin is far more than a new form of money. *Coindesk.* www.coindesk.com/layer2/2022/03/24/bitcoin-is-far-more-than-a-new-form-of-money/

Human Rights Foundation. (2022). 2021 HRF annual report. *Human Rights Foundation.* https://hrf.org/wp-content/uploads/2022/03/2021-HRF-Annual-Report-Final.pdf

Human Rights Watch. (2022). Colombia. *World report 2022.* www.hrw.org/world-report/2022/country-chapters/colombia

Hutabarat, S. P. H. (2023). *Essays on bitcoin mining and renewable energy: Exploring sustainability and profitability.* Dissertation, Colorado State University. https://mountainscholar.org/items/39313b43-8d2e-42fe-afe9-3d427e827769

Hütten, M., & Thiemann, M. (2017). Moneys at the margins. In M. Campbell-Verduyn (Ed.), *Bitcoin and beyond.* Taylor and Francis.

Ibañez, J. I., & Freier, A. (2023). *SoK: Bitcoin, energy consumption and environmental impact.* arXiv preprint arXiv:2304.04578.

Imbert, F. (2016). Coke criticisms are one-sided, 'immature and stupid': Berkshire's Munger. *CNBC.* www.cnbc.com/2016/04/30/coke-criticisms-are-one-sided-immature-and-stupid-berkshires-munger.html

Innes, A. M. (1914). Credit theory of money. *The Banking Law Journal*, *31*(2), 151–168.

Jackson, R. B., Solomon, E., Canadell, J., Cargnello, M., & Field, C. (2019). Methane removal and atmospheric restoration. *Nature Sustainability*, *2*, 436–438. https://doi.org/10.1038/s41893-019-0299-x

Jaggar, A. M. (2019). Thinking about Justice in the unjust meantime. *Feminist Philosophy Quarterly*, *5*(2). https://doi.org/10.5206/fpq/2019.2.7283

Jahal, J. (2021, November 5). Palestinian banks accused of colluding with Israel. *Al-Monitor*. www.al-monitor.com/originals/2021/11/palestinian-banks-accused-colluding-israel

Jakobson, R. (1962). Why 'mama' and 'papa'? In R. Jakobson (Ed.), *Selected writings, vol. I: Phonological studies* (pp. 538–545). Mouton.

Jarvis, C. (2021). Cypherpunk ideology: Objectives, profiles, and influences (1992–1998). *Internet Histories*, 1–27.

Jones, C. (2018, November 15). Bank of England to offer real-time gross settlement service for cryptocurrencies. *Financial Times*. www.ft.com/content/92c4737e-e8ed-11e8-885c-e64da4c0f981

Jones, D. (2021). Switzerland approves ban on face coverings in public. *NPR*. www.npr.org/2021/03/07/974630640/switzerland-approves-ban-on-face-coverings-in-public

Joy, J. (2013). Cyprus bank deposit tax: Robbery or smart move? *CNN*. www.cnn.com/2013/03/19/business/cyprus-deposit-tax-robbery

Kahan, D. M. (2016). The politically motivated reasoning paradigm, part 1: What politically motivated reasoning is and how to measure it. In R. A. Scott & S. M. Kosslyn (Eds.), *Emerging trends in the social and behavioral sciences*. Wiley. https://doi.org/10.1002/9781118900772.etrds0417

Kahn, A. (2018). Payment systems and privacy. *Federal Reserve Bank of St. Louis Review*, *100*(4), 479–499. https://doi.org/10.20955/r.100.479-499

Kahn, C. M., McAndrews, J., & Roberds, W. (2005). Money is privacy. *International Economic Review*, *46*(2), 377–399.

Kaplan, E. (2022). Cryptocurrency goes green: Proof-of-stake offers solution to energy concerns. *NBC News*, *1*(1). www.nbcnews.com/tech/tech-news/cryptocurrency-goes-green-proof-stake-offer-solution-energy-concerns-rcna1030

Kavanagh, D., & Dylan-Ennis, P. J. (2020). Cryptocurrencies and the emergence of blockocracy. *The Information Society*, *36*(5), 290–300.

Keating, R. (2018). Operation Choke Point reveals true injustices of Obama's Justice Department. *The Hill*. https://thehill.com/blogs/congress-blog/politics/415478-operation-choke-point-reveals-true-injustices-of-obamas-justice/

Kelly, J. (2021a). On bitcoin's fee-based security model – part 1: Beware the Turkey fallacy. https://joekelly100.medium.com/on-bitcoins-fee-based-security-model-part-1-beware-the-turkey-fallacy-4285e18d41ea

Kelly, J. (2021b). On bitcoin's fee-based security model – part 2: Security vs. what? https://joekelly100.medium.com/on-bitcoins-fee-based-security-model-part-2-security-vs-what-54024a958ad1

Keynes, J. M. (1920). *The economic consequences of the peace*. Harcourt, Brace & Company.

King, R. (2009). Lessons from the data breach at heartland. *Businessweek.* https://web.archive.org/web/20140608030215/www.businessweek.com/stories/ 2009-07-06/lessons-from-the-data-breach-at-heartlandbusinessweek-business-news-stock-market-and-financial-advice

Klein, B. (1974). The competitive supply of money. *Journal of Money, Credit and Banking, 6*(4), 423–453.

Kochkodin, B. (2023). Who is Balaji Srinivasan and why should we care about his $1 million bitcoin prediction? *Forbes.* www.forbes.com/sites/brandonkochkodin/ 2023/03/20/who-is-balaji-srinivasan-and-why-should-we-care-about-his-1-million-bitcoin-prediction

Koerth, B., & Thomson-DeVeaux, C. (2021). Our radicalized republic. *FiveThirtyEight.* https://fivethirtyeight.com/features/our-radicalized-republic/

Kollewe, J. (2018). Bitcoin is 'noxious poison', says Warren Buffett's investment chief. *Guardian.* www.theguardian.com/technology/2018/feb/15/bitcoin-is-noxious-poison-says-warren-buffett-investment-chief

Koning, J. P. (2019). *Is bitcoin getting less volatile?* http://jpkoning.blogspot. com/2019/06/is-bitcoin-getting-less-volatile.html

Koomey, J. (2017). Epilogue. In *Turning numbers into knowledge: Mastering the art of problem solving* (3rd ed.). Analytics Press.

Koomey, J., & Masanet, E. (2021). Does not compute: Avoiding pitfalls assessing the Internet's energy and carbon impacts. *Joule, 5*(7), 1625–1628. https://doi. org/10.1016/j.joule.2021.05.007. www.sciencedirect.com/science/article/pii/ S2542435121002117

Kristoufek, L. (2020). *On the role of stablecoins in cryptoasset pricing dynamics.* https://papers.ssrn.com/sol3/papers.cfm?abstract_id=3672909

Krugman, P. (2011, September 7). Golden cyberfetters. *The New York Times.* https://krugman.blogs.nytimes.com/2011/09/07/golden-cyberfetters/

Krugman, P. (2018, March 1). [Tweet]. https://twitter.com/paulkrugman/status/ 959801709794078720

Krugman, P. (2021, May 20). The cryptocurrency bubble is a gigantic nothing-burger. *The New York Times.* www.nytimes.com/2021/05/20/opinion/crypto-currency-bitcoin.html

Krugman, P. (2022, June 6). The fraud that is cryptocurrency. *The New York Times.* www.nytimes.com/2022/06/06/opinion/cryptocurrency-bubble-fraud.html

Kubát, M. (2015). Virtual currency bitcoin in the scope of money definition and store of value. *Procedia Economics and Finance, 30*, 409–416.

Kumar, R., & O'Brien, S. (2019). 2019 findings from the diary of consumer payment choice. *Fednotes/Federal Reserve Bank of San Francisco.* www.frbsf.org/ cash/publications/fed-notes/#2018

Kumble, S. P., Epema, D., & Roos, S. (2021). *How lightning's routing diminishes its anonymity.* https://arxiv.org/pdf/2107.10070.pdf

Kunda, Z. (1990). The case for motivated reasoning. *Psychological Bulletin, 108*(3), 480–498. https://doi.org/10.1037/0033-2909.108.3.480

Kwecka, Z., Buchanan, W., Schafer, B., & Rauhofer, J. (2014). "I am Spartacus": Privacy enhancing technologies, collaborative obfuscation and privacy as a public good. *Artificial Intelligence and Law, 22*(2), 113–139.

Kydland, F., & Wynne, M. (2002). The great inflation of the 1970s: What have we learned? *Federal Reserve Bank of Dallas Economic and Financial Policy Review, 84*(1), 1–16.

Lagos, R. (2008). Inside and outside money. In M. Vernengo, E. P. Caldentey, & B. J. Rosser, Jr., (Eds.), *The new Palgrave dictionary of economics*. Palgrave Macmillan. https://doi.org/10.1057/978-1-349-95121-5_2740-1

Lal, A., Zhu, J., & You, F. (2023). From mining to mitigation: How bitcoin can support renewable energy development and climate action. *ACS Sustainable Chemistry and Engineering, 11*, 16330–16340.

La Roche, J. (2021). Charlie Munger: 'Of course, I hate the bitcoin success'. *Yahoo Finance*. https://finance.yahoo.com/news/buffett-and-munger-on-bit-coin-213317653.html

Laurent, L. (2022). *Celsius crypto FOMO proved irresistible to finance pros too.* www.bloomberg.com/opinion/articles/2022-06-13/celsius-crypto-blowup-fomo-proved-irresistible-to-finance-pros

Lawson, B. (2013). Individual complicity in collective wrongdoing. *Ethical Theory and Moral Practice, 16*(2), 227–243.

Lei, N., Masanet, E., & Koomey, K. (2021). Best practices for analyzing the direct energy use of blockchain technology systems: Review and policy recommendations. *Energy Policy, 156.* www.sciencedirect.com/science/article/pii/S0301421521002925

Levy, S. (2001). *Crypto*. Penguin.

Lew, J. (2016, October 19). Remarks of Secretary Lew on the evolution of sanctions and lessons for the future at the Carnegie Endowment for International Peace. *United States Department of the Treasury.* www.treasury.gov/press-center/press-releases/Pages/jl0398.aspx

Lewis, D. (1969). *Convention: A philosophical study*. Wiley-Blackwell.

Lewis, D. (1970). How to define theoretical terms. *Journal of Philosophy, 67*, 427–446.

Lewis, D. (1979). Counterfactual dependence and time's arrow. *Noûs, 13*, 455–476.

Lewis, D. (1986). *On the plurality of worlds*. Wiley-Blackwell.

Lewis, S. J. (2017). *Queer privacy*. MIT Press.

Lewis-Beck, M. S., Norpoth, H., Jacoby, W. G., & Weisberg, H. F. (2008). *The American voter revisited*. University of Michigan Press.

Li, F., & McMillin, B. (2014). A survey on zero-knowledge proofs. *Advances in Computers, 94*, 25–69.

Lipman, M. (2023). On bitcoin: A study in applied metaphysics. *The Philosophical Quarterly, 73*, 783–802.

Liu, Z., & Papa, M. (2022). *Can BRICS de-dollarize the global financial system? Elements in the economics of emerging markets*. Cambridge University Press. https://doi.org/10.1017/9781009029544

Lopp, J. (2018). Who controls Bitcoin core? *Lopp*. https://blog.lopp.net/who-controls-bitcoin-core-/

Lopp, J. (2022). Bitcoin information & educational resources. *Lopp*. www.lopp.net/bitcoin-information.html

Lorenzoni, G. (2021). *The prudential use of capital controls and foreign currency reserves. National Bureau of Economic Research Working Paper 29476.* www. nber.org/papers/w29476

Luther, M. (2017, September 14). How much cash is used by criminals and tax cheats? *American Institute for Economic Research.* www.aier.org/article/ how-much-cash-is-used-by-criminals-and-tax-cheats/

Luther, W. J. (2016). Cryptocurrencies, network effects, and switching costs. *Contemporary Economic Policy, 34*(3), 553–571.

Luther, W. J. (2018a). Is bitcoin intrinsically worthless? *The Journal of Private Enterprise, 33*(1), 31–45.

Luther, W. J. (2018b). In defense of cash. *Reason Magazine,* 36–41.

Luther, W. J. (2019). Review of Golumbia (2016). *Review of Austrian Economics, 32*(1), 85–88.

Luther, W. J. (2022). *Pornhub and the Value of Bitcoin. AIER Sound Money Project Working Paper.* https://papers.ssrn.com/sol3/papers.cfm?abstract_id=4036795

Lyons, R., & Viswanath-Natraj, G. (2022). What keeps stablecoins stable? *Journal of International Money and Finance.* https://papers.ssrn.com/sol3/papers. cfm?abstract_id=3508006

Machin, J. (2014). *Manchin demands federal regulators ban bitcoin.* Press Release. www.manchin.senate.gov/newsroom/press-releases/manchin-demands-federal-regulators-ban-bitcoin

Mafi-Kreft, E. (2003). The relationship between currency competition and inflation. *Kyklos, 56,* 475–490. https://doi.org/10.1046/j.0023-5962.2003.00234.x

Makarov, I., & Schoar, A. (2021). *Blockchain analysis of the bitcoin market.* Working Paper 29396. National Bureau of Economic Research. https://doi.org/10.3386/ w29396. www.nber.org/system/files/working_papers/w29396/w29396.pdf

Malik, N., Aseri, M., Singh, P. V., & Srinivasan, K. (2022). Why bitcoin will fail to scale? *Management Science, 68*(10), 7065–7791. https://pubsonline.informs. org/doi/abs/10.1287/mnsc.2021.4271?journalCode=mnsc

Mallin, A. (2020). US charges North Koreans, Chinese nationals in multi-billion dollar money laundering scheme. *ABC News.* https://abcnews.go.com/Politics/ us-charges-north-koreans-chinese-nationals-multi-billion/story?id=70932712

Manley, D. (2019). *Reason better.* TopHat.

Manne, R. (2011). The cypherpunk revolutionary. *The Monthly.* www.themonthly. com.au/issue/2011/february/1324596189/robert-manne/cypherpunk-revolutionary

Manskar, M. (2019). PayPal turns off payments to Pornhub models. *New York Post.* https://nypost.com/2019/11/15/paypal-turns-off-payments-to-pornhub-models/

Masanet, E., Shehabi, A., Lei, N., Vranken, H., Koomey, J., & Malmodin, J. (2019). Implausible projections overestimate near-term Bitcoin CO_2 emissions. *Nature Climate Change, 9,* 653–654. www.nature.com/articles/s41558-019-0535-4

Mason, R. (2016). The metaphysics of social kinds. *Philosophy Compass, 11*(12), 841–850.

Matsakis, L. (2019). How the West got China's social credit system wrong. *Wired.* https://www.wired.com/story/china-social-credit-score-system/

Matthews, S. (2010). Anonymity and the social self. *American Philosophical Quarterly, 47*(4), 351–363.

Maxwell, G. (2013). CoinJoin: Bitcoin privacy for the real world. https://bitcoin-talk.org/index.php?topic=279249.0

May, T. C. (1994). Blacknet worries. *Cypherpunk Mail List*. https://mailing-list-archive.cryptoanarchy.wiki/archive/1994/02/e6a43588522aa402985d-90327d9c5f277b55752676f702030c4920b87f635a1b/

McAfee, J. (2017, July 17). [Tweet]. https://twitter.com/officialmcafee/status/887024683379544065

McAfee, J. (2019, August 6). [Tweet]. https://twitter.com/officialmcafee/status/1158739823852527619

McAfee, J. (2020, January 7). [Tweet]. https://twitter.com/officialmcafee/status/1213839069681205254

McCauley, R. (2021). Why bitcoin is worse than a Madoff-style Ponzi scheme. *Financial Times*. www.ft.com/content/83a14261-598d-4601-87fc-5dde528b33d0

McCook, H. (2023). Drivers of bitcoin energy use and emissions. In S. Matsuo, L. Gudgeon, A. Klages-Mundt, D. Hernandez, S. Werner, T. Haines, A. Essex, A. Bracciali, & M. Sala (Eds.), *Financial cryptography and data security. FC 2022 international workshops. FC 2022. Lecture notes in computer science, vol. 13412*. Springer. https://doi.org/10.1007/978-3-031-32415-4_2

McDowell, D. (2020). Payments power: The overlooked role of the dollar as top international payments currency. (Part of the symposium: Global monetary order and the liberal order debate.) *International Studies Perspectives, 21*, 109–153.

McIntyre, A. (2023). Doctrine of double effect. In E. N. Zalta & U. Nodelman (Eds.), *The Stanford encyclopedia of philosophy*. Metaphysics Research Lab, Stanford University. https://plato.stanford.edu/archives/win2023/entries/double-effect/

McKinney, J. (2018). Bitcoin security: A Negative exponential. https://medium.com/coinmonks/bitcoin-security-a-negative-exponential-95e78b6b575

McLeay, M., & Thomas, R. (2014). Money creation in the modern economy. *Bank of England Quarterly Bulletin, 54*(1), 14–27. www.bankofengland.co.uk/-/media/boe/files/quarterly-bulletin/2014/money-creation-in-the-modern-economy.pdf

Menati, A., Zheng, X., Lee, K., Shi, R., Du, P., Singh, C., & Xie, L. (2023). High resolution modeling and analysis of cryptocurrency mining's impact on power grids: Carbon footprint, reliability, and electricity price. *Advances in Applied Energy, 10*. https://doi.org/10.1016/j.adapen.2023.100136

Menger, K. (1892). On the origin of money. *The Economic Journal, 2*(6), 239–255. https://doi.org/10.2307/2956146

Merrill, T. W. (2015). Ownership and possession. In Y. Chang (Ed.), *Law and economics of possession* (pp. 9–39). Cambridge University Press.

Messias, J., Böhme, R., Edelman, B., Moore, T., & Henrique, L. (2021). *Selfish & opaque transaction ordering in the bitcoin blockchain: The case for chain neutrality*. https://dl.acm.org/doi/pdf/10.1145/3487552.3487823

Messina, J. P. (2023). *Private censorship*. Oxford University Press.

Metzger, P. E. (2022). [Tweet]. https://twitter.com/perrymetzger/status/1515783994192896009

Michaelson, R. (2022, January 21). Tales from the crypto: Lira crisis fuels Bitcoin boom in Turkey. *The Guardian*. www.theguardian.com/business/2022/jan/21/tales-from-the-crypto-lira-crisis-fuels-bitcoin-boom-in-turkey

Mikerah. (2022). Awesome privacy on blockchains. https://github.com/Mikerah/awesome-privacy-on-blockchains

Mill, J. S. (1989). On liberty. In C.L. Ten (Ed.), *'On liberty' and other writings*. Cambridge University Press. (Original work published 1859)

Mills, C. (1998). *Blackness visible: Essays on philosophy and race*. Cornell University Press.

Milman, O. (2022). Bitcoin miners revived a dying coal plant – then CO_2 emissions soared. *Guardian*. www.theguardian.com/technology/2022/feb/18/bitcoin-miners-revive-fossil-fuel-plant-co2-emissions-soared

Ming, C. (2018, March 5). Bitcoin more likely to be $100 than $100,000 in 10 years, Kenneth Rogoff says. *CNBC*. www.cnbc.com/2018/03/05/bitcoin-more-likely-to-be-100-than-100000-in-10-years-kenneth-rogoff.html

Mitchell, W. C. (1944). The role of money in economic history. *The Journal of Economic History*, 4(2), 149–175. https://doi.org/10.1017/S0022050700022331

Modderman, G. (2022). Who accepts bitcoin as payment?. *Cointelegraph*. https://cointelegraph.com/explained/who-accepts-bitcoin-as-payment

Mooradian, N. (2009). The importance of privacy revisited. *Ethics and Information Technology*, 11(3), 163–174.

Moore, A. D. (2018). Privacy, interests, and inalienable rights. *Moral Philosophy and Politics*, 5(2), 327–355.

Mora, C., Rollins, R., Taladay, K., Kantar, M., Chock, M., Shimada, M., & Franklin, E. (2018). Bitcoin emissions alone could push global warming above 2°C. *Nature Climate Change*, 8, 931–933. www.nature.com/articles/s41558-018-0321-8

Mora, C., Tittensor, D. P., Adl, S., Simpson, A. G. B., & Worm, B. (2018). How many species are there on earth and in the ocean?. *PLoS Biology*, 16(8), e2003586. www.nature.com/articles/s41558-018-0321-8

Moroz, G., Perez, P., & Zohar, A. (2020). *Double-spend counterattacks: Threat of retaliation in proof-of-work systems*. https://arxiv.org/pdf/2002.10736.pdf

Motlagh, M. S., Abdul Rahman, A. S., & Bagheri, B. (2021). *The impact of selfish mining on bitcoin network performance*. www.researchgate.net/publication/348249694_The_Impact_of_Selfish_Mining_on_Bitcoin_Network_Performance

Mullan, P. C. (2014). *The digital currency challenge: Shaping online payment systems through US financial regulations*. Palgrave Macmillan.

Mullan, P. C. (2016). *A history of digital currency in the United States*. Palgrave Macmillan.

Murch. (2022). [Tweet]. Retrieved from https://twitter.com/murchandamus/status/1608136693638373378

Nair, M., & Cachanosky, N. (2017). Bitcoin and entrepreneurship: Breaking the network effect. *The Review of Austrian Economics*, 30(3), 263–275. https://doi.org/10.1007/s11138-016-0348-x

Nakamoto, S. (2008a). *Bitcoin: A peer-to-peer electronic cash system*. https://bitcoin.org/bitcoin.pdf

Nakamoto, S. (2008b). Bitcoin P2P e-cash paper. *Cryptography Mailing List*. www.metzdowd.com/pipermail/cryptography/2008-November/014863.html

Nakamoto, S. (2009a). Bitcoin open source implementation of P2P currency. *Forum Post*. https://satoshi.nakamotoinstitute.org/posts/p2pfoundation/1/

Nakamoto, S. (2009b). Bitcoin v0.1 released. *Email*. https://satoshi.nakamotoinstitute. org/emails/cryptography/17/#selection-103.0-111.57

Nakamoto, S. (2009c). Bitcoin v0.1 released. *Email*. https://satoshi.nakamotoinstitute. org/emails/cryptography/16/#selection-9.0-9.21

Nakamoto, S. (2010). Re: Bitcoin minting is thermodynamically perverse. https:// satoshi.nakamotoinstitute.org/posts/bitcointalk/337/#selection-9.0-9.49

Nambiampurath, R. (2023). Lebanon's soaring inflation rate fuels crypto adoption amid economic turmoil. *BeInCrypto*. https://beincrypto.com/lebanons-inflation-rcrypto-adoption-economic-turmoil/

Narayanan, A., Bonneau, J., Felten, E., Miller, A., & Goldfeder, S. (2016). *Bitcoin and cryptocurrency technologies: A comprehensive introduction*. Princeton University Press.

Narayanan, A., & Clark, J. (2017). Bitcoin's academic pedigree. *Communications of the ACM, 60*(12), 36–45.

Nature Climate Change. (2022). Article metrics for "bitcoin emissions alone could push global warming above 2°C". www.nature.com/articles/s41558-018-0321-8/metrics

Nawyn, S., Gjokaj, L., Agbényiga, D., & Grace, B. (2012). Linguistic isolation, social capital, and immigrant belonging. *Journal of Contemporary Ethnography, 41*(3), 255–365.

Negy, K. P., Eyal, I., Juels, A., Kosba, A., Wattenhofer, R., & Wattenhofer, R. (2019). *Selfish mining re-examined*. www.cs.cornell.edu/~kevinnegy/Selfish%20 Mining%20Re-Examined.pdf

Neumueller, A. (2023). *Bitcoin electricity consumption: An improved assessment*. University of Cambridge Judge Business School. www.jbs.cam.ac.uk/2023/ bitcoin-electricity-consumption/

Newman, L. H., & Greenberg, A. (2022). Bitcoin fog case could put cryptocurrency tracing on trial. *Wired*. www.wired.com/story/bitcoin-fog-roman-sterlingov-blockchain-analysis/

Ney, A. (2014). *Metaphysics: An introduction*. Routledge.

Niaz, H., Liu, J. J., & You, F. (2022). Can Texas mitigate wind and solar curtailments by leveraging bitcoin mining? *Journal of Cleaner Production, 364*. https://doi.org/10.1016/j.jclepro.2022.132700

Nicas, J., & Lankes, R. (2022). Inflation in Argentina. *The New York Times*. www. nytimes.com/2022/08/06/business/inflation-argentina.html

Nolan, C. (2022). JPMorgan chase pulls ads after Kanye West's "anti-semitic" comments. *Business Insider*. www.businessinsider.com/jp-morgan-chase-kanye-west-ye-antisemitic-comments-2022-10

Nuzzi, L. (2020). Bitcoin: An unprecedented experiment in fair distribution. *Coin-Metrics Report*. https://coinmetrics.io/bitcoin-an-unprecedented-experiment-in-fair-distribution/

NYT Editorial Board. (2010). The Cyprus crisis. *The New York Times*. https://web. archive.org/web/20101230122600/www.nytimes.com/2010/12/26/opinion/ 26sun3.html

Ohuocha, C., & George, L. (2021). Crypto trading thrives in Nigeria despite official disapproval. *Reuters*. www.reuters.com/business/crypto-trading-thrives-nigeria-despite-official-disapproval-2021-10-12/

Onu, E., & Osae-Brown, A. (2022). Nigeria caps ATM cash withdrawals at $45 daily to push digital payments. *Bloomberg.* www.bloomberg.com/news/articles/2022-12-06/nigeria-limits-cash-transactions-to-push-enaira-and-other-payments

Orji, C. (2022). Bitcoin ban: These are the countries where crypto is restricted or illegal. *Euronews.* www.euronews.com/next/2022/08/25/bitcoin-ban-these-are-the-countries-where-crypto-is-restricted-or-illegal2

Osae-Brown, A., Fatunde, M., & Oluroundbi, R. (2022). Digital-currency plan falters as Nigerians defiant on crypto. *Bloomberg.* www.bloomberg.com/news/articles/2022-10-25/shunned-digital-currency-looks-for-street-credibility-in-nigeria

Osborn, A. (2019, December 30). Russia freezes bank accounts linked to opposition politician Navalny. *Reuters.* www.reuters.com/article/us-russia-politics-navalny/russia-freezes-bank-accounts-linked-to-opposition-politician-navalny-idUSKC-N1UY1ER

OSTP. (2022, September 8). *Climate and energy implications of crypto-assets in the United States.* Washington, DC: White House Office of Science and Technology Policy. Retrieved from www.whitehouse.gov/wp-content/uploads/2022/09/09-2022-Crypto-Assets-and-Climate-Report.pdf

Packard, J. M. (2003). *American nightmare: The history of Jim Crow.* St Martin's Publishing.

Paez, M., & Cross, T. (2022). *Bitcoin and the energy transition.* Bitcoin Policy Institute. www.btcpolicy.org/articles/comment-to-the-white-house

Partz, H. (2021). 0.01% of bitcoin holders control 27% of all circulating coins: Study. *Cointelegraph.* https://cointelegraph.com/news/0-01-of-bitcoin-holders-control-27-of-all-circulating-coins-study

Passinsky, A. (2020). Should bitcoin be classified as money? *Journal of Social Ontology, 6*(2), 281–292.

Pearlman, J. (2017). *Gunslinger: The remarkable, improbable, iconic life of Brett Favre.* Mariner Books.

Perlroth, N. (2021). Daniel Kaminsky, a security expert who lived on the edge, dies at 42. *New York Times.* www.nytimes.com/2021/04/27/technology/daniel-kaminsky-dead.html

Pew Research Center. (2021). Demographics of mobile device ownership and adoption in the United States. *Fact Sheet.* www.pewresearch.org/internet/fact-sheet/mobile/

Pines, M. (2022). *Bitcoin and U.S. National Security: An assessment of bitcoin as a strategic opportunity for the United States.* Bitcoin Policy Institute Whitepaper. www.btcpolicy.org/articles/bitcoin-and-us-national-security.

PlanB. (2021, May 11). [Tweet]. https://twitter.com/100trillionUSD/status/1406577006230245376

Platt, J., & Skerritt, A. (2022). Convoy leader denied bail as Canadian officials warn of unrest. *Bloomberg.* www.bloomberg.com/news/articles/2022-02-22/convoy-leader-denied-bail-as-canadian-officials-warn-of-unrest

Polimeni, J. M., Mayumi, K., Giampietro, M., & Alcott, B. (2008). *The myth of resource efficiency: The Jevons paradox* (1st ed.). Routledge.

Poon, J., & Dryja, T. (2016). *The bitcoin lightning network: Scalable off-chain instant payments.* https://lightning.network/lightning-network-paper.pdf

Popescu, M. (2015). There's a one bitcoin reward for the death of Pieter Wuille. *Details Below*. http://trilema.com/2015/theres-a-one-bitcoin-reward-for-the-death-of-pieter-wuille-details-below

Popescu, M. (2019). I own erotica like Zeus owns Olympus. http://trilema.com/2019/i-own-erotica-like-zeus-owns-olympus/

Popper, N. (2015). *Digital gold: The untold story of bitcoin*. Penguin.

Protess, B., & Silver-Greenberg, J. (2014). JPMorgan is penalized $2 billion over Madoff. *The New York Times*. https://archive.nytimes.com/dealbook.nytimes.com/2014/01/07/jpmorgan-settles-with-federal-authorities-in-madoff-case/

Quiggin, J. (2013, December 11). The bitcoin bubble: A bad hypothesis. *The National Interest*. https://nationalinterest.org/commentary/the-bitcoin-bubble-bad-hypothesis-8353

Quiggin, J. (2015). *Predictions for 2015*. https://johnquiggin.com/2015/01/15/predictions-for-2015/

Quiggin, J. (2018). *Bitcoin's belated bust*. https://johnquiggin.com/2018/11/23/bitcoins-belated-bust/

Quiroz-Gutierrez, M. (2022). Crypto is fully banned in China and 8 other countries. *Fortune*. https://fortune.com/2022/01/04/crypto-banned-china-other-countries/

Rachels, J. (1975). Why privacy is important. *Philosophy and Public Affairs*, 4, 323–333.

Rahn, R. (1999). *The end of money and the struggle for financial privacy*. The Discovery Institute.

Raskin, M. (2021). A global first: Bitcoin as national currency. *The Wall Street Journal*, 15.

Rathje, S., Shariff, A., & Schnall, S. (2022). Ideology trumps self-interest: Continued support for a political leader despite disappointing tax returns. *Journal of Elections, Public Opinion and Parties*, 33, 479–496.

Rawls, J. (1999). *A theory of justice* (Rev. ed.). Harvard University Press.

Read, C. L. (2022). *The bitcoin dilemma*. Palgrave Macmillan.

Reid, F., & Harrigan, M. (2012). An analysis of anonymity in the bitcoin system. In Y. Altshuler, Y. Elovici, A. B. Cremers, N. Aharony, & A. Pentland (Eds.), *Security and privacy in social networks* (pp. 197–223). Springer.

Renteria, N. (2022). A year on, El Salvador's bitcoin experiment is stumbling. *Reuters*. www.reuters.com/technology/year-el-salvadors-bitcoin-experiment-is-stumbling-2022-09-07/

Reserve Bank of India. (2022, May 18). *Speech by Dr. B.P. Kanungo, Deputy Governor, Reserve Bank of India at the International Institute of Digital Technologies, Tirupati*. https://rbi.org.in/Scripts/BS_SpeechesView.aspx?Id=1196

Reuters. (2014). JPMorgan hack exposed data of 83 million, among biggest breaches in history. *Reuters*. www.reuters.com/article/us-jpmorgan-cybersecurity-idUSKCN0HR23T20141003

Reuters. (2018, December 3). Nigerian court orders seizure of assets linked to former oil minister. *Reuters*. www.reuters.com/article/ozatp-us-nigeria-politics-idAFKBN1O90MR-OZATP

Reuters. (2022, October 7). Lebanese banks close again after depositor hold-ups, bankers say. *Reuters*. www.reuters.com/world/middle-east/lebanese-banks-close-again-after-depositor-hold-ups-bankers-say-2022-10-07/

Ribeiro, M. H., Ottoni, R., West, R., Almeida, V. A. F., & Meira, W. (2020). Auditing radicalization pathways on YouTube. In *Proceedings of the 2020 Conference on Fairness, Accountability, and Transparency (FAT* '20)* (pp. 131–141). New York: Association for Computing Machinery. https://doi.org/10.1145/3351095.3372879

Rizzo, P. (2021). 10 years ago today, bitcoin creator Satoshi Nakamoto sent his final message. *Forbes*. www.forbes.com/sites/peterizzo/2021/04/26/10-years-ago-today-bitcoin-creator-satoshi-nakamoto-sent-his-final-message/

Rogan, J. (2021). Joe Rogan experience podcast – JRE MMA Show #99, Interview with Francis Ngannou. https://jrelibrary.com/jre-mma-show-99-francis-ngannou/

Rogoff, K. (2016). *The curse of cash*. Princeton University Press.

Romiti, M., Judmayer, A., Zamyatin, A., & Haslhofer, B. (2019). *A deep dive into bitcoin mining pools*. https://arxiv.org/abs/1905.05999

Rosenbaum, K. (2019). *Grokking bitcoin*. Manning Press.

Rössler, B. (2005). *The value of privacy*. Polity Press.

Rothschild, S. (2021). Poll: Political polarization is worse among younger students. *Axios*. www.axios.com/2021/12/08/poll-political-polarization-students

Roubini, N. (2014, March 19). [Tweet]. https://twitter.com/Nouriel/status/442725510423248897

Roubini, N. (2018a, March 6). [Tweet]. https://twitter.com/Nouriel/status/960743853748883456

Roubini, N. (2018b, May 11). [Tweet]. https://twitter.com/nouriel/status/994994180299640832

Rudd, M. (2022). 100 important questions about bitcoin's energy use and ESG impacts. *Challenges, 14*(1). https://doi.org/10.3390/challe14010001. www.mdpi.com/2078-1547/14/1/1

Rudd, M. A. (2023). Bitcoin is full of surprises. *Challenges, 14*(2), 27. https://doi.org/10.3390/challe14020027

Rybarczyk, A., & Fabiano. (2021). On bitcoin's energy consumption: A quantitative approach to a subjective question. *Galaxy Digital*. https://medium.com/@galaxydigitalmining/on-bitcoins-energy-consumption-a-quantitative-approach-to-a-subjective-question-d107f46c8cc5

Saad, W., He, Y., Al-Rubaiee, W., & Ochieng, E. (2019). Exploring the attack surface of blockchain: A systematic overview. https://arxiv.org/pdf/1904.03487.pdf

Sabaghi, D. (2023). How Lebanon was plundered by its own central bank. *DW News*. www.dw.com/en/how-lebanon-was-plundered-by-its-own-central-bank/a-66613994

Sai, A. R., Buckley, J., & Le Gear, A. (2021). Characterizing wealth inequality in cryptocurrencies. *Frontiers in Blockchain, 4*, 730122. https://doi.org/10.3389/fbloc.2021.730122

Salter, A. W., & Luther, W. J. (2019). Adaptation and central banking. *Public Choice, 180*(3/4), 243–256.

Samuelson, P. A. (1938). A note on the pure theory of consumers' behaviour. *Economica. New Series, 5*(17), 61–71.

Samuelson, P. A. (1948). Consumption theory in terms of revealed preference. *Economica. New Series, 15*(60), 243–253.

Sandor, K., & Genç, E. (2022). The fall of terra: A timeline of the meteoric rise and crash of UST and LUNA. *Coindesk*. www.coindesk.com/learn/the-fall-of-terra-a-timeline-of-the-meteoric-rise-and-crash-of-ust-and-luna/

Schrepel, T. (2021). Blockchain: From ideology to implementation. In *Blockchain + Antitrust*. Edward Elgar Publishing.

Scott, B. (2022). *Cloudmoney: Cash, cards, crypto, and the war for our wallets*. Harper Business.

Sears, D. O., & Citrin, J. (1982). *Tax revolt: Something for nothing in California*. Harvard University Press.

Selgin, G. (2010). Boom and bust banking: The causes and cures of the great recession. *Independent Review*, *14*(4), 481–509.

Selgin, G. (2015). Synthetic commodity money. *Journal of Financial Stability*, *17*, 92–99.

Selgin, G. (2021). A three-pronged blunder, or, what money is, and what it isn't. https://www.alt-m.org/2021/10/27/a-three-pronged-blunder-or-what-money-is-and-what-it-isnt/

Selgin, G., Lastrapes, W. D., & White, L. (2012). Has the fed been a failure? *The Journal of Macroeconomics*, *34*(2), 569–596. https://doi.org/10.1016/j.jmacro.2012.01.002

Selgin, G., & White, L. (2005). The case for free banking. *The Journal of Economic Issues*, *39*(1), 1–25. https://doi.org/10.1007/s10602-005-5853-z

Semple, K. (2014). Immigrants who speak indigenous languages encounter isolation. *New York Times*. https://web.archive.org/web/20220613153849/www.nytimes.com/2014/07/11/nyregion/immigrants-who-speak-indigenous-mexican-languages-encounter-isolation.html

Seth for Privacy (Pseudonym). (2022). Reviewing privacy-enhancing proposals for bitcoin. *Bitcoin Magazine*. https://bitcoinmagazine.com/technical/list-of-bitcoin-privacy-proposals

Shepperd, J., Malone, W., & Sweeny, K. (2008). Exploring causes of the self-serving bias. *Social and Personality Psychology Compass*, *2*, 895–908. https://doi.org/10.1111/j.1751-9004.2008.00078.x

Shin, L. (2017). How bitcoin solved this serial entrepreneur's problems. *Forbes*. www.forbes.com/sites/laurashin/2017/08/08/how-bitcoin-solved-this-serial-entrepreneurs-problems/?sh=3dec8149309c

Shin, L. (2022). *Cryptopians: Idealism, greed, lies, and the making of the first big cryptocurrency craze*. PublicAffairs.

Shinobi. (2021a). How centralized is bitcoin mining really? *Bitcoin Magazine*. https://bitcoinmagazine.com/business/is-bitcoin-mining-centralized

Shinobi. (2021b). Defining and discussing "bitcoin security." https://medium.com/block-digest-mempool/defining-and-discussing-bitcoin-security-38f35cc80c18

Silver-Greenberg, J. (2012). HSBC to pay record fine to settle money-laundering charges. *The New York Times*. https://archive.nytimes.com/dealbook.nytimes.com/2012/12/11/hsbc-to-pay-record-fine-to-settle-money-laundering-charges/

Sinaee, M. (2022). Iran confiscates 6,000 bitcoin mining machines. *Iran International*. www.iranintl.com/en/202207250260

Sinclair, E. (2022). It's over 9000: Crypto mining rigs seized in Iran this year. *Blockworks*. https://blockworks.co/its-over-9000-crypto-mining-rigs-seized-in-iran-this-year/

Singh, R. (2022). Ukraine has received close to $100 million in crypto donations. *Coindesk*. www.coindesk.com/business/2022/03/09/ukraine-has-received-close-to-100-million-in-crypto-donations

Skidelsky, R. (2019). *Money and government: The past and future of economics*. Yale University Press.

Slothuus, R., & Bisgaard, M. (2021). Party over pocketbook? How party cues influence opinion when citizens have a stake in policy. *American Political Science Review*, 1–7.

Song, J. (2019). *Programming bitcoin*. O'Reilly.

Song, Y., & Aste, T. (2020). The cost of bitcoin mining has never really increased. *Frontiers in Blockchain*, 3, 565497. https://doi.org/10.3389/fbloc.2020.565497. www.frontiersin.org/articles/10.3389/fbloc.2020.565497/full

Soros, G. (1988). *The alchemy of finance: Reading the mind of the market*. Simon & Schuster.

Stancel, D. (2020). Coin perspective. https://medium.com/coin-story/coin-perspective-7-douglas-jackson-913d1985e9fa

Statista. (2022a). *Daily number of e-mails worldwide*. www.statista.com/statistics/456500/daily-number-of-e-mails-worldwide/

Statista. (2022b). *Spam e-mail traffic share*. www.statista.com/statistics/420391/spam-email-traffic-share/

Statista. (2022c). *Total damage caused by cyber crime in the US*. www.statista.com/statistics/267132/total-damage-caused-by-by-cyber-crime-in-the-us/

Stewart, N. (2020). Planned parenthood in N.Y. disavows margaret sanger over eugenics. *New York Times*. www.nytimes.com/2020/07/21/nyregion/planned-parenthood-margaret-sanger-eugenics.html

Swarns, R. L. (2020a). Race discrimination at bank? Check it out. *The New York Times*. www.nytimes.com/2020/01/23/us/race-discrimination-check-sauntore-thomas.html

Swarns, R. L. (2020b). Banks face racial bias lawsuits over 'discriminatory' treatment of Black customers. *The New York Times*. www.nytimes.com/2020/06/18/business/banks-black-customers-racism.html

Szabo, N. (2001). *Trusted third parties are security holes*. https://nakamotoinstitute.org/trusted-third-parties/

Szabo, N. (2002). *Shelling out: The origins of money*. https://nakamotoinstitute.org/shelling-out/

Szabo, N. (2007). Nanobarter. *Blog Comments*. http://unenumerated.blogspot.com/2007/06/nanobarter.html

Tabuchi, H. (2020). Oil and gas may be a far bigger climate threat than we knew. *New York Times*. www.nytimes.com/2020/02/19/climate/methane-flaring-oil-emissions.html

Tas, E., Tse, D., Gai, F., Kannan, S., Maddah-Ali, M., & Yu, F. (2022). *Bitcoin-enhanced proof-of-stake security: Possibilities and impossibilities*. https://arxiv.org/pdf/2207.08392.pdf

Tavani, H. T. (2007). Philosophical theories of privacy: Implications for an adequate online privacy policy. *Metaphilosophy*, 38(1), 1–22.

Taylor, L. (2022). The world's first bitcoin republic. *New Scientist*, 253, 14.

Tham, E., & Pollard, M. Q. (2022). China's Henan bank customers face harassment, job loss over protests. *Reuters*. www.reuters.com/world/china/chinas-henan-bank-customers-face-harassment-job-loss-over-protests-2022-07-12/

Throuvalas. (2022). Bitcoin energy concerns are lobbyist propaganda, says Michael Saylor. *Cryptopotato.com*. https://cryptopotato.com/bitcoin-energy-concerns-are-lobbyist-propaganda-says-michael-saylor/

Touryalai, H. (2013). Yes, banks are reordering your transactions and charging overdraft fees. *Forbes*. www.forbes.com/sites/halahtouryalai/2013/06/11/yes-banks-are-reordering-your-transactions-and-charging-overdraft-fees/

Treasury. (1999). Treasury department releases study on illicit money flows. *U.S. Department of the Treasury*. https://home.treasury.gov/news/press-releases/ls230

Treeck, T. (2022, January 20). Crypto assets "worth nothing", says ECB's Christine Lagarde. *Politico*. www.politico.eu/article/crypto-assets-worth-nothing-ecb-christine-lagarde/

Troianovski, A. (2020, September 24). Navalny poisoning exposes Russia's ability to freeze assets. *The New York Times*. www.nytimes.com/2020/09/24/world/europe/navalny-poisoning-russia-frozen-assets.html

Tsabary, O., & Eyal, I. (2018). *The gap game*. https://arxiv.org/pdf/1805.05288.pdf

Tugend, A. (2015). Speaking freely about politics can cost you your job. *New York Times*. www.nytimes.com/2015/02/21/your-money/speaking-about-politics-can-cost-you-your-job.html

UNODC. (2022). Money laundering and financing of terrorism. *United Nations Office on Drugs and Crime*. www.unodc.org/unodc/en/money-laundering/overview.html

Valentini, L. (2012). Ideal vs. non-ideal theory: A conceptual map. *Philosophy Compass*, 7(9), 654–664.

Valfells, S., & Egilsson, J. H. (2016). Minting money with megawatts. *Proceedings of the IEEE, 104*(9), 1674–1678. https://ieeexplore.ieee.org/document/7547426

van den Hoven, J., Blaauw, M., Pieters, W., & Warnier, M. (2020). Privacy and information technology. In E. N. Zalta (Ed.), *The Stanford encyclopedia of philosophy* (Summer 2020 Edition). https://plato.stanford.edu/archives/sum2020/entries/it-privacy/

Vander Laan, D. (2022). Creation and conservation. In E. N. Zalta (Ed.), *The Stanford encyclopedia of philosophy* (Spring 2022 Edition). https://plato.stanford.edu/archives/spr2022/entries/creation-conservation/.

Varon, J., & Peña, P. (2021). Artificial intelligence and consent: A feminist anti-colonial critique. *Internet Policy Review*, 10(4). https://doi.org/10.14763/2021.4.1602. https://policyreview.info/articles/analysis/artificial-intelligence-and-consent-feminist-anti-colonial-critique

van't Klooster, J. (2019). Central banking in Rawls's property-owning democracy. *Political Theory*, 47(5), 674–698. https://doi.org/10.1177/0090591718810377

Van Wirdum, A. (2018). The genesis files: How David Chaum's eCash spawned a Cypherpunk dream. *Bitcoin Magazine*. https://bitcoinmagazine.com/culture/genesis-files-how-david-chaums-ecash-spawned-cypherpunk-dream

V-Dem. (2020). Autocratization surges–resistance grows. www.v-dem.net/static/website/files/dr/dr_2020.pdf

Véliz, C. (2019). The Internet and privacy. In D. Edmonds (Ed.), *Ethics and the contemporary world* (pp. 149–159). Routledge.

Visa. (2022). Visa fact sheet. *Visa.com.* www.visa.co.uk/dam/VCOM/download/corporate/media/visanet-technology/aboutvisafactsheet.pdf

Void and Alper. (2022). Bitcoin mining energy use inconsequential, rapidly becoming more efficient – Saylor. *Cryptonews.com.* https://cryptonews.com/news/bitcoin-mining-energy-use-inconsequential-rapidly-becoming-more-efficient-saylor.htm

Volpecelli, R. (2021, February 22). China confirms it will "severely crack down" on bitcoin mining and trading. *Wired UK.* www.wired.co.uk/article/china-ban-bitcoin-cryptocurrencies

Voreacos, D. (2022). Millions in cryptocurrency vanished as agents watched helplessly. *Bloomberg.* www.bloomberg.com/news/articles/2022-10-03/feds-seized-311m-in-bitcoin-btc-the-crypto-hacker-stole-it-back

Voskuil, E. (2019). Censorship resistance property. https://github.com/libbitcoin/libbitcoin-system/wiki/Censorship-Resistance-Property

Wagner, C. (2022). Impossible for Russia to evade sanctions with crypto, FinCEN rep says. *Blockworks.* https://blockworks.co/impossible-for-russia-to-evade-sanctions-with-crypto-fincen-rep-says/

Walch, A. (2019). Intermediaries that must not be named? A legal and policy research agenda for crypto miners. *Presentation.* https://speakerdeck.com/angelawalch/intermediaries-that-must-not-be-named-a-legal-and-policy-research-agenda-for-crypto-miners

Wales, J., & Ovelman, D. (2019). Bitcoin is speech: Notes toward developing the conceptual contours of its protection under the first amendment. *Journal of Information Technology & Politics, 16*(4), 395–406.

Warmke, C. (2021). What is bitcoin? *Inquiry, 67,* 25–67.

Warmke, C. (2021, January 17). [Tweet]. https://twitter.com/craigwarmke/status/1349712696401387520

Warmke, C. (2022). Electronic coins. *Cryptoeconomic Systems, 2*(1). https://cryptoeconomicsystems.pubpub.org/pub/warmke-electronic-coins

Warren, E. (2022, March 1). Letter to the U.S. Department of the Treasury regarding OFAC's enforcement of crypto sanctions. United States Senate. www.warren.senate.gov/imo/media/doc/2022.03.01%20Letter%20to%20Treasury%20re%20OFAC%20crypto%20sanctions%20enforcement.pdf

Warren, M. (2023). *Bitcoin: A game-theoretic analysis.* DeGruyter.

Weatherford, J. (1998). *The history of money: From sandstone to cyberspace.* Three Rivers Press.

Wells Fargo. (2022). *Cryptocurrencies – Too early or too late?* Wells Fargo Investment Institute. www.wellsfargo.com/investment-institute/cryptocurrencies-too-early-or-too-late/

White, L. H. (1989). *Competition in currency: Essays on free banking and money.* New York University Press.

White, L. H. (1999). *The theory of monetary institutions.* Blackwell Publishers.

White, L. H. (2023). *Better money: Gold, fiat, or bitcoin?* Cambridge University Press.

White, L. H., Vanberg, V. J., & Köhler, E. A. (Eds.). (2015). *Renewing the search for a monetary constitution.* Cato Institute.

Whitesell, W. (2006). Interest rate corridors and reserves. *Journal of Monetary Economics*, *53*, 1177–1195.

Wieczner, J. (2022). The crypto geniuses who vaporized a trillion dollars. *New York Magazine Intelligencer*. https://nymag.com/intelligencer/article/three-arrows-capital-kyle-davies-su-zhu-crash.html

Wilcox-O'Hearn, B. Z. (2002). Experiences deploying a large-scale emergent network. In P. Druschel, F. Kaashoek, & A. Rowstron (Eds.), *Peer-to-peer systems*. Springer.

Wile, R. (2014, April 3). Interview with David Andolfatto. *Business Insider*. www.businessinsider.com/interview-with-david-andolfatto-2014-4

Woo, W. (2020, December 2). [Tweet]. https://twitter.com/woonomic/status/1333826686257831936

World Bank. (2017). *Global Findex database 2017: Measuring financial inclusion and the Fintech revolution*. https://openknowledge.worldbank.org/bitstream/handle/10986/29510/9781464812590.pdf

World Bank. (2022). *Ponzi finance?* https://openknowledge.worldbank.org/server/api/core/bitstreams/0d0ca056-f041-5a8f-95f5-276225248b7e/content

Yermack, D. (2015). Is bitcoin a real currency? In D. K. C. Lee (Ed.), *The handbook of digital currency* (pp. 31–44). Elsevier.

Young, I. (1990). *Justice and the politics of difference*. Princeton University Press.

Zeigler, C. (2009, January 29). Favre won't speak to Aaron Rodgers. *Outsports*. www.outsports.com/2009/1/29/4047054/favre-wont-speak-to-aaron-rodgers

Zelmanovitz, L. (2016). *The ontology and function of money: The philosophical fundamentals of monetary institutions*. Lexington Books.

Zimmerman, J. B., & Anastas, P. T. (2015). Opportunities and challenges in the chemistries of sustainability. *ACS Sustainable Chemistry & Engineering*, *3*(10), 2383–2389. https://pubs.acs.org/doi/10.1021/acssuschemeng.0c09435

Zuboff, S. (2019). *The age of surveillance capitalism*. Hachette Book Group.

Zverev, A., & Belton, C. (2021). Bitcoin donations surge to jailed Kremlin critic Navalny's cause: Data. *Reuters*. www.reuters.com/article/us-russia-politics-navalny-crypto-curren/bitcoin-donations-surge-to-jailed-kremlin-critic-navalnys-cause-data-idUSKBN2AB2GR

INDEX

www.ingramcontent.com/pod-product-compliance
Ingram Content Group UK Ltd.
Pitfield, Milton Keynes, MK11 3LW, UK
UKHW022309250125
454108UK00018B/194